# CHRISTENDOM DIVIDED

## THE PROTESTANT REFORMATION

*THEOLOGICAL RESOURCES* is a series of books taking its impulse from the striking renewal of interest in theology to-day. That renewal is unique in theological history, because its impetus derives from all the churches and because evidence for it abounds in all countries. The contributors to the series have been chosen, therefore, for their suitability to particular subjects rather than for denominational uniformity. There are two General Editors, John P. Whalen, formerly acting head of the Catholic University of America, and Jaroslav Pelikan, a prominent Lutheran Pastor, at present the Titus Street Professor of Ecclesiastical History at Yale University.

In commenting on the current theological revival, the General Editors write—'this interest, vital though it is, stands in danger of being lost in superficiality and trivialized into a fad. The answer to this danger is greater depth. *THEOLOGICAL RESOURCES* is intended to supply that depth.'

*HANS J. HILLERBRAND*

# CHRISTENDOM DIVIDED

## THE PROTESTANT REFORMATION

CORPUS OF NEW YORK
WESTMINSTER OF PHILADELPHIA
HUTCHINSON OF LONDON

CORPUS INSTRUMENTORUM

EDITORIAL OFFICES
110 East 59th Street, New York, N.Y. 10022

SALES & DISTRIBUTION
2231 West 110th Street, Cleveland, Ohio 44102

THE WESTMINSTER PRESS
Witherspoon Building, Philadelphia, Pa. 19107

Library of Congress Catalog Card Number: 70-93573
*First printing, 1971*
MANUFACTURED IN GREAT BRITAIN

# Contents

# Editors' Foreword

The Protestant Reformation was a kind of cultural and religious time bomb that had a double detonation. Its first explosion rocked Christendom, an institution that had contributed to a cultural stability that had come to be recognized as a stagnation, and caused Christendom to be divided in a way from which it has not recovered even until this day. The second explosion seems to be taking place at the present time.

Questions were raised by Luther and Calvin and Hooker and others that demanded immediate answers, so basic were they. But the questions also provoked a long and introspective, if fearful, self analysis for Christianity that required four hundred years and three 'Ecumenical Councils' to permit Christianity to recognize what had happened. For the spirit of question and challenge that characterizes Christianity in the last part of the twentieth century is the same spirit that revolutionized the Church in the sixteenth. It is startling to look back and discover features of soul and of its expression that one today is used to finding in religious journals and newspapers. It is not possible to understand the present trends and upheavals without understanding the theological transformation of the Christian faith that was brought about by the Reformation.

This is not simply another account of the Reformation. Inclusion of *Christendom Divided* in the series *Theological Resources* is necessary because it sets the stage for a development of doctrine and of the history of the theological enterprise. It is not possible to understand theology nor to evaluate its present or future thrust without an appreciation of what happened to Christendom four hundred years

ix

ago. A sensitive theological evaluation of the events of the Reformation based on a thorough grasp of the facts makes *Christendom Divided* a key theological resource.

Any effort on the part of the Churches to come to basic agreements on doctrines and the life styles that derive from them must be rooted in an understanding of the basic disagreements on doctrines and life styles that have contributed to the calling into existence of these very Churches. *Christendom Divided* provides this understanding. It is a theological book with historical and cultural insights that are crucial to the self understanding of all the Churches and persons who claim to be Christians.

J.P.W.
J.P.

# Preface

Reformation histories are almost as numerous as pebbles on a beach, and the publication of yet another requires a measure of self-confidence on the part of any author. The fact that virtually all of these histories tell their stories the same way (as is so obvious to the specialist) seems to imply a certain rigidity and to doom each new attempt from the outset. In any case, the reader is entitled to a word of explanation.

Two considerations have prompted this narrative of the Reformation. I felt deeply gratified by the invitation to contribute a volume to this distinguished project, especially since it must be the first time a book on the Reformation has been written by a non-Catholic under Catholic auspices. I hope that the book justifies the invitation. A second consideration has been the opportunity to put forth my interpretation of the Reformation, which in some respects differs from the customary perspective. Reformation scholarship has often suffered from certain vices, one being the assumption that Martin Luther and the German Reformation were the *umbilicus mundi* in the 16th century, and another being the notion that the new Protestant ecclesiastical tradition can be understood simply on theological grounds.

It is impossible to understand the Reformation fully apart from the general developments of the time, notably the political factors. Of course, this is hardly a new insight; Ranke argued it in his *German History in the Time of the Reformation* with acumen and brilliance, when he noted that authentically religious forces are continuously intertwined with political ones. However, Ranke perceived the relationship of religion and politics very much in a formal way, viewing the Reformation virtually as a chapter in 16th-century diplomatic history. That is a somewhat narrow understanding. It should be broadened so as to include the roles of the respective rulers and nobles, the presence of constitutional problems and issues, etc. Indeed, the term 'politics' should include, in a broad definition economic, cultural, and intellectual forces as well, for the course of the Reformation was intimately related to these elements.

Usage of the term Reformation must distinguish between three specific aspects of the course of events. There were what we might call the religious, the theological, and the political Reformations. The first two, in particular, need to be kept apart. We need not belabor the fact that the Reformation was a significant theological achievement (though Catholics and Protestants have vehemently disagreed over its Biblical character): Luther's tract on Christian freedom, Calvin's *Institutes*, and Hooker's *Laws* are monumental documents. But even the sum total of the theological opinions propounded does not necessarily afford the best clue to the religious character of the time. Thus, what did the popular pamphlets say about Luther and about his 'gospel'? How did they interpret his teaching? We today are invariably very wise concerning the 'real' Luther, but at the same time, we are a bit farther from the historical pulse of things: the 'real' Luther, as he emerges from sophisticated analysis of his lectures, letters, and tracts, may not be the 'historical' Luther who made such a momentous impact on his contemporaries. A large number of additional matters could be noted, such as the spirituality of the new hymns or the new forms of worship. In short, there was a religious Reformation of considerable significance.

There was also the political Reformation—the involvement of religion in the power politics of the time: the utilization of the sacred in order to achieve the profane, and the utilization of the profane in order to accomplish the sacred. The two went hand in hand. The struggle to obtain the legal recognition of Protestantism in Germany, for example, was a development quite different from the drafting of the first (or second) Book of Common Prayer in England. This book seeks to distinguish, by its particular sequence of chapters, between these three usages of the term Reformation.

The underlying assumption of the narrative here presented is that it was the proclamation of Martin Luther that precipitated, inadvertently, the religious controversy. While there were discontent and disaffection with the Church, nothing suggests that either was widespread or intense. Had Martin Luther died in his cradle, the

Church would have survived in all probability without any major disaster. But it was not so much Luther's theological proclamation that effected this large-scale dissent from the Catholic Church; it was rather his religious intensity. Moreover, this proclamation promptly became embedded in a variety of psychological, political, and ecclesiastical factors that led, on the one hand, to its speedy condemnation by the Church and, on the other, to its widespread popular acceptance.

This narrative will also argue that the response to Luther was widespread and genuine, at least in the early phase of the controversy; that those who supported him had initially no intention of breaking with the Church; that the European expansion must be attributed to the direct stimulus of Luther; that two developments must be distinguished, the theological (religious) and the political; and, finally, that the Reformation was as successful as it was because political considerations added their weight to the religious ones.

The reader is reminded that, in its present form, this work on the Reformation will be augmented by other books in the Theological Resources series. This has made it possible—and to some extent necessary—to exclude certain themes and developments that ordinarily would need to be included. For example, an account of the state of ecclesiastical affairs in the early 16th century is omitted, as are detailed considerations of the theological emphases and characteristics of the major reformers and the traditions that they founded. Were it not for such corollary augmentation, these omissions, especially the former, at a time when the examination of late nominalist thought is so lively, would be hard to justify. My purpose has been not so much to sketch the theological characteristics of the Protestant Reformation as to show the actual historical matrix in which Protestantism, both as a theological and a historical phenomenon, had its beginning. Indeed, if there is a moral to the story, then it lies not in the various theologies, no matter how profound, but in the reality of their interaction with the whole range of man's human, all-too-human concerns.

H. J. HILLERBRAND

*Duke University*

---

# CHAPTER ONE

# The Prelude

On July 17 1505, a young student knocked at the door of the monastery of the Eremites of St. Augustine at Erfurt and asked to be admitted as a novice.[1] Such commitment to monastic life occurred countless times in those days and was thus neither spectacular nor unusual. Still, this particular case was noteworthy, for the student was Martin Luther, the man destined not only to become a great theologian but also to precipitate in Western Christendom the great schism we call the Reformation. It was Luther's spiritual struggle in the monastery that led him to the formulation of the theology that altered so dramatically the history of the Christian Church. Within the cloister walls that were to have separated him forever from the world, Luther pondered those thoughts that were to shake the very foundations of that world. His life began when it was to have ended.

Thus, at the beginning of the Reformation of the 16th century stands Martin Luther—not the condition of society or the Church at the time, not even the state of theology, but this one man and his spiritual pilgrimage. To study the Reformation is like listening to a Wagnerian opera, exciting, tedious, long, involved, and full of pathos. Its *leitmotif*, recurring again and again, is Martin Luther. The Reformation is unthinkable without him. His thought precipitated the controversy that divided the Church in Germany and indeed throughout Europe. To be sure, there were other factors at work, and the point can be made that but for them Luther would have died an early and ignominious death had he persisted with his novel ideas, and his words, no matter how striking or profound, would have been written as on water. He was blessed with high

1

qualities of intellect and an agreeable temperament. He was also born at a propitious time. This combination of character and circumstances was what elevated him to greatness.

The irony of the matter is that Luther became a reformer unintentionally and much against his will. He always thought little of his own person and his role in the course of events. He wanted his writings burned at his death, and he spoke with painful acrimony about himself. 'I am but a stinking bag of worms,' he said on one occasion. 'The teaching is not mine. I was crucified for no one.'[2] And in the year before his death he announced that he would prefer to see all of his books committed to oblivion.[3]

### Martin Luther

Born in 1483 at Eisleben on the eastern slope of the Harz Mountains in central Germany, Martin Luther was the son of a hard-working middle-class entrepreneur who was determined to give him the benefits of his newly acquired prosperity. His father, Hans, appears in his recollections as a stern and opinionated character, but if the details of the relationship between father and son intimate significance, they are also quite enigmatic. The cursory evidence available has prompted a psychoanalyst to see the oppressive father as a major factor in Martin Luther's theological development, suggesting that Martin pictured God in the same oppressive way he saw his father— that his theological problems were, in other words, merely an extension of his personal ones.[4] The thesis is intriguing, but, since the evidence is scarce, we do well to exercise restraint in this regard, lest the temptation to practice good psychoanalysis leads us to indulge in bad history.

Luther's childhood and youth seem to have been routine enough for a time in which life was as Brueghel's canvasses depict it— earthy, hard, exuberant, each day a new struggle of joy and sorrow. Luther's few recollections from his childhood take us into a strange world of credulity—he reports, for example, that a woman at Eisenach gave birth to a mouse or that he never heard any exposition of the Lord's Prayer and the Ten Commandments—but otherwise are without worthwhile substance.[5]

In 1501 'Martinus Luther ex Mansfeld' matriculated at the University of Erfurt. He was declared *in habendo*—not eligible for scholarship aid—an indirect testimony to the economic success of his father. He pursued the customary course of study in the liberal arts, and received, probably in 1503, the baccalaureate and in 1505 the master's degree. That summer, in line with the wish of his father, he began the study of law, proudly clutching his copy of the *Corpus juris*, which his father had bought for him. Less than 3 months later, however, he had entered the monastery. The explanations vary. It is possible, of course, that the decision was an impulsive one, but more likely there were serious reasons. In later years Luther himself observed that he had entered the monastery in order to obtain *salutis meae*, 'my salvation.'[6] But even if we acknowledge that spiritual anxieties prompted Luther's decision, we can leave room for catalytic events—the death of a close friend, an injury that easily might have been fatal, or the realization that his legal studies were an erroneous vocational choice. In his own mind, however, one incident stood out as decisive: the experience of a thunderstorm near Stotternheim that mortally terrified him and brought about his vow to become a monk.

In the fall of 1506 Luther made his monastic profession and for the next 20 years or so he was an Augustinian monk, an unusual one, if his own recollection may serve as a trustworthy guide.[7] With scrupulous determination he sought to find the resolution of his spiritual problem. 'If ever a monk came to heaven through monkery, it should have been I,' he observed on one occasion, and added, 'in the monastery I lost both the salvation of my soul and the health of my body.'[8] These words indicate that there was an unusual quality about the monk Martin Luther: he was overwhelmed with the realization of his sinfulness; he brooded endlessly over his inescapable damnation; he was perturbed by the question of whether he had done enough penance, prayer, and fasting to be acceptable to God; and he always concluded that he had not. If Luther was perturbed because he had committed actual sins, perhaps of a sexual sort, as Catholic biographies of Luther contended until the 20th century, the evidence is completely lacking; indeed, the argument points in the opposite direction: Luther's nagging problem was that despite his outwardly proper demeanor he still thought himself unacceptable by God. The problem was not actual sin, *peccatum actuale*, but the underlying disposition, *concupiscentia*, concupiscence, which is self-centeredness.[9]

At last Luther found the answer, though when he did remains disputed in scholarship. The sinner is justified before God not by what he does or is, but by something else. Man must acknowledge his sinfulness: thereby he 'justifies' God who has called him a sinner and he can claim the forgiveness that God has offered to sinners.[10] Justification takes place by faith, because the sinner appropriates by faith the divine promise of forgiveness as it is found in the Gospel, and also because it is contrary to experience.[11] Man is thus justified, but he remains a sinner—*simul justus et peccator*.[12] 'I felt as though I had been born again and entered the gates of paradise,' Luther reported later in life about this discovery.[13] The key scriptural passage was Rom 1.17, 'For in it the righteousness of God is revealed through faith for faith; as it is written, "He who through faith is righteous shall live." ' From this passage Luther concluded that God's righteousness, as revealed in the Gospel, does not give man what he deserves, but offers him forgiveness.[14] As far as he was concerned, it was new, dramatically new, 'contrary to the opinion of all the doctors,' nothing less than a reformulation of the doctrine of the Apostle Paul. The exuberance over having found his spiritual delivery made him overlook what modern scholarship has clearly established, namely, that the medieval commentators on St. Paul (though not the systematic theologians) interpreted the Pauline passage the way he did, and that the theology against which he was struggling was not, as Joseph Lortz pointedly put it, catholic.[15] This is to say that in considerable measure Luther's spiritual dilemma had been created by the theological atmosphere of the late 15th and early 16th centuries, with its stress on man's ability to contribute to his salvation. Thus Gabriel Biel wrote, 'Man's free will can, of its own nature and without grace, elicit a morally good act'[16] and coined the famous phrase that 'God will not withhold his grace from him who does what he can (*facere quod in se est*).'[17] This perspective placed much emphasis on man's natural ability to do the good and thus lacked the balance of the exposition of earlier theologians, such as St. Thomas Aquinas.

Two important comments must be made at this point. The first is that Luther's insight had ramifications on several other theological points. It was as if he had discovered the crucial word in a puzzle: all other words fell readily into place. Grace was no longer the supernatural ontological change of man from sinner to saint; it was simply the divine word of forgiveness. Faith was the acceptance of this word, and consequently faith assumed crucial importance. In short, the implications of Luther's 'evangelical discovery' went far beyond a single point of theology. A second comment is equally relevant. Did Luther mean to oppose the Church? The answer must be negative. Not only did Luther give no indication of restlessness in the years before the outbreak of the indulgences controversy (and most Luther scholars agree that he attained his new understanding at least by 1515), he also gave no indication of dissent in the first phase of that controversy; on the contrary, he outdid himself with expressions of subservience to the Church.

Alongside Luther's spiritual pilgrimage took place the more or less routine career of a brilliant monk. He was ordained to the priesthood in April 1507, and afterward began formal theological studies, first at Erfurt, then at the recently founded University of Wittenberg, a town of which he said that it was situated 'on the edge of civilization.'[18] In the fall of 1512 he received the doctorate in theology at Wittenberg and assumed the *lectura in Biblia*, the professorship in Biblical studies there. Professor Luther was 'a man of middle stature,' reported a student, 'with a voice that combined sharpness in the enunciation of syllables and words and softness in tone. He spoke neither too quickly nor too slowly, but at an even pace, without hesitation and very clearly, and in such fitting order that every part flowed naturally out of what went before.'

During the next few years Luther lectured twice on the Psalms, as well as on Romans, Galatians, and Hebrews. Though some of his lectures are extant only in the form of student notes (which, one fears, must be used with caution), they are important evidence of how he departed from the traditional fourfold exegetical scheme of the medieval expositors, stressed the literal meaning of the text, and increasingly gave expression to his new theological stance. After an initial conflict with his Wittenberg colleagues, notably Andreas Bodenstein Carlstadt, he was able to bring them to his side. A collection of 97 theses 'against scholastic theology,' of September 1517, constituted a public manifesto of his new theological perspective.[19] Suddenly an innocuous event catapulted the unknown professor into the public limelight. Infuriated by certain claims made in the sale of indulgences by the Dominican Friar Johann Tetzel, Luther drafted a set of 95 theses dealing with the topic of indulgences, planning an academic disputation on the matter. On October 31 he sent a copy of his theses, together with a covering letter, to Archbishop Albert of Mainz, Tetzel's ecclesiastical superior, asking that his preaching be stopped.[20] Traditionally, it has been assumed that he posted a copy of the theses in Wittenberg, but on close examination the evidence is rather thin. That he sent copies of the theses to several friends can, however, be established.

The response was dramatic, and no one was more astounded than Luther. The theses had been moderate (certainly in comparison with those of September), calling only for a reinterpretation of indulgences that had not as yet been defined by the Church. What Luther did not know was that he had put his head into a hornet's

nest: Tetzel was not a lone indulgence preacher, but part of an
elaborate financial and political scheme that involved the Curia,
Archbishop Albert, the banking house of the Fuggers, and possibly
even the next German Emperor. Luther could not have chosen a
more inopportune occasion to express a theological concern. At
stake was the jubilee indulgence for the reconstruction of St. Peter's
in Rome, first promulgated by Pope Julius II in 1505 and renewed,
after his death, by Pope Leo X. It was surely a worthwhile purpose,
though its sale was anything but a success. Virtually all territories in
northern Germany had prohibited the sale, and one suspects that
this indulgence would have fallen into the nescience of history had
there not been an unexpected turn of events.

In 1514 Albert of Hohenzollern, 24 years of age, was elected
Archbishop of Mainz, after having already been elected the previous
year Archbishop of Magdeburg and Administrator of Halberstadt.
Such accumulation of ecclesiastical offices, especially on the part
of someone who had not as yet attained the prescribed age for the
episcopacy, violated the provision of Canon Law. After lengthy
negotiations between the Curia and Albert agreement was reached
that the payment of a special sum in addition to the customary pal-
lium would procure a papal dispensation. To make the payment
attractive to Albert the Curia proposed that the jubilee indulgence
should be sold in North Germany for a period of 8 years, with half
of the proceeds accruing to Albert and the other half to the Curia.
The assumption was that Albert's brother, Elector Joachim of
Brandenburg, could open most of North Germany for the sale. This
was a financial transaction of major proportions and the young archbishop may well have had sleepless nights, though the anticipation of
substantial income from his new ecclesiastical benefice, his political
stature (the archbishop of Mainz was also a German elector), and
the realization that the indulgence buyers would assume the major
share of his debt, must have made him pleased about the matter. On
paper everyone was to profit: Albert for the reasons just cited and
the Curia for the anticipated income and for the hope of political
influence in Germany through Albert's electorship.

Luther, of course, knew only about the practical side of the matter—the way Johann Tetzel, the chief salesman of the indulgence in
North Germany, was reported to be going about his activities. When
Luther obtained a copy of the *Instructio summaria*, the instructions
for the indulgence, he was shocked by its mercenary spirit.[21] His reflection on the place of indulgences in the Church resulted in the
drafting of 95 propositions. 'When our Lord and Master Jesus Christ

said "Repent," he meant the entire life of his faithful to be one of repentance.' Thus the first thesis set the tone for what followed. Succeeding theses defined key terms and then considered the effectiveness of indulgences for the dead (theses 8–29) and for the living (theses 30–80). A summary of various popular arguments against the sale of indulgences, together with a few repetitions, brought the total number to 95.

Written in Latin, clothed in proper academic form, intricate in theological argumentation, Luther's theses were not meant as a clarion call for an ecclesiastical revolution. They were merely the basis for an academic discussion. Even where Luther deviated from the theological consensus—as in his insistence that indulgences can free one only from canonically imposed punishment—he did so in the form of suggestions and possibilities rather than categorical assertions. 'This I presented for debate and did by no means put into emphatic affirmations,' he wrote a few months later.[22] Indulgences, purgatory, and papal power were acknowledged and not rejected. Only occasionally were the words those of a man in anger: 'Those preach man-made doctrine who assert that, as soon as the coin rings in the coffer, the soul departs from purgatory;' or, 'to say that the crucifix erected with the papal coat of arms can do as much as the cross of Christ is blasphemy.'[23]

Friedrich Myconius, a stanch partisan of Luther, wrote many years later that the 95 Theses spread throughout Germany within weeks 'as if angels from heaven themselves had been their messengers.'[24] One must be skeptical about the accuracy of this statement, in regard both to its metaphysical implications and its breathless chronology. Luther's fame (or notoriety) was long in coming. The speed with which he became a public figure has surely been overestimated. When the year turned, Luther was still widely unknown and awareness of his Theses restricted to a small circle of officials and scholars. The spread of the Theses was a slow process; only during the early months of 1518 did they become known to a wider public.

They also became quite notorious, for upon learning of them Tetzel launched a vehement, if superficial, counterattack, in which he asserted that souls were freed more quickly from purgatory than the falling of a coin (in payment of an indulgence) in the coffer; after all, the coin required time to fall! At the same time, the German nationalists applauded Luther for his forceful attack against Rome. By the spring of 1518 a theological controversy was clearly in the making. It involved the theologians and drew wider circles among

the humanists, but generally remained confined to a few. Luther contributed to the debate with his immensely successful *Ein Sermon von
dem Ablass und Gnade* (Sermon on Indulgence and Grace), his first
tract in German, and also published his Heidelberg Theses, written
for a disputation in connection with a meeting of the German congregations of the Augustinian Order at Heidelberg.

The Heidelberg Theses were a bold statement of his Theology of
the Cross: 'the theology of glory calls evil good and good evil: the
theology of the Cross calls things by their name.'[25] The difference
was between man's search and God's answer, between self-'glory'
and self-'humiliation,' between speculation that fails to perceive God
and the true knowledge of God in the 'Cross.' At the same time
Luther attacked an erroneous understanding of God: 'He is not a
true theologian who beholds God's invisible being in created things,
but who beholds and knows God as he has visibly manifested himself through suffering and the Cross.' God is found, Luther argued,
'only in his sufferings and the Cross,' not through works, effort, striving, but through *'humanitas, infirmitas, stultitia.'* God, in other
words, is other than man thinks and expects, and Christ's death on
the Cross provided the supreme illustration.

Luther's foremost antagonist in the controversy proved to be
Johann Eck. Three years younger than Luther, Eck was a brilliant
and widely known scholar. He had jotted down a few 'obelisci,'
comments on the 95 Theses, and circulated them among friends.
When Luther saw them, he composed an aggressive reply, labelled
'asterisci,' in which homely comparisons with the animal kingdom
made their entrance into Reformation polemics. Eck had called
Luther a 'Bohemian,' a follower of Jan Hus; Luther, in turn, insisted on his orthodoxy, and for the time being this settled the matter. But there was Andreas Carlstadt, Luther's senior colleague at
Wittenberg, whose exuberance carried the controversy forward.
During Luther's Heidelberg sojourn Carlstadt had compiled 379
theses, which he subsequently enlarged to 405, an exhausting and
exhaustive delineation of the new Wittenberg theology. Eck responded with theses of his own, and since Carlstadt was unwilling to
let his opponent have the last word, he published another set of
theses against Eck in late summer. One round of controversy followed another and with each round the tone became more bitter
and vehement.

In August 1518 Luther published the *Resolutiones*, or
'Explanations Concerning the Theses on the Power of Indulgences,'
a lengthy exposition of the 95 Theses.[26] In a way, they were his own

response to the invitation in the preface of the 95 Theses, where he had asked for a scholarly disputation of his propositions. Theologically, the *Resolutiones* showed Luther in a state of transition. He affirmed the centrality of Scripture but allowed a place for tradition. He acknowledged papal primacy but suggested certain restrictions of papal power.

Together with the theological controversy was a second development, feeble at first, but of incisive, if tragic, significance in the end: the official ecclesiastical proceedings against Luther.[27] One cannot note emphatically enough that from the very beginning the controversy was not a matter of theological opinion only, but was an affair of state. There was an ominous awareness on the part of all that every word was placed on a golden scale in Rome in order to enforce orthodoxy and to suppress heresy. The first step in this connection had come with surprising speed. On December 1 1517, Archbishop Albert asked the University of Mainz to assess Luther's theses. Two weeks later, without having heard from the academicians, he reported the matter to Rome, asking for the commencement of the *processus inhibitorius*, the first step in heresy proceedings, against Luther.

In the spring of 1518 came the actual opening of the proceedings. The Master of the Sacred Palace, Sylvester Mazzolini Prierias, was assigned the task of investigating the theological aspects of the case. He hastily composed a treatise, angrily noting that it had kept him from the more serious task of continuing a commentary on St. Thomas Aquinas. Entitled *Dialogus in praesumptuosas M. Lutheri conclusiones de potestate Papae* (Against the Presumptuous Theses of Martin Luther Concerning the Power of the Pope), the treatise was superficial and characterized by an unwillingness to take Luther seriously. It was basically a defense of the authority of the pope, but it failed to distinguish between normative dogma, where this authority had to be accepted, and theological opinions, where freedom of discussion was permissible. There was a goodly portion of theological flair in the tract, as, for example, the remark that Luther's words suggested that he was about to emigrate to Bohemia—a fateful suggestion concerning the supposed proximity of Luther to Hus.[28]

Early in August 1518 Luther was served the *admonitio caritativa* to appear in Rome as a reputed heretic within 60 days, and toward the end of that same month the head of the Saxon province of the Augustinian Order and Cardinal Cajetan, the papal legate in Germany, were instructed to have Luther apprehended as a notorious

heretic. Pope Leo X wrote Elector Frederick of Saxony to be mind-
ful of the faith of his fathers and to turn the 'son of iniquity' over to
the ecclesiastical authorities. The wheels of ecclesiastical machinery
had moved swiftly and with determination. The case of Martin
Luther, Augustinian monk and professor of theology, writer of bold
theological theses—possibly a heretic—was about to be closed.

At this juncture extraneous considerations impinged upon the
course of theological and ecclesiastical events. A German Diet was
in session in Augsburg. Emperor Maximilian I was preoccupied with
the question of his succession, but the most important matter before
the German Estates was the financing of a campaign against the
Turks. The papacy was greatly interested in this venture and its
concern was underscored by the presence of Cardinal Cajetan as
papal legate. The Estates were reluctant to shoulder the necessary
tax. They agreed that a crusade was an honorable matter and a
Christian responsibility, but insisted that the mood among the
people did not allow for levying a new tax. On August 27 they
formally declared a new tax out of the question. They called attention to the widespread complaint about moneys already contributed
to various worthy causes and, for good measure, added a long list
of grievances against Rome that should be alleviated, such as the
appointment of foreigners to ecclesiastical positions in Germany and
the increasing financial burdens. In the end, however, the bark was
worse than the bite. The recess of the Diet provided that for 3 years
communicants should pay a tax to be used for financing a crusade
against the Turks, though the Estates announced that they must first
consult with their subjects about this matter.

Such was the setting for the next phase of Luther's case. Im-
mediately upon receiving the *admonitio* Luther had appealed to his
Elector to secure a hearing in Germany, and the active interest of
Elector Frederick caused the matter to take a different turn.
Frederick supported Luther's request and received Cajetan's con-
cession that Luther be examined at Augsburg.[29]

The Saxon Elector's concern for Luther was thus exceedingly
important; but it is easier by far to acknowledge this fact than to
offer an explanation. Without Frederick's protecting hand over him,
Luther would not have survived the first year of the controversy.
But why did Frederick protect him? Was he a partisan of Luther?
Luther's attack on indulgences had been implicitly directed against
Frederick's own collection of relics in the Castle Church at Wittenberg, and so there was every reason for the Elector to be cool toward
his audacious professor. Frederick did not know Luther per-

sonally, though there was indirect contact between the two men through George Spalatin, Frederick's chaplain and secretary. What is more, there is no evidence that Frederick, who continued the celebration of the Mass in his private chapel until 1525, shared Luther's religious orientation. In his mid-fifties when the storm broke loose, he was set in his religious ways. Religious considerations hardly suffice as explanation. What about considerations of diplomacy and politics? Given the public sentiment in Germany, Frederick's support of Luther was a gesture to the gallery that could be sure of applause. Even if nothing more than a forceful indication that the Curia could not proceed unilaterally and that the cooperation of the secular arm was necessary, Frederick's persistent support was an understandable act of political prudence. But there is yet another side to the matter. His contemporaries agreed that Frederick was a man of simple virtues. He believed in justice—and so in a fair treatment of Martin Luther, his professor, of whose sincerity he was persuaded, even if he did not share his views. Frederick's knowledge of ecclesiastical procedure may have raised doubts in his mind as to the fairness of the action against Luther. Fairness was his primary concern, and he was willing to go to considerable trouble to achieve it. But whatever the motivation, his stand in the summer of 1518 made him the saviour of Luther and thereby of the Reformation.

The Church was represented at Augsburg by Cardinal Thomas de Vio, known as Cajetan. One of his early biographers related his mother's dream that St. Thomas Aquinas himself taught her son and carried him to heaven. Such pious anticipation may have guided the childhood and youth of her son, who could soon boast of a brilliant career. His theological eminence was celebrated and his ecclesiastical achievements distinguished. He was general of the Dominican Order and one of the most learned men of the Curia. Indeed, his nine-volume commentary on St. Thomas's *Summa Theologiae* continues to this day as an impressive exposition of the magnum opus of the Angelic Doctor. Cajetan's legatine assignment to Germany was to influence the German Estates to a vigorous suppression of the Hussites and a war against the Turks, while keeping a watchful eye on the paramount political issue in Germany—the question of the successor to the Emperor. Precisely on this point Elector Frederick's request to have Luther examined in Augsburg was bound to fall on fertile ground: as German Elector, Frederick occupied an important role. The Church, vitally interested in the new Emperor, could hardly afford to slight him.

Three times—on October 12, 13, and 14—Luther and Cajetan

met at Augsburg. Cajetan had done his homework well. He had
written a treatise on indulgences and had attempted to read Luther's
writings. He was not disposed to deal with Luther offhandedly.[30]
Their meetings ranged through the whole diapason of politeness,
subtle argumentation, theological discussion, and explosive anger.
Neither was impressed by the other. Cajetan thought Luther an obstinate and uncouth monk, with 'ominous eyes and wondrous fanta-
sies in his head,' who did not revoke because of fear of personal
shame rather than because of his conviction. Luther, on the other
hand, held that Cajetan 'possibly might be a famous Thomist, but
he is an evasive, obscure, and unintelligible theologian and Christian.'[31]

If the encounter remained fruitless, it was for the reason that the
two men did not speak the same theological language. Cajetan, willing to engage in theological discussion with Luther, told Luther of
his two errors: he had denied the treasure of merit as the basis of
indulgences, contrary to the bull *Unigenitus Dei filius* of 1343, and
he had argued that faith was indispensable for justification. The
problem was that the two men depended on different authorities.
Luther, in stating his case, cited Scripture; Cajetan used scholastic
theology and Canon Law. Agreement was difficult, for the fateful
distinction between 'Scripture' and 'tradition,' between the 'Word of
God' and 'human additions,' came to the fore in Luther's words.
Luther argued bluntly that Cajetan's authorities—the scholastics
and Canon Law—did not measure up to the eminence of Scripture.
The point was that the traditions of the Church were not Biblical.
But precisely this assumption formed the heart of Cajetan's argument: he saw the Church as a mystical body that was more than its
empirical expression in the hierarchical structure. It was an organism
nurtured by sacramental union with Christ. The traditions embedded
in the bosom of the Church could not be but authentic testimonies to Scripture. The Fathers were authentic interpreters of
Scripture.

At the end of their third meeting Cajetan dismissed Luther with
the exasperated comment that he need not return unless he was ready
to recant. Luther thereupon appealed to 'a not-well-informed pope
so that he be better informed,' in which he explained that ill-health,
poverty, and the threat of sword and poison made his journey to
Rome impossible. He volunteered not to write anything against
Scripture, the Fathers, and Canon Law, and then fled from Augsburg. There was good reason for his nervousness. Papal instructions
of the end of August had empowered Cajetan—even though the 60

days given Luther in the 'charitable admonition' had not expired—
to have Luther apprehended and sent to Rome.

Back in Wittenberg, Luther published an account of his conversation with Cajetan, the so-called *Acta Augustana*, and drew up
an appeal to a general council. Then he settled back into academic
routine to await the future, his belongings packed, ready to flee Wittenberg at a moment's notice. His appeal to a general council was
in line with the conciliar notion that a council was superior to the
pope. Though such appeals had been condemned in the 15th century, Luther's act had precedents, such as a statement of the Paris
faculty of the spring of 1517. Indeed, at points Luther followed the
Parisian document almost word for word. Luther's appeal was
printed so that it would be ready if needed; it was not intended for
immediate distribution. But his printer, who sensed its sensational
character, promptly put it on the market. Luther's distress at this
indiscretion was but a pretense, however; publicity could only aid
his cause.

On November 9 the bull *Cum Postquam* defined the doctrine of
indulgences and the authority of Church and pope in absolving from
temporal punishment. The mentor of the bull was clearly Cajetan.[32] Luther's view was now incompatible with that of the Church.
At this point Karl von Miltitz, a young Saxon nobleman and papal
chamberlain, appeared. He had been entrusted with the delivery of
the Golden Rose, a papal decoration, and special indulgences for the
Wittenberg Castle Church to Elector Frederick. He was not officially
involved in the controversy, nevertheless he tried to resolve it. His
efforts failed, and compared with the increasingly complex interweaving of ecclesiastic and political scheming, this one-man *tour de
force* possessed only peripheral significance. Yet Miltitz was one of
the few men who had a realistic notion as to how the controversy
might be resolved. His plan was to use a period of silence to calm
tempers and to reduce the matter to a purely academic controversy.

Some will say that the theological divergence between Luther
and the Church made a split inevitable. But in 1518 there was no
reason why Luther's teaching could not have been made a legitimate
option within the Catholic Church. Historical parallels can be cited;
they suggest that partial disagreement with the Church did not always lead to a break. St. Augustine was not condemned for his anti-
Pelagian writings, and Erasmus, despite denunciation and partial
condemnation, died in peace with the Church. Why could not Luther
have followed Erasmus's example? Possibly, he was the more
orthodox of the two. The reason is twofold: Luther, we noted,

chose a most inopportune time to propound a theological point. He became embroiled in both theological controversy and ecclesiastical proceedings, whereas Erasmus always skillfully managed the former so as to avoid the latter. There is also a psychological point. In 1519 the specter of a schism in Western Christendom was not very real. There had been heretics before and the Church had successfully dealt with them. Even Jan Hus's dissent had remained geographically restricted. Why should Luther's case be different? There seemed no need to be overly concerned and no reason to make accommodations. This is not to say that action of the Church should be guided by prudence. It is to suggest, however, that a different course of action was surely possible.

After his meeting with Miltitz at Altenburg early in January 1519, Luther wrote the pope a letter in which his deep religious concern, his awareness of the problems and anxieties caused by his teaching, and his desire to find an acceptable solution found graphic expression. Luther declared himself willing to be silent, if his opponents were silent, and to write a treatise exhorting everyone to honor the Church. Clearly, Luther was not a revolutionary, and at Altenburg he gave evidence that he would respond to conciliatory gestures. Still, the agreement came to naught, and in the annals of Reformation history the encounter with Miltitz is only a fleeting and even comic interlude in the swiftly moving course of events. Indeed, Miltitz has been called 'a kind of ecclesiastical Von Ribbentrop,' a combination of diplomatic ineptitude and arrogant self-conceit. How pathetic a verdict on a man who sought to light the candle to dispel darkness! The agreement failed not because it was the wrong solution (on the contrary, it seems to have been the right one), but because some men are never in favor of any solution. Miltitz should be chided not so much for his solution but for his inability to understand the temper of the protagonists.

The silence was broken by two men with brilliant minds but limited perspectives: Eck and Carlstadt. Their feud once again dominated the theological controversy and eventually brought Luther back into the arena. They had agreed to settle their theological differences with a disputation, for which Eck had published 12 theses. Upon reading them Luther felt that they were directed against him rather than Carlstadt and posthaste retorted with a set of 12 theses of his own. The Altenburg agreement was thus thrown overboard, though Luther was able to say that his opponent had broken the silence. The range of issues in this controversy was wide, but the emphasis unmistakably lay on the question of papal authority. Therefore, one of Eck's theses had been, 'We deny that the Roman Church was not superior to other churches in the time of Sylvester,' an assertion which had sent Luther to extensive historical studies.[33]

The disputation between Eck, Carlstadt, and Luther took place at Leipzig in June 1519. A High Mass and academic convocation formally opened the debate on June 27. For those who delighted in the splendor of academic festivities, the day must have been memorable. A Leipzig academician delivered the oration for the occasion —a 2-hour exercise that pompously belabored the obvious, the learned man evidently thinking the opportunity too good to pass without giving an exhibition of his rhetorical and scholarly competence. He covered the range of history as well as of religion, and spoke of the great debates of the past and of the need for truth and modesty. Duke George of Saxony expressed surprise that theologians were so godless as to need such exhortations. The debate itself began inauspiciously. Carlstadt, who had insisted on debating first, cut a poor figure beside the eloquent and flamboyant Eck, who cited his authorities, several at one time, from memory (whether accurately or inaccurately proved to be a contested question), whereas Carlstadt had to look up his citations, causing tedious delays. The topics were free will and grace. Both Eck and Carlstadt succeeded in obtaining minor concessions from one another, but on the whole the interchange, no matter how profound, was listless. During Luther's encounter with Eck the discussion shifted to the question of papal supremacy, and Eck at once reiterated his charge of Hussite heresy. This sent chills up and down the spines of those who heard it, for the University at Leipzig had been founded by German emigrants leaving Prague in opposition to Hussitism. Luther issued an emphatic denial, adding he did not care about what Hus had or had not taught. Later in the debate, however, Luther remarked that not all of Hus's views had been heretical, some had been Christian, such as his assertion that there is one holy Christian Church.

At this point the character of the disputation changed. Again and again Eck accused Luther of being a Hussite, while Luther each time asked Eck to tell him what was wrong with the statement that there is one holy Christian Church. In exasperation, Luther finally noted that the condemnation of some statements of Hus at Constance showed that councils, too, can be in error. Upon hearing Luther's words, Duke George burst out *das walt die Sucht* (a loose rendering would be, 'I'll be damned!') and left the room, an indication that he recognized the implications of Luther's words. Eck announced that Luther was a 'heathen and publican,' a much milder statement than his earlier denunciation that Luther was 'heretical, erroneous, blasphemous, presumptuous, seditious, and offensive to pious ears.' There was no doubt as to his sentiments.

Eck and Luther debated for several days about purgatory, indulgence, penance, and the forgiveness of sins. But the climax of the debate had passed, and the minds of the two disputants must have wandered back more than once to the incisive interchange concerning conciliar authority. To everybody's relief, one suspects, the debate was concluded on July 15. Both sides claimed victory in letters to friends and in public pronouncements that spread the news of the disputation far and wide. Officially, the universities at Erfurt and Paris had been asked to render a decision—the debate had been an academic affair, a scholarly exchange. But in addition to its ecclesiastical overtones, word about it spread even in the vernacular, so that instead of remaining an esoteric affair among professionals the Leipzig disputation became a widely known event, that symbolized Luther's defiant rejection of ecclesiastical authority. In actual fact, however, Luther had tempered his rejection of councils with the crucial qualification—'in matters not(!) *de fide*'—but that got lost in the shuffle.

All this time, the theological controversy had been overshadowed by political developments. Emperor Maximilian had died, not unexpectedly, in January 1519, and the powerful in Europe began to involve themselves in the election of his successor. Formally the election lay in the hands of the seven German electors, but in reality it was the *cause célèbre* of European politics during the first 6 months of 1519. At least four candidates were mentioned at one time or another: Henry VIII, Frederick of Saxony, Francis I, and Charles I; but only the latter two were serious contenders. The most obvious candidate was a young man 18 years of age who had never been in Germany and could not speak German: Charles I of Spain. As grandson of Maximilian, he possessed a nominal claim, and indeed his grandfather had almost succeeded in formalizing his succession before his death. Charles ruled Spain and the Habsburg territories—the Netherlands, Burgundy, and Austria. The imperial crown suggested itself as a means to consolidate these geographically heterogeneous possessions. The other serious candidate, Francis I of France, was bound to enter the race if for no other reason than to keep the prize from Charles who, as German Emperor, threatened to control lands along virtually all of the French border. The papacy saw serious danger in Charles's candidacy, and a glance at the map quickly tells the reason. Charles already ruled Naples, to the south of the Papal States, and the prospect of his rule in northern Italy meant worse things to come. French domination in northern Italy also was problematic, but, compared with Charles, Francis seemed the lesser of two evils. Leo X marshalled his influence in support of Francis; he promised cardinal's hats to the electors of Cologne and Trier and a permanent legateship for the elector of Mainz. But the strength of the papal support for France only alienated the German electors. German nationalism, antipathy toward things French, and warm memories of Emperor Maximilian became important elements as the election approached. But in the end, the election turned into a financial transaction with the prize going to the higher bidder. The sums expended by Charles and Francis staggered the imagination, but the Spaniard's figures were more impressive and, in the end, persuasive.

Charles's election was unanimous. A *Wahlkapitulation*, election agreement, specified the relationship between the Emperor and the territorial rulers: imperial offices were to be occupied only by Germans; the German language was to be used exclusively in official matters; all Diets were to be held in Germany; no foreign soldiers were to be brought to Germany; no one should be outlawed without a hearing. A *Reichsregiment*, imperial regiment, was to be established for the purpose of administering imperial affairs during the Emperor's absence from Germany, though the exact nature of this institution was left to subsequent agreement.[34] The German people hailed the new Emperor enthusiastically. Poems, sermons, and odes sang his virtues. It was like a spring morning, with signs of budding and flourishing everywhere; the German people looked forward eagerly to Charles's rule. Luther remarked in his Open Letter to the Christian Nobility that 'God has given us a young, noble blood to be our head and thereby awakened many hearts to great and good hopes.'[35] Soon these 'great and good hopes' vanished.

## The Wild Boar in the Vineyard

In the fall of 1519 the ecclesiastical proceedings against Luther, slowed down on account of the imperial election, received new stimulus. Johann Eck had sent self-confident accounts of the Leipzig debate to Rome together with pessimistic prophecies about the spread of Luther's ideas in Germany. This gloomy picture incited action.

In January 1520, a consistory heard the demand that Luther's orthodoxy be examined and, if necessary, his heresy condemned.

One month later a papal commission hastily condemned several of Luther's teachings, but then some members of the Curia counseled for more extensive deliberations in this case. Consequently another commission, comprised of the heads of several monastic orders, was appointed to examine Luther's teachings anew. The commission rendered the surprisingly mild verdict that some of Luther's propositions were erroneous, but only some were heretical; they were mainly 'scandalous and offensive to pious ears.' Then Johann Eck appeared himself in Rome and poured oil on the fire. 'It was appropriate that I came to Rome at this time,' he wrote a friend, 'for no one else was sufficiently familiar with Luther's errors.' He made sure that such ignorance was promptly dispelled. The bull *Exsurge Domine*, promulgated on June 15 1520, rejected 41 propositions culled from Luther's writings.[36] This bull is known as are few items in Reformation history. There is the picturesque, if Biblical, flavor of its language: 'the wild boar which has invaded the Lord's vineyard'; and the appeal to Christ, St. Peter, St. Paul, the Apostles, the saints, indeed the entire Church, to arise and defend their cause against the onslaught of Luther, whose past history is described, whose 41 condemned propositions are called 'heretical, offensive, erroneous, objectionable to pious ears, misleading to simple minds, and contrary to Catholic teaching,' and whose stubborn refusal to recant is bewailed. The bull claimed that, like all heretics, Luther scoffed at the scriptural interpretation of the Church and substituted views of his own. Luther was given 60 days during which to recant; otherwise he and his supporters were to be declared heretics.

*Exsurge Domine* is a strange summary of Luther's teaching. True, most of the 41 condemned sentences can be found in Luther's writings, but a curious procedure characterizes the quotations. Thus, the bull compressed into a single sentence what Luther wrote at different places on a given page.[37] In one instance Luther merely cited the opinion of others, and in another he only expressed his hope what a general council might do. If Luther's teaching were extant only in the form provided by the bull, we would be sorely misled about it. Justification, for example, was not mentioned at all, except that Luther's denial of free will was rejected. More than half of the 41 propositions came from the 95 Theses and the *Resolutiones*; most of the others were taken from the proceedings of the Leipzig disputation. Again, some of the condemned propositions dealt with peripheral points, such as that 'the spiritual and temporal rulers would be well advised to do away with begging' or, 'the burning of heretics is against the Holy Spirit.' There were also outright contradictions. At one place the bull stated that all of Luther's writings were to be burned, at another only those containing any of the 41 condemned errors. In short, the bull seemed to give little evidence of a willingness to take Luther seriously. Those familiar with Luther's writings (above all, of course, Luther himself) were bound to observe that they had been neither seriously considered nor fully understood. Far from clarifying the situation, the bull intensified the uncertainty, and many people became obsessed with the notion that Luther had not been fairly treated. Ever more loudly the demand was made that Luther should receive a 'real' hearing.

This was the time when three of Luther's most famous tracts came off the press: *An den christlichen Adel deutscher Nation von des christlichen Standes Besserung* (The Open Letter to the Christian Nobility); *De captivitate Babylonica ecclesiae praeludium* (The Babylonian Captivity); and *Von der Freiheit eines Christenmenschen* (Freedom of a Christian Man).

The Open Letter to the Christian Nobility was telling indication of how Luther juxtaposed the yearning for reform and his teaching (which would have found fault with the Catholic Church even if no abuses existed). Accordingly, these were the two themes of the treatise. At the beginning came the repudiation of the 'three walls of the Romanists': that ecclesiastical power was superior to temporal power; that no one can properly interpret Scripture except the pope; and that no one can convene a general council except the pope. Luther's repudiation utilized the fullness of his theological insight. The postulate of the priesthood of all believers was relevant here, since faith and Baptism make all Christians 'priests.' On the basis of such universal priesthood Luther admonished the Christian nobility to take its place in the reform of the Church. When the pope fails to convene a council, the Christian congregation has the right and the duty to do so. The second part of the tract contained 26 reform proposals addressed to the secular authorities. Some of them were echoes of the traditional German *gravamina* against the Church, and a few dealt with matters of general concern, such as the restriction of the spice traffic and the need for laws against extravagance and excess in dress.

The Babylonian Captivity of the Church, written in Latin, was a scholarly discussion of the sacramental teaching of the Catholic Church. 'I know another little song about Rome and about them,' Luther had written at the end of the Open Letter, 'and if their ears itch for it I will sing them that song too, and pitch the notes to the

B

top of the scale.'[38] The criterion for assessing the sacramental teaching of the Catholic Church was fidelity to the Scriptures. Luther defined the sacrament as a divine promise to which a sign is attached.
He concluded that there are only two—Baptism and Communion.
And the latter was erroneously observed in the Catholic Church:
the cup was withheld from the laity; the philosophical notion of
transubstantiation was used to explain Christ's presence; and the
Mass was understood as a sacrifice. 'The Holy Spirit is greater than
Aristotle,' Luther wrote, and added that 'in order that the real body
and the real blood of Christ may be present in the sacrament, it is not
necessary that bread and wine be transubstantiated and Christ be
contained under their accidents.'[39] Luther's positive description of
the nature of the sacrament noted that the faithful must turn their
'eyes and hearts simply to the institution of Christ and to this alone,
and set naught before us but the very word of Christ by which he
instituted this sacrament.'[40] The word of Christ is a word of promise
—the remission of sins—and the proper approach to the sacrament
must therefore be that of faith.

The treatise on the Freedom of a Christian Man, finally, discussed the principles of Christian morality. The Christian life,
Luther asserted, is a life of freedom, and the Christian—'a perfectly
free lord over all things'—is subjected only by love. Today this
sounds simple and even a Christian commonplace; to Luther's contemporaries it was no less than revolutionary, for the medieval
Church had thought to express the Christian ethos with specific and
detailed rules. Luther offered the world 'freedom.' The Christian,
bound only by love, is a 'free lord over all.' 'It will not hurt the soul,'
Luther wrote, 'if the body is clothed in secular dress, dwells in un-
consecrated places, eats and drinks as others do.'[41] No more detailed
rules; no more minute prescriptions—but freedom. 'A Christian,'
Luther observed, 'is free from all things and over all things, so that
he needs no works to make him righteous and to save him, since
faith alone confers all these things abundantly. But should he grow
so foolish as to presume to become righteous, free, saved, and a
Christian by means of some good work, he would at once lose faith
and all its benefits.'[42] In the second part of the treatise Luther spoke
about those who, 'misled by the word "faith" and by all that has
been said, now say, "If faith does all things and is alone sufficient
unto righteousness, why then are good works commanded?" ' Freedom does not mean license. The Christian, though free from rules, is
called upon to be 'Christ' unto his neighbors—to serve them in their
needs, even as Christ served all men by his life. God calls man to be

both free and a servant: free because God has loved him and servant because he is called upon to love his neighbor.

More than anything else Luther had written up to that time, these three treatises showed the range of his reinterpretation of the Christian faith. One reader angrily threw the Babylonian Captivity to the 'ground upon finishing reading it' and another reported that it made him shiver from head to toe. Luther showed that his concern was not the correction of abuses or the alleviation of grievances, but a new understanding of the Gospel.

It made little difference that some readers of the three treatises enthusiastically endorsed their content, or even that others found words of vehement rejection. The overpowering event in the late summer of 1520 was the bull and, after weeks of anxious uncertainty, the official notification to Luther indicated that it was neither rumor nor forgery. Luther was persuaded that the bull was the work of Antichrist, and he proved this to his own satisfaction in a tract *Adversus execrabilem Antichristi bullam* (Against the Execrable Bull of the Antichrist), of which the title gave a sufficient hint as to its content. This tract appeared almost on the last day granted by the bull for revocation, and thus constituted his indirect, though unmistakable, response. At the same time he issued an appeal to a general council. On the morning of December 10 1520 Luther, accompanied by a throng of eager students, burned a copy of the bull outside the Magpie Gate at Wittenberg. A number of second-rate theological works and a copy of the Canon Law were also burned: 'Because you have grieved the saints of the Lord, may eternal fire grieve you,' Luther said as he committed the books to the flames.[43] To the students it was a great hoax, and it must have been painful for Luther to see the seriousness of the occasion made ridiculous by collegiate pranks. The next day Luther, who had 'trembled and prayed' at the occasion, told his students that 'now things will turn serious.' One contemporary called the burning 'a crime such as has not been seen for centuries, a *lèse* majesty.' It was not so much the burning of the bull that was so offensive, although papal authority had been dramatically defied with this act, but the burning of Canon Law, the very foundation of medieval law and order.

On January 3 the bull *Decet Romanum pontificem* was promulgated.[44] Since Luther had not heeded the *admonitio caritativa* and had not recanted his erroneous views, he was excommunicated. In contrast to the *Exsurge Domine*, the bull of excommunication was not made public until later in the year. This created little uncertainty, however, since the stipulation of the first bull had been clear and unmistakable: no revocation meant excommunication. And so the Church had spoken. The next step was to seek the cooperation of the secular authorities to execute the ecclesiastical verdict. But once again alien considerations encroached upon the case. Emperor Charles V, who had assured the papal nuncio that he would gladly give his life for the Church, recognized that, for better or for worse, the resolution of the matter depended on more than his sentiment. His *Wahlkapitulation* had stipulated that no one in Germany should be outlawed without a proper hearing. And many thought that Luther had not received such a hearing. Those who yearned for ecclesiastical reform felt that Luther's plea in this regard, despite its vehemence and theological danger, deserved more careful consideration than it had been afforded. The German nationalists resented the Curial condemnation as foreign intrusion, while some territorial rulers saw unilateral imperial action against Luther as a fateful step in the direction of imperial autocracy. In short, for a variety of reasons people in Germany were bound to be unhappy with the resolution of Luther's case. But, whereas many agreed that the matter should not be considered closed, the solutions and suggestions as to what should be done varied widely. One proposal was that Luther should receive a hearing, though the details—the form of such a hearing, and who should conduct it—were left somewhat nebulous. Erasmus proposed that the rulers of Germany, England, and Hungary appoint a committee to arbitrate the dispute. Increasingly the suggestion gained acceptance that Luther should appear before the forthcoming German Diet. The Emperor's chancellor, Gattinara, in particular argued such a course of action, and he was supported by the Saxon Elector Frederick, who formally asked the Emperor for an examination of Luther by learned men.

The papal nuncio Aleander emphatically asserted that a condemned heretic could not receive a hearing and that a mandate against Luther should be issued at once. The Emperor shared Aleander's sentiment for prompt action, but for diplomatic reasons he was willing to explore alternate means that would achieve the same end. Gattinara urged him repeatedly not to issue a mandate against Luther without prior consultation of the German Estates. Gattinara was influenced less by benevolence for Luther than by the realization that the Emperor needed the Estates for future support. In February the Estates refused to pass a bill suppressing Luther's writings and demanded, in view of the restlessness of the common people, that Luther should be cited before the Diet 'to the benefit and advantage of the entire German nation, the Holy Roman Empire, our Christian faith, and all Estates.'⁴⁵ At this juncture Emperor Charles recognized that the sentiment prevailing among the Estates made Luther's citation the only practicable option. The Estates' concession that Luther should not be allowed to engage in a disputation, but should only be permitted to recant, made it easier for the Emperor to accept this solution. On March 6 the formal citation went out to Luther, who was called 'honorable, dear, devoted' (a strange ascription for a condemned heretic!), and who was informed that 'information is requested from you concerning your teachings and your books.'⁴⁶ Though some, notably Aleander, had bitterly opposed Luther's citation, in the end everybody gained by it. The Emperor conformed to the stipulation of his *Wahlkapitulation*; Elector Frederick demonstrated his continued interest in his professor; the territorial rulers asserted their autonomy; the humanists and others desiring reform of the Church could assure themselves that the Church had not had the final word. And even Aleander must have recognized that Luther's coming was in the ecclesiastical interest: his revocation might resolve the whole controversy, whereas his condemnation by the Diet, in case he did not revoke, would put the blame on the Germans rather than on the Curia.

Luther's journey to Worms turned into a march of triumph. Wherever he paused along his route he was feted at banquets and toasted with wine. He was warned that he would be burned to ashes, as had been done with Hus at Constance. Before he reached Worms, Spalatin warned him not to proceed since the Saxon Elector could not protect him and his case had already been decided. 'We will come to Worms,' retorted Luther, 'in spite of all the gates of hell'— a phrase which he afterward changed into the more picturesque statement 'even if there were as many devils to spring upon me as there are tiles on the roofs.'⁴⁷

Then, on April 17 1521, shortly after 4 o'clock in the afternoon, came the confrontation: the monk and the Emperor, the lonely dissenter and all the rulers of the Empire. When Luther was escorted into the hall, Charles remarked that this man would never turn him into a heretic. Luther was told that he had been cited for two reasons: to acknowledge the books placed on a table as his own and to repudiate their content. Luther acknowledged himself as the author of the books, but 'in a very soft voice' requested time to ponder his answer to the second question. This caused consternation, but after a brief consultation Luther was given 24 hours, after which he was to state his answer.

One suspects that Luther had been taken by surprise by the

directness of the questions.[48] His citation to the Diet had said nothing of a revocation. Indeed, in March he had written Spalatin that he was not interested in going to Worms merely to recant, 'which I could do here as well as there.' He had no idea what would take place when he was ushered into the hall. To his dismay he was asked only two questions. During the 24 hours given him to consider his answer to the second question, he formulated a careful response. On the following day Luther appeared once more before the dignitaries of the Empire. Darkness engulfed the room, and the wavering light of the torches added a dramatic mood. Luther had overcome his timidity of the previous day and, when recognized, gave his answer. His writings fell into three groups, he stated. Some dealt with faith and morals, some with papal tyranny, some were written against literary opponents. At times he had been vehement in tone, more vehement than became a Christian; for this he apologized. But revoke? If he were convinced by scriptural texts he would do so and be the first to burn his own books. He was told that his answer had not been clear enough. Thereupon Luther gave the famous response: 'Since your majesty and your lords demand a simple answer, I shall give one without horns and teeth. Unless I am convinced by the testimony of Scripture and evident reasoning I am convinced by the Sacred Scripture I have cited—for I believe neither solely the pope nor the councils, for it is evident that they have erred often and contradict one another. My conscience is captured by the Word of God. Thus I cannot and will not revoke, since to act against one's conscience is neither safe nor honest.'[49] The official retorted that Luther should forget about his conscience; he could never prove that councils had erred. Luther insisted that he could, but at this point the Emperor interjected that enough had been said, and Luther was escorted from the hall. Aleander reported to Rome that Luther, on leaving, raised his arms 'as is the custom of German soldiers when they rejoice over a good hit.'[50]

The following day Charles asked a group of territorial rulers for their opinion in the matter. When they expressed the need for further reflection, he told them that he for one needed not to ponder his position. His ancestors, he said, had been faithful sons of the Catholic Church and had bequeathed their faith to him. A single monk had set his own opinion above the consensus taken by the Church for more than 1,000 years. 'I am therefore determined to use all my dominions, possessions, and friends, my body and blood, my life and soul to settle this matter.'[51] This principle was to guide Charles's German policies until the day of his abdication 35 years later; it proved to be his destiny. Indeed, when speaking to the members of the Spanish *consejo real* and *consejo de estade* a few years later, Charles remarked that while future historians would note the outbreak of the Lutheran heresy during his reign, they would also acknowledge *que con mi favor e industria se acabo*—that it was 'extinguished through my help and eagerness.' Charles abhorred heresy and at Worms set out to suppress it.

When Charles demanded the concurrence of the Estates, he found them reluctant. They suggested that further conversations be held with Luther since he had not been told his specific errors. Luther had expressed his willingness to be shown his errors and this should be done; God did not want the death of the sinner, but that he convert himself and live. The Emperor agreed. In subsequent negotiations Luther was confronted with the arguments that he was dividing the Christian Church; that pious men had read the Gospel before him and had not broken with the Church; that, by not revoking, the good that he had written would also be condemned. But Luther remained immovable or, as some would say, stubborn. He insisted that his scriptural interpretation was correct and boldly declared that he could accept a decision of a general council only if it agreed with the Word of God. Obviously, the situation was hopeless. When Luther was finally asked, in exasperation, how the matter was to be resolved, he responded with the elusive scriptural passage: 'If it is a work of men, it will perish; is it from God, ye will not quench it.' On his way back to Wittenberg Luther was captured and secretively taken to Wartburg castle, where he was to spend 10 months. At first few people knew of Luther's fate and whereabouts. Even Elector Frederick, who had instigated the capture, made sure that he himself was not told where Luther was being held so that he could truthfully claim ignorance.

Frederick's action had come in time. On May 8 the Emperor ordered an edict against Luther, drawn up by Aleander several days earlier, put into proper legal form. Four days later he was ready to sign, with pen in hand, when he decided to take counsel once more with the Estates in order to gain their approval, but this attempt was unsuccessful. Afterwards the Diet adjourned and many of the rulers departed from Worms; yet this bit of unfinished business remained. Finally, on May 25, Elector Joachim of Brandenburg assured the Emperor of the consent of the Estates, whereupon Charles signed the edict of May 8.[52] It enumerated Luther's errors in line with *Exsurge Domine*. Luther and his supporters were declared political outlaws. His books were to be burned. This edict proved to be an ambiguous matter (rather like the bull *Exsurge Domine*), for doubts about its legality were raised at once. Indeed, this dubious legality may well have constituted a major factor in its practical insignificance in the subsequent course of events. One consideration in particular evoked questions. The edict was issued after the adjournment of the Diet and the phrase 'with the unanimous counsel and will of the electors, rulers, and estates' was plainly inaccurate. Most of the rulers, such as Frederick of Saxony, had left Worms by the middle of May. The authority of the Emperor stood behind the document, but not much more. Before Luther's coming to Worms the Estates had assured the Emperor that he could act if Luther did not revoke; this was an important consideration for him, and, indeed, his justification for what appeared to be unilateral action. But what Charles had conveniently overlooked was that during the negotiations in May the Estates had clearly reversed their earlier sentiment. It was an open question whether Charles had the authority to proceed unilaterally. Moreover, since the signature of the imperial chancellor, Albert of Mainz, was lacking, the edict was of dubious legality if taken as imperial law. If, on the other hand, the edict was considered an imperial mandate, its applicability was definitely restricted. In short, a fateful uncertainty prevailed.

With the edict the curtain fell on what should have been the final act of the drama of Martin Luther. Surely, most of his contemporaries thought this was the end. But it was not, and from the vantage point of subsequent events the reason is not difficult to discern. None of Luther's opponents recognized the vitality and explosive exuberance of his teaching. They may have done their best to settle an exceedingly complicated situation in faithfulness to the Church. None of them seemed to have sensed, however, that the situation called for new ways and new solutions. They all tried—Charles, Gattinara, Aleander, and the others—but they all failed to sense the profundity of the hour.

Worms was the last real hope for bringing together Luther and his Church. But Luther's obstinacy and the unwillingness of his opponents to see the religious reasons in such obstinacy made this impossible. From that point on, Luther's work proceeded along its own lines—much to the fateful development of Germany and, indeed, of Europe. Luther himself was hardly dismayed: 'Easter will come also for us and then we will sing hallelujah! . . . "A little while and ye shall not see me, and again a little while and ye shall see me," Christ said. I pray that this will be the case again. But may God's will be done, as the best in heaven or on earth.'[53]

# CHAPTER TWO

# The Beginning
# of the Reformation

The year 1521 marks an important break in the history of the Reformation, and nothing symbolizes this more aptly than Luther's move from Worms, the very center of power in the Empire, to the solitude of the Wartburg. Events after 1521 assumed a different character. One might even suggest that only then did the Reformation in the proper sense begin.

The events between 1517 and 1521 had pertained to the fate of one man—Martin Luther. They had had many facets: political maneuvering, ecclesiastical action, and theological discussion had variously intertwined. But in the center stood Martin Luther, and the story of those 4 years was his story, from the publication of his 95 Theses in 1517 to his excommunication and political condemnation in 1521. At issue were certain theological propositions, their theological discussion, ecclesiastical assessment, and political overtones. The situation was complex; if it had any peculiar feature, it was its intimate ecclesiastical and political involvement. Luther's Theses were not a purely academic document but were ominously related to power, politics, and money.

To label these events 'Reformation' means to employ a risky kind of scholarly shorthand. The full ecclesiastical implications and theological significance of the controversy were by no means clear and its political dimensions not yet obvious. Indeed, the 4 years between 1517 and 1521 brought little that corresponded to the happenings during the remainder of the century. The delineation of confessional standards, the establishment of Churches and the political involvement of these Churches were the themes that dominated events after

27

1521, and the term 'Reformation' describes this broader and more comprehensive development.

But before new creeds were drawn up or new Churches organized, something else had happened: the controversy turned into a movement. No longer was there only a single man, supported by a few friends; increasingly supporters appeared on the scene, men who had read Luther's pamphlets and who had been touched by their content. These 'Martinians' were not restricted to a single corner of Germany or to a section of the people. They were everywhere, north and south; they were learned and illiterate; young and old. Thus Luther's proclamation did not remain confined to the circle of learned theologians, but touched the very core of society.

This course of events, so remarkably obvious after 1521, was characterized by two features. It took place in the face of both the ecclesiastical and political censures pronounced over Luther—and all his followers. To take up the cause of Luther was not, therefore, a kind of neutral option, the support of one theological position over another; rather it was the support of a man labeled heretic by the Church, a support that invoked of the wrath of Christendom. A second feature of the ensuing development was its increasing legal and political involvement. Precisely because a legal verdict had been pronounced against Luther at Worms, a legal component was introduced that made itself felt with increasing intensity.

And Martin Luther? The chronicler will accompany him for a while, since for a brief time he continued in the public eye. Then the focus will change.

The stage was occupied by different men, a few of them theologians, such as Philipp Melanchthon and Martin Bucer, but most of them statesmen and diplomats, such as Philip of Hesse and Maurice of Saxony. Once the time of storm and stress had passed, when theological words could be uttered without regard for practical consequences, new questions of a practical sort arose and had to be answered—from the problem of how to train ministers to that of upholding proper doctrinal standards.

To the time of the Edict of Worms events had been only prologue. Afterward the controversy turned into an affair of state. The curtain lifted on the Reformation. No longer stood one man on the stage; a chorus was exuberantly taking his place.

### Worms and Beyond

The news of Luther's disappearance spread quickly. Only a few knew what had actually happened and most people thought of foul play—that Luther had been arrested, perhaps even killed. Albrecht Dürer, on a visit to Holland, penned some stirring lines in his diary upon learning of Luther's disappearance. 'O God,' he wrote, 'if Luther is dead, who will henceforth proclaim to us the holy Gospel?'[1]

Emperor Charles observed many years later that it had been a major mistake of his rule to have honored Luther's safe conduct. There is persuasive logic in this reflection; had Luther been apprehended and punished as a heretic, the storm might have yet proved to be a tempest in a teapot. But Charles's comment confirms that even in retrospect he failed to understand what had happened at that time. For all practical purposes it seemed indeed as though Luther were dead. But at issue was not, as Charles erroneously assumed, a single monk with heretical ideas, but a phenomenon of increasingly widespread dimension. Thus, neither the honoring of the safe conduct, nor even Elector Frederick's decision to 'kidnap' Luther was the decisive factor. The action of neither man, however important, saved the Lutheran cause. What did save it was enthusiasm for Luther's message. In the months following the Diet the *affaire Luther* became the German Reformation. Everywhere people began to take up Luther's slogans and to echo his sentiments. From the pulpits in Saxony, in Nuremberg, Augsburg, Ulm, Strassburg, in The Netherlands and East Frisia came the new proclamation and from the pews a response.

While this electrifying windstorm was going through Germany, Luther was at the Wartburg, 'the realm of the birds and air,' as he himself called it. Today the tourist can still see the *Luther-Stube* of the castle, the rounded door leading to the room, the stone floor, a small table on which a pious tradition put a 'Luther Bible' under glass. A small window opened on the woody hills and the world. Luther's presence was kept secret. He called himself 'Junker Jörg,' wore knightly attire and sported a beard.

One day he had faced the Emperor and the dignitaries of the realm, had argued with churchmen and theologians; the next day he rested in the solitude of a castle nestled in woods, all alone, his only contact with the keeper of the castle who brought his food. There was nothing to do, no one to talk with, only the gentle breeze over the woodland hills and the chirping of the birds! At long last he had time to reflect upon the turbulent events. He had repudiated centuries of Christian tradition and had divorced himself from the Church. The full impact of such thoughts weighed heavily on him.

'My heart often trembled and pounded and reproached me,' Luther wrote. 'Are you alone wise? Is everyone else in error? Have so many centuries been in ignorance? What if you have been wrong and dragged many with you into error and eternal damnation?'[2] It was then that spiritual assaults, *Anfechtungen*, beset him.

One can hardly talk about Luther without speaking of those *Anfechtungen*, his temptations or 'assaults,' pronounced on the Wartburg and the constant companion of his spiritual pilgrimage. 'Should I live longer,' Luther remarked once across the dinner table, 'I should like to write a book about temptations, for no one can understand the Scriptures, faith, the fear or the love of God without them.'[3] Indeed, he related the formulation of his theology to his experience of the *tentationes*: 'I did not learn my theology all at once. I had to brood and ponder over it with increasing depth. My temptations have led me to my theology, for one learns only by experience.'[4]

His were not temptations in the ordinary sense of the word, but spiritual agonies and struggles, affecting the core of his faith. Luther was persuaded that faith must always run counter to experience. The dualism between faith and experience constituted a fundamental insight into the nature of God's dealing with man. The definition of faith was found in Hebrews 1.1—'the evidence of things not seen.' Therefore the object of faith was hidden and beyond experience, indeed contrary to experience. Such an understanding means that one always lives in the face of conflicting experiences and principles.

Vigorous work turned out to be both a therapeutic help and a theological necessity. Luther assembled a *Kirchenpostille* (Church Postill), a collection of exegetical 'sermons,' to be read privately or used in the pulpit by illiterate ministers. He wrote his treatise on *Monastic Vows*, which contained a trenchant consideration of the monastic profession. Luther rejected monastic vows because they were a denial of faith and against Christian freedom. Luther also countered the Louvain theologian Latomus with a treatise, *Rationis Latomianiae confutatio*, that ranks high as an expression of his understanding of justification and the proper approach to Scripture. Luther's main work, however, was the translation of the New Testament into German, a task to which he addressed himself quite consistently.[5] His claim that Scripture was the norm of faith made it mandatory that he turn to the practical side of the matter. How could the common man use this norm unless it was available in his own tongue? Even Friedrich Nietzsche, the master of German prose, had words of commendation: 'In comparison with Luther's Bible, almost everything is just literature, that is, it is a thing which has not grown in Germany and has not grown, and is not growing, into German hearts as the Bible has done.'[6] German translations of the New Testament existed before Luther; therefore his work was neither linguistically nor philologically a pristine feat. If his translation was a sensation, it was because he himself had prepared the ground. That 15th-century translations had a way of falling into oblivion, whereas Luther's was a revolution, must be attributed to the different temper of the times. Luther had succeeded in persuading the people of the importance of Holy Writ, of its eminence in formulating religious convictions. As important as the translation itself, then, was Luther's sharpening of the sensitivity of the people in regard to the importance of Scripture. Theretofore, the people had been content to let the Church expound the Scriptures; Luther persuaded them to read for themselves.

Luther's translation was a creative accomplishment. His use of the Saxon dialect aided in the development of the modern German tongue, but, more than that, he made his German version live and breathe an authentic spirit. Luther transformed Galilee into Saxony and Jerusalem into Wittenberg. The personages of the Gospels, their speech, their customs, their environment, became those of the 16th century. When Jesus spoke to his disciples, he spoke as the man in Wittenberg or Nuremberg would speak to his neighbors. Lucas Cranach's woodcuts, which accompanied the text, conveyed the same message by providing a 16th-century setting for the Biblical events. More than 50 printings within 4 years attested to the phenomenal popularity of Luther's translation. It is true that in a few places Luther translated rather loosely. He made Rom 3.28 read by 'faith alone,' even though the Greek said only by 'faith.' Holy Writ in its German version explicitly proclaimed Luther's gospel. But Luther did not intend to falsify the text: even St. Thomas Aquinas had rendered the passage the same way. Luther made the change, as he wrote later on in his tract *Sendbrief vom Dolmetschen* (On Translating), because his rendition reflected not only the meaning of the passage but also conformed to the temper of the Greek language.

When the translation was published in September 1522—it is known as the 'September Bible'—it included a preface on the nature of Scripture. Perhaps this preface outranks the translation in importance, for in it Luther delineated some basic hermeneutic principles. The controversy with Latomus, who extensively quoted

Scripture, had caused him to reflect that *sola scriptura* was an insufficient source of authority. Scripture was heterogeneous; a principle was necessary to transform the complexity of Scripture into a consistent whole. It was not enough to quote Scripture; it had to be quoted properly. Or was the Catholic Church right when it insisted on the need for authoritative interpretation? In the preface Luther gave his answer. To be a genuine source of faith a passage must *Christum treiben*—'proclaim Christ.'[7] Luther argued that not all of Scripture did so: certainly not the Epistle of James (a 'strawy epistle'), certainly not the Apocalypse; Luther was also uncertain about the Synoptics and spoke highly only of John's Gospel, of Romans, Galatians, Ephesians and 1 Peter.

Such an unconstrained, though profound, attitude toward Scripture was problematic. Luther eased his blunt differentiation in later years to make sure that no one understood him to advocate a revision of the canon. The Epistle of James was in the canon and Luther always affirmed the decision of the early Church. What he meant to discount was the notion of proof-texts to undergird any proposition. A principle of interpretation was necessary, and Luther found this principle in Paul, or, more particularly, in Rom 1.17. This was the key to the New Testament and indeed to the Bible. Luther recognized that Paul's assertion of justification by faith and James's stress upon justification by works needed to be harmonized —without invoking the external authority of the Church—and his conclusion was that such harmony could be accomplished with the hints of Scripture. It was in keeping with the sentiment of the entire Bible, Luther felt, to interpret all of it through Paul: James or the Synoptics were thus viewed through the eyes of Paul, rather than vice versa.

Late in 1521 the pastoral idyll of the Wartburg was disturbed by perplexing news from Wittenberg, where ecclesiastical life was increasingly characterized by tumult and uproar. Luther had disappeared to the Wartburg at a crucial moment. A thousand practical questions demanded an answer. Should current ecclesiastical practice be changed in the light of the new Biblical insight? Should one wait for the Church? Should one go ahead independently? Luther had denounced the bases of Catholic religion—the monastic vocation, the ecclesistical benefices, the sacraments, the sacrifice of the Mass. Should these practices be continued? Luther had given no answer. His sojourn on the Wartburg kept him removed from the daily involvement in ecclesiastical practices that for some Wittenbergers led to disturbed consciences. At Wittenberg traditional ecclesiastical practices continued as if nothing had happened: the Mass continued to be celebrated, monks remained in the monasteries, the Communion cup continued to be withheld from the laity. What should be done? There was more to this situation than met the eye. It was one thing to call for a conformity of ecclesiastical practice with Biblical theory, and quite another to know exactly what practice was specified on Biblical grounds. The easiest, and most consistent, answer is to say that everything is specified, the more difficult one is to make distinctions.

The questions that perturbed many minds were practical and theological and dealt with principle as well as expediency. Both the *what* and the *when* of ecclesiastical change were problems. The first practice to come under attack was the Mass, in particular the withholding of the cup from the laity, the so-called 'private Masses', and the notion of sacrifice in the Mass. Carlstadt announced that he would observe an 'evangelical mass' on New Year's Day. When the Saxon Elector prohibited this, Carlstadt held the 'mass' at Christmas. The occasion was memorable. First came a Communion meditation, then a new liturgy that had been stripped of anything that suggested sacrifice. The words of institution were spoken in German, and Carlstadt performed the ceremony in simple clothes. An ancient ceremony had disappeared. Other changes occurred in rapid succession. Carlstadt volunteered to read daily a chapter from the Bible. More alterations were made in the liturgy. Images were taken from churches and the elaborate singing in the service was discontinued. Carlstadt made news with the announcement that rather than celebrate Mass he would purchase a house in Wittenberg and earn his living as a beer brewer and innkeeper.

The Wittenberg city council finally decided that things were getting out of hand. Elector Frederick, informed of the situation, issued an instruction demanding that the sacrament be treated in a 'most orderly and Christian fashion,' that the images remain in the churches, and that Carlstadt, who seemed to represent the rabble-rousers, be kept from preaching. In the background loomed the mandate of the *Reichsregiment* of January 20, which had prohibited all changes in established Catholic practices.

Luther had initially not been opposed to the course of events in Wittenberg and after a clandestine visit to the city had written that he was pleased with what he had seen. But then came the January mandate and the perplexity of Elector Frederick, and Luther recognized that the exuberance of the Wittenberg reformers endangered by its legalistic attitude the work of reform itself. He said 'no.' There was danger that the Gospel was once again being perverted. External changes were undertaken too rapidly, without the awareness that inner change must precede the outer. Moreover, the innovations disturbed the distinction between law and Gospel by transforming the Gospel once again into law. The prohibition of the cup, the celibate priesthood, the fasting, were matters of Christian freedom, if the Old Church had erred by positing certain regulations, the impatient reformers in Wittenberg were in error by establishing new ones of their own. Early in March Luther returned to Wittenberg. Two days after his return he preached for the first time in almost a year. What would Luther say? Even before he spoke a single syllable the answer was clear. There he stood in front of them in the habit of an Augustinian monk. The beard and long hair of Junker Jörg were gone; a newly shaven tonsure had taken their place. It was as if nothing had been said about monasticism, nothing about man-made vows that need not be kept, nothing about the abomination of the papal system. 'We are all called upon to die,' Luther began, 'and no one will die for the other, but each one will for himself fight with death. We can well shout into one another's ears, but each one must himself be prepared for the time of death.'[8] Therefore, Luther continued, man must know the faith by which he lives and dies, namely, the recognition of sin and of God's grace, and the love of one's neighbor. These are the main matters, Luther asserted, and he recalled how he himself had needed many years to grasp them. All else was secondary. To pretend that the secondary matters were the most important ones was naïvely erroneous.

The nature of Luther's reforming temper was expressed in his sermon, and everyone in Wittenberg must have recognized this. Outer form can never be as important as faith. First the idols in man's heart must be torn down; only afterward can the same be done to those in the churches. Christian freedom dare not be turned once again into slavish rules; the Biblical 'may's' must not be turned into rigoristic 'must's.' About some matters no clear Biblical directive was available, and they may be handled in Christian freedom. Of course, Luther's understanding of the Gospel did entail practical consequences and the need for ecclesiastical change. Yet Luther could never admit that these practical consequences were crucial. The turbulence in Wittenberg during his absence had increased his theological antipathy against reform undertaken by coercion. 'By their fruit ye shall know them' was the scriptural dictum, and the iconoclasm in Wittenberg left no doubt that the fruit had been evil. Upon Luther's return to Wittenberg several of the ecclesiastical changes undertaken during his absence were undone. The Mass was reintroduced and continued, though purged of its elements suggesting sacrifice. Reform in Wittenberg was slow in coming. To deal with the pressing issue of the worship of the congregation, Luther wrote *Formula missae et communionis* (Form of the Mass and Communion), a Latin order of worship. His *Taufbüchlein verdeutscht* (Order of Baptism) was the first German order for the administration of Baptism. Another tract, *Dass eine christliche Versammlung oder Gemeine Recht und Macht habe, alle Lehre zu urteilen* (That a Christian Gathering or Congregation Has the Authority and Power to Judge All Doctrine and to Call Teachers), asserted the centrality of the congregation in the ordering of its affairs. He meant to offer only suggestions or example, for this, too, was a matter of Christian freedom, and slavish conformity was not necessary.

So, by the middle of the decade several changes had been made in the ongoing ecclesiastical life and practice. But these changes were few and pertained mainly to the grey no-man's-land that did not affect incisively the Catholicity of ecclesiastical life. The ties had not been cut. No new Church had replaced the old. The question was, all the same, how long this equilibrium could last.

## The Message

In his *Von den guten Werken* (Sermon on Good Works) of 1520, Luther remarked that he had been accused of 'writing only small tracts and German sermons' and retorted that 'I am not ashamed that I preached and wrote in German for the unlearned laity—even though I can also do it the other way—for I do believe that if we had heretofore been more concerned about this, Christendom would show more improvement than it does from the high and mighty books and questions typical of the academicians of the universities.'[9]

In so writing Luther espoused a definite program for ecclesiastical transformation that consisted in a direct appeal to the common man in order to alter the ecclesiastical state of Christendom. He himself had made the beginning with his German Sermon on Indulgence and Grace of 1518, which saw no less than 23 reprints during the first 3 years of the indulgences controversy. Most of Luther's subsequent tracts, especially those in German, enjoyed a similar popularity. 10, 15, and even 20 reprints of a tract were not at all unusual: if there had been the kind of stringent prohibitions of reprints as exist in our own day, the popular appeal of Luther would have been

notably less. All in all, one million copies of Luther's tracts may well
have been in circulation by 1524.

A host of tracts issued from the printing presses, flooding the
countryside and making Luther's tenets common household words.
In the 5 years after 1518 Luther undoubtedly was the most popular
German writer. One may well single out the printing press as the
foremost factor in the colportage of the new religious ideas. Without the press, Luther and the Reformation would not have been
successful. The press was the mouthpiece of the new evangel, the
means of its spread into towns, hamlets, and homes. The reformers
recognized this contribution, and none more superbly than the John
Foxe who introduced his narrative of the Reformation in his *Actes
and Monuments* with a discussion of the invention of printing:
'. . . the Pope, that great Antichrist of Rome, could never have been
suppressed . . . except this most excellent science of printing had
been maintained.'[10]

The quantity of the materials was phenomenal. Between 1518
and 1522 the character of the publications in Germany underwent a
far-reaching change. The earlier preponderance of secular writings,
from astrological prognoses to current-events pamphlets, disappeared and religion became the most important subject. Nuncio
Aleander reported in February 1521 that 'daily there is a veritable
downpour of Lutheran tracts in German and Latin . . . nothing is sold
here except the tracts of Luther.'[11] Here, as on other occasions, he
may have overdramatized the issue, but one needs to look only at
the quantitative evidence to become aware of the obvious impact.
There was Luther's own impressive literary production (now found
in no less than 100 volumes of the so-called Weimar edition of his
works). And the other reformers were equally prolific, though not
always equally profound, doing their share to swell the number of
publications. The writings of Melanchthon, Bucer, and Bullinger
fill several volumes, and one reason for the lack of scholarly editions
of the minor reformers is surely that they simply wrote too much.
Carlstadt wrote more than 50 tracts, and the edition of Schwenckfeld's works comprises some 19 formidable volumes. Such quantity
was more the rule than the exception. Capito, Bugenhagen, Cranmer, Calvin, and their confreres can claim credit for publication lists
that today would persuade any university tenure committee. Not all
of these writers were on the scene in the early 1520s, of course, nor
did all address themselves to the 'popularization' of the new Gospel.

But there were a host of partisans of Luther's cause, men who
had neither the brilliance nor the creativity to become figures of

lasting significance. Still, they wrote prolifically on behalf of the Lutheran Gospel. Mere numbers reveal how dramatically the quantity of religious publications increased in Germany: In 1517 there were less than 20; in 1522, approximately 100, excluding those of Erasmus and those of Luther. Of course, not all of these were partisans of Luther's cause, but most were. While one must treat such figures with a great deal of caution (the size of the individual editions, for example, is enigmatic, as is the more obvious question whether the people who bought them did actually read them), the basic conclusion seems inevitable. There was great interest in the Lutheran writings, and society, not merely its educated segments, but the common people as well, was reading extensively. It was as if people were awaking from a slumber. Earlier they had had no opportunity or no desire to read. Now they read voraciously.

This ecstatic reading was made possible by several developments. We have already noted the contribution of the printing press, without which the circumstances of publication would have been simply impossible. Another important factor was the drastic change in format. Most of the publications prior to the Reformation had been weighty, voluminous, and in Latin. The new literature was different. Most of it was in pamphlet form—8, 16, perhaps 32 pages in length, convenient to use, decorated with woodcuts, and low in price. More than that, there was no linguistic obstacle to widespread distribution, for the language was the vernacular. To be sure, some of the publications prior to 1517 were also in the vernacular—astrological calendars, news broadsheets, or travel accounts—but the real change came with Luther. While some of his incisive theological tracts were in Latin—one thinks of the Babylonian Captivity or *De servo arbitrio* (The Bondage of the Will)—his most significant works certainly were in German. And even his Latin works were promptly translated into the vernacular and thereby exerted an influence among all the people.

Such use of the vernacular to propound religious ideas had no precedent. With rare exceptions the religious and theological literature before the Reformation was in Latin, as were the writings of the humanists, such as Erasmus's *Encomium Moriae* (Praise of Folly), the tract *Julius a coelo exclusus*, and the *Epistolae obscurum virorum*. The medium the humanists chose was Latin, the language of the learned. In so doing they were concerned about more than the revival of an elegant and versatile language; they expressed a program of reformatory renewal. The appeal for change and reform was addressed to the educated circles and the elite, in the hope of influencing them and, through them, society at large. Luther and the reformers, on the other hand, chose to speak to the common people and to persuade them directly of the new proclamation. Initially, this may have come about by accident, though Luther's Sermon on Indulgence and Grace, his first publication in German, revealed several of his characteristic qualities: his concern to enlighten the common people about indulgences and grace, his marvelous command of language, his ability to summarize essential points, and his genius in singling out incisive issues. These qualities were to characterize the literary controversy for the next decades. Luther's presupposition was that religious issues were to be pursued not only in the circle of the theological experts, but also among the common people. This, in turn, meant that it was needful for the common people to be involved and that they were thought capable of considering religious issues. The Protestant publishing effort was thus a large-scale attempt to confront society with religious issues, as Luther had argued in his Letter to the Christian Nobility, where he had written that the laity should help in the reform of the Church. The reformers were concerned about the common people—about the artisans and the burghers in the towns, about the peasants in the country. Erasmus had waxed lyrical about his desire to have the peasant recite the words of Sacred Writ behind his plough, but he had himself always written in Latin. Theretofore neglected and considered incompetent to deal with religious issues, the common man found himself in a different role.[12] He was wooed and exposed to fervent appeals to embrace the new teaching. Nothing is more symptomatic of this temper than the dramatically new position occupied by the lowliest of the lowly, the peasant. Some Lutheran tracts addressed themselves directly to the peasant, depicting him as a wise and perceptive observer of the religious controversy. The tract *Karsthans*, first published in 1521 and reprinted no less than nine times, made a simple peasant the judge of a theological disagreement between Luther and his Catholic opponent, Murner. That Luther's arguments triumphed (predictably) was of less importance than the significant part given to the peasant.

The Lutheran tracts sought to accomplish two purposes—to expound, in simple terms, the Lutheran understanding of the Christian Gospel, and to respond to possible objections from proponents of the old faith. This latter purpose explains the widespread popularity of the dialogue, which made it possible to voice certain objections (in as vulnerable a form as possible) to the Lutheran teaching, and then to dismiss them with a skillful combination of logic and

Biblical references. Today's reader will find all of these dialogues a bit stilted and less than fully convincing, especially since their outcome is all too obvious from the very beginning. But man in the 16th century, unaccustomed to reading anything in his own language but simple devotional tracts, found it all both exciting and persuasive. Besides dialogues a variety of other literary forms was used, such as sermons, open letters, and poems. There were also satires, such as Satan's declaration of war against Luther, and parodies, such as an account of Luther's appearance at Worms clad in the form of the Gospel narratives of Jesus's passion. Literature in the broader sense carried the banner of the new faith. The visual arts played an important role also from the time the first crude woodcut of Luther made its appearance on the title page of a published sermon of 1519 to Cranach's drastic, if vulgar, cartoons depicting the 'abomination' of the papacy. Luther naturally was a favorite object of such artistic endeavors, now shown with a saintly halo, now in knight's armor, whereas his opponents were transformed into replicas of the lower animal kingdom. The most popular of these pictorial propaganda efforts was the *Passional Christi und Antichristi*, which depicted in parallel woodcuts the contrast between the simplicity of Christ and the splendor of the papacy—Christ washing his disciples' feet, the pope having his feet kissed; Christ wearing a crown of thorns, the pope wearing the tiara.

This takes us to the question concerning the content of the Lutheran tracts in the early years of the Reformation. Their enormous quantity makes any generalization difficult, though it is obvious that they were not 'Lutheran' in the full sense of the word. Of course, Luther was not either. This is to say that Luther's German publications during the first years of the controversy by no means portray the 'entire' Luther, as modern scholarship might reconstruct him. There is painfully little on the doctrine of justification. The overwhelming quantity of Luther's literary pronouncement of the time (his sermons, his exposition of various psalms, his tracts on confession, marital life, and temporal government) propound his religious views, but in very simple form. The 'entire' Luther was not known to contemporaries, for his letters, his academic lectures (especially the unpublished early ones), and even his Latin works were hidden in the solitude of Wittenberg, known only to a few. A few key themes were sounded and could be heard over and over again with the simplicity of a Gregorian plain song. There was the insistence on the scriptural basis of the Christian faith, the notion that the Bible rather than ecclesiastical tradition must form the ground for religious truth. This was in opposition to 'human traditions,' including not only the official pronouncements of the Church but the views and opinions of scholastic theologians as well. There was the insistence on the centrality of faith, the assertion that salvation was not by works, but by faith, not by striving, but by grace. There was the rejection of the complex edifice of the medieval understanding of the Christian faith in favor of a 'simple' faith. Indeed, simplicity may well be said to have been the key slogan. Reform was to be simplification. The repristination of the Gospel was to be accomplished by removing the welter of 'traditions.'

The message of the Gospels was simple; it had nothing to do with externals and ritual; it concerned the life of faith and trust. True religion knew of no real difference between clergy and laity, of the superiority of the clerical profession over the vocation of the laity. This was the message. Its persuasiveness lay in its simplicity. It could be easily comprehended and, moreover, it was meaningful to all those who had grown discontented and restless with the Church and who felt, without ever voicing overt criticism, that true religion somehow or other was different. We need to remind ourselves that the acceptance of this perspective did not, at least at that time, mean a repudiation of the Roman Church, though it did mean the unlearning of beliefs and practices familiar since childhood.

It is as misleading to label the enormous pamphlet literature 'Lutheran' as it is to suggest that the writers (many of whom were trained theologians) failed to understand Luther's real theological intent. The crux of the matter is that they meant to be supporters of Luther—and this is what they were. They hailed him as a pious man and servant of God, 'herald of the true teaching,' indeed as Elijah or as the angel of the Book of Revelation. No other figure—neither Zwingli nor Müntzer nor Carlstadt—shared this immense popularity.

### The Response

Whatever may be uncertain about Luther's proclamation, there can be little doubt that it called forth a widespread response. One may question the religious sincerity of those who embraced Luther's cause; that people did embrace it, however, cannot be contested. Luther became a reformer and his personal religion became a historical movement because his contemporaries responded to his message.

To do so was no easy thing. It meant the repudiation of the Church and of centuries of Christian tradition. It meant the rejection of one's religious heritage. But so it happened, not in isolated instances, but thousands of times. Monks who had vowed obedience to the pope became his mortal enemies. Nuns who had pledged themselves to lives of celibacy entered matrimony. Priests who had thought the Mass the very heart of the faith denounced it as the abomination of abominations. To do all this required courage. The change of loyalties could hardly have been lighthearted. Those who embraced Luther's cause set out to live their religious lives diametrically opposite from previous practice. Still, the number of Luther's partisans was legion. In 1521 the nuncio Aleander remarked that nine-tenths of the German people had rallied around Luther and 2 years later Ferdinand of Austria reported that 'Luther's teaching is so firmly embedded in the Empire that among a thousand persons not a single one is completely untouched; it could be hardly worse.' While both comments may be too general, they express tellingly the psychological atmosphere at the time. And there are other means to gauge Luther's impact. The spectacular increase in the enrollment at the University of Wittenberg—from 162 in 1516 to 579 in 1520—can be cited here, as can the widespread distribution of Luther's writings already noted. The free imperial cities in Germany provide further persuasive evidence for the popularity of Luther's message. Most of the cities embraced the new faith because in the cities a measure of democracy prevailed that gave the burghers a voice in the conduct of civic business. Popular agitation for an alteration of ecclesiastical affairs was thus bound to find relatively easy expression in the cities, in contrast to the territories, in which the ruler made all the difference. It has been shown that the acceptance of the Protestant faith in the Swiss cities was most delayed where there was little popular participation in municipal affairs. Zurich, with a contingent of artisans on its city council, moved with relative ease, whereas Berne and Basel, where patrician families dominated the council, required almost a decade to make the change.[13]

Everywhere the city councils were initially the retarding forces, whereas agitation for change came from the burghers and the guilds. Had the issue been one of greater control of ecclesiastical affairs by the secular authorities, the councils would have been anxious to repudiate the ecclesiastical status quo. The fact is that they did not and, on the contrary, strove to thwart the propagation of the new faith. The Protestant cause was advocated by those who were to derive no obvious political advantage from any change.

Why did the people respond positively to the Lutheran proclamation? The answers vary. One may cite non-religious factors:
economic greed for wealth of the Church; resentment over the legal
prerogatives of the Church; desire to control all affairs in a given
commonwealth, including those of the Church. It is surely noteworthy that at some places the demand for discontinuation of pay-
ments to the Church and for 'evangelical' ministers was made in the
same breath as that for greater popular participation in governmental affairs. On the other hand, one may insist on the pre-eminence
of religious and spiritual concerns. The evidence is ambiguous. Obviously, the historian will never know what went on in the minds of
people in the third decade of the 16th century. Even where religious
reasons were given, a word of caution is in order, for religious conviction and verbal demonstrance are not necessarily one and the
same.

Two considerations must be kept in mind here. One is that in all
probability there was no single factor. Some men acted for this
reason, others for that; some did not act at all. The other is a chronological caveat. To throw all men and all religious decisions of the
Reformation into one grab-bag from which to derive one generalization is highly precarious. One must differentiate between the situations prevailing at different times and in different places. In the
1530s, when Protestantism in Germany had attained political
strength, political prudence may have made the acceptance of the
new faith an understandable decision. In the early 1520s, however,
the situation was different: both ecclesiastical and political authorities had condemned Luther and his followers. The Emperor, while
temporarily absent from Germany, had left no doubt about his intention to suppress heresy in the realm. To support Luther meant to
support heresy—and heresy had never prevailed, but had always
been suppressed. No matter how many hundreds of pamphlets hailed
Luther's cause, he was still a heretic against whom the universal
Church had rendered its verdict. Few, if any, heretics had ever been
successful.

The historian knows that in the end the bark proved worse than
the bite, that Luther and the other major reformers died peacefully
in bed, and that acceptance of the new faith, far from entailing loss
of property or life, could be economically profitable as well as
politically prudent. But all this could not be known in 1523 or 1524.
when the prospects for anyone accepting the new faith seemed
rather grim. If, in the face of such difficulties, many were willing to

embrace the new faith, genuine religious enthusiasm must have been present. At the same time, we must note that the support of Luther, or what we have called the embracing of the new faith, did not mean categorical rejection of the Catholic Church or a deliberate attempt at a parting of the ways. It was merely a challenge to the Church to reform, a plea for the true Church against the perverted one. And even where individual sentiment jelled into collective agitation for ecclesiastical change, the situation was not different. As a rule, the first and most persistent demand of the proponents of the new faith was for 'evangelical' preachers. This would suggest that the goal was not to repudiate the Church, or to break away from it, but to make changes within it. Few actual changes were undertaken before 1525, and even those were, deliberately, one feels, of a marginal character, such as the removal of images from the churches, that did not affect the heart of traditional religion.

In short, people saw the situation as fluid, flexible, and without the kind of finality that a view *ex post eventu* does so easily suggest. After all, the call was for 'reform,' which meant a change within the Church rather than its split. The situation after 1521 was one of extemporization and improvisation. The absence of the Emperor made this virtually inevitable, and the repeated demands on the part of the German Diets between 1522 and 1524 for the convening of a general council indicated that the hope for resolution of the controversy lay with the Church. Still, any support of Luther was the support of a man condemned as a heretic by the Church. And this was not only politically precarious; it was also spiritually abominable. Those who saw loyalty to the Church as represented by the pope as the noblest expression of religious devotion, could not but oppose the heretic from Wittenberg, no matter how widespread his support and how popular his tenets. The existence of two groups of people was, from the very beginning, the hallmark of the controversy. Indeed, the situation was fluid enough to make it possible for some of Luther's supporters to divorce themselves from him in the end and for erstwhile Catholics to accept his tenets.

The question of possible patterns of 'conversion' or 'loyalty' remains. It would be splendid, if this matter of becoming (or not becoming) a supporter of Luther followed a discernible pattern—so that all people in the cities (or in the country), in the north (or in the south), with education (or without), with wealth (or without) became Lutheran. Alas, no such pattern exists—or, if it does, this writer at least has been unable to discern it. A few comments, however, may be made. One pertains to the humanists, from whose ranks had initially come Luther's most ardent supporters. In the end, most humanists chose to remain Catholic. One thinks here at once of Erasmus, of course, but also of men such as Mutian or Budé, and others too numerous to mention. The humanists had wanted the correction of ecclesiastical abuse and a reformed religion. They had employed their pens to precipitate it, and at first they had given their vigorous support to Luther. But soon they abhorred Luther's theological reformulation as too radical and too tumultuous. None expressed this sentiment better than Erasmus when he wrote in 1527 that 'the reformers should have not heedlessly wrecked anything without having something better ready to put in its place. As it is, those who have abandoned the Hours do not pray at all. Those who have put off pharisaical clothing are worse in other matters than they were before. Those who disdain the episcopal regulations do not obey the commandments of God.'

If a goodly number of the humanists remained cool toward Luther and his cause, the universities and the established theologians were even more so.[14] By and large, the academic community remained closed to the new faith. Wittenberg was an exception; at most other universities the reaction of the academicians was uniformly negative. At Leipzig, a phalanx of theologians opposed Luther; at Erfurt, Luther's own alma mater, he had a few supporters, but the eminent members of the faculty, such as Trutvetter, Usingen, and Mutian, did not make Luther's cause their own. Cologne, Ingolstadt, Heidelberg, Freiburg, Tübingen, and Frankfurt likewise remained Catholic. In later years Basel, Leipzig and Tübingen became Protestant, and Landgrave Philip of Hesse founded a Protestant university at Marburg in 1527. The fact remains that virtually all established academic theologians died as good Catholics. In some instances personal or academic rivalry may have influenced the negative reaction and the conservatism of academicians, most of whom were advanced in years, can also be cited as a reason. Moreover, the universities were related to the Catholic Church in a number of ways. At Wittenberg, for example, the Augustinian Order provided several professorships and a repudiation of Catholicism there destroyed the structure of academic life. A more fundamental reason for academic coolness toward the new faith was the radical rejection of the scholastic method and of scholasticism on the part of the Protestants, by which the very character of the university was altered and Aristotle was deprived of his place of authoritative prominence. To accept such a radical reorientation would have been an undue expression of ideological mobility on the part of the academicians. The new Protestant universities were influenced by humanism rather than by scholasticism. Naturally, they failed to earned their distinction by expounding scholastic notions. In short, the new theology, no matter how learned, was not university oriented; the Protestant theologian was not a professor of theology, but a minister and a preacher.

If the university community showed itself immune to the challenge of the Reformation, the clergy proved a different picture. The higher clergy generally remained faithful to the Catholic Church, whereas the lower clergy joined the Protestant ranks in large numbers. Indeed, the men who first carried the new evangel to success had formerly been Catholic priests and monks. They were the foot soldiers of the Reformation and without them no lasting achievement would have been possible. The persuasiveness of the printed word alone would never have sufficed to effect a socialization of the new faith. They were the 'Little Luthers' who exposed their congregations to the new proclamation and restructured ecclesiastical life in their communities.

The common characteristic of the advocates of the new theology was youth. Luther was 34 years of age at the outbreak of the indulgences controversy and Zwingli just a few months younger; Melanchthon was 20. These are typical figures to which the dates of other reformers are easily added: Wenzeslas Link was born in 1483; Friedrich Myconius, in 1491; Jacob Strauss, in 1485; Andreas Osiander, in 1498; Johann Brenz, in 1499; Johann Oecolampadius, in 1482; Martin Bucer, in 1491; Wolfgang Capito, in 1478; Bugenhagen, in 1495; Urban Rhegius, in 1489; Thomas Müntzer, in 1490. Virtually all were young men in their 20's and 30's when the controversy broke out, a fact that helps to explain the vitality of the new faith. The Reformation was a movement of youth, of exuberance, of a bold disregard for consequences.

## The Political Sequel

With the Diet of Worms began a new and different chapter in the ecclesiastical controversy. And this was not only for the reason already noted, namely, that the proclamation of a single man was increasingly echoed and re-echoed throughout Germany. More important was the fact that the Edict of Worms turned the affair of Luther into an affair of state. Any resolution of the matter from then on had to be in the realm of politics and law as much as of religion.

But the man who was to undertake the administration of the Edict was absent. All the splendid oratory of Worms, when Charles had confronted the territorial rulers with his uncompromising assertion that he was ready to pledge his life and property to the eradication of the Lutheran heresy, had disappeared like smoke. Charles departed from Germany to travel to Spain in what seemed a wise and necessary move after he had attended, at his first German Diet, to the pressing political problems. He had settled the problem of the *Reichsregiment*; he had turned over the Austrian lands and the claims to Bohemia and Hungary to his brother Ferdinand; he also had disposed (on paper, that is) of the heretical menace. Accordingly, he thought it proper to direct his attention to Spain. There his election to the imperial throne had been received with ill-concealed dismay. The prospect of an absentee-ruler and of higher taxes, necessary for Charles's exercise of the imperial office, was hardly calculated to arouse warm feelings. In May 1520, the so-called *comuñeros* revolt had broken out and, even though it was quickly suppressed, there is little doubt that Charles's return was necessary. Moreover, the renewed conflict with France diverted Charles's attention from Germany.

Germany was therefore like a pilotless ship, a fact that was to have profound consequences for the subsequent course of events. But at the time Charles could see no reason why the Lutheran menace would not be swiftly crushed. Heresy had always been crushed. One suspects that Charles left Germany in the spring of 1521 with a feeling of satisfaction and accomplishment. But he had overlooked two important facts: the intensity of popular support for Martin Luther and the inability of the *Reichsregiment* at Nuremberg to enforce the Edict of Worms. Part of the trouble lay in the cumbersome way in which the *Reichsregiment* functioned. Its representation rotated all too frequently for any long-range policy to be practicable. There was also a disposition to stay aloof from such a heated controversy and to let events run their course. Only the dogged determination of Duke George of Saxony kept the matter alive and in January 1522 led to a mandate that prohibited all changes in existing ecclesiastical practice.[15] Since the Edict of Worms had declared the same prohibition, the mandate was probably gratuitous, and it was certainly as ineffective.

Meanwhile the Curia was becoming annoyed or frustrated (perhaps both) over the absence of swift action against Luther and his followers. The nuncio Francesco Chieregati, in Germany to further the cause of a crusade against the Turks, spoke to the German

Estates in January 1523 about the religious controversy. He read a brief from Pope Adrian VI expressing consternation over the tardy administration of the Edict of Worms and rejecting the insinuation that Luther had been condemned without a proper hearing. This was not unusual, but the brief included also a confession that 'God sent this tribulation to his church on account of the sins of men, especially of priests and prelates.' Such frank words had not been heard before, nor had there been anything similar to Adrian's pledge 'that we shall reform the Curia from which possibly all evil matter had emanated.'[16] The response from the Estates differed from what the nuncio must have anticipated. The clergy was cool and the supporters of Luther were reserved. One year later a similar statement by Cardinal Campeggio (though without the blunt admission of curial shortcomings) encountered a similar response. This was understandable, perhaps, since Campeggio was rigid in his demeanor, being unwilling even to talk about the traditional German *gravamina* which the Estates were itching to throw at him. Campeggio's lament that some rulers had given up the religion of their forebears in order to accept a seditious doctrine should have fallen on fertile ground, for most of the Estates were loyal to the Church and a formal acknowledgment of the Edict of Worms could be expected. Still, dissatisfaction with ecclesiastical affairs prevailed and gave rise to the demand for a council as the means to settle the religious issues: a *gemeine Versammlung deutscher Nation*, a general assembly of the German people, should convene at Speyer in November to arrive at a temporary settlement.[17] Campeggio protested, as did the Curia when informed of this action. Clement VII told the Emperor that only force would subdue the heretics and demanded that the proposed gathering be prohibited. The Emperor complied, whether on account of his Catholic orientation or because he saw his imperial authority threatened, or even because he hoped for the pope's support for his own policies is hard to tell. He was shocked, Charles wrote to Germany, by this incredible venture proposed by the 'pious German people.' He demanded that the Edict of Worms be administered and that 'all discussion, explanation, or interpretation of the Christian faith' be stopped. In cooperation with the pope he would seek to bring about a general council.

The Emperor's prohibition settled the matter and November 1524 came and went, and no council gathered at Speyer. But some Germans did gather at that time, casually at first, but then with increasing intensity and determination: the German peasants, restless and discontented, rallied to express their grievances. Germany, already in the throes of violent religious controversy, became the site of the political and social turmoil of the 'Peasants' War.' The conflict had not come overnight. From the late 14th century onward Germany had been beset by periodic peasant unrest. Though the peasant demands and grievances were many, one single theme ran through them. It was the demand for the 'Old law,' the restoration of traditional custom and law. The peasants resented the new way of life, the new taxes and obligations, the new laws, the new judicial procedures, and, above all, the increasingly autocratic tendencies of the territorial rulers. What evoked their indignation was not economic need or social oppression, but a changing and alien legal order. Later appeared a demand for the 'divine law,' voiced by those who wished for more than the removal of the recent social and legal innovations. Here was a vision of a society governed by the principles of the divine law, in which the peasants' place would be determined not by arbitrary laws but by the very law of God. Thus vassalage was to be done away with, for God had created all men free; and the fruits of creation were to be used by all, for God had created them for all. When the storm broke in southwest Germany in the fall of 1524 there was at first no outright war. There were a few skirmishes and numerous acts of brutality on both sides, but that was all. The final outcome half a year later, however, was disastrous. Though exact figures are beyond reconstruction, the number of casualties among the peasants may well have been about 100,000. The peasants were militarily naïve and lacked competent leaders; they never had a chance.

The multitude of peasants killed, the number of houses burned and the amount of land devastated, left little doubt that the toll had been heavy, indeed catastrophic. Initially, the peasant demands had been moderate and one wonders if the possibility of a pacific resolution of their grievances existed.[18] Here and there agreements were actually reached between peasants and lords. But by and large violence, not compromise, determined the course of events. Increasingly, both sides became more unyielding until resort to force was the only solution. Details of the uprising need not concern us here. Important for our narrative, however, is that in the grievances of the peasants Lutheran notions seemed to make an appearance, thereby suggesting a connection between religious reform and social grievance. Thus the famous *Twelve Articles* (*Die grundlichen und rechten hauptartickel aller baurschaft*) summarized the peasant grievances along the lines of the 'divine law.'[19] Some 60 Scripture references provided unmistakable evidence for the impact of the

Reformation. 'The minister thus chosen should teach us the gospel pure and simple, without human additions, doctrine, or ordinance,' the First Article announced, and continued, 'Being taught continually in the true faith will prompt us to pray God that through his grace his faith may increase within us and be confirmed in us. For if his grace is not within us, we always remain flesh and blood which is without avail. Scripture clearly teaches that only through true faith can we come to God and only through his mercy can we become holy.' The other Articles reiterated familiar economic demands. Congregations should be allowed to elect their own ministers. The use of woods and waters ought to be free, and the services rendered to the lords should be restricted. At the end, the document pledged that if any demand was found to be contrary to the Word of God, it would be withdrawn.

The outcome of the peasants' uprising was destruction, suffering, and bloodshed. More than ever, the peasants were the neglected ones of society. But there was also the matter of Luther's alleged involvement. It was an ironic situation, for Luther abhorred violence and had a high regard for law and order. But when all was over Luther found himself indicted on two counts: the rulers charged that he had been the spiritual mentor of the peasants—they could point to the *Twelve Articles* in support of their contention; whereas the peasants lamented that he had double-crossed them—and they could point to the closing words of his tract *Wider die räuberischen und mörderischen Horden der Bauern* (Against the Murderous and Plundering Hordes of the Peasants), in which he had exhorted the rulers to 'slay, stab and kill' the peasants as God-pleasing work.[20]

What shall we make of Luther's involvement? We do well to recall that Luther was a religious, not a social, reformer. But some of the pamphlets that appeared in the early 1520s called for a reform of society no less than of the Church. Although not actively pursuing this sentiment, Luther had paid lip-service to it in his Open Letter to the Christian Nobility and had never openly dissociated himself from it. It was inevitable that the peasants should take up his words. There was a connection between the proclamation of Martin Luther and the aspirations of the peasants, who with halberds and sickles went forth to translate their dreams into reality. Exciting new thoughts and slogans, such as the common man had not heard before, had come out of Wittenberg. Luther had spoken about the freedom of the Christian man, who was a 'perfectly free lord of all, subject to none.' Luther had asserted that even the simple could understand the Gospel and that the high and mighty of the world had perverted this precious treasure. Luther had proclaimed the priesthood of all believers, had insisted that all Christians were spiritual equals. The tracts expounding the new Lutheran evangel no longer derided the peasant, but presented him as paradigm for an authentic insight into things spiritual.

After the initial peasant uprising Luther sought to clarify his relationship to the peasants with his *Ermahnung zum Frieden auf die 12 Artikel der Bauern* (Friendly Admonition to Peace Concerning the Twelve Articles of the Peasants) of April 1525. He was bitter toward the stubborn rulers and favorably disposed toward the peasants' demands, which seemed right and proper to him, though as a minister of the Gospel he felt not competent to adjudge. Experts in the fields of law and economics should do this. What evoked his indignation, however, was that the peasants supported the demand for the alleviation of economic grievances with references to the Gospel. This was an abomination and Luther spared no words of vehement denunciation. 'And even if they [the demands] were proper and right according to the natural law, you have forgotten the Christian law, since you do not seek to attain them with patience and prayer to God, as becomes Christian men, but with impatience and blasphemy to force the authorities.'[21]

Three weeks later Luther took to the pen again. His tract Against the Murderous and Plundering Hordes of the Peasants was of a different tone. The peasants had proceeded to violence, insurrection, and bloodshed; law and order were disrupted. This was bad enough, but what made it demonic was once again the peasants' utilization of religion for their political purposes, an abominable misunderstanding of the Gospel, which admonishes man to turn the other cheek, and a repudiation of political authority as well, which had been ordained by God to provide for law and order. Luther used some harsh and almost hysterical words in the tract, but this he always did when he thought fundamental issues at stake. He sought to quench the negative reaction to his second tract with a third pamphlet, the *Sendbrief von dem harten Büchlein wider die Bauern* (Letter Concerning the Harsh Pamphlet Against the Peasants), which reiterated his earlier position and chided the rulers who, not content with the restoration of order, were exercising a terrible revenge upon the peasants. But the damage had been done. It was as if Luther had written his second pamphlet with indelible ink. Theologically his case may have been consistent as well as sound; linguistically, it was a failure. No wonder that the peasants found little love lost between themselves and the man who wished for their stabbing, slaying, and killing. One cannot measure the religious allegiance of the 16th-century peasant who had no leader, no platform, and no literary expression. To talk about what he did after the Peasants' War is therefore as gratuitous as to suggest what he had done before. The assertions are many, but the facts lamentably few. Whether the Peasants' War signified the end of the popular dimension of the early Reformation cannot be said. That general enthusiasm waned is incontestable, but at the same time natural: the exuberance of the initial period of storm was bound to end sometime; the turmoil of the Peasants' War may have been rather incidental in this respect.

## Luther's Controversy with Erasmus

The year 1525 was a most significant one for the Reformation. It brought the confrontation between Luther and the peasants, and brought also the first indication of a clash between him and the Zurich Reformer Huldrych Zwingli, for the adherents of the new faith, far from being of one mind with regard to the interpretation of the Gospel, bitterly feuded with one another. And then there was the controversy between Luther and Erasmus. Rather like Luther's encounter with the Peasants' War, it had ramifications that went far beyond the specific case, for after the ink of the two protagonists had dried, a goodly number of humanists who had theretofore upheld Luther's banner felt that their home was with the Catholic Church after all.

This was a significant turn of events, because during the first years of the Reformation the humanists constituted a formidable and enthusiastic phalanx of Luther's supporters.[22] Men such as Ulrich Zasius and Christoph Scheurl endorsed the new Wittenberg theology (as they understood it), and their pens and influence did much to catapult Luther into the position of prominence that he enjoyed after 1520. The support of the humanists therefore was an important element in the early years of the ecclesiastical controversy. It was both direct and indirect: not only did many of the humanists openly endorse Luther; there was also a benevolent neutrality on the part of many humanist-oriented officials, a fact which had great significance for the official deliberations concerning Luther from 1520 onward. Furthermore, humanism provided the Lutheran cause with some welcome tools. Luther, perhaps routinely, acknowledged this when he wrote in his tract against Erasmus, 'I confess that I am

C

greatly indebted to you.'[23] The Biblical work of Jacques Lefèvre and the linguistic efforts of Erasmus were indispensable prerequisites for the theological formulations of Luther and his fellow reformers. Luther could hardly have translated the New Testament without the help of Erasmus's Greek text of 1516! In short, Christian humanism and Lutheran reform were comrades-in-arms in what seemed to be a common cause. For a short while the two great movements went hand in hand—whether by accident or intent was another question that was answered in 1525, when Erasmus and Luther clashed in literary battle.

Contrary to most of his followers, Luther was never a humanist and hardly ever an admirer of Erasmus. As early as 1517 he had spoken critically about the great humanist, though at that time many thought that Erasmus stood behind Luther's theological pronouncements. Erasmus seemed at first not displeased about such unsolicited fame, but he became of a different mind when the nature of Luther's temper became known. Still, he made it clear that while he disapproved of Luther, he was also displeased with the way the Church dealt with him. Convinced, as he was, that the Church did stand in need of reform, he was perturbed by the seemingly nonchalant way Luther was treated. 'Your responsibility,' he wrote to Elector Frederick, 'is to protect religion and you must not allow an innocent man to fall into the hands of the godless in the name of religion.' In 1520 he remarked that he disapproved of Luther's writings since 'they seem to lead to uproar,' and a few years later he observed that the 'wildness of Luther's writings' offended him.[24]

Erasmus's negative reaction was based not so much on any doctrinal divergence, but on the detestable manner by which Luther renewed religion. Erasmus was persuaded that peace and tranquility were the indispensable prerequisites for change and reform. He believed in the power of education, in the orderly rational process of persuading men, not in agitation, emotions, or appeals to the common man. But as time passed, the theological divergence between him and Luther became more and more apparent. Erasmus preferred to remain silent, to be merely 'an onlooker of the tragedy,' confiding only to a few friends, hoping that the storm would pass, calm return, and true religion once again increase. When it did not, Erasmus was urged from all sides to write against Luther. At first he thought of a dialogue among three persons, representing the Catholic Church, Luther, and compromise. His concern was not to attack the Wittenberg Reformer, but to write for peace and accord. By November 1523 Erasmus had changed his mind. He was going to write against Luther and do so directly and to the point. The topic: free will. The result was entitled *De libero arbitrio* and was a slender tract of less than 100 pages. The introduction stressed the ethical purpose of religion, and the main part considered the Scripture passages dealing with free will. Erasmus's principal argument was that Scripture taught man to have a free will, 'the ability which allows man to turn to or desist from that which leads to eternal salvation.'[25] To deny this free will was unbiblical as well as dangerous, since it made God a tyrant and paralyzed human effort. At the end of his treatise Erasmus used an illustration to explain his views: 'A father lifts up a child who, since it is unable to walk, fell down, despite its determined effort. The father points to an apple. The child is anxious to get to it, but the weakness of his legs would cause him to fall again. Surely, the father will reach out his hand to support and guide the child. Aided by his father, the child reaches for the apple. Tenderly, the father puts the apple into his hand—as a reward for his walking. Without the father's help the child could not have stood up, nor would he have seen the apple. . . . Can the child claim anything as his own accomplishment? He did do something, but owes everything to the father.'

Why did Scripture praise man's obedience and denounce his disobedience? In so arguing Erasmus did not mean to deny the significance of divine grace. Indeed, he sought to propound a middle course between Pelagianism, with its denial of grace, on the one hand, and determinism, with its denial of man's responsibility, on the other. His definition of free will was a cautious one indeed: man can turn to or desist from that *which leads* to eternal salvation. He stated explicitly that he preferred the opinion of those who attributed much to grace, but some to free will!

A year passed before Luther responded. His answer, *De Servo Arbitrio*, was four times the size of Erasmus's pamphlet and perhaps four times as vehement. The list of epithets Luther reserved for Erasmus was long and passionate, e.g., atheist, skeptic, destroyer of Christianity. Luther wanted to safeguard man's utter inability to contribute to his salvation, and he did so by stressing God's omnipotence: God's 'will has neither cause nor reason.' Man must acknowledge 'that God is good, even if he should condemn all men.' Man's relationship to God is that of 'a saw or an ax used by a carpenter.' God 'works even in the godless. For even as he created everything, so he moves everything through his omnipotence.'[26] Luther rejoiced that God had so ordained it. He did not want a free will, he said, even if it were possible, for the certainty of God's election would be replaced by the uncertainty of having fulfilled enough of God's commands.

In part, the difference between the two men was one of approach: Luther probed deeply, whereas Erasmus resigned himself to pious skepticism. Erasmus doubted that all of Scripture could be clearly understood, whereas Luther affirmed that it could. Erasmus doubted the wisdom of discussing all the questions raised by Scripture, whereas Luther affirmed it. And even if Luther's views were right, what advantages to true religion and morality would there accrue from a public discussion? Sometimes men—both wise and foolish men—step where angels fear to tread. Luther stepped boldly and asserted that the teaching of Scripture was clear: 'He who denies that Scripture offers clear insights, takes from man all light and any possibility of illumination.'[27] Both Erasmus and Luther talked about man and God. Erasmus was primarily concerned with man, Luther with God. Accordingly, Erasmus argued that 'Luther attributes little to erudition and much to the Spirit,'[28] even as Luther had remarked earlier that for Erasmus 'human considerations are more important than divine.'[29] We must not suggest that the controversy was solely over different emphases, but to a large extent it was. Luther was not really opposed to erudition, nor was Erasmus really a disciple of Epicurus. Both extolled God, though one approached him *sub specie aeternitatis*, whereas the other saw his clue in man. There is a telling passage in Erasmus's treatise. What, he asked, is the value of man if God works in him as a potter works in the clay? Luther quite likely would have put it the other way around, seeing value and dignity only if God guides man.

Erasmus answered Luther with the tract *Hyperaspistes*, reiterating his argument that not all passages in Scripture can be understood. But it was like the final sparkler after a big firework: the main words had been spoken. Neither protagonist had convinced the other, but Lutheran reform and Erasmian humanism reached a parting of the ways. Many of the older humanists reaffirmed their allegiance to the Catholic Church, and the Reformation was deprived of a good measure of support. As matters turned out, however, humanist ideals and aspirations, pushed out the front door, were to return through the back door before too many decades had passed. Educational ideals in Protestant lands were unthinkable without them.

# CHAPTER THREE

# The Division
# of the Reformation

Martin Luther dominated the Reformation scene for several important years and nothing illustrates this centrality better than the label 'Martinian' or 'Lutheran' ascribed to all those who took up Luther's cause or expressed a yearning for ecclesiastical reform. Not that every last tract published merely echoed his sentiment, for there was much variation in detail. But there were no real theological alternatives to what he taught and wrote.

Then it became evident that there did indeed exist a good deal of diversity among those who had taken up Luther's banner. Most of this had little bearing on the larger course of events, being but the private opinions of theologians and churchmen, uttered from the pulpit and printed in pamphlets, in the 16th century prompting an occasional raised eyebrow, in our own day exciting the fancies of dissertation writers. Of the many reformers few, if any, agreed completely with Luther. Most of them had their own particular slant and interpretation.

Perhaps this is the lifeblood of the theologian. To engage in his own formulation of the meaning of the Christian Gospel may be as necessary for him as the air he breathes. No period in the history of the Church was exempt from such dynamic vitality; at no time did theologians A, B, C, and D ever agree completely with one another. The theological scene during the initial phase of the Reformation was not different in this regard and most of the theological diversity is of importance primarily for the understanding of individed theologians rather than of the Reformation as a whole.

Some of the divisions were enormously important, however,

55

since theological difference could lead to sociological differentiation. The exposition of different theological positions meant in several instances the emergence of different factions among the followers of Luther. One suspects that the seriousness of the differences proved the key to the matter so that lesser differences were resolved (or ignored) and bigger ones led to division. But was this really the case?

The fact is that extraneous considerations also entered the picture. In some instances—notably in Sweden and England—geographic factors played a major role in the unfolding of different ecclesiastical bodies. Moreover, the temperament of the protagonists, the timing of the controversy, certain political factors—these, and others, were at times as influential as outright theological differences. In other words, there was a kind of irrationality to what we might call the 'theological consolidation' of the Reformation.

## Huldrych Zwingli

The Zurich reformer Huldrych Zwingli is a good case in point. His proclamation agreed with that of Luther, yet it possessed its own distinct emphases. Zwingli's monument at Zurich depicts him with Bible and sword, as a man of the Word and of deed. More than pious patriotism of Zurich burghers fashioned this monument: Zwingli was as much a Swiss patriot as he was a Christian theologian. Thus his program of reform was informed by elements alien to that of Luther. For Zwingli, 'reform' meant not only reform of theology and the Church, but also of society in light of the Gospel. Though there were social and economic consequences of Luther's work, these were more direct and immediate in Zwingli.

Huldrych Zwingli was born on New Year's Day, 1484, at Wildhaus, then as now a small village amid impressive mountains on the eastern edge of Switzerland. Zwingli's first biographer, Oswald Myconius, suggested that the high altitude of the reformer's birthplace possessed theological significance: the nearness of heaven, he wrote, made God a profound reality. One need not pay homage to such geographic determinism to acknowledge the truth of this statement: Zwingli's appreciation of nature, his reserved character, and his rustic language betray the setting in which he grew to manhood—in the sight of the grandeur of the mountains, where man and nature appear to exist in unbroken continuity. After studies at Vienna and Basel he received the baccalaureate degree in 1504, and

2 years later he concluded his studies in the liberal arts with the *magister artium*. The years at Basel were important and exerted considerable influence on him, especially through his teacher, Thomas Wyttenbach, to whom in later years he attributed a great deal of theological indebtedness. The intellectual climate of Basel was that of the *via antiqua*, which thought the truths of revelation to be beyond proof, but coherently related to the insights of natural reason; revelatory truth was the proper extension of reasonable truth. Recent scholarship has tended to minimize Zwingli's dependence on the *via antiqua*, and surely his mere presence in an academic atmosphere saturated by the 'old way' does not, in itself, offer sufficient proof for a relationship. Nonetheless, the notion of Zwingli's indebtedness is both a reasonable conclusion about his studies at Basel and also provides a satisfactory, if partial, explanation for his subsequent theological orientation.

In 1506, Zwingli came as *kilchher*, or parson, to Glarus, where he spent 10 important years pursuing his ministerial responsibilities in the village and several outlying hamlets, and visiting with the villagers over a glass of *zyger*, the local wine. But instead of falling prey to what Shakespeare called the 'insolence of office' in the small village, Zwingli applied himself to serious intellectual pursuits. His interests were humanistic. He attained a high competence in classical learning and became conversant with theological scholarship, even though, not having had formal training, he was theologically a self-made man. Even at this early phase of Zwingli's career an important and characteristic element made its appearance: his political interest. His very first literary effort, the *Fable of an Ox and Other Animals*, was an allegory on Swiss political involvement in the affairs of the Papal States, France, and Germany. And he did not confine himself to literary reflections. On several occasions he accompanied Swiss mercenaries to northern Italy. He was present at Marignano in 1515, the bloodiest battle of the century, where the Swiss suffered bitter defeat at the hands of Francis I. For Zwingli, who was anti-French, the French victory came as a disastrous shock. The bloodshed of that day, the awareness of Swiss drudgery, and a growing openness for Erasmian ideas influenced him profoundly and made him a pacifist. His new sentiment found expression in a new literary effort, the *Labyrinth*. A distinctly religious attitude became discernible. The difference between Zwingli's two patriotic poems was an outgrowth of a new theological interest, stimulated by Erasmus's Christian humanism. For several years Zwingli's concern for *Christianismus renascens*—a revived Christianity—received its impetus from the thought of the great humanist. Even his initial enthusiasm for Luther may have been prompted by the assumption that he was a disciple of Erasmus.

In 1516 Zwingli moved to Einsiedeln and 2 years later to Zurich, where he was appointed *Leutpriester*, people's priest, a prestigious post that offered opportunities for scholarly studies and a welcome proximity to humanist friends. Zurich had some 6,000 inhabitants; it was prosperous and politically influential among Swiss cities. In line with a constitutional agreement of 1498, government lay in the hands of a Large Council, the 'Two Hundred,' and a Small Council, with 50 members. Power was wielded by the Large Council, which dealt with foreign affairs and basic policy; the Small Council super-vised domestic administrative matters. Membership on the two councils was by election. Such was the backdrop of Zwingli's re-forming work. The political climate of Zurich was different from that of Wittenberg. Zurich was a small city-state, with a democratic form of government; Wittenberg was a city, part of a large terri-tory, under autocratic rule. Luther's partner was his territorial ruler, whose benevolence and support were needed to carry out the Reformation. Zwingli, on the other hand, had to pursue his plans within the far more direct and complex context of the two Zurich councils.

Zwingli began his ministerial responsibilities in Zurich with some startling homiletical innovations, but before their impact was felt, the indulgences controversy began to overshadow everything else. In December 1518 Luther's name made its first appearance in Zwingli's correspondence. Zwingli sought to obtain his writings; he praised them, and furthered their colportage. A 'new Elias' had been given to the world, he exclaimed exuberantly, and later he wrote that Saul (Erasmus) had slain a thousand, but David (Luther) ten thousand. And yet, when asked about Luther's influence, Zwingli denied it. 'I do not want to be called Lutheran,' he wrote in 1522, 'for I did not learn the teachings of Christ from Luther, but from the Word of God.'[1] If Zwingli's assertion is correct, the Reformation in Zurich was an independent phenomenon, free from outside in-fluence. At least as far as this particular instance is concerned, the history of the ecclesiastical transformation in the 16th century would relate the simultaneous emergence of reform efforts at several places in Europe. What can be said?

Political considerations oriented to some extent Zwingli's ex-pression of aloofness from Luther. The Edict of Worms had de-clared Luther's followers outlaws and to acknowledge himself as

Luther's disciple would have meant a threat to his own work. His demurrer was an act of understandable prudence. But more was involved. Zwingli was convinced that he had proclaimed the Gospel before he had ever heard of Luther. Obviously, the question hinges on the meaning of 'Gospel.' When Zwingli used it to describe his early thought, he gave it a connotation that it later did not possess. His 'Gospel' was that of Erasmus; his call for pure faith, the program of the Christian humanists. Later these elements persisted, but a new strain was added: the Pauline *theologia crucis*. Christ was central in Zwigli's theology before and after, but in a different way: Christ's initial prominence was that of the great exemplar, the giver of the Sermon on the Mount. Later came Zwingli's emphasis on Christ as redeemer and liberator from the Law. Moreover, Zwingli's theological orientation was anything but static between 1516 and 1521; it matured considerably during those crucial years. His preoccupation with patristic and scriptural texts modified his theology in the direction of St. Paul, and Luther was the guide along the way. The Wittenberg reformer was the catalyst, confirming here and suggesting there, but never overpowering. Zwingli saw it this way, for he wrote that Luther 'propelled me to eagerness.'[2]

Zwingli could argue the independence of his religious insight all the more forcefully since an intensely personal experience in 1519 wove his life and thought into one invisible pattern. In August 1519 the Black Death struck Zurich. Zwingli contracted the dreadful disease and for weeks wrestled with death, until slow recovery restored his health. From the experience came a personal religious document, the *Pestlied*, or Hymn of Pestilence. But no comment concerning the righteousness of faith graces this testimony, which is hardly evidence of a dramatic conversion or of a profound reorientation of life. The matter was far simpler. Zwingli, in facing the reality of death, became persuaded of the reality of God. Personal experience had merged with theological insight.

> Help, Lord God, help
> In this distress!
> Death stands at the door.
> Stand thou before me, Christ,
> For thou hast overcome him!
> To thee I cry:

. . .

Yet if thou wilt
That Death should take me
In the midst of days.
So let it be!
Do what thou wilt,
I am completely thine,
Indeed, thine vessel.[3]

Four factors, then, converged to lift the unknown *Leutpriester* of
Zurich to historical prominence: Erasmus, an increasing theological maturity, Luther, and a personal experience. Not all of these
may have been of equal importance, but all were present.


## The Reformation in Zurich

On the face of things, the ecclesiastical transformation in Zurich
differed little from that at other places; only the specific occasion
was a bit unusual. Two pork-sausages stood at the beginning, eaten
in 1522 during Lent by several eager partisans of Luther's cause, who
thereby violated the rule of the Church.

The harmless culinary feat became an *affaire d'état*. An extensive investigation followed and revealed additional instances of
violation of the fast. Zwingli's proclamation, or perhaps Luther's,
had borne its fruit. The apology of the culprits pointed to a basic
consideration: 'We must keep all our lives and our doings in accord
with the Gospel,' one of them wrote, 'or else we are not Christians.'[4]
Repercussions came promptly. The city council appointed a committee of four, including Zwingli, to examine the contested practice. The report, submitted early in April, was evasive, but this was
less significant than the fact that a secular body, the Zurich city council, had claimed it to be its jurisdiction to assess an ecclesiastical
practice. The bishop of Constance promptly informed the city council that to deal with violations of ecclesiastical practice was his
responsibility, not that of the council. Early in April the city council
asked the bishop for a general council to render a decision in accord
with the institution of Christ. At the same time the council issued a
mandate that 'until further notice' meat should not be eaten during
Lent nor should there be any public disputation concerning 'the eating of meat, preaching or other matters.'

One week after this mandate Zwingli published a sermon entitled *Von Erkiesen und Freiheit der Speisen* (Concerning Choice

and Liberty of Food), the first public statement of his theological position.[5] The theme was the relationship between faith and works, between inward piety and outward prescription; its motif was that of the freedom of the Christian man. The Christian does not stand under the law, but above it, Zwingli asserted. Genuine morality does not stem from external observations but from free and joyful commitment.

Late spring and summer brought renewed demands on the part of the bishop of Constance for the suppression of heretical teaching, further literary pronouncements from Zwingli, and the decision of the city council that a theological disputation should solve the contested issues. If the Church at large did not convene a council, then the Christian congregation of Zurich was at liberty to proceed on its own, to ponder the issues, and come to its proper conclusions. A dramatic step! Not because the invitation to the disputation had been extended by the city council, for there was precedent for such a move. The revolutionary step was the claim to ecclesiastical and theological independence. In a way it was not more than the conciliar principle applied to a single congregation, but, needless to say, such drastic geographic limitation obviated the basic notion of conciliarism. Moreover, the proposed gathering was to consider the full range of the Christian faith *de novo*—as if previous doctrinal statements did not exist—and this was revolutionary.

In preparation for the disputation Zwingli compiled a list of propositions, 67 in number, delineating his understanding of the needed reform of the Church. These 67 *Schlussreden*, or Conclusions, covered the full range of religion and morality, ceremonies and faith.[6] Two basic assertions set the tone for the document: the centrality and self-sufficiency of the Scriptures; the centrality of Christ and the need for the proclamation of his gospel. 'Those who assert that the gospel is nothing without the confirmation of the church are in error and blaspheme God.' The main part of the treatise contained reflections about the papal office, ecclesiastical practices, church property, clerical celibacy, and monasticism. The one throughout was aggressive, as is exemplified by Conclusion 30, which stated that 'those who vow celibacy promise too much in childish and foolish fashion. From this one learns that those who accept such vows act blasphemously with pious men.'

The disputation took place on January 29 1523. More than 600 persons were present, though few of them were defenders of the old faith. The delegates of the bishop of Constance insisted that theological questions had to be argued at a general council and then fell into studied silence. After a somewhat listless morning the city council announced that 'Master Huldrych Zwingli should continue, as heretofore, to proclaim the Holy Gospel and the Sacred Scriptures.'[7] The same exhortation was given to the clergy of Zurich. Zwingli rose to utter appropriate words of thanks and the disputation seemed over. But at this point Johann Faber, one of the bishop's representatives, took the floor and insisted that Zwingli's 67 Conclusions were against the 'praiseworthy glory and splendor of the Church.' A brief, but lively, debate followed. The point of contention was whether Scripture needed an interpreter. Faber affirmed this and cited Scripture in support, whereas Zwingli asserted the self-sufficiency of Scripture. The exchange remained inconclusive. At the end there was a humorous note, when a country parson asked how he, a poor man, could afford to purchase a New Testament. Zwingli retorted that none was so poor as not to afford one; a pious benefactor might make the purchase for him or at least lend him the money. No obstacles here to the Protestant principle!

As a consequence of the disputation several minor changes took place in Zurich. The request of the bishop of Constance to publish the Edict of Worms was rejected. Monks and nuns were allowed to leave the monasteries. The endowments of the Minster church were to be used for charitable purposes. By and large, however, ecclesiastical life continued unchanged. The Mass was observed in its traditional form, as was most of the ritual, and statues and pictures of the saints remained in the churches. Since some of the Reformers considered both practices particularly offensive, restlessness beset the city. In one church the 'eternal light' was torn down by some fanatics 'while everyone was at supper' and in another a painting of Jesus disappeared. A crucifix wound up in a ditch outside one of the city gates. Toward the end of September the city council appointed a committee to examine the lingering religious problems. This committee suggested a second disputation to deal specifically with the problem of the images and the Mass.

If the January disputation had been a lame and uninspiring affair, this second gathering, held in October, brought a lively meeting of minds. In January the controversy had been between the proponents of the old faith and those of the new faith; this time it was among the followers of the new faith. Although general agreement prevailed that images and the Mass were contrary to Scripture, there was bitter dispute as to when they should be abolished. The conclusion was to make haste slowly. The images must first be taken down from the hearts of man, Zwingli argued. Then the external removal would come without turmoil in its own time. First had to come the proclamation of the Gospel, or, as Zwingli put it, 'the people must first of all be instructed with the Word of God that neither vestments nor singing is a proper part of the Mass. If presently anyone would celebrate Mass without vestments uproar will result.' The October disputation temporarily calmed the religious excitement. But by the middle of December the absence of concrete changes revived the earlier restlessness. The city council announced that at Whitsuntide 'the matter should be taken up again and brought to a conclusion agreeable to God and his holy word.' Political prudence prompted the delay. The second disputation had evoked repercussions among those Swiss cantons loyal to the Catholic Church and the Zurich council did not want to add fuel to the fire. At a meeting of the *Tagsatzung* at Lucerne in April 1524, the bishops of Basel, Chur, and Constance demanded that ecclesiastical changes should be undertaken only with the approval of the proper political and ecclesiastical authorities. At the same time the cantons decided to punish all heretical innovations, such as the marrying of priests or the breaking of the fast.

On Whitsuntide, 1524, the date set by the Zurich council for a decision concerning religious change, it was ordered that the images be removed from the churches 'so that all would turn completely from idols to the living and true God.' For two weeks workmen were busy. When they were done, the Gothic magnificence of richly ornamented shrines had been transformed into the cool austerity of simple worship houses. The walls were white, the windows clear, the view unobstructed. Precious works of art, priceless objects of religious devotion, had disappeared under the chisel, the hammer, and the paintbrush. Treasures of art no less than man's soul were gone forever.

The abolition of the Mass took longer. Not until the spring of 1525 did the city council rule that the Mass should be discontinued and 'the remembrance of the institution and the table of God as practiced by the Apostles' observed instead. For ears accustomed to the chanting of the Mass and for eyes used to its ritualistic splendor, the Communion service, then introduced, was a radical innovation. The new service was utterly simple. After the sermon Zwingli took a place behind a table 'covered with a clean linen cloth.' Wooden bowls and goblets contained the bread and wine, which were carried by helpers to the congregation. The liturgy was in the vernacular. Although it followed the traditional pattern, there were changes: one of the Scripture lessons was read by one of the lay helpers, and the Gloria and the Creed were recited antiphonally by minister and congregation. The mystery of the Mass had become the simple communal gathering of a Christian congregation commemorating Christ's death on the Cross.

In a way the course of events in Zurich was hardly spectacular— no flaming oratory, no dramatic encounter, no heroic deeds. One might almost find the Swiss temper expressed in this development. And yet what happened in Zurich was noteworthy for two reasons: Zwingli's specific theological contribution and the paradigmatic character of events in the city. What took place in Zurich between 1522 and 1525 was to recur in countless places throughout Germany: the proclamation of ideas that were vaguely 'Lutheran' and thus at odds with the Catholic Church; the agitation for certain change in ecclesiastical practice; the intervention of governmental authority, at first with the call for a confrontation between the old faith and the new, then with the statutory introduction of ecclesiastical change. Thereby the fabric of the one Church was torn and a rival form of Christianity established itself against the Church represented by the pope. The beginning was made with the insistence that fundamental questions concerning the faith could be decided on a local level: even if the outcome of the January disputation in Zurich had been a routine affirmation of the Catholic faith, this affirmation would have rung hollow for its denial of the hierarchy and the pope.

Again we must face the question of the ultimate rationale in the minds of those who demanded ecclesiastical change: did they want to break with the Church? Did they seek to go their own way? Some of the changes were marginal ones (the closing of the monasteries or the removal of images); others were more crucial, for example, the discontinuance of the Mass. But always there was the conviction on the part of the reformers that they were propounding the true Gospel and that this true Gospel would be victorious—not in the sense of a defeat of the Catholic Church but rather in its acceptance of this true Gospel. This was what mattered. Their boundless enthusiasm may have prompted the reformers to be naïve about the future. After all, how could a small city-state hope to confront Western Christendom? A more realistic appraisal of the situation was bound to anticipate the future with ominous forebodings.

## The Emergence of Radical Movements of Reform

Triumph or defeat of the Reformation: the emergence of radical movements of reform has been interpreted as either. If interpretations thus differ, the actual facts are simple: in most centers of the Reformation a new kind of reformers appeared, men who at one time had been under the sway of Luther's or Zwingli's teaching and had been their disciples. But they had grown dissatisfied. They began to question, to denounce, to 'out-Luther' Luther and to 'out-Zwingli' Zwingli—and eventually to go their own ways. Although their impact upon the contemporary scene was modest and does not compare with that of Luther or Calvin, they must be neither ignored nor caricatured, a fate that has been theirs ever since the 16th century. In some ways they were heralds of the modern age, advancing principles that, though fiercely disputed in their own time, have become the common possession of Christendom. Some insisted on religious freedom and tolerance, for example, claiming that government should not interfere with religion, whereas others argued that most theological disagreements pertained only to secondary matters and could therefore be disregarded.

Doubtless the new movements received their impetus from the Reformation, since radicals flirted with the Lutheran or Zwinglian program of reform before they grew dissatisfied and went their own way. The Reformation provided the initial religious stimulus. The radicals were as emphatic in their repudiation of Catholicism as were the reformers. Nonetheless, the Reformation hardly suffices as full explanation for the emergence of Protestant radicalism. There were other factors, such as humanism, especially of the Erasmian variety, the mysticism of Tauler, Thomas à Kempis, and the *German Theology*, as well as the enigmatic underground of medieval apocalyptic and philosophical speculation. And there was the Bible, which these radicals read in the vernacular and with a disarming freshness and from which they may well have received some of their insights.

In contrast to the other ecclesiastical groupings in the 16th century, these dissenters did not obtain the support of governmental authority, which at most places was grimly determined to crush all deviating religious sentiment. The story of the radical reformers is therefore the story of persecution, of an underground movement suppressed with countless mandates, ordinances, and edicts. The radicals were the outcasts of a society that, having closed its ranks against them, offered them neither the opportunity to worship nor the status of citizenship. Michael Servetus, the Spanish antitrinitarian radical, was burned by Catholics in desire and by Protestants in reality. Such a spectacular demise symbolizes the fact that there was no place for the radical in the 16th century.

The radicals were a company of martyrs. All religious groupings supplied the stake and the executioner's block in the 16th century —the Calvinists no less than the Lutherans, and the Catholics no less than the English Protestants. The radicals, however, supplied martyrs in larger numbers and with a unique motivation. How many there were can only be conjectured. The several martyrologies from the time sought to provide devotional inspirations rather than compile exact statistical information. A total of some 4,000 victims appears as a likely estimate for the entire century, a greater number than for any other grouping.

The radicals were martyr-minded. Persecution, martyrdom, and even death were not accidental misfortunes but the essence of the Christian confession. Christ himself had walked the way of suffering and death, and he beckoned his disciples to come and follow him. Often the radicals did not know subtle points of theological argumentation or the answers of Biblical interpretation. When they were interrogated, they were pathetically ill-equipped to match the sophisticated theological wits of their opponents. Still, they were persuaded that they had been called to follow in Jesus' steps, to do as he had commanded them to do, to suffer, to die. They quoted Jesus' words that the 'disciple is not above his master, nor the servant above his lord,' and held that the disciple was called upon to be like his master in his rejection, suffering, and death. Martyrdom was a test of obedience, and they would not shrink from it. What did they lose? The sufferings were not to be compared with the eternal bliss that awaited them. They were on a pilgrimage and looked beyond the flames of the stake and the executioner's sword to the promised land.

One of the moving documents coming from an Anabaptist martyr is this letter written prior to her execution by a Dutch woman to her infant daughter:

> I have borne you under my heart with great sorrow for nine months, and given birth to you here in prison, in great pain. They have taken you from me. Here I lie, expecting death every morning. . . . And I, your dear mother, write to you, my dearest child, something for a remembrance. . . .
>
> I must through these lines cause you to remember, that when you have attained your understanding, you endeavor to fear God, and see and examine why and for whose name we both died; and be not ashamed to confess us before the world, for you must know that it is not for the sake of any evil. Hence be not ashamed of us; it is the way which the prophets and the apostles

went, and the narrow way which leads into eternal life, for there shall no other way be found by which to be saved. . . .

Further, my dear child, I pray you, that wherever you live when you are grown up, and begin to have understanding, you conduct yourself well and honestly, so that no one need have cause to complain of you. And always be faithful, taking good heed not to wrong any one. Learn to carry your hands always uprightly. . . . Do not accustom your mouth to filthy talk, nor to ugly words that are not proper, nor to lies; for a liar has no part in the kingdom of heaven; for it is written: 'The mouth that lieth slayeth the soul.' Hence beware of this, and run not in the street as other bad children do. Take up a book, and learn to seek there that which concerns your salvation. . . .

So I must also leave you here, my dearest lamb. The Lord that created and made you now takes me from you in His Holy will. I must now pass through the narrow way which the prophets and martyrs of Christ passed through, the many thousands who put off the mortal clothing, who died here for Christ, and now wait under the altar till their number shall be fulfilled. Your dear father is one of them and I am on the point of following him, for I, too, am delivered up to death. . . . If it were not the will of the Lord, He could yet easily deliver me out of their hands and give me back to you, my child. Even as the Lord returned to Abraham his son Isaac, so He could still easily do it. He is the same God that delivered Daniel out of the lion's den, and the three young men out of the fiery furnace. He could easily deliver me out of the hands of man. . . .

And now, Janneken, my dear lamb, who are yet very little and young, I leave you this letter, together with a gold real, which I had with me in prison, and this I leave you for a perpetual adieu, and for a testament. Remember me by it, as also by this letter. Read it, when you have understanding, and keep it for your edification as long as you live in remembrance of me and of your father. I bid you adieu, my dear Janneken Munstdorp, and kiss you heartily, my dear lamb, with a kiss of peace.[8]

One reason for the stubborn vitality of the radicals was that when tried by fire and iron, there were no fellow travelers in their midst. Theirs was the enthusiasm of those who had deliberately elected to travel the narrow road. They were a community of true believers who professed seriousness of religious commitment. Accordingly, their number was small. The fear of the authorities that the radicals were conspiring to overthrow the established order clearly was behind some of the severity of the persecution. Though doctrinal deviation alone entailed grave legal consequences, torture

and other measures of suppression often were used in an effort to
unmask a political 'conspiracy.' Most of the radicals were peaceful
and altogether other-worldly. When some of them talked about the
apocalyptic upheaval of society, theirs was more the naïve speculation of men heavy with the mysterious language of Holy Writ than
the manifesto of committed revolutionaries. But there were also a
few exceptions, men who, carried away by their fancies and aspirations to alter society instantly, justified the suspicion of the authorities. Moreover, in one striking sense the accusation of disrupting
law and order was correct: the radicals rejected the identity of the
political and religious community that was universally accepted by
Protestants and Catholics alike. They argued that Church and state
were different, and that to be a citizen of a commonwealth did not
necessarily mean automatic identification with an ecclesiastical
community.

Although the number of the radicals was probably quite small,
their theological emphases were legion. In some instances this meant
the outright splintering into various groupings, in others a baffling
constellation of affinities. All in all, it is easier by far to determine
what the radicals opposed than what they advocated. They opposed
both the Reformation and the Catholic Church, hurling charges of
compromise against the former and of perversion against the latter.
They wanted a reformation of the Reformation. As one of them remarked picturesquely, 'Luther broke the pope's pitcher, but kept
the pieces in his hand.'[9] The radicals were going to drop the pieces
also. Did they possess a common vision of what constitutes the
Christian religion? There is no answer, at least none on which
scholars would presently agree. Current nomenclature speaks of the
'radical reformation,' suggesting that the radicals ventured to go to
the very 'root' of the Christian faith for its restoration. But this is
delicate language, for the major reformers claimed to do the same,
only defining the 'root' of the faith differently from the radicals. The
label thus begs the question. Another suggestion speaks of the 'left
wing' of the Reformation, thereby utilizing a term taken from political parlance, stressing the radicals' disavowal of governmental interference in religious affairs. Both suggestions contain accurate insights. If our purview is to encompass the full spectrum of Protestant
dissent in the Reformation, however, a somewhat more general
characteristic suggests itself. The common denominator of all
radicals was their simple insistence that the Reformation, too, had to
be reformed. In their opinion, the reformers had not gone far
enough, had left unquestioned what should have been challenged,

and had affirmed what should have been rejected. But the specific criticism differed from radical to radical. The Antitrinitarians were particularly concerned about the ancient christological dogma, whereas the Anabaptists and Spiritualists stressed what may be called 'practical Christianity.' The Scriptural statement 'by their fruit ye shall know them' served as their motto. There were elaborate and at times emphatic theological assertions, especially from the Anabaptists—comments about Baptism, Scripture, the Lord's Supper, or the Church. But their recurrent theme was the assertion that the Christian profession had to manifest itself in the daily walk of life.

If the specifics thus differed, from radical grouping to radical grouping, there were also intriguing common bonds. The Anabaptists wrestled with the problem of spiritualism, whereas the Spiritualists thought rather little of infant Baptism. Nor were the Antitrinitarians any more orthodox about infant Baptism than they were about christology. Still, the kinship was more psychological than theological. In a religiously restless age the radicals had been imbued with a questioning spirit. In this sense they were similar branches of the same tree.

## The Deserting Disciples

Despite the presence of a variety of factors, the eminent influence in the emergence of the dissenting reform movements was none other than Martin Luther. This was so for two reasons. Luther had intensified the religious concerns of his contemporaries and virtually all of the subsequent dissenters owed their real religious awakening to his proclamation. More specifically, Luther's proclamation raised more questions that it seemed to answer. The full implications of his theological pronouncements were not immediately obvious. He had spoken about the centrality of faith, insisting that faith was the key to the sacraments. But once this assertion had been made, the question arose concerning the Baptism of infants: did infants possess the necessary faith? Another point of uncertainty pertained to the locus of authority. Luther had argued for the centrality of Scripture, stressing that the guidance of the Spirit was necessary for its proper interpretation. Did this mean the priority of the Spirit over the Letter?

These two issues, in particular, were bound to receive further attention. And this they did, with two figures who appeared out of the sky of the Reformation like comets, burning brightly but disappearing quickly: Andreas Bodenstein Carlstadt and Thomas Müntzer. Though their immediate impact on the scene was slight indeed, their significance for the crystallization of radical dissent can hardly be underestimated. Carlstadt, a quarrelsome character, was also a thoroughly competent and brilliant theologian. A senior member of the Wittenberg faculty, he never avoided controversy; on the contrary, he sought it out. The consequences were disastrous. At first reluctant to follow the lead of his junior colleague Luther, he quickly became an enthusiastic partisan and played a significant and vociferous role in the indulgences controversy.

During Luther's stay at the Wartburg, Carlstadt showed himself sympathetic with those who demanded extensive ecclesiastical reform at Wittenberg. But after Luther's return he lacked the diplomacy to adjust to his colleague's conservative temper and the flexibility to reconsider his position. For a while he continued as dean of the theological faculty, gave well-attended lectures, and wrote pamphlets, but otherwise was outside the current of events. Early in 1523 he went to Orlamünde, south of Wittenberg, where he proceeded to undertake ecclesiastical reform in the manner that he had desired to do at Wittenberg. The parish church was stripped of images, Communion was observed in simple form, and infants were no longer baptized. Complications arose, since Carlstadt continued to issue prolific propaganda for his brand of ecclesiastical reform. Had he confined his activities to spreading manure as 'Brother Andrew,' as he did proudly at times, or had he only expounded his evangel to peasants under an oak tree in the manner of Breughel, there would have been no problems. But he meant to change the course of ecclesiastical reform at large. In September 1524 Carlstadt was expelled from Orlamünde. For half a year he moved restlessly from place to place, hoping to influence the course of events. He was unsuccessful, became tangled up in the Peasants' War (how deeply we do not know), and was eventually permitted, after a haphazard recantation, to return to Wittenberg. A few years later he found his way to Basel, where he died in 1541.

Carlstadt was an important figure in the rise of Protestant dissent. He argued for a speedier and more comprehensive alteration of ecclesiastical life and thought than Luther and most other reformers were disposed to undertake. His pamphlet *Ob man gemach faren* (If One Should Tarry) propounded in classical form the argument that Biblical insight must at once be translated into actual ecclesiastical reform. Moreover, Carlstadt went beyond Luther in what may be called the 'spiritualizing' of the Gospel, the move away from the empirical to the spiritual. Accordingly, the sacraments had to be reinterpreted, since they could be only symbols and were not central. He desperately sought to reinterpret Communion so as to deprive it of its sacramental character, and he was sufficiently perplexed by the Baptism of infants to discontinue the practice in Orlamünde.

The other early radical was an erstwhile priest by the name of Thomas Müntzer. Long neglected by scholarship, Müntzer is currently much in vogue, an indication, perhaps, that historical reputation can always take a new turn. He, too, became a devoted follower of Luther in the course of the indulgences controversy and moved around as a kind of traveling evangelist for the Wittenberg gospel, although there may have been more of the strange amalgamation of ideas culled from medieval sources that were to characterize him subsequently. He found his way to Bohemia, where at Prague on All Saints' Day of 1521, he published a *Manifesto*, a self-conscious and vehement ultimatum on behalf of the new faith.[10]

The people failed to rally to Luther's cause as proclaimed by Müntzer, and soon thereafter Müntzer left Prague. Where he went and what he did, we cannot tell, although the temptation is great to conjecture contact with Hussite ideas. In the spring of 1523 he became minister in the Saxon town of Allstedt, where he stayed for more than a year and had the opportunity to translate his theological theory into ecclesiastical practice. He wrote three church orders (*Deutsche Kirchenampt*, *Deutsch Evangelisch Messze*, and *Ordnung und Berechnung des Teutschen Ampts*), for all practical purposes the first orders of worship of the Reformation. Though adhering to traditional form, they embodied new content, suggesting a creative reformation of the worship of the congregation. The Scripture lesson was lengthened, for example, and the entire congregation joined in the recitation of the words of institution at the celebration of the Lord's Supper. More important was his theological estrangement from Luther. Early in 1524 Müntzer published two pamphlets, *Vom getichten Glauben* (Concerning Faked Faith) and *Protestation und Erbietung* (Protestation and Declaration). The former theorized about the nature of true faith, the latter offered a specific application.

Müntzer argued that the Gospel was not merely the promise of God's forgiveness, but also the acceptance of God's law. Man must accept his cross in suffering and obedience, and he must fulfill the law. Christendom had perverted this true Gospel as was evidenced by the practice of the Baptism of infants who lacked both the pre-requisite faith and the ability to fulfill the law.

After leaving Allstedt in the fall of 1524, not altogether voluntarily, Müntzer came into contact with the simmering peasants' unrest, and somehow he identified the peasants' cause with his own. Persuaded of the rightness of his position, he saw the rulers who had opposed him at Allstedt as godless. Since the peasants opposed the same rulers, he thought (erroneously, as it turned out) their opposition and his own identical. What exact role he played in the camp of the rebelling peasants, that of a revolutionary firebrand or simply that of one of the crowd, is not certain. After the peasants went down to defeat at Frankenhausen in May 1525, he was arrested, tortured —it was then he made the cryptic statement that among Christians 'all things should be held in common'—and executed. A bold man and a creative theologian passed from the scene. Müntzer contributed two emphases to the incipient program of Protestant dissent. He criticized Luther's view of the norm of authority, rejecting the motion of the 'paper pope,' the Bible, replacing it with the notion of the Spirit speaking directly to man. Secondly, he condemned Luther's soteriological view by propounding an alternative, the commitment to fulfill God's law as a consequence of God's gracious forgiveness.

### Anabaptism

Anabaptism began in Zurich in January 1525 with the administration of believer's Baptism. Its real beginnings, however, lie shrouded in darkness. Some of those who became Anabaptists had been influenced by Erasmus, and the impact of Carlstadt and Müntzer cannot be fully discounted. Nor must we overlook the obvious, that they read Zwingli and Luther. In short, the picture is complex, and the most accurate conclusion would need to be that a conflux of influences—Erasmus, Müntzer, and Zwingli—molded the theological temper.

Initially, there was only a growing impatience with the slowness of ecclesiastical reform in Zurich. Probably early in 1524 the dissatisfied among Zwingli's followers gravitated toward one another, talked theology and reform, and attained theological sophistication. Eventually the break with Zwingli was over Baptism, but there were issues of more fundamental importance. At stake was soteriology. Zwingli remarked later that the future Anabaptists had approached him to form 'a church in which there would be only those who knew themselves without sin.' If that is an authentic recollection, it shows that the nature of Christian commitment stood at the center of the disagreement. To be a Christian meant a voluntary and deliberate decision, which expressed itself in reception of adult Baptism and separation from the 'ungodly.'

After fruitless conversations with Zwingli in the fall of 1524 the break came in January of the following year with the mutual administration of believer's Baptism by a small group led by Conrad Grebel and Felix Mantz. This act constituted a flagrant violation of the criminal code no less than of mandates of the Zurich city council. The small group had two alternatives—either to yield to the authorities or to remain true to their conviction. What a dramatic gathering it must have been when they met to talk about the future! Their decision was to defy the authorities. The circumstances of the sacrament were highly unusual: a living room was the sanctuary, and a kitchen ladle was used for pouring the baptismal waters. There were no scruples over the absence of an ordained person or even about the fact that the one who administered the first believer's Baptism had himself not received it. Within 2 weeks, more than 30 people had been so baptised. In a way this was a spectacular success, but it must not be assumed that Anabaptism represented more than a minute percentage of the populace. It never had a chance of becoming truly popular. Still, the threat to the principle of a religiously monolithic society existed. The exuberance of the Anabaptists added to the tensions (one of them disrupted a church service in Zollikon near Zurich by offering audible annotations to the minister's sermon), and promptly the Anabaptists were arrested. Since most of them recanted, they were soon released; the few who did not were expelled from Zurich territory.

From the outset there was present in the Anabaptist movement a centrifugal tendency that prompted its spread throughout Central Europe. Expulsion from Zurich left some Anabaptists with no alternative but to move elsewhere, where they continued to proclaim their message. The Anabaptists perceived the difference between their own view of the Gospel and that propounded by others in radical terms. Theirs alone was the true Gospel; the world at large was in utter darkness. Therefore men everywhere had to be called to follow Christ and to signify their commitment with the reception of adult Baptism. Even if the Anabaptists had experienced no persecution in Zurich, they would have taken their message to other places. That there was persecution made the carrying out of the principle expedient as well as necessary. Obvious factors influenced the geographic direction of the expansion of Anabaptism into South Germany. Only in German-speaking areas could the Anabaptist message be communicated. Moreover, it was easier to follow the well-established roads to the north than to move eastward across the mountain ranges into Austria. Everywhere their missionaries enjoyed an initial period of toleration. By the time the authorities moved to suppressive action, the Anabaptist evangelists had formed the nucleus of a congregation by administering believer's Baptism. Persecution quickly forced this congregation underground and made further expansion virtually impossible.

Some people were ready for the Anabaptist message. They were the spiritually sensitive ones, dissatisfied with the course of the ecclesiastical transformation and religiously aroused by the Lutheran proclamation but bewildered by its increasing theological sophistication. The Anabaptist message seemed to supply their need by combining the message of the Reformation with something new— the insistence that, even as a tree brings forth its fruit, the Christian believer must bring forth the fruit of his commitment. The Anabaptist message was simple: repentance, faith, Baptism, new life. Everyone could understand it. Since the denunciation of the reformers was an important part of the Anabaptist proclamation, many of those who joined the movement shared this, but nothing more. The expansion of Anabaptism meant at once the loss of the homogeneity of the movement.

Its expansion was unsystematic, sporadic, haphazard, and theologically unsophisticated. With few exceptions, the Anabaptist missionary was theologically illiterate. To be sure, there were sophisticated men such as Balthasar Hubmaier, Hans Denck, and Hans Hut, but most Anabaptist evangelists were simple men whose religious enthusiasm had to compensate for the lack of theological training. The consequences were inescapable. The Anabaptist message was reduced to its essentials. Subtle points of theological argumentation had to be ignored. The simplicity of the message proved to be its strength, for the common people could understand its significance and face its challenge.

Once a nucleus of believers had been formed, the missionary who had introduced the message moved on and the new congregation was on its own. It would study the Bible and read the few Anabaptist pamphlets that were available. But by and large its contacts were limited: the congregation was like an island in an ocean, part of a universal brotherhood, yet basically living its own

life. The proclamation of the reformers initially encountered the
same difficulty, for the exposition of Luther's theology by thousands
of well-meaning clerics, all of whom had been Catholic priests, was
bound to lead to diversity and problems. The pulpits in Lutheran
territories hardly propounded uniform Lutheran doctrine. Yet the
Reformation had the advantage of the dissemination of its ideas by
the printed page and a formal ecclesiastical structure; Anabaptism
did not.

About the success of this Anabaptist evangelistic effort we know
little. A network of Anabaptist congregations throughout Austria
and South Germany was established and a relatively small number of
Anabaptists can be identified through court records, etc. The evidence available, however, suggests that Anabaptism was never a
mass movement. The details of the continuing expansion of the Anabaptist movement need not be recounted. Important were the intensity of the movement, its geographic spread, and the increasing persecution. But, as we noted, the expansion proved to be a mixed blessing. Anabaptism ceased to be the homogeneous phenomenon that
it had been at its inception. The larger the movement, the greater its
doctrinal diversity and the greater also the need for theological clarification. Such clarification occurred in three places in 1527: at
Nikolsburg in Moravia, at Augsburg in South Germany, and at
Schleitheim on the Swiss-German border. Unfortunately, in all three
cases the sources are enigmatic.

At Nikolsburg the issue at stake was the proper attitude toward
governmental authority. Hans Hut and Balthasar Hubmaier were
the two chief antagonists, the former arguing for non-resistance, the
non-swearing of oaths, and non-participation in governmental
offices, the latter advocating a political ethic identical with that of
the Reformers. Hut's followers were called *Stäbler*, as they were
those who would carry only a *Stab*, or staff, while Hubmaier's followers were the *Schwertler*, those with the *Schwert*, or the sword.
The gathering at Augsburg dealt with Hut's chiliasm and apocalyptic preaching. Though most Anabaptists did not share this emphasis,
the gathering seems to have modified Hut's teaching only slightly,
affirming the imminent return of Christ and the need for emphatic
missionary effort. From the gathering at Schleitheim a remarkable
theological document has come down, perhaps the most incisive
formulation of early Anabaptist thought, the *Brüderliche Vereinigung*, or Schleitheim Confession of Faith, which deals with Baptism, excommunication, Communion, separation, the ministry, the
sword, and the oath. The opening section of the Confession noted

that 'a very great offense has been introduced by certain false brethren among us, so that some have turned aside from the faith,' thereby indicating that the meeting had sought to resolve tensions within the Anabaptist brotherhood. The inclusion of Baptism suggests that even this seemingly basic tenet had not been uncontested in some Anabaptist circles. The paragraphs on the 'sword,' and the oath, and governmental authority elaborated the Anabaptist view that, although government had been instituted by God, involvement in it, by participating in war on government or by the swearing of oaths, was contrary to the commandment of Christ. By its incisiveness and comprehensiveness the Schleitheim Confession emerged as a doctrinal statement probably of major significance for Anabaptism in South Germany.

When talking about Anabaptism we must keep in mind that it was an underground movement. Nowhere did it enjoy official recognition; everywhere it was persecuted by the authorities. It had no organizational structure, but consisted of more or less autonomous congregations scattered throughout central Europe. It had no generally binding confessional statements. Some confessions received partial recognition. The one that was widely accepted, the Dodrecht Confession, was not promulgated until 1632. In a way, the situation of Anabaptism was similar to that of Protestantism in France or Scotland during the struggle for official recognition, though there was the important difference that the Protestants in those countries received support from abroad, notably from Geneva, and were numerically large enough to establish early organizational structures and confessional standards.

The absence of organizational structures in Anabaptism entailed two consequences. First, one can hardly write the history of Anabaptism as a 'movement.' With the exception of its Hutterite branch, which did possess an organizational structure (and confessional norms), there is an open-ended complexity about Anabaptist history which makes it difficult to do more than expound the thought of the eminent leaders. A second consequence was the perpetuation of theological strife among factions.

Anabaptism was a network of loosely knit congregations. There was no formal training for the leaders. Occasionally a figure of charismatic qualities would appear and through organizational ability or theological exposition make his mark. Since the theological contribution often took the form of clandestinely printed tracts, it is not surprising that historical nescience has frequently obscured it. The South German Anabaptist Pilgram Marpeck is a good case in point. Virtually unknown to historians until the beginning of the 20th century, the discovery of his extensive literary production established him as the most prolific Anabaptist writer in the first half of the 16th century. Even quantity aside, the content of his tracts revealed his substantial contribution to the delineation of the Anabaptist message.

Marpeck first appeared as an Anabaptist spokesman during his residence in Strassburg between 1528 and 1532, when he engaged in debates with representatives of what was to him the right and the left: the mainstream Reformation, represented by Martin Bucer, and Spiritualism, represented by Hans Bünderlin. This corresponded to the twofold challenge facing the Anabaptist movement—on the one hand, the legitimacy of its dissent from the mainstream Reformation and, on the other, the validity of its position over Spiritualism. The relevant questions were whether the rejection of infant Baptism could be Bibically sustained and whether Baptism, after all only a symbol, could not be dispensed with altogether. Marpeck delineated a penetrating Anabaptist position by addressing himself to the proper understanding of Scripture. He held that the unity of Old and New Testament was rather like the unity of promise and fulfillment, and he suggested that the New can cancel the stipulations of the Old. In Baptism Marpeck sought to combine inner spirit Baptism and outer water Baptism, and thereby, in a sense, inner and outer forgiveness also. His second major contribution to Anabaptism came in the early 1540s in his controversy with Caspar Schwenckfeld, the eminent Spiritualist of the German Reformation. The *Verantwurtung über Casparn Schwenckfelds Judicium*, a weighty tome of 800 pages, reiterated the basic points Marpeck had made against Bünderlin a decade before.

Marpeck was the most perceptive of the Anabaptist spokesmen in the early part of the 16th century. Like his confreres he was an untrained theologian (he was a mining engineer by vocation), and the specific dates of his public activity (from the early 1530s to his death in 1556) remind us of John Calvin. It was Pilgram Marpeck's historical role to define in a sophisticated fashion the basic Anabaptist emphases and thereby to safeguard its theological identity. This he did splendidly, even though not all the branches of Anabaptism availed themselves of his contribution. The issues were brought to him in a concrete way: the relatively tolerant atmosphere of Strassburg meant that a host of dissenters found their ways to this city, men such as Sebastian Franck, Melchior Hofmann, Hans Bünderlin, and Caspar Schwenckfeld. The obvious theological ferment among the dissenters in the city brought inevitable confrontations as well as clarification of the various positions.

The spread of Anabaptism from its Swiss cradle into South Germany was paralleled by a northward expansion into Central Germany and the Low Countries. A South German furrier and lay preacher played the crucial role: Melchior Hofmann, at once a quiet man ready to suffer for his conviction and a brooding dreamer who became increasingly preoccupied with the evasive arithmetic and imagery of Scripture. He was obsessed with what he called the 'figure,' the meaning of the allegorical and figurative parts of Scripture.

After several years as a traveling evangelist, Hofmann arrived in Strassburg in 1529. There he had contact with Anabaptists and received believer's Baptism. He petitioned the city council for a church to be used by the Anabaptists, unsuccessfully, as might have been expected, and then moved to North Germany, where he preached and administered believer's Baptism. In 1531 he extended his activities to Holland. For all practical purposes, Hofmann and the other Anabaptist evangelists were the first ones to proclaim the Protestant faith there. But in Holland, too, persecution set in promptly. The prisons were filled, the fires kindled around the stakes, and the executioner's axe sharpened. A bitter price had to be paid. As the number of followers was high, so was the number of victims. In itself this turn of events was not particularly noteworthy; it was but a repetition of widespread practice. Important, in this particular instance, however, was the reaction of Hofmann, who interpreted the outbreak of persecution as the obvious sign of the last days. Promptly he announced that all Baptism of believers (the external cause of the persecution) should be suspended for 2 years. The Biblical justification was Ezra 4.25, which described the interruption of the construction of the temple for two years under Zerubbabel. The peripheral place of Baptism in Hofmann's thought is evident here; he was certain that even those who would die unbaptized during this time could be assured of their salvation. The commitment to follow Jesus was more important than the external administration of the baptismal rite.

Hofmann himself became his own pathetic victim. In 1533 a man told him that he would be in prison for half a year before God would call him. This prediction proved to be of crucial importance, for Hofmann's Biblical arithmetic had led him to see 1533 as the time of the Second Coming. He hurried to Strassburg, the 'New Jerusalem,' to fulfill the prophecy. Upon his arrival he was arrested, but he rejoiced over this turn of events. 'And he praised God that the hour had come and he lifted his hat from his head . . . raised his fingers to heaven, swearing to the living God that he would take no other food or drink than water and bread.'[11] The first part of the prophecy had come true, but Hofmann was not to witness the Second Coming, for he died in his Strassburg cell. When Hofmann left Holland for Strassburg, Anabaptism in the North was a heterogeneous movement, heavily influenced by his chiliasm and allegorical interpretation of Scripture, but uncertain as to the real thrust of the Anabaptist message. Hofmann had been able to maintain some balance, but the subsequent course of events showed that it could not be kept permanently.

Hofmann's two main lieutenants in Holland were Obbe Philipps and Jan Matthijs. Both shared his eschatological emphasis; both were persuaded that the day of God's establishment of the New Jerusalem was at hand. But there they parted company. Jan Matthijs advocated a vigorous assertion of the divine will. God's law had to be fulfilled no matter what the cost. Obbe Philipps, on the other hand, advocated passive suffering and forbearing. In the city of Münster Matthijs found a dramatic field of activity.

Münster was a milestone in the history of Anabaptism; neither the Anabaptists themselves nor the ecclesiastical and governmental authorities were to be the same afterward. In this city in Northwest Germany the Anabaptists succeeded in what they had failed to do elsewhere; they attained political control and proceeded to establish the New Jerusalem. A strange one it was, at least for outsiders, characterized not only by adult Baptism, but also by polygamy and communism. Contemporaries considered it the abomination of abominations, the proof that all Anabaptists were evil, immoral, and heretical. It mattered little that there were significant differences between the Anabaptists in Münster and those elsewhere. The common affirmation of adult Baptism obscured these differences for both the authorities and the reformers.

At the beginning stood a relatively harmless transformation of ecclesiastical life in Münster along Anabaptist lines. Like many cities in the early years of the Reformation, Münster had passed through a period of ecclesiastical tension between proponents of the old faith and the new. The agitation of Bernhard Rothmann, a former priest, brought about ecclesiastical change, and in February 1533 Münster officially became Protestant. Since many cities in Germany were then taking the same step, the course of events in Münster was none too unusual. But Rothmann increasingly favored more drastic change, and he was able to pull the city along with him. In May 1533 he publicly denounced infant Baptism. The news of this development spread abroad and prompted many Anabaptists to flock to Münster. Most of these newcomers were devout and peaceful people who forsook their worldly possessions to come to the city. But there were also some fanatics, men who sought to fish in muddy waters, unstable characters who always find their way to scenes of controversy.

In January 1534 two followers of Jan Matthijs arrived in Münster and proclaimed that believer's Baptism should be administered. Rothmann and many others—a contemporary spoke of more than 1,400 people—were baptized. This Baptism and the other changes in Münster made a deep impact upon Anabaptists in the North. Believer's Baptism had been suspended upon Melchior Hofmann's exhortation that the end was imminent. Hofmann himself lay in a Strassburg prison, impatiently awaiting that Great Day. Then occurred the dramatic change at Münster, the seeming victory of the true Gospel, surely the vindication of Hofmann's prophetic views. In Münster, persecution had ceased, the elect were unmolested, the city had changed its face to conform to the vision of the New Jerusalem. Jan Matthijs's exhortation that believers' Baptism could be administered again ushered in an atmosphere of spiritual exuberance. Matthijs arrived in Münster soon thereafter, and his presence denoted the occasion for extensive change. Elections to the city council brought an Anabaptist majority. All who were unwilling to be baptized had to leave the city.

When the last of these emigrants had disappeared outside the city walls, Münster had become the New Jerusalem, for the 'ungodly' had been driven away and only the 'elect' remained. On the face of things, Münster was Anabaptist, but actually a basic deviation from Anabaptist principles had taken place. The notion of the Church as a suffering minority within society was replaced by the assertion of the identity of Church and society. The *corpus christianum* was re-established. The difference lay in the fact that whereas earlier the Church had been Catholic or Lutheran, now it was Anabaptist.

Neither the bishop of Münster nor the rulers of the surrounding territories were willing to accept the change in the city, and only the intense eschatological orientation of the Anabaptists affords an explanation as to why they were oblivious of this fact. A siege of Münster commenced. Jan Matthijs was killed in battle, but the loss of the prophet of the New Jerusalem created only a temporary vacuum, since his place was taken by another Dutchman, Jan van Leyden. A tailor by trade, with a keen awareness of political reality and an extraordinary sense of spiritual vocation, Jan was convinced that

God had called him to rule over his elect at Münster and throughout the world. He was the third David, whose pretentious emblem was a globe with the inscription 'king of righteousness over all.'

Jan introduced communism in Münster. The precarious economic situation created by the siege was undoubtedly a major factor in this step, but there was also the determination to follow the Biblical precedent of the Book of Acts. Afterward polygamy was introduced, again against the backdrop of practical necessity and theological insight. Women outnumbered men in Münster, and since in those days single women were (legally) helpless creatures, a way had to be found to deal with their problem. The claim to Biblical precedent was supported by reference to the patriarchs of the Old Testament, who demonstrated that polygamy was evidently practiced without divine disapproval. The Old Testament was indeed taken as the epitome of spirituality, quite in contrast to the other reformers, who thought that the new dispensation heralded by Christ had obviated the old. Whatever the purported spiritual justification, contemporaries saw the innovation as Jan van Leyden's rationale for covering up his sensuality. In August 1534 Jan van Leyden proclaimed himself king. Psychological factors may have played an important part in this respect, for the difficulties created by the siege suggested the need for the demonstration that the full restitution of the Biblical ideal had indeed occurred in the city.

Actually, the siege made little progress. When famine broke out in the winter, Jan had to allow those who wished to leave to do so. The stalemate continued during the early months of 1535, until aided by treason the besieging forces fought their way into the city. A bloody battle followed, and when it was over the New Jerusalem had come to its unbiblical, if not unexpected, end. Jan van Leyden and two of his associates were captured, tried, and executed.

And the significance of this tale of horror, bloodshed, and spiritual exuberance? It lies in the relationship of Münster Anabaptism to the Anabaptist movement at large. Both affirmed adult Baptism, but there were also differences, for example, the interpretation of the nature of the Church or the use of force. That the Münster Anabaptists affirmed believer's Baptism is itself not sufficient to make them part of Anabaptism, for this same logic would require that all advocates of infant Baptism be grouped together. But there were ties between Münster and Anabaptism at large. Not only did the South German Anabaptists use a tract of Bernhard Rothmann; more importantly, both thought of the Christian faith as deliberate commitment to fulfill the divine law. The emphasis of both was nomistic and consisted in the effort to realize this law in daily life. Anabaptism at large saw this as commitment to the *nova lex Christi*, to discipleship, to the following after Christ. It was intensely personal and devoid of real eschatological considerations. Münster Anabaptism thought in terms of 'restitution,' as expressed in the title of Rothmann's magnum opus (*Restitution rechter und gesunder christlicher Lehre*): the restitution of the divine plan for the world, eminently prefigured in the Old Testament and reiterated in the New. Demands made upon the individual are only part of the more comprehensive plan for the restitution of society. Such restitutionist theology was necessarily eschatological: one can hardly imagine how Jan van Leyden envisioned the survival of the New Jerusalem at Münster against the world unless he thought the end of the world imminent. Undoubtedly, Jan van Leyden had been a compelling charismatic figure who left a formidable imprint on his followers; the other important factor in this story was the grim reality of the seige.

After the dramatic demise of the New Jerusalem at Münster, the question began to haunt Anabaptists as to how this happening was to be interpreted. Had Münster been an authentic expression of Anabaptist ideals, or had it been a perversion?

Three answers vied for acceptance among the bewildered Anabaptists. The followers of Melchior Hofmann, still replete with apocalyptic anticipation and allegorical interpretation of Scripture, but peaceful and willing to suffer, were persuaded that the end— and thus the New Jerusalem—was imminent. Münster had been a false step in the right direction. Other Anabaptists, notably one Jan van Batenburg, felt that Münster had been a genuine expression of Biblical religion, which called for the destruction of the godless with the sword. A third group of Anabaptists decried the eschatological-apocalyptic orientation of Hofmann and the use of force advocated by the Münsterites. They emphasized pacifism and a peaceful way of life. The last view was to dominate. In great measure this was the accomplishment of Menno Simons, the outstanding Anabaptist leader in the North. He was not a great theologian, though the enormous quantity of his writings may convey this impression. His writings lack tightly knit argumentation and often strain to make a point. But his many pamphlets offered a simple message. At a time when many Protestant writings had become theologically sophisticated, written more for theologians than for the common man, Menno's tracts were simple. His mood was devotional, his style that of an exposition of Biblical passages, his theology that of the Zurich Anabaptists. His theology was not new, though the absence of demonstrable ties between the South and the North suggests that Menno may have shown more creativity than one suspects.

At the heart of Menno's theology stood the marvel at the new birth that was made possible by divine grace and enabled man to lead a life of obedience. God did not only declare the sinner righteous; he actually made him righteous. Thus Menno's theology was a theology of deeds, of life, of sanctification. Menno was persuaded that God called his people to a life of holiness. Faith was trust in God's offer of forgiveness as well as obedience.

Menno's christology departed from general Anabaptist thought (and orthodox doctrine, for that matter) in one important way. Influenced by Melchior Hofmann, Menno held that Christ had not been born *of* Mary, but *in* her. 'Christ Jesus, as to his origin,' Menno wrote, 'is no earthly man, that is, a fruit of the flesh and blood of Adam. He is a heavenly fruit of man.'[12] Menno sought to safeguard Christ's sinlessness and was persuaded that it could be done only by keeping Jesus' flesh free from possible stain by Mary.

If Jesus had received his flesh from Mary he could not have been sinless, and thus he could not have reconciled man with God. In his later years Menno's theological concern focused on the Church, its purity and its challenge to be without 'spot or wrinkles.' He shared the general Anabaptist notion that the Anabaptist congregations were the true Church of Christ or, as he observed on one occasion, 'it is sufficiently proved that our hated, despised, and small church is the true, apostolic and Christian Church.'[13] This assertion entailed the corollary insistence that this Church was kept pure through discipline and the ban. This easily stated theory involved complications in practice. The ban meant the breaking of social ties no less than religious ones. What was to happen in the case of a couple where one spouse was banned? Should the other separate from the banned party? One Anabaptist, Leenaert Bouwens, argued that the believing spouse should do so, since the 'heavenly marriage' between Christ and the believer was more sacred than earthly marriage between husband and wife. Menno at first thought more tolerantly, but eventually concurred, perhaps unwillingly, with the rigoristic position.

These two emphases on the part of the outstanding Anabaptist leader illustrate at once the doctrinal divergencies that increasingly beset North German and Dutch Anabaptism. Factions emerged, an understandable development, especially since the movement at large never possessed organizational coherence. Moreover, governmental

D

authority could not be used to resolve arising differences in favor of one faction or another. The factions survived. And the more time passed, the more the movement became respectable and the more the authorities turned weary, and persecution at long last faded away.

## The Hutterite Communities

The climate encountered by Anabaptism in Moravia was unique, for there the authorities were tolerant and offered a haven of rest for Anabaptists bitterly persecuted elsewhere. Had this been the only distinction of Moravian Anabaptism, it would have been note-worthy. But there was another: in Moravia the Anabaptists estab-lished communities, thus forming a 'state church' of Anabaptist pro-pensity. The unique feature of these communities was their com-munist form of socialization. Though periodically beset by external oppression and internal uncertainty, these Hutterite Anabaptists flourished throughout the century and survived into the next.

The Anabaptist message was brought to Moravia by Balthasar Hubmaier in 1526. At first the character of the movement was not different from that elsewhere. Then a far-reaching change occurred, reported by a contemporary chronicler with these words: 'In light of their need, they took counsel with one another and named "ser-vants of temporal needs". . . . These men spread a cloak in front of the people and everyone brought his belongings, willingly and un-coerced, so that the needy might be provided for, according to the teaching of the prophets and apostles.'[14] This account shows that two considerations were important in the move to communal sharing: economic necessity and Biblical precedent. It is difficult to say whether a permanent practice was contemplated; probably not.

The man whose name was to designate Anabaptism in Moravia saw communal living as the eminent mark of the true faith: Jakob Hutter, a leader of charismatic qualities, who put his stamp on Mora-vian Anabaptism. Under his guidance Anabaptism flourished. Most Anabaptist congregations, as a result of circumstances, had gone their own way, but he brought them together to form a large com-munity. He was a simple man, without education, lacking even a rudimentary theological competence, the symbol of the peasant whose calloused hands took the Bible and, uninformed by theo-logical learning and linguistic competence, sought to understand it. The scope of his activity was restricted (perhaps to one or two thousand people at best), and we can hardly compare him with the outstanding figures of the century. Yet, one must admire him for the warmth of his religion, expressed in letters that echoed apostolic simplicity and style. If Anabaptism elsewhere was a heterogeneous phenomenon, in Moravia it was unified, and the tribute belongs to this strong leader.

Repercussions of the debacle of Anabaptism at Münster brought the Hutterites to the brink of catastrophe. A provincial Diet ordered in 1535 the expulsion of all Anabaptists, who had to pack their belongings and start on a journey without destination, wandering from place to place, hoping, much against hope, somewhere to find toleration. They were the outcasts of a society that had no place for them. They were refused lodging, even food and water, and were accompanied by the suspicion that they, like their supposed Münster kinsmen, were political revolutionaries. To defend his followers against such charges. Jakob Hutter wrote a touching *apologia pro vita sua* to the governor of Moravia. He recapitulated the Anabaptist commitment to follow Jesus, told of the persecution they had suffered, mentioned their peacefulness, and their expulsion. 'Now we lie in this vast heather, according to God's will. We do not wish to hurt or wrong anybody, not even our greatest enemies, such as Ferdinand. All men know our doings, know our words and deeds. . . . We would gladly give our lives. We have no weapons, neither lancets nor rifles, as everybody knows. In short, we strive to talk and walk, live peaceably and harmoniously in God's truth and righteousness.'[15] But the plea went unheeded. Reluctantly, the Anabaptists divided into smaller groups and continued their search for toleration. Gradually they found it. Once a group had been given a noble's permission to settle, others arrived on the scene and enlarged the contingent. For a while external conditions remained precarious, but in the end Moravian Anabaptism survived its most serious threat.

The life of a Hutterite colony was painstakingly organized. Each member had a specific place, each performed a specific task. The result was a community at once egalitarian and totalitarian, though deeply spiritual in purpose and commitment. In the center stood the 'congregation' and all activity and effort were directed toward it. It was the true visible Church, here—and here only—restored according to the Biblical pattern. 'There was no one who went idle,' wrote a Hutterite chronicler, 'everyone did what he was commanded and what he was able to do, no matter whether he had been rich or poor. Even the Ministers, who joined our brotherhood, performed manual labor. . . . As in the artful mechanism of a clock one wheel moves and helps the others and makes them turn, or as in a hive all bees work together, so it was here. For where there is no order, there is disorder and disruption, where God is absent everything will soon break apart.'[16]

In a striking way the Hutterite communities constituted a return to the notion of the *corpus christianum*, to a society in which the civic and the religious communities were identical. The Hutterite communities were numerically much smaller, of course, than those of Hesse or Württemberg, of Augsburg or Strassburg, which they had left behind. Moreover, the point could be made that this civic and religious identity was the result of the fact that all had received believer's Baptism. To the untrained eye, however, there was little difference between a Hutterite *Haushabe* (community) and an ordinary peasant village in Moravia. The Hutterites had to organize their communities in such a way as to provide both for the economic well-being and the general civic responsibilities.

The Hutterite way of life was not static, and it evolved throughout the 16th century. It flourished during the second half of the century, when the Hutterites numbered about 12,000. About 200 people, men, women, and children, comprised one *Haushabe*. Such a *Haushabe* was, for practical purposes, a village, consisting of several large and sturdy houses. C. A. Fischer, one of the Catholic antagonists of the Hutterites, conceded that they 'have the most beautiful houses.' The first floor of the houses was comprised of the public rooms—kitchen, dining halls, laundry, nursery. On the second and third floors were small rooms that served as bedrooms for married couples and their infant children. Once the children had turned two, however, they lived in 'schools,' supervised by 'schoolmasters' and nurses. A remarkable *Address to the Schoolmasters*, of 1568, by Peter Walpot, impresses the reader by its extraordinary attention to detail and by its obvious concern for the children. Here the frequency of bathing was spelled out, as was the manner of their punishment and their treatment during sickness.[17] The Hutterite communities were situated on the estates of the nobility and most of the Hutterites worked for the nobility, some directly, others by providing services, such as tailoring, to the nobility and to their own group. Wages received were put into a common chest. Detailed instructions were drawn up and prescribed the work of the artisans—what they could manufacture, what was prohibited as 'worldly,' the prices to be paid, and so on. The *Hutterite Chronicle*, frank about the inner life of communities, indicates that there were periods of difficulty. But the ideal of communal living was always embraced with vigor and conviction. Outsiders occasionally remarked about the legalism and haughtiness of the Hutterites, but they themselves were always persuaded that they had found the better way.

## Protestant Spiritualism

The Protestant spectrum in the 16th century included a group of radicals for whom the label 'Spiritualists' has become accepted nomenclature. These radicals neither got excited about adult Baptism —or infant Baptism, for that matter—nor did they take the trinitarian dogma as the apex of theological perversion; therefore they have been distinguished from both Anabaptists and Antitrinitarians. Since they denounced the Catholic Church, they may be classified as Protestants, and since they also found fault with the Protestant reformers, they must bear the label 'radical.' In contrast to all other religious groupings in the 16th century, however, they made no real attempt to alter the prevailing ecclesiastical status quo. They criticized the existing forms of religion, but they never were concerned to form a new ecclesiastical tradition or a new Church. Deep in their hearts they were individualists. This meant that they are without history. They are outsiders, forgotten men, who live on only in the pages of their prolific writings. Most of them conformed to the expected external routine of their respective communities. Only a few made bold to testify to their conviction, and thus they appeared in the limelight of Reformation history. These few are the sole evidence we have of their kind, though there must have been many who thought like them, but who lacked the courage or the determination to stand up and be counted. The Spiritualists were children of the Reformation, though Luther and his colleagues disowned them and cited Scripture to prove their point. Some of their roots undoubtedly can be found in the medieval mystic tradition; the decisive stimulus and the personal awakening, however, derived from the Reformation.

'In the beginning was the Word': this Biblical dictum can be inscribed over the Spiritualists. But theirs was a unique definition of the 'Word': they did not refer to the outer word, the Bible, which they considered an obscure and enigmatic book, where one part disagreed with the other, where interpretation stood against interpretation. As a matter of fact, they delighted in collecting scriptural passages that, as they claimed, contradicted one another. Their 'Word' was God's immediate and direct communication to man, the 'Spirit' speaking to man. Scripture was of this only the external witness and record. This basic insight prompted the Spiritualists to label all empirical manifestations of religion as peripheral and insignificant. They preferred the living voice of God to the dead record of Scripture. They considered spiritual Baptism more important than the Baptism of water at whatever age, and the spiritual partaking of Christ more meaningful than the eating of bread and the drinking of wine. Outer form was rejected in favor of inner spirituality. The Bible and ceremonies, the Sacraments and the Church, creeds, and ecclesiastical polity were unimportant, for they were externals. Such emphasis meant the rejection of a great deal of traditional dogma, or, at any rate, a reversal of priorities, so that the doctrines that were not outrightly questioned were relegated to a place of insignificance.

The Spiritualists were verbal exhibitionists who endlessly committed their ideas to paper. In the case of David Joris, for example, it is almost impossible to count the tracts he wrote. Philipp Melanchthon, no mean writer himself, marvelled at the inexhaustible quantity of Caspar Schwenckfeld's literary output and called him *centimanus*, a 'hundred-handed man.' There may have been good reason for such prolixity, for to entrust their thoughts to paper was the only safe way to propagate their teachings.

Sebastian Franck, a soapmaker, printer, historian, and theologian, was the first Spiritualist. His versatility may be considered characteristic, for the Spiritualists were laymen, jacks-of-all-trades, and amateur theologians of boundless exuberance and endurance. Franck traversed the full spectrum of religious options in the early 16th century, beginning as a Catholic, turning Lutheran, then Anabaptist, and finally deciding it best to walk his own way. 'I do not want to be a papist,' he wrote, 'I do not want to be a Lutheran, I do not want to be an Anabaptist.'[18] His reason was that he found fault with all. His was a brief life and, considering the turbulence of the time, a tranquil one. But beneath the tranquillity lay revolutionary thoughts that altered the Christian religion beyond recognition. Franck saw Christianity as another expression of man's universal religion—to use language made popular by English Deist Matthew Tindal 200 years later, 'a republication of the religion of nature.' Accordingly, religious insight was valid regardless of where it was found, within or without the Christian Church, within or without the Christian tradition. The great events of the Bible were seen as timeless symbols of God's dealing with man. Eternal truth expresses itself in historical form, Franck argued, and only the former is important. 'The histories of Adam and Christ are not Adam and Christ,' he remarked, and added, 'The external Adam and Christ are but the expression of the inward, indwelling Adam and Christ.'[19]

Caspar Schwenckfeld, another Spiritualist layman, was unconcerned about the external forms of the Christian faith. In contrast to Franck, his concern was to spiritualize not doctrine but religion, that is, to assert that true religion consisted in piety and the right inner attitude. Schwenckfeld sought to establish the true Church, and he parted with Luther because he charged that the Wittenberg Reformer had not been sufficiently serious in this regard. Schwenckfeld's view of Communion became the crucial expression of his theology. Communion had emerged as the painful issue of division among the various proponents of the new faith. But the proper understanding of Communion meant an understanding of the Christian faith, namely, the distinction between externals and internals, and preference for the latter. The old Church and the new were both in error, as were the Anabaptists, for their stress on externals destroyed the immediacy of the relationship between God and man. Having taken such a position, Schwenckfeld proposed in April 1526 the suspension of the celebration of Communion until agreement had been reached among all parties concerning its meaning and significance! The devotional character and the quantity of Schwenckfeld's writings explain why he was able to gather a small group of followers. They called themselves 'confessors of the glory of Christ,' the term was Schwenckfeld's, whereas outsiders preferred the simpler and theologically less objectionable label 'Schwenckfelders.'

A third Spiritualist, Sebastian Castellio, made compassion a theological principle. He paid for it with a life of personal hardship, an early death, well-nigh universal repudiation by his contemporaries—and a famous place in history. His compassion for the Antitrinitarian Michael Servetus was expressed in an eloquent repudiation of governmental suppression of deviate religious opinion. The work was entitled *De haereticis, an sint persequendi* (If Heretics Are to be Persecuted?) and was published in 1553, in response to Michael Servetus's execution in Geneva. This book was neither an emotional appeal nor a tightly knit argument; rather it was a simple anthology of statements of famous theologians, from Augustine and Jerome to Erasmus and Luther, on the treatment of heretics. Its single theme, repeated with many variations, was that the noblest minds of Christendom through the centuries had been against the persecution of heretics. Persecution was wrong, because it contradicted the principles of Christ. Moreover, who is a heretic? 'If you are reputed in one town a true believer, you will be reputed in the next town as a heretic. Accordingly, if anyone wants to live today, he must have

as many confessions of faith and religions as there are towns and
sects, just as a traveler has to change his money from one day to the
next.'[20] Although Castellio's primary motivation was the simple virtue of compassion, horror over the pain and anguish of a fellow
human being, underneath stood the same dichotomy of 'external'
and 'internal' that we have already encountered in Franck and
Schwenckfeld. Castellio assumed that differences over the interpretation of certain doctrines did not touch on the essence of the Christian faith. Therefore, such differences should be disregarded. The
practice of virtue and a moral life were of greater importance than
agreement over the proper interpretation, for example, of the
mystery of the Trinity. In short, Castellio's religion was undog-
matic, latitudinarian, and practical, a strange departure from the
norms so universally observed in the 16th century.

Sebastian Franck, Caspar Schwenckfeld, Sebastian Castellio: the
list is not complete and hardly can be. Still, they are examples of
what must have been a much larger number of their contemporaries
—men who had neither the capacity nor the interest to concern
themselves with intricate theological questions, who felt that the
competing ecclesiastical factions differed only over subtle points of
doctrine, and who were persuaded that in the final analysis one of
these factions was as good as the other. One suspects that even
before the Reformation there had been such thinkers. It was the
significance of the 16th century that such sentiment rose to the
surface.

## The Antitrinitarian Dissent

A third and final expression of radical reform consisted of those men
who attacked the trinitarian dogma of the Church. They have received the label Antitrinitarians.[21] Like the Anabaptists and the
Spiritualists, they were heirs of the late medieval tradition as well
as of the Reformation. Antitrinitarian soteriology was not Catholic,
though it was a far cry from what may be called the Protestant
consensus. Interestingly, the early representatives of antitrinitarianism appear to have nurtured their radicalism while yet in the bosom
of the Catholic Church. To trace the phenomenon exclusively to the
Protestant Reformation does not explain a complex situation. That
the Reformation exerted a powerful stimulus cannot be doubted.
however, both by its calling into question many traditional notions
and by insisting on the primacy of the Scriptures as source for Chris-

tian theology.[22] By all odds, those who harbored radical notions would have preferred to be secretive about them, knowing full well the fate inescapably befalling a solitary heretic. The extensive religious turmoil precipitated by the Reformation made for a different situation. And once one theological point had become exposed to biting criticism, it was not surprising that the Trinitarian dogma should be similarly attacked.

The Antitrinitarians may be classified with both the Anabaptists and the Spiritualists not only because they exhibited certain theological similarities, such as the repudiation of infant Baptism, but also because they shared the characteristic attitude of denouncing the old Church and the new as equally perverted and divorced from scriptural truth. Yet there were differences, the principal one being that virtually all Anabaptists and Spiritualists were orthodox Trinitarians. The Anabaptists viewed the person of Christ in traditional terms, and although the Spiritualists wrote rather obscurely—one almost feels that at times they themselves did not understand their beliefs—their essential orthodoxy also is certain. Moreover, the Anabaptist and the Spiritualist concern was primarily religious—their watchwords were 'commitment,' 'obedience,' and 'new walk of life'—rather than theological. The Antitrinitarians were concerned about theology.

The epic of 16th-century antitrinitarianism began with solitary individuals. Decades later came the relatively unmolested establishment of Antitrinitarian congregations in eastern Europe. The story was halted, at least temporarily, with the virtual extinction of these congregations in the first half of the 17th century. Since antitrinitarianism was basically a theological phenomenon, it had a lively theological history, from the repudiation of the orthodox Trinitarian dogma to the painful groping for positive alternatives, which often led to assertions, e.g., tritheism, that were more complicated than what had been repudiated. The impact of antitrinitarianism went beyond a single doctrine. The rejection of the Trinitarian dogma was a direct attack on traditional soteriology, and this entailed different views of Jesus and of anthropology. Not since the days of Pelagius had notions of this sort been so forcefully presented within the Christian framework. Adolf von Harnack argued in his famous *History of Dogma* that Unitarianism was a watershed in the history of Christian thought because it dissolved dogma in favor of reason.[23] It is true, but in this sense the Arians of the early Church had already 'dissolved' dogma. The Unitarians did not advance any essential argument that had not already appeared in the great christological debates of the early Church. That they were called 'new Arians' was an apt expression of their connection with the past. Their ideas were hardly novel; they had been considered in the doctrinal controversies of the early Church and had been found wanting.

A Spanish humanist, physician, geographer, and lay theologian stood at the beginning: Michael Servetus. As with so many other Reformation figures, we know little about his childhood and youth: history had not yet reached out and made him prominent.[24] His first piece of writing shows him conversant with the Biblical languages as well as theology, an indication that his schooling must have been thorough and extensive. In the 1520s he studied law at the University of Toulouse, where he entered the service of Juan de Quintana, the famed Franciscan preacher to Emperor Charles V. In 1529 he accompanied Quintana to Italy and spent half a year at Bologna. The sojourn at Bologna possibly brought him into contact with the religious skepticism of late 15th-century Italy: the brilliant youth could have assimilated such notions rather quickly. In the fall of 1530 he moved to Basel and there began to nettle John Oecolampadius with bothersome questions concerning the Trinity. Servetus, barely turned 20, must have been an *enfant terrible*, more concerned about scoring a theological point than the pursuit of truth. During the 6 months he spent at Basel, Servetus worked on a tract dealing with his Trinitarian views. Early in 1531, he succeeded in securing a printer for his manuscript, which he entitled *De Trinitatis Erroribus* (Errors of the Trinity). Servetus's position was Sabellian modalism: Father, Son, and Holy Spirit were seen as the three 'modes' or 'dispositions' of God. Jesus was divine, indeed the Son of God, but not in the orthodox sense.[25] The following year Servetus published a second treatise, entitled *Dialogorum de Trinitate libri duo*, which, despite a number of minor modifications, reiterated the earlier position.

Two decades later, in 1553, came the publication of Servetus's magnum opus: *Christianismi Restitutio*. Within months, he was arrested in Geneva, brought to trial, and in October of that year burned at the stake. Before the flames consumed his body he was heard to cry, 'O God, save my soul; O Jesus, Son of the eternal God, have mercy on me.'[26] As one bystander remarked, if he had placed the adjective 'eternal' before 'Son', his life would have never been in danger. The flames of Geneva burned his name indelibly into the annals of European history—and his reference to the pulmonary circulation of the blood, put down casually in the *Restitutio*, entered his name in the pages of medical history as well. His death raised the question of religious freedom and his theology laid the seed for the dissolution of the Trinitarian dogma.

The execution turned into a *cause célèbre*, evoking the resolute sentiment of a few voices of dissent, notably Sebastian Castellio's *De haereticis, an sint persequendi* and Guillaume Postel's *Apologia pro Serveto Villanovano*. Michael Servetus, instead of being an epilogue, proved to be the beginning of a lengthy line of critics of the Trinitarian dogma. His ideas were picked up, echoed, and spread by disciples who succeeded, in the end, in translating his theological theory into ecclesiastical practice. The critics were strikingly similar. They were men of the second generation of the Reformation and of strong humanist orientation. None was a trained theologian. All were Italian.[27]

The first was Matteo Gribaldi, born around the turn of the 16th century, professor of law at the University of Padua. After Servetus's trial he asserted that no man should be put to death on account of his belief. He could see nothing wrong with Servetus's teaching and indeed had held the same views from childhood. It is hard to say what he meant by this remark; perhaps it was to underscore the harmlessness of Servetus's thought. Afterward he studied Servetus's pamphlet on the Errors of the Trinity and concluded that it contained the proper understanding of the doctrine. Gribaldi, like Servetus, was an amateur theologian. He found the orthodox Trinitarian doctrine objectionable, but his own reconstruction landed him in a worse dilemma. To compound the difficulty, his writings were ambiguous. Even his various confessions are not very helpful, though they do convey a rough outline of his thought. Only God the Father deserved the divine attributes; Jesus and the Holy Spirit owed their divinity to the Father.

Among Gribaldi's disciples was a fellow Italian, Giorgio Biandrata. A renowned specialist in gynecology, he was invited in 1540 to Poland to serve as personal physician to the Polish queen. He stayed for more than a decade, returned to Italy for a few short years, then moved to Geneva, where his piety made him an eminent member of the Italian congregation. After a period of uneasy patience he began to nettle Calvin with theological questions about the Trinity. No matter how many answers he received, he always came back with new questions. Since the Trinitarian dogma does need explanation—the proper definition, for example, of such terms as person, essence, property, and substance makes an enormous theological difference—Calvin at first complied. But his patience ran out, especially after Biandrata had raised the question whether it was not sufficient to assert simply faith in 'one God the Father, one Lord Jesus, and one Holy Spirit,' and whether it was not preposterous 'to undertake an examination of the essence of God.'[28] At this point the story of antitrinitarianism took a different course. Thus far it had related the fates of individuals, men of strong conviction but of little success, burned at the stake but not convicted, expelled but not persuaded. From the late 1550s onward, however, it took on a sociological dimension. Moreover, the site of agitation shifted to Poland.[29] Protestantism in Poland was Calvinist and the rise of antitrinitarian sentiment occurred within the ranks of the Calvinist Church. Biandrata returned to Poland in 1558 and his arrival stimulated criticism of the Trinitarian dogma. The relative religious freedom in Poland was important, and the country increasingly became a haven for weary theologians.

Lelio Sozzini—Laelius Socinus, as he was known in the Latinized form of his name—born in 1525, was scion of a distinguished family. Melanchthon, who met him, was full of praise for his erudition, honesty, and uprightness. Early in his youth he was converted to Protestantism. For over a decade, from 1547 to 1559, he traveled throughout Europe, studied at Basel and Wittenberg, and corresponded with Calvin, whom he annoyed with theological questions. Some were harmless, such as whether one could marry a Catholic. Others were more disturbing, such as whether it was necessary to believe in the resurrection of the flesh.

In 1552 Socinus came to Zurich, where he continued his epistolary inquiries about the faith. Somehow rumors about his orthodoxy cropped up and Bullinger, the Zurich reformer, urged him to clear the air with a confession of faith. This Socinus did and the Zurich reformer found the statement acceptable. No wonder! It minced no words about condemning the Arians, the Anabaptists, and the followers of Servetus, but the positive delineation of the author's views was on the enigmatic side. Still, it settled the question of his orthodoxy and for the next several years he lived a quiet life in the city, withdrawn in his contacts with others, taking to the pen to commit his thoughts to paper. Lelio Sozzini died in 1562 at 37, a perfect example of a 'Nicodemite,' outwardly conforming to the prevailing theological sentiment, while inwardly questioning it persistently.

With Socinus's passing, the site of the antitrinitarian drama shifted. Gone were the Italian humanists, who moved from Italy to Geneva, there to experience an uncertain fate. The new place of action was Poland, already in the throes of an antitrinitarian controversy, fanned to increasing intensity by the presence of Biandrata and others. The quintessence of the subsequent development was a successful effort on the part of Antitrinitarians to reorient a segment of the Reformed Church in Poland along antitrinitarian lines. Biandrata, whom Calvin called a 'treacherous troublemaker,'[30] brought about an open consideration of the antitrinitarian issue. At a synodal meeting at Piotrków in 1565 the issue came to a head. The Trinitarian dogma was extensively debated, but neither side was able to persuade the other, and so they parted. An antitrinitarian Church therefore became a reality in 1565. Initially, it had no name. The Antitrinitarians preferred to call themselves 'brethren in Poland and Lithuania who have rejected the Trinity,' or simply 'Christians,' but the latter designation was too simple and theologically challenging to attain widespread use. In the end the name Minor Reformed Church of Poland was accepted, though their opponents always called them Arians.

The Minor Reformed Church of Poland experienced an interesting history. Outwardly it strove to resist encroachment from governmental authority. Theologically, the Minor Church was characterized by a lively and strenuous effort to arrive at a distinctive antitrinitarian theology. The first issue to arise was Baptism, precipitated by contacts with Anabaptists. A synod discussed the question at length in 1565, without reaching a decision. Sentiment against infant Baptism was strong, but not strong enough to sway the gathering. The decision was astoundingly tolerant: no one should be forced to act against his conscience and the two factions should live harmoniously until the next synod, when God would reveal his will.

A subsequent synod discussed the question again and, once more, did not reach a consensus. This meant that nothing was to be done except to repeat the original exhortation to brotherly love. But the threat of a schism over the issue of Baptism had been avoided. For a while the question of participation in governmental offices occupied the center of attention, but more and more the major issue became the clarification of the understanding of the person of Christ. The first reformulations of the doctrine had resulted in tritheism. Thereby the paradox of the orthodox assertion that God was 'three in one' had been avoided, but since the unity of God had been sacrificed, the answer was hardly satisfactory. Christ's pre-existence, a crucial aspect of the orthodox doctrine, soon became a matter of controversy. The Di-theists, or Arians, held that Christ had existed before the creation of the world, though he was inferior to the Father. These Arians did not share the historical Arian sentiment concerning the creation of Christ, and therefore the nomenclature was a bit faulty. To complicate the situation, some Antitrinitarians denied any pre-existence of Christ and thereby any divinity in the strict sense. A synodal meeting in 1567 brought vehement disagreement, though harmony eventually prevailed: 'All separated with love unimpaired, mutually promising that they would cultivate harmony.' The rejection of Christ's pre-existence raised the problem whether he was to be adored. Some argued that he had become divine by his baptismal adoption and thus deserved adoration; others insisted that Christ should not be worshiped: Adorants and non-Adorants stood against one another.

At this juncture, Fausto Sozzini, the great figure of 16th-century Unitarianism, appeared.[31] Born about 1539, Fausto had an early religious life, nominally Catholic, without deep commitment. In 1561 he left his native Italy for Lyons, and a year later he traveled to Zurich to obtain the papers of his uncle Lelio. It was a case of *tolle, lege* ('take and read'), for the encounter with the ideas of his uncle meant his 'conversion' to Protestant and, indeed, antitrinitarian beliefs. Fausto's first piece of writing was entitled *De Scriptura auctoritate* (Concerning the Authority of Scripture) and appeared in 1568.[32] The title page named 'Dominicus Lopez, S.J.' as the author, a skilful, though not necessarily sophisticated, device to confound the Inquisition. The work saw several editions and was translated into other languages. It was significant because of its novel approach. Fausto undertook an extensive exposition of the credibility of Scripture. He addressed himself both to Christians and non-Christians, considered possible objections raised by both, and concluded that no matter how cogent the argumentation some men would remain unconvinced, for incontestable proof was not possible. *De Scripturae auctoritate* contained a curious mixture of rationalist concern and a pious willingness not to try to penetrate impenetrable mysteries.

In 1574, Fausto left Italy for Basel, where he remained for 3 years and became involved in a running disputation with a French minister named Jacques Couet over the meaning of the work of Christ. Fausto's contribution, circulated in manuscript form, bore the title *De Jesu Christo Servatore*. Part of it found its way into print in 1583 and the entire work was published 11 years later. It advanced a new view of the work of Christ, traditionally seen as satisfaction for the sins of mankind. Fausto considered inappropriate the notion that the sins of one person can be transferred upon another. Christ's work consisted in the full revelation of God's will, in the proclamation of 'the way of eternal life.'[33] Man's response was to be not faith but obedience, the following of the example set by Christ. Such discipleship did not mean slavish imitation; rather it was a commitment to the kind of life that was lived by Jesus. Between Jesus and the believer exists a 'similitude,' and 'both can be said to have qualities of the same kind.'[34] Fausto was a moderate in his christological perspective—Christ was divine through the Father. He was tolerant and argued that, in contrast to differing concepts of God, differing concepts of Christ cannot endanger salvation. Tolerance within the Christian brotherhood was therefore necessary.

Word about his book spread to Poland, and in 1578 Fausto went there at the invitation of Biandrata, who wanted support against the non-Adorants. For almost a quarter of a century, from 1580 to 1604, Fausto was the inspiration of the Minor Reformed Church. He wrote numerous tracts and countless letters, debated with Catholics and Calvinists, and ably represented the antitrinitarian cause. The Minor Church came to be called the Socinian Church, and although this tribute fails to acknowledge that the tradition was already strong when Fausto appeared on the scene, it does bestow honor where honor is due. Without Fausto Sozzini, antitrinitarianism in Poland would never have taken the form it did. When he died, in March 1604, he left behind him a relatively homogeneous Minor Church. One year later the *Racovian Catechism*, the programmatic theological pronouncement of the Minor Reformed Church, appeared.[35] It took its name from Racov, the center of Polish Socinianism, where the synods of the Minor Church were held and where its polemical books and pamphlets were published. Probably Fausto himself had supplied the first draft.

The catechism is an interesting piece of theological writing. Its title called it the 'Catechism of the assembly of those people who in the Kingdom of Poland, and in the Grand Duchy of Lithuania . . . affirm and confess, that no other than the Father of our Lord Jesus Christ is the only God of Israel; and the man Jesus of Nazareth, who was born of a virgin, and no other besides him, is the only-begotten Son of God.' Interestingly, the first section of the *Racovian Catechism* was not devoted to a discussion of God, as was customary, but to the problem of authority—the authenticity of Scripture.

A large section of the catechism dealt with christology. Jesus was seen as 'a true man by nature,' though he was more than mere man, for he was conceived of the 'Holy Spirit and born of the Virgin Mary.' That he had a divine nature was found 'repugnant not only to sound reason, but also to the holy Scriptures,' for reason shows that 'two substances indued with opposite properties cannot combine into one person, and such properties are mortality and immortality; to have a beginning, and to be without beginning.' Scripture, in turn, confirms that 'whatever divine excellency Christ hath, the Scripture testifieth that he hath it by the gift of the Father.'

The discussion of the work of Christ by the *Racovian Catechism* was equally startling. The view that 'Christ by his death merited salvation for us and fully satisfied for our sins' was denounced as 'fallacious, erroneous, and very pernicious,' and as 'repugnant both to Scripture and reason.' Accordingly, justification 'is nothing but the transformation of our mind and will, and composure of them to the doctrine of our Saviour Christ as the very word does intimate.' Faith is primarily obedience, namely, 'that we be obedient unto God, not only in those things only which he has commanded in the law delivered by Moses, and are not abrogated by Christ; but also in those things which Christ has added to the law.'

Here was indeed a new way of theologizing. It had its basis in the intellectual difficulties of the orthodox doctrine, as well as in the mood of religious questioning ushered in by the Reformation. After decades of probing, the Antitrinitarians had at long last formulated positive and constructive assertions concerning the person and work of Christ. Thereby the history of antitrinitarianism in the Reformation came to its conclusion.

# CHAPTER FOUR

# John Calvin

In March 1536, a slender book was published under the long and somewhat nondescript title *Christianae religionis Institutio totam fere pietatis summam et quicquid est in doctrina salutis cognitu necessarium, complectens: omnibus pietatis studiosis lectu dignissimum opus ac recens editum.* The author, a Frenchman by the name of John Calvin, had worked hard and fast on the manuscript, and had produced a competent, if inconspicuous, work. The book was a success, but hardly more so than dozens of Protestant theological tracts published in that age of religious ferment. The author, however, made his entrance upon the stage of the Reformation, which he was to dominate for the next three decades.

John Calvin would become one of the most eminent reformers. Such distinction is worthy of note. While many other reformers were either ignored by historical scholarship or even deprived of their theological originality, Calvin's stature has always been recognized. In the Anglo-Saxon world his impact has been widespread and his thought has often been synonymous with the Protestant tradition. He was the great theological system-builder of the Reformation, quite in contrast to Luther, who rambled through the theological thicket with the vigor of an exuberant genius, more concerned with the exposition of certain issues than with overall consistency, neither fearful of paradox nor hesitant of overstatement.

This historical significance must be rightly understood. By all accounts Calvin's site of reform activity was modest and insignificant. Geneva, no matter how influential in the Swiss Confederation, was a small city-state, picayune when compared with the real centers

99

of power in Europe, with England, Spain, or France. What took place in that small commonwealth, even with regard to the matter of ecclesiastical change, was quite secondary. Although histories of the Reformation recount the course of events in Geneva in striking detail, there is no more justification for doing this than for narrating the events in Strassburg, Basel, Augsburg, Nuremberg, or any other of the numerous towns in Central Europe. The history of the Reformation in Geneva can well be slighted. Of primary significance is the thought of the Genevan reformer, the formulation of what he took to be the essence of the Protestant evangel. There was also the remarkable transfer of Calvin's ideas from the town on Lake Leman to the four corners of Europe, to France no less than to Scotland, Poland, Hungary, and Holland. A centrifugal quality about Calvin's thought made it, within a few short years, normative for the vocabulary of those who adhered to the new faith. Calvin's life constituted the prelude to this dynamic expansion, even as a generation earlier Luther's life had formed the prelude to the beginnings of the Protestant Reformation. Throughout Europe Calvin's thought took on flesh and blood. Men formed new churches, suffered pain and martyrdom, went into exile, because they were persuaded that John Calvin, who had never taken a formal course in theology (and who had, perhaps, never been ordained) propounded the authentic and genuine Christian message. In several European countries, notably in Scotland, France, and the Low Countries, the fabric of Calvinist thought interwove intricately with the political aspirations of the people so that the cause of the Reformation (which was Calvin's Reformation) became, once again, inextricably linked to the broader development.

When bidding farewell on his deathbed to the Genevan citizens with whom he had labored—city councilors, ministers, teachers— Calvin recalled the struggles during his years at Geneva and then added that 'the Lord our God so confirmed me, who am by no means naturally bold (I say what is true), that I succumbed to none of their attempts.'[1] 'Who am by no means naturally bold'—no description of Calvin sounds more unbelievable: we envision him as a cold, stern, even tyrannical person. Perhaps Calvin himself sensed the astounding character of his words and added, 'I say what is true.' What he meant by those words was that his natural disposition was alien to the demands of the official responsibilities that he exercised in Geneva. But he had been persuaded God had called him to do the work, and he was going to do it. The notion of a strong and direct divine vocation hovers over Calvin's life and work.

Like his great reforming counterparts, John Calvin had a penchant for work. His literary output does not quite equal that of Luther (who often wrote while he was still clarifying his thinking), but still it was enormous. In addition, Calvin was involved in the routine of ecclesiastical affairs in Geneva, corresponded prolifically, and preached countless sermons from the pulpit of St. Peter's. Some 2,000 of these sermons are extant, preached over a 10-year period, which makes for the highly impressive average (especially when one is aware of the content) of 200 a year. Such activity, coupled with a persuasive theology, carried Calvin's message far beyond the city walls of Geneva. Its success was, paradoxically, the success of a rigoristic and almost sectarian brand of Protestantism. Calvin insisted that the Gospel required resolute commitment and comprehensive conformity of life and work; the Calvinist path to the kingdom, in short, was straight and narrow. Since there had emerged a new and dynamic Catholicism by that time, the qualities exhibited by Calvinism constituted an intriguing parallel.

No comment on the dynamic expansion of Calvinism from the middle of the century onward can quite overlook the characteristic interlocking of religious and political concerns. France, Scotland, and the Low Countries were the sites of intense political activity and Calvinist agitation, a fact that raises the question whether there was a particular quality to Calvin's political thought which made this unique connection possible or necessary. Calvin's understanding of the relationship of Christianity to political life may have made his interpretation of the Gospel particularly attractive to sites of political turmoil. Moreover, it has already been observed that it was Calvinist Protestantism that proved to be dynamically expansionistic throughout Europe, whereas Lutheranism, its potential rival, failed to exhibit this quality. Accordingly, only Sweden, the country in which ecclesiastical change had occurred early in the Reformation, embraced Lutheranism; the other countries accepted Calvinism, or came close to doing so. Naturally one wonders if these two characteristics are more than accidental and causally related.

It was noted earlier that more obvious factors help to explain the phenomenon of the interaction between Calvinist thought and the success of Calvinism. During the time of Calvin's ascendancy Lutheranism was not only engaged in a bitter life-and-death struggle (as the result of the War of Schmalkald) but also had to deal with serious theological dissensions within its own ranks. By the force of external circumstances Lutheranism, for all practical purposes a

German phenomenon, became inner-directed. In the German situation the alignment of religion and politics, so typical of the Reformation, meant simply the pursuit of certain ecclesiastical concerns on the part of the territorial rulers in the Diet. The only issue of real constitutional import had been in connection with the founding of the League of Schmalkald in the early 1530s and had then involved the issue of the right of resistance on the part of the territorial rulers against the Emperor, an issue of obviously limited significance.

From the beginning Calvinism found itself in a different situation for two basic reasons: the French background of John Calvin and the geographical proximity of Geneva and France. Calvin was a Frenchman and he had no greater hope nor a more fervent aspiration than to lead his native land to the true understanding of the Christian Gospel. And in addition to this emotional involvement was the practical fact that the language of his theological tracts and his letters of counsel, inspiration, and exhortation were, as a rule, in French. He could speak directly to the French people, in the way Luther had been able to speak to the Germans at the outset of the Reformation. The geographic location of Geneva added its own particular significance.

Another element entered the picture. The places of vigorous Calvinist expansion became also places of constitutional turbulence, and this had profound consequences for the inner history of Calvinism. This constitutional turmoil can best be understood by recalling that virtually all reformers had agreed on the right of the lower magistracy to resist the upper magistracy. In Germany this line of thought had provided the theological rationale for the founding of the League of Schmalkald, whereas elsewhere, notably in France, the issue was considerably more complicated, for there prevailed not only a prolonged and frustrating struggle for the legal recognition of the Protestant faith, pursued under intermittent persecution, but also a very real constitutional crisis. This situation precipitated considerable reflection on the relationship of the Christian to the secular authorities. Calvinist theologians offered some striking suggestions to make their tradition congenial to political upheaval and change. Calvinism, in other words, was at the right time and place when certain issues arose and demanded an answer. This was its destiny and its historical significance.

### Calvin's Theology

What a strange man Calvin was—timid and stern, modest and aggressive, an unusual combination of opposites. The second generation of the Reformation may have called for men of this type and Calvin brought impressive credentials, foremost, of course, a profound theological mind. Much has been written about Calvin's theology and there can be little doubt that it was one of the eminent achievements of the century—and one can say this without engaging in the kind of parochial hagiography that so often inflates denominational founding fathers to positions of historical prominence. Compared with the other outstanding reformer, Luther, Calvin's thought was more systematic and less paradoxical.

Opinions differ as to what is the core of Calvin's theology.[1a] Most frequently predestination—the *decretum quidem horribile,* as Calvin himself called it—has been mentioned. The notions of God's honor and sovereignty and of man's sanctification have also been suggested. The observation has been made that Calvin was a Biblical theologian who meant to convey to his readers Christ as the heart of Scripture. The starch for a single theme has given way to the suggestion that there are two focuses, such as the notion of the sovereignty of God and the worthlessness of man, or the freedom of God and the certainty of man. In actual fact, several themes occupy more than a cursory place in Calvin's theological exposition. The assertion of divine sovereignty is one; predestination is undoubtedly another; the righteousness of faith, yet another. The difficulty is not so much the acknowledgment that these are important, but the assessment of their relative significance. Possibly the common thread is the systematic delineation of the theological ramifications of a radically understood notion of justification *sola gratia.* The spectrum of Protestant opinion in the 16th century shows that this principle lent itself to a variety of expressions, and Calvin's exposition is therefore neither the only nor the authentic one.

There is an interesting phrase in Calvin's dedicatory epistle to Francis I: 'How does the kingdom of Christ come to us and remain among us?'[2] The majesty of divine sovereignty is the *leitmotif* of Calvin's theology. This theology is Biblical—'our wisdom cannot consist in anything but our humble acceptance of everything (without exception) which is made known to us in Scripture.'[3] God's sovereignty over little things as well as big ones, over good as well as evil, over man's damnation as well as his salvation, forms the constant theme of Calvin's *Institutes of the Christian Religion,* creation and man point to the glory of God.

Calvin saw predestination as the radical application of justification *sola gratia.* To the assertion that God's grace, and not man's

works, effects man's redemption, Calvin added the insistence that
God is utterly free to bestow this grace upon whom he pleases. 'We
say rightly that [God] foresees all things, even as he disposes of them;
but it is confusing everything to say that God elects and rejects according to his foresight of this or that. When we attribute fore-
knowledge to God, we mean that all things have always been and
eternally remain under his observation, so that nothing is either
future or past to his knowledge: he sees and regards them in the
truth, as though they were before his face. We say that this fore-
knowledge extends throughout the circuit of the world and over all
his creatures. We call predestination the eternal decree of God by
which he decided what he would do with each man. For he does not
create them all in like condition, but ordains some to eternal life,
the others to eternal damnation.'[4] This was Calvin's notion of predestination. God did not merely allow the fall of Adam; He willed
it. Calvin saw this as the clear teaching of Scripture, but he conceded
the difficulties: 'We ought not to seek any reason for it because
in its greatness it far surpasses our understanding.'[5] Calvin was persuaded that this doctrine was taught in Scripture. Quite a few of his
contemporaries disagreed with him on this contention, but he was
not able to accept their argument. He asserted not only that the
doctrine was scriptural, but also that it vouchsafed man's redemption as nothing else could. The certainty of redemption was related
to the certainty of election, which, in turn, was the consequence of
Christ's redemptive work. And this redemptive work of Christ—
the death on the Cross of God's only begotten son—was as impenetrable a mystery as the mystery of predestination. Man's redemption inevitably entailed sanctification, not by way of some sort of
instant change, but as a gradual process—'our entire life remains
penance.'[6] Although Calvin was reluctant to speak about the possible verification of divine election, he cautiously acknowledged that
there were signs of it, fallible, to be sure, but indications nonetheless. Among these were the acceptance of the Gospel and the reception of the Lord's Supper. And there was also the new life of the
believer. Calvin emphasized the fruit of the Spirit. 'The reflection on
our works strengthens, since they are testimonies that God lives and
reigns within us.'[7]

In Geneva and those places where Calvin's religion gained entrance, there prevailed a serious determination to follow the rule of
Christ. It might well be that the other reformers gave in a bit too
easily, or were too greatly overcome by theological scruples about
the use of the magistracy to achieve moral reform. Calvin, however,

saw his goal and pursued it relentlessly. No wonder that John Knox found Geneva 'the most perfect school of Christ since the days of the Apostles.' Geneva was different, and those who went there were quite aware of it. Calvin taught his followers to be Soldiers of the Cross. There was a spirit of militancy among the Calvinists. The world was the battlefield between the forces of God and Satan, and they were determined to do their share in assuring the victory of God. The 'Kingdom of Christ' was to be maintained. Thus Calvin molded an ethos. He did more than proclaim a theology; he changed a people.

### Calvin's Life and Labors

John Calvin was born in 1509, the son of Gerard Calvin, secretary to the bishop of Noyon, and procurator of the cathedral chapter of the town. Both year and parental background are important. Calvin was a man of the second generation of the Reformation who reached theological maturity when the period of storm and stress had passed. Moreover, he spent his youth in the urbane and cultured setting of a cathedral town, the *haut monde* of ecclesiastical life. He could never sense the loneliness encountered by the first reformers when they opposed the Catholic Church.

In line with his father's desire he pursued the study of law. This was an erroneous vocational direction, however, and his humanistic orientation prompted him to study Greek. His tutor, Melchior Wolmar of Germany, was a man of Lutheran sympathies and, although there is no concrete evidence, it seems plausible to assume that more was discussed by master and pupil than Greek declensions.

After the unexpected death of his father in 1531 John moved to Paris, where he undertook humanistic studies at the college newly founded by Francis I. His main preoccupation was work on a commentary on Seneca's treatise *De Clementia*, which was published in April 1532. 'At length the die is cast,' he wrote a friend. 'My commentaries on the books of Seneca, *De Clementia*, have been printed, but at my own expense, and have drawn from me more money than you can well suppose. At present, I am using every endeavor to collect some of it back.'[8] Since this work was not theological in its orientation and antedated Calvin's Protestant orientation, it has generally been overlooked by scholarship. Yet it offers a telling clue to understanding Calvin. Stoic ideals were in vogue among the humanists of the day. Calvin did not show himself a blind admirer of the Roman philosopher, but his sympathies were obvious. Calvin's notion of natural law undoubtedly was derived from Stoic thought, and the exegetical approach of the commentary—using grammar and parallel passages—laid the foundation for his subsequent mastery of Biblical hermeneutics.

In the fall of 1533 Calvin became involved in a *cause célèbre* centering on Nicolas Cop, rector of the University of Paris, who on All Saints' Day delivered an oration on Mt 5.1–2 that smacked of Protestant heresy, though it actually was a rather harmless melange of Erasmian ideas. In the ensuing uproar Calvin hurriedly left the city, since, according to tradition, he had been the author of Cop's address, the Saul behind the voice of Paul. He buried himself in scholarship and pursued theological studies.

In May 1534 Calvin traveled to Noyon to surrender his ecclesiastical benefices. An event of importance must have compelled him to cut his ties with the Church, and there is good reason to believe that a conversion had been the precipating factor. Scholarly opinion has placed this conversion anywhere between 1527 and 1534. The sources are scarce, and the most pertinent document is Calvin's own *Commentary on the Psalms* of 1557, in which he wrote that 'God by a sudden conversion subdued and brought my mind to a teachable frame.'[9] No date is offered, nor any theological detail. Much depends on the meaning of 'conversion,' and varying definitions obviously will suggest different dates. If we take the term to mean a radical religious reorientation and simultaneous break with Catholicism (as seems most obvious), the event must have occurred sometime between August 1533, when Calvin attended a chapter meeting at Noyon, and May 1534, when he resigned his benefices.[10] In any case, Calvin's Protestant conviction made a continued stay in France increasingly dangerous. In the fall of 1534 he moved to Basel. He read further in theological works and corresponded with some of the reformers, but mainly he worked on the *Institutes of the Christian Religion.* This book, first published in 1536, proved to be his destiny. He was truly *vir unius libri*, a man of one book. In 1539 a second edition appeared, substantially enlarged—the original 6 chapters were expanded into 17—and this new edition revealed the theological brilliance of the author. Further editions appeared in 1543, 1550, and 1559, each followed by a French translation. Calvin worked on the *Institutes* for almost a quarter of a century, until he had satisfied himself that the 80 chapters of the 1559 edition were as definitive a statement of the Christian faith as he could hope to make.

In the summer of 1539 Calvin happened to travel through Geneva, then a small town on the westernmost tip of Lake Leman, relatively unimportant and undistinguished. The woodcut in Sebastian Münster's *Cosmographey* of 1564 shows a few dozen houses, together with the steeples of three or four churches, among them, most prominently, St. Peter's. Geneva had its share of political problems in the opening decades of the 16th century (mainly caused by the oppressive policies of the dukes of Savoy), but in addition the city experienced religious ferment. At issue was the propagation of Protestant ideas, personified by Guillaume Farel, who arrived in the fall of 1532. He was a Protestant firebrand with a tendency to put his left foot forward, or, to use language of today, to employ the tactics of confrontation politics. There was a bit of explosive and ebullient Gallic temper in him; he knew neither weakness nor patience— only a zealous pursuit of the things of God. 'At no time did any man preach the Sacred Word of God purely without being persecuted and denounced by the world as a rogue and an impostor,' he said on one occasion and his life provided abundant illustration for his own contention. The monument erected in his memory in front of the cathedral of Neuchâtel shows him with arms raised high, holding a Bible: the figure could be Moses hurling the Ten Commandments against the Golden Calf, and the similarity is more than coincidence. Some would have called him a rabble-rouser, for he always left traces of tension, strife, and turmoil, in Neuchâtel no less than earlier in Geneva. He was the prototype of the militant Protestant.

During Farel's initial stay in Geneva Catholic sentiment was strong, and he did his best to agitate against it. In March 1533 the City Council, with curious ambiguity, ordered that nothing be said against the sacraments, that the citizens live in peace and harmony, and that the ministers not preach anything that could not be proven from Scripture. Such recourse to Scripture plainly smacked of Protestantism. The stage was set. The intervention of Berne, already Protestant, secured a church for the Protestants early in 1534 and allowed Farel's preaching there. Finally, on May 21 1536, the Protestant faith was officially introduced in Geneva. With upraised arms, the citizens voted for the new faith. An edict of the City Council extolled the 'Gospel and the Word of God' as the norm of life and faith.

John Calvin passed through this city 2 months later. When he stopped that day, he must have wondered if he would ever return. But before the day was over his life had been altered and Geneva had become his destiny. Not given to saying much about himself, he later spoke with characteristic reticence. He recalled that Farel sought to keep him at Geneva, proceeding 'to utter an imprecation that God would curse my retirement, and the tranquility of the studies which I sought, if I should withdraw and refuse to give assistance, when the necessity was so urgent. By this imprecation I was so stricken with terror that I desisted from the journey which I had undertaken.'[11] Calvin was persuaded that God had called him to Geneva. The tenacity with which he clung to this city, to which he returned after his expulsion and stayed within despite opposition, is explained by this conviction.

Soon thereafter Calvin began his activities, interpreting the Pauline Epistles 'with great praise and profit.' He spoke of himself as '*professor sararum literarum in ecclesia Genevensi,*'[12] a somewhat high-sounding title that obscured his modest role in the ecclesiastical affairs of the city. It was more aptly expressed in the minutes of the City Council for September 5 1536: 'Master Guillaume Farel points out the necessity of the lectures begun by that Frenchman at St. Peter's and requests that he be retained and supported. He was told that such support would be taken under advisement.'[13] Calvin drafted a church order that dealt with worship, as well as with such matters as marriage and the celebration of the Lord's Supper.[14] One of the significant features of the order was its stress on church discipline. Men 'of good reputation among all the faithful' were to be appointed to supervise the citizens. Those whose lives were 'disorderly and unworthy of a Christian' were to be excluded from the Lord's Supper. A catechism, based upon the *Institutes*, and a confession of faith, based upon the catechism, were completed by Calvin a short time later.

A provision in the church order stipulated that all the citizens should publicly subscribe to this confession of faith 'so that it can be seen who agrees with the Gospel and who would rather belong to the Kingdom of the Pope than of Jesus Christ.' In March 1537 the large and small Councils approved the order, modifying only the proposed frequency of the celebration of Communion. The subscription to the confession, however, proved to be a different matter and despite repeated efforts most burghers showed themselves recalcitrant and refused to subscribe. Still, ministers' zeal to get a general subscription to the confession continued. Farel's rashness and Calvin's inexperience precipitated a fateful development. Geneva had been exposed to the Protestant proclamation for only a short time, and Catholicism continued strong. Farel, with the eagerness of the zealot, and Calvin, with the impatience of youth, sought to accomplish overnight what should have taken months and years.

In February 1538 came elections to several municipal offices, and the opponents of the recent ecclesiastical changes made a clean sweep. The four new syndics, or mayors, were opponents of Farel and Calvin, as was the new majority of the small council. Calvin called it a 'most miserable situation,'[15] forgetting that in part it had been caused by his own obduracy. From Basel, the reformer Simon Grynäus counseled to make haste slowly, but Calvin and Farel persisted. Then came the showdown. At issue was the use of ordinary or unleavened bread at Communion and the use of the baptismal font. Calvin and Farel admitted that these were insignificant matters, but they saw a basic principle at stake. Mainly for political reasons, the City Council favored the use of unleavened bread and the baptismal font; both were used in Berne, which sought liturgical uniformity among Swiss Protestants. The Genevan Council thought it prudent to follow this Bernese liturgical precedent and voted to adopt the Bernese 'ceremonies.' The ministers, who were not consulted, were furious over this governmental usurpation of ecclesiastical authority.

Communion was to be celebrated on Easter. Farel and Calvin refused to use the Bernese form and were promptly forbidden to preach. Calvin preached anyhow. He acknowledged that the matter at issue was insignificant and remarked that it was *en la liberté de l'église*—within the freedom of the Church—to do one or the other. But there was a larger issue, whether the affairs of the Church should be guided by the Council or the ministers. Communion was not celebrated that day and thus neither leavened nor unleavened bread was distributed. 'A holy mystery would be profaned,' said Calvin, since disorder, abomination, execrable blasphemy, and mockery of God and his Gospel ruled in the city.[16] By not celebrating Communion the two ministers had excommunicated an entire city. Farel and Calvin were ordered to leave the city 2 days later. Calvin, after a delay of 2 years, continued his journey. His public ministry, reluctantly begun, but vigorously pursued, had ended in failure. Farel found a home at Neuchâtel and Calvin accepted an invitation from Martin Bucer to serve a congregation of French refugees at Strassburg.

For 3 important years that city was his home, indeed, more than that. It was his school of theology and ecclesiastical statesmanship. He could hardly have chosen a better time for his Strassburg sojourn. Important religious colloquies were then held at Hagenau, Worms, and Regensburg. Martin Bucer was one of the eminent participants and Calvin learned a great deal. At Strassburg Calvin saw a Protestant community in action, without the kind of problems that had perturbed Geneva. Calvin also found time for extensive theological studies. In 1539 he published a commentary on Romans, the first of an impressive series of exegetical works. He also revised his *Institutes*. It was still the same book, but its character had changed considerably. A detailed and comprehensive exposition of the important points of doctrine had taken the place of the brief catechism of 1536. Several new chapters were added on the knowledge of God, the Trinity, the relationship of the Old and New Testaments, and predestination; others were substantially enlarged and revised, as, for example, the chapter on justification.

During his Strassburg years Calvin published another important work, *The Reply to Sadoleto*.[17] Archbishop Sadoleto of Carpentras, learned and devout, had been prompted by the chaotic situation in Geneva early in 1539 to write to the Genevan Council. He made a persuasive plea for the unbroken tradition of the Catholic Church, which, no matter how extensive its abuses, laid claim to the divine promise of the presence of the Holy Spirit. Though the argumentation was neither new nor brilliant, it was to the point. Sadoleto thought the issue simple: to believe either 'what the Church throughout the whole world has approved with general consent for more than fifteen hundred years or the innovations introduced during the last twenty-five years by crafty or, as they think themselves, wise men.'[18] Calvin's reply, prompted by the Genevan Council, repudiated the charges of a lack of personal integrity and countered Sadoleto's insistence upon tradition with the 'threefold ground' of the true Church: doctrine, discipline, and sacraments. The book was a powerful apologia for the Reformation, perhaps the most incisive ever written.

In July 1539 Calvin received Strassburg citizenship. Without doubt he had every intention of making the city his permanent home. Geneva was meanwhile experiencing tensions. The summer of 1539 had brought a bitter dispute over a treaty with Berne. The city was divided between two factions, the Artichauds, who approved of the article of the treaty, and the Guillermins, the followers of Guillaume Farel, who opposed them. Early in 1540 the Guillermins succeeded in obtaining the majority on the small Council. In June riots occurred over this issue and shortly thereafter one of the leaders of the Artichauds was executed in an enigmatic exercise of justice. The relationship between Berne and Geneva deteriorated and the threat of conflict was real.

If the political situation of Geneva was in a precarious state, religious affairs were hardly better. No strong leadership existed and the clergy were a sorry lot, characterized by shocking behaviour and professional incompetence. Some Genevan citizens thought wistfully of Calvin, who had demonstrated his theological competence (and interest in Geneva) by his *Reply to Sadoleto*. His return to Geneva began to be advocated by the Guillermins and in September 1540 the City Council issued its first invitation. Calvin could not have been less interested: 'I would prefer a hundred other deaths to that cross.'[19] But eventually he yielded, as he always did when responsibilities were thrust upon him. On September 2, 1541, he left the city that had been his home for 3 years and journeyed into an unknown future. He carried a letter from the Strassburg authorities, who gave him a leave of 6 months. Did he mean to stay only until calm and order had returned to the Genevan Church? The 6 months stretched into 23 years, a difficult time, and more than once Calvin must have wondered about the wisdom of his return.

### Calvin and the Genevan Church, 1541–64

Calvin was still a young man in 1541—32 years of age. But he came as the leader of the Genevan Church, a far cry from the subordinate position he had occupied when he first went there. A vigorous Protestant tradition emerged from his decision, for Geneva gave him an opportunity to translate his theological theory into ecclesiastical practice. To be sure, even in Geneva the real always fell short of the ideal, and Calvin's relationship with Geneva was never more than a *mariage de convenance*, an arrangement where neither of the partners was particularly happy, though both found it acceptable and valuable. Calvin was too one-sidedly concerned about religion to be fully appreciated by the Genevan citizenry, whereas Geneva was far too worldly to gain Calvin's full respect.

On the day of his return Calvin asked the city fathers to consider an *ordre sur l'église*—a church order. Thus he left little doubt about what was foremost on his mind, namely, the formulation of a comprehensive order for the Genevan Church. The Council appointed a committee to consider such an order. Serious disagreement arose over only one question, but that was the one dearest to Calvin's heart: the practice of church discipline and the right of the Church to excommunicate. The Council was reluctant to approve this provision, for it did not wish to surrender its jurisdiction over public morality and it feared a form of ecclesiastical tyranny. The difficulty lay in the fact that morality was also understood as a responsibility of the Church: as soon as this was asserted, problems arose. The identity of the ecclesiastical and the political community made this inevitable. A citizen of Geneva was a burgher of two worlds, and a moral offense automatically evoked the censure of both the ecclesiastical and political authorities.

Calvin stood firm. The exercise of church discipline constituted the cornerstone of his conception of the Church. Finally the magistrates realized his determination and yielded, inserting, however, a provision in the order denying 'civil jurisdiction' to the Church and requiring that whenever it was necessary to 'inflict some punishment or constrain the parties' the matter be referred to the City Council. The principle was thereby acknowledged, but procedural matters kept the clergy from unilateral procedure. Tensions were inevitable, in a way, and characterized the situation. Not until 1555 was the right of the Church to excommunication unquestioningly acknowledged by the City Council. *Sans contredicte*—without opposition—did the people of Geneva on November 20 1541, approve the new order. Surely, there must have been doubting Thomases that day, but the hope of ecclesiastical peace may have silenced the doubters and quickened the faithful.

The *Ordonnances ecclésiastiques* were Calvin's contribution to the issues of practical churchmanship.[20] Influenced by Martin Bucer and the practice of the Strassburg church, the assumption of the *Ordonnances* was that the New Testament contained a clear-cut and explicit paradigm as to how a local congregation should be structured. Four congregational offices were specifically noted: ministers (*pasteurs*); teachers (*docteurs*); elders (*anciens*); and deacons (*diacres*). The ministers, collectively known as *venerable compagnie des pasteurs*, were responsible for preaching and the administration of the Sacraments. They also were entrusted with the proper interpretation of doctrine. The teachers saw to the religious instruction of the congregation, taught the young, and trained future ministers. The elders supervised the lives of the faithful to assure that the principles of Christian demeanor were properly exhibited. The deacons, finally, 12 in number, cared for the sick and the poor. One important feature of the *Ordonnances* was the method of appointment of the holders of the four offices: although the *compagnie des pasteurs* had an important nomination right and the people also were involved in certain ways, the decisions were made by the Council.

Of all the provisions of the *Ordonnances ecclésiastiques* none has been as famous—or infamous—as the institution of the consistory, composed of the ministers and the elders. It was the heart of the *Ordonnances*, the instrument, as Calvin observed, for 'the supervision of the congregation of the Lord so that God might be honored purely.' It met weekly and considered a large variety of offenses: Catholic practices, blasphemy, immorality, dancing, non-attendance at Church, some trivial, others important. There is pathos, sadness, and even humor in these records; for example, a *femme fatale* who, cited before the consistory because of improper dress, retorted that those who did not want to see her that way should close their eyes. The number of excommunications was large; between 1555 and 1561 more than 1,300 persons were excommunicated.

A careful ecclesiastical supervision of the lives of the citizens was thus established in Geneva. This fact must not lead to the conclusion that there existed a clerical tyranny. The consistory was not a clerical body. The majority of its members were laymen. Calvin aptly remarked that they represented *totum corpus ecclesiae* (the entire congregation). Moreover, the supervision by the consistory was hardly new, for public regimentation of morality was generally carried out in late medieval society. The uniqueness of the Genevan situation was that such regimentation was administered by a body that spoke for the ecclesiastical and the political community. In any case, the prerogative of the Church to supervise the lives of the citizens was asserted in forceful fashion. There were long, difficult, but successful battles to establish this prerogative. The opposition came from the secular authorities, who objected to what seemed to be an ecclesiastical usurpation of civic jurisdiction. More problematic, however, was something else. Excommunication and church discipline ceased to be merely spiritual matters. The consistory and the magistracy worked hand in hand; the citizen who talked boisterously during the service had to endure the wrath of the police as well as that of the Church.

The *Ordonnances ecclésiastiques* were accepted by the Genevan citizenry with a minimum of opposition. Soon much that was familiar to the Genevan burghers was changed as a result of the new religious spirit. The taverns were closed, though for a short time a harmless version that would have won the approval of any temperance society was tried out. Theaters also were closed; gambling was prohibited. The Genevan citizens accepted these changes without much ado. This is noteworthy and cannot be solely explained by the passivity that characterizes most common folk. There was a dynamic persuasiveness about Calvin, who engendered support and, perhaps, even a restrained enthusiasm. And this all the more so since he was more than a minister. He helped to revise the Genevan constitution, a task for which his legal background proved to be of great value. His participation encompassed small matters even as large ones, regulations for the Genevan fire department and a treaty with Berne in February 1543. He counseled concerning matters of international diplomacy no less than legal affairs, educational proposals no less than religious problems, and always did so competently and astutely. But the 'man of Geneva,' as diplomatic correspondence referred to him, was a stranger within its gates. Not until December 1559 did he receive Genevan citizenship. Calvin had never requested it, and the Council never offered it, perhaps fearful that it would constitute an irreversible *fait accompli*.

A new chapter began in 1555. Only after that year was Calvin's authority in Geneva eminent, though even then Geneva hardly was a theocracy. Calvin's manuscripts always had to be submitted to a censor, a fact sufficient to discount any undue exaggeration of his role in Geneva, which was molded by the persuasiveness of his ideas rather than the force of his hand. The next years saw the continuation of Calvin's varied tasks and responsibilities. The establishment of the right of the consistory to excommunicate was a major accomplishment, though even then the difficulties were by no means over. Calvin always thought the city too lax in its pursuit of Christian morality. Three times between 1555 and 1558 he voiced his protest against the inadequate opposition to immorality. 'The evil has increased,' he observed on one occasion, 'the city has been greatly contaminated, and above all God has been insulted.'

Calvin's eminent achievement of these years was the founding of the Genevan academy in 1559. The realization of the plans was no easy matter, for Geneva was a small town and not very prosperous. The plans for the academy were ambitious; the institution was to include not only a school of liberal arts but also schools of theology, law, and medicine. A phalanx of eminent and capable teachers joined the faculty, notably the theologians Theodore Beza and Pierre Viret. The impact of the Genevan academy was especially significant in religion. Students came from many European countries, from France, Holland, Scotland, Hungary, and Poland, to study and prepare themselves for the proclamation of Calvin's message. At stake was nothing less than the future of this message. Who was to provide for continuity? The early reformers had possessed theological training, whether on account of their formal academic background or rigorous self-discipline. But what about the future? The Genevan academy provided the answer for the Calvinist Reformation. 'Send us wood, and we shall send you arrows.' So Calvin had written to the French Protestants, and so it happened. Less than 200 students were enrolled the first year, and some not-so-well-meaning friends thought that the undertaking would fail for lack of students. But within 5 years the number had swelled to over 1,500.

If the academy was one facet of Calvin's activities extending beyond the walls of Geneva, his ecumenical efforts were another. He had grown to theological maturity during the time of the colloquies of Worms, Hagenau, and Regensburg. And although he was skeptical about the possibility of Catholic-Protestant concord, he was deeply concerned about the doctrinal divisions among Protestants, especially those in Switzerland. After extended negotiations a consensus was reached in May 1549, the *Consensus Tigurinus*, an outgrowth of Calvin's and Bullinger's theological magnanimity. It was a genuine agreement, which meant the union of Swiss Protestantism, the merger of Zwingli's tradition with that of Calvin; and hardly any event has had greater significance for the Calvinist tradition.

Death came to Calvin on May 27 1564, and Theodore Beza, his successor, recorded that 'as the sun went down, the greatest light in this world was taken up into heaven.'[21] The funeral was simple, for so Calvin had wanted it—no hymns, no eulogies, no tombstone —expressing Calvin's conviction that his person possessed no significance. As one contemporary put it, 'No man knoweth his resting-place until this day.' Those who would seek out John Calvin in Geneva today may walk from the university, the successor of the academy, across the Promenade des Bastions to the famous Reformation Monument, where the statues of Calvin, Farel, Beza, and Knox symbolize the events of the 16th century and the tradition which Calvin founded. The figure of Calvin is only slightly taller than the others, a striking expression of the way Calvin himself wanted his place understood.

E

# Political Consolidation in Germany

The year 1525 had brought unusual turbulence to Germany, and many saw the violence and bloodshed of that spring and summer to be a sign of the last days. Luther thought so, as did Elector Frederick of Saxony, who died during the height of the Peasants' War. The many victims of the peasants' uprising, the destruction and devastation, helped create a widespread feeling of despondency.

This turbulence symbolized the significance of the year in the German Reformation, for in several important ways 1525 was a watershed. It was a year of clarification, for Luther's involvement in the Peasants' War, his controversy with Erasmus, the emergence of radical dissent, and the disagreement over Communion tended to define more sharply the movement for ecclesiastical reform. The period of ecstatic exuberance, during which Luther's camp was overcrowded with well-meaning, if uninformed, partisans, came to its end.

Of crucial importance was the Peasants' War—not only for Luther's loss of popular support, but also for the larger course of the Reformation. The 'Lutheran' ring of the peasants' demands had seemingly made Luther the real culprit of the whole matter. Naturally, the rulers were concerned about preventing a future uprising and, with a kind of self-evident logic, a rallying together of the rulers suggested itself as the best means to achieve this end. What complicated matters was that Luther was widely viewed as the spiritual mentor of the rebellion. Consequently, any protective effort was bound immediately to have an anti-Lutheran character. What on the face of things was directed against the peasants, could easily

116

be interpreted as aimed at the suppression of Lutheranism. This fact proved to be of utmost consequence for the subsequent development, for it suggested to those rulers with Lutheran propensity the need for collective action. The ominous rallying together of Catholic rulers made this virtually inevitable.

Therefore, the two sides of the religious controversy faced one another not merely as proponents of differing theological points of view, but also as warriors preparing for battle. Thus the Reformation became a political phenomenon and the character of the course of events changed. If the first phase had been the spontaneous popular response to Luther's proclamation, and if the second phase had been characterized by the haphazard administration of the Edict of Worms in individual territories, the third phase brought the emergence of two political blocs, the one loyal to the Catholic Church, the other committed to the new faith. Neither side consciously precipitated this development. To be sure, the Catholic rulers were determined to enforce the Edict of Worms in their territories; the so-called Convent of Regensburg, a meeting of South German rulers in July 1524, had led to the avowed pledge to administer the Edict of Worms, though there is no reason to believe that this was meant as anything other than an indication that the rulers involved would do so in their territories. The Lutheran rulers in turn sought to retain their freedom of action. Neither side, however, seems to have pursued a policy of strength to settle the religious controversy by force. Rather, the development was prompted by the confusion of Lutheran ideas with the ideology of the peasants, which had marked the Peasants' War. Measures directed against the peasants were accordingly, at least by implication, also directed against the Lutherans; understandable political action led to far-reaching consequences. Since a Diet had been called to meet at Speyer early in 1526, the Lutherans naturally sought counsel and a clear understanding as to what seemed advisable under the circumstances. In February 1526 Philip of Hesse and John Frederick of Saxony agreed at Gotha that if either was attacked for religious reasons, the other would render support. This agreement, ratified soon thereafter at Torgau, became known as the Gotha-Torgau Agreement. In June several North German rulers joined the ranks.

## Speyer, 1526

That same month the Diet opened. On the first day Mass was celebrated in the cathedral, as this had always been the custom; yet there was a difference. Some of the Lutheran sympathizers had the initials VDMIE on their coat sleeves, the abbreviation for *Verbum Dei Manet in Eternum* (The Word of God Remains Forever). This was a new spirit, illustrated by Landgrave Philip when he deliberately had an ox butchered and roasted on a Friday, the day the Church exhorted the faithful to abstain from meat.

The most important item on the agenda was the enforcement of the Edict of Worms. In the deliberations the cities stated bluntly that it simply could not be done and afterward proposed that the Emperor, Charles V, should be informed of this situation. Their point was obvious: in the Emperor's absence no decision could be made, neither for nor against the Edict of Worms. The decree of the Diet expressed this sentiment. It proposed a delegation to the Emperor to acquaint him with conditions in the Holy Roman empire, requested a 'free general council or at least a national council,' and advised the territorial rulers how the religious issues should be handled in the meantime: 'In matters concerning the Edict so to live, rule, and act as each estate could hope and trust to answer before God and the Emperor.'[1] The proposed delegation to the Emperor never materialized, and the most important matter to come from the Diet was the sentence just cited. Here, needless to say, everything depended on interpretation. The Diet had meant the provision as a temporary solution, as a truce until the religious problem could be solved: nothing here of a recognition of Lutheranism, nothing of an acknowledgment of a right of the territorial rulers to do as they pleased. At issue was only the enforcement of the Edict of Worms.

Yet the essence of any truce is its brevity. If it lasts too long it becomes unalterable. So it was with the Recess (decree) of Speyer. The continuing absence of the Emperor, together with the absence of a council, postponed the resolution from month to month and year to year. This, in turn, made the organizational consolidation of Lutheranism inevitable, and the recess of Speyer formed the rationalization for this development. The decree of Speyer, and thereby the history of the Reformation, might have been altered by a new turn of events: the Emperor's intervention or return to Germany, the convening of a council. But nothing happened, and the truce became a peace. Then and there the religious schism of Germany developed into a state beyond repair.

Here lies the tragedy of Charles V for the unity of Christendom. His absence from Germany, prompted by his complex involvement in Spanish and, indeed, European politics, created a vacuum in the German ecclesiastical scene and decisively influenced the fate of the Reformation. If anyone, Charles should have been the one to stem the tide of the Lutheran heresy. But he was far away in Spain, waging war against his archfoe Francis I. Charles won a splendid battle at Pavia, but afterward he lost the peace at Madrid. In short, his concerns were those of the *rey catholico* of Spain rather than of the *Kaiser* of Germany. It is a moot question whether his presence in Germany would have altered the course of events, but his absence —this much is obvious—did not make matters better.

Soon after the Diet of Speyer came a spectacular demonstration of the deterioration of the atmosphere in Germany: the so-called *affaire Pack*, which took Germany to the brink of war. Otto von Pack, a councilor in the service of Duke George of Saxony, confided to Landgrave Philip of Hesse in 1527 the existence of a secret treaty between Duke George and several other rulers for the purpose of waging war against Hesse and Saxony. Philip accepted the story because it agreed with his own disquieting assessment of the situation. He informed the Saxon Elector, and the two agreed, in March 1528, to go to war against Duke George. Philip was persuaded that in light of such a threat the way to solve the religious problem was to use force against force. He never bothered to verify Pack's claims, as he sought to kill two birds with one stone. He was in difficulties at the time because of his persistent support of the deposed Duke Ulrich of Württemberg and he clearly intended to use the religious issue to improve his political situation.

At the last moment none other than Martin Luther poured oil on the troubled waters. Luther argued that an offensive war was against the Gospel and emphatically advised against it: the Catholics should be warned to desist from their evil ways. After some hesitation Philip agreed to publish the 'treaty,' which was promptly denounced as a forgery by Duke George. Peace prevailed and the matter appeared to have been a tempest in a teapot. But it had also been ominous. War had almost made its debut as the means to resolve religious and theological differences. And even though no gun was fired and all had ended well, the fact remained that some seemed to think that war was a potential element of the ongoing controversy.

### Speyer, 1529

After an interval of 3 years the German Estates gathered again, in

March 1529. The Emperor's summons had singled out action against
the Turks as the principal item for consideration, though it also
noted that the religious situation had deteriorated and therefore required action. Accordingly, the two main tasks of the Diet were to
consider military assistance for a campaign against the Turks and
to settle the religious problem.

The deliberations among the Estates revealed substantial disagreement. The first draft of a decree called for the convening of a
general council within 18 months; until that time the territories
that had accepted the new teaching should undertake no further
changes. The Lutheran Estates voiced opposition, but they soon
realized that they were in the minority. The majority clearly favored
a tough line. The situation was different from 1526, when affairs had
been in a state of flux. In 1529 the issues were clearly defined: the
long duration of the controversy and the temporizing that increasingly turned into permanent arrangements called for a definitive
resolution. Such was the sentiment of the majority of the Estates,
which in April proposed a decree that rescinded the decree of 1526,
renewed the Edict of Worms until a general council, and prohibited
ecclesiastical change.

The adherents of the new faith promptly voiced a protest: since
the Recess of 1526 had been passed unanimously, they argued that
it was 'honorable, proper and legal' to rescind it only by a unanimous vote. They would not accept the proposed decree, 'since in
matters pertaining to the honor of God and the salvation of our
souls each man must himself stand before God and give an account
so that no one can excuse himself with the decision and doings of
others, be they many or few.'[2]

The occasion was hardly spectacular. Legally it was an open
question whether majority opinion could be imposed upon the
minority. But more was at stake than a legality. The protestation
of the minority indicated that the voice of conviction was raised
against political odds. The medieval world, with its ideal of the
*corpus christianum,* the *one* Christian body, fell apart when the
minority thought faithfulness to its spiritual ideals more important
than peace and harmony.

The historian, aware of the lasting significance of the decisions
reached at the Diet, wonders what must have been on the minds of
the chief actors of the drama as they left Speyer. On the face of
things Charles's brother Ferdinand was the victor. He had been able
to marshal a majority among the Estates for the repudiation of the
Recess of 1526. The adherents of the new faith clearly were a

minority, but they showed, as Ferdinand observed, *mauldite ob-
stinacion* (cursed obstinacy) in their determination not to yield in
their faith. The Protestants, as they could now be called, demanded
acceptance of the status quo and the recognition of the ecclesiastical
changes undertaken in their territories.

In 1521 a single monk had faced the dignitaries of the empire
and had demanded freedom for the exercise of his conscience as it
was bound to the Word of God. Almost to the day 8 years later a
group of territorial rulers echoed this sentiment and therefore his
cause. To be sure, theirs was first of all a protest. Still, there were also
positive implications, as their appeal to the Emperor pointed out,
when it referred to the 'honor of God,' the 'salvation of our souls,'
and 'our consciences' as the ground of the protestation.

The official Recess of 1529 called for the convening of a German council within a year and the administration of the Edict of
Worms, and it prohibited ecclesiastical changes.[3]

Politically, the situation had become explosive. Would the
majority tolerate the minority? What would the minority do?
Answers came slowly. While the Diet was still in session, negotiations were conducted between several Protestant rulers. In April a
plan for a defensive alliance was proposed. If any partner was attacked 'for the sake of the Word of God,' the others would come to
its assistance. Many questions went begging since not all the parties
had the same understanding of the significance of the proposal.
Moreover, the Emperor was not mentioned, which meant that the
critical problem as to what should be done if he were to suppress
them was ignored. Also, the alliance had been put forward without
consultation of the theologians. What they would say was uncertain, especially since a fateful split had arisen in the Protestant ranks
that seemed to have implications for the unity of the Protestant
cause. Philip of Hesse, who realized the seriousness of the split, felt
that the political future of Protestantism depended on its resolution.
During the final days of the Diet he asked the chief antagonists to
meet with him in an effort at conciliation. The issue was Communion.

### The Communion Controversy

For several years one theological issue commanded the attention of
the adherents of the new faith: the proper interpretation of Communion. It was a feud among Protestants; the Catholics stood at the

sidelines and watched the spectacle of bitter Protestant division. The issue had come out into the open almost accidentally, but once it had become a point of controversy a violent and bitter polemic ensued. It involved not only theology; political factors were at times equally important. Both sides mixed religion and politics, each in its own way placing politics before religion. At the heart of the matter, however, lay a theological issue.

Luther's repudiation of the medieval understanding of the Sacrament of the Altar formed the point of departure. In his treatise on The Babylonian Captivity of the Church Luther had found the medieval teaching wanting. 'From this you will see that nothing else is needed for a worthy holding of the Mass than a faith that relies confidently on this promise, believes Christ to be true in these words of his and does not doubt that these infinite blessings have been bestowed upon it.'⁴ Aside from his insistence on the primacy of faith in the sacrament, Luther voiced three objections to the Catholic teaching: it was incomplete, since the cup was not offered to the laity; it offered a false philosophical interpretation of the miracle through the notion of transubstantiation; the teaching of the sacrifice of the Mass was unscriptural.

There the matter rested until a letter of the Dutchman Cornelis Hoen confronted both Luther and Zwingli with a radical alternative to the Catholic teaching. Going back to the tradition of Wycliff, Hoen suggested that Christ's words of institution, 'This is my body,' should be interpreted symbolically to mean, 'This *signifies* my body.' In his view the Lord's Supper was a memorial event in which Christ was present only in the subjective recollection of the believer.⁵ At about the same time, Andreas Carlstadt published five tracts, proposing that Christ had pointed at himself while saying 'This is my body.' The argument was hardly convincing to anyone except himself, though his concern was to repudiate any connection between bread and body, wine and blood. Carlstadt denied that Christ was 'really' present in the Communion elements. Moreover, Carlstadt called attention to the christological argument that Christ's place at the 'right hand of the Father' made his presence in the Communion elements impossible. Above all, Carlstadt argued that faith in Christ, nothing more, was necessary to obtain forgiveness of sins; a sacrament was, therefore, superfluous.

The publication of Carlstadt's tracts brought the lingering uncertainty about how the adherents of the 'new faith' understood Communion into the open. Luther summarized his position with *Ein Brief an die Christen zu Strassburg wider den Schwärmergeist* (A

Letter to the Christians at Strassburg), of December 1524, and his *Wider die himmlischen Propheten* (Against the Heavenly Prophets), of January 1525. Both tracts repudiated Carlstadt's interpretation with an impressive arsenal of Biblical, theological, and linguistic arguments. Luther not only rejected Carlstadt's interpretation of the words of institution, he also argued for the need of external means of grace and asserted Christ's real presence in the Communion elements. Zwingli's *Commentarius de vera et falsa religione* (Commentary on True and False Religion), of March 1525, on the other hand, pointed at a different direction. Zwingli accepted both Hoen's explanation of the words of institution and Carlstadt's christological argument concerning Christ's place at the right hand of the Father. This divergence of the two major reformers precipitated a lively controversy, involving not only Luther and Zwingli but also their respective disciples—Brenz, Bugenhagen, Oecolampadius, and Bucer. The pamphlets contained theological argumentation regarding the contested doctrine as well as the whole range of theology.

Luther was persuaded that the plain sense of the words of institution—'one has to take the words just as they are'[6]—taught the real presence of Christ in Communion. On various occasions he used the prepositions 'in,' 'with,' and 'under' to describe how the body and blood of Christ were present in bread and wine. It was a bodily and objective presence, not dependent upon subjective feelings and considerations. The presence (or absence) of faith on the part of the recipient made only the difference between a salvatory and a damning use of the Sacrament: Luther did not hold that the believer received body and blood and the unbeliever merely bread and wine. The objectivity of God's offer meant that both received body and blood—albeit with different consequences. The benefits of the Sacrament were many—gratitude, recollection, communion, but above all forgiveness of sins. Christ offered his body and blood to the faithful, and this body and blood guaranteed forgiveness.

Zwingli parted company with Luther over the interpretation of the words of institution, which in his view had to be interpreted as 'this *signifies* my body.' The examination of Jesus' last supper with his disciples, a consideration of the passage Jn 6.26–60, and the centrality of Christ's death on the Cross suggested to him that Communion was an act of memory, of gratitude, of brotherly love. 'Faith is the food of which Christ speaks.'[7] Still, it was more than an act of eating. Even the symbolic act had far-reaching consequences: 'Whoever eats, with the believer, the symbolic bread and flesh, has to live henceforth according to Christ's commandment, for he has proved to others that he trusts in Christ and he who trusts in Christ must walk even as he walked.'[8] The controversy with Luther brought Zwingli to the acknowledgment of a spiritual presence of Christ since there is, as he put it, no 'faith in Christ Jesus without the concept of his body and blood.'[9]

The antagonists wrote hard and furiously. They convinced no one but themselves. As the years passed, the suggestion was variously made that a personal encounter between Luther and Zwingli might resolve the controversy. Nothing came of this until political factors intruded. An alliance of five Catholic cantons with Austria foreshadowed difficulties for Zurich and the recess of the Diet of Speyer in 1529 ominously raised the specter of the use of force as a means to settle the religious question. The ramification of this political development for the theological disagreement was not inescapable: only if force was to be met by force did the Protestant division caused by the vehement controversy over Communion make any difference. Landgrave Philip sought to safeguard the Protestant cause by a policy of strength; therefore he was solidly behind efforts to resolve the theological disagreement in order to pave the way for a comprehensive political alliance of Protestant territories that would force the Emperor and the Catholic Estates to agree to religious concessions. The premise was the assumption that the split between the old and the new faiths was irreparable. Not all Protestants shared this assumption; some saw reconciliation with Catholics still as a possibility. Melanchthon, for example, was deeply concerned about the unity of the Christian faith. He meant to restore ecclesiastical calm by stressing the orthodoxy of the Wittenberg theology. If political ties were necessary at all, they were to be established only with those whose theological orthodoxy was unquestionable.

Orthodoxy was here defined by the so-called Schwabach Articles, probably drafted by Luther in September 1529. Modeled after the statement of faith Luther had appended to his *Vom Abendmahl Christi, Bekenntnis* (Confession Concerning the Last Supper of Christ) of 1528,[10] the Articles condemned a number of Catholic practices, such as obligatory confession, celibacy, and the sacrifice of the Mass, and outlined the Lutheran interpretation of Communion. Compared with Luther's statement of 1528, however, the tone was moderate, and the reason was not so much a change in theological sentiment as a modest political concession. Even Saxony was not on principle opposed to political alliance—but only with those Protestants whose theological propensity would not come into conflict with the basic policy of how to effect reconciliation with the Catholics.

Despite this handicap Philip of Hesse pursued his goal of a meeting between Zwingli and Luther. Zwingli was immediately in favor; Luther at first was skeptical, but then agreed to come. The colloquy took place at Marburg in October 1529. At the very outset Luther dramatically indicated his own position, when he took a piece of chalk and wrote the words of institution on the table—*hoc est corpus meum*. Though a tablecloth quickly covered his autograph, the words were always there, an invisible reminder of Luther's literal interpretation. Then followed 2 days of forceful arguments on both sides. Luther affirmed the real presence of the body and blood of Christ and insisted on the *manducatio corporalis*, the bodily eating of Christ's body and blood both by believer and unbeliever. Zwingli and Oecolampadius, on the other hand, argued for a symbolic interpretation and emphasized the spiritual partaking of Christ by the believer. Luther conceded that metaphorical passages were found in Scripture, but he demanded proof that the words of institution were a case in point and pushed aside Oecolampadius's Biblical parallels and patristic interpretation.

Toward the end of the colloquy Luther remarked that Christ was not *localiter* present in the bread and wine, and Oecolampadius acknowledged that *verum corpus Christi*, the true body of Christ, was present by faith. There may have been here a chance to explore conciliation, but as matters turned out the colloquy ended in failure. Landgrave Philip made a last-minute effort to bring about a compromise. The Lutherans proposed the formulation that the body of Christ was 'substantially' present. Though there was no detailed explanation as to the nature of this presence, the phrase, as it stood, was Lutheran in its implication and thus unacceptable to the Zwinglians. That seemed the end, until Philip appeared on the scene again and suggested that, no matter what the disagreement, a common confession should be signed. Reluctantly, Luther drafted a statement. Its 15 paragraphs affirmed the major articles of the faith—Trinity, incarnation, original sin, redemption, and so on—and noted those aspects of the Lord's Supper concerning which agreement prevailed: Communion under both kinds, the repudiation of the sacrifice of the Mass, the objectivity of the gift of grace in the Sacrament, the eminence of spiritual eating, and the pedagogical function of Communion for those weak in faith. The unresolved disagreement was put into a dependent clause: 'And although at present we are not agreed as to whether the true body and blood are bodily present in the bread and wine, nevertheless each party should show Christian love to the other, so far as conscience can permit, and both should fervently pray Almighty God that he, by his Spirit, would conform us in the right understanding.'[11] The statement was signed by all participants, and to this day the extant copies show the signatures of the eminent theologians of the Reformation in peaceful harmony. Once back home, both Luther and Zwingli insisted that the document expressed their particular position. Each one assumed that the antagonist had come around to his view—erroneously, for the crucial sentence that 'the Sacrament of the Altar is a sacrament of the true body and blood of Jesus Christ'[12] was interpreted differently by Luther and Zwingli, not as concord, but as confirmation of their own positions.

Zwingli and Luther came to Marburg with two different notions as to the nature of faith. During the colloquy Luther asserted that he knew no God other than the one who had become man. God was never abstract, but always concrete, always *in* something—*in* Christ, *in* his Word, *in* the sacraments. God reveals himself concretely, often in lowly and unexpected ways. This was the meaning of the Incarnation. God is always appropriated in tangible form. For Oecolampadius and Zwingli, however, God was spirit—and spirit was opposed to matter. Oecolampadius challenged Luther 'not to cling to the humanity and body of Christ, but to lift the spirit upward to the divinity of Christ.'[13] To be sure, Zwingli had a place for material elements in religion, but they only signified, symbolized, and represented, never did more. Luther, on the other hand, understood the Sacrament as the means by which God's offer of forgiveness could be empirically and personally appropriated by the believer. In receiving the body and blood of Christ the faithful were tangibly assured that forgiveness was theirs. The Sacrament thus was an indispensable means of grace. Zwingli had no need for this, for faith in the Cross was all that was necessary and a Sacrament constituted a degradation of the Cross. Redemption and forgiveness were found only in the Cross.

A second area of disagreement between Zwingli and Luther was over the relationship of reason and faith. Zwingli was concerned to weave rational arguments into a coherent theological pattern: a body by definition had to be finite, discernible, located at one place. Christ's body was not exempt from such requirements. Luther, on the other hand, thought differently. He responded to all of Zwingli's nagging queries with the insistence that God had spoken and his Word must be accepted. The question was not what is possible, but what *is*: God's command was crucial. 'If he would command me to eat manure, I would do it, since I would know that it would be to my salvation. A servant must not ponder about the will of his master. You must close your eyes.'[14] Oecolampadius gave the characteristic Zwinglian response: 'Dear doctor, where is it written that we must walk through Scripture with closed eyes?' Zwingli himself remarked a little while later: 'The oracles of the demons are dark, but not so the words of Christ.'[15]

The Marburg colloquy was a failure. Theologically, it had confirmed that Protestantism was a divided house. This fact, bitter though it was, gave lie to the exuberant Protestant assertion that men everywhere would agree to the meaning of Scripture if they were only of good will. Now it turned out that evidently such good will was absent among some Protestants or that Scripture did not quite lend itself to the easy interpretation that had been assumed. And which of these two options to favor was surely a painful decision.

The failure to attain agreement meant that both sides clung to their respective theological positions with unwavering determination. The consequences were both far-reaching and disastrous. Protestantism remained a divided house, a fact that influenced the Reformation era no less than subsequent centuries. But more was at stake than theological consensus or brotherly affection. Zwingli and Luther had come to Marburg also as representatives of political courses of action, even as Landgrave Philip had convened the colloquy for reasons both political and theological. Theological conciliation was to be the steppingstone to a political alliance: this was the way both Zwingli and Philip saw it. To them the political situation was exceedingly ominous. There was the recess of the recent Diet, the peace concluded at Cambrai between Charles V and Francis I, as well as the fact that the relations between Charles and Pope Clement VII were warmer than they had been before. Charles's return to Germany was imminent and there was no doubt that he would seek to resolve the religious conflict by enforcing the Edict of Worms. For the time being there were no other pressing issues.

If the failure of Marburg meant the failure of the political plans of Philip and Zwingli, the situation was different as far as Saxony was concerned, for there not a policy of strength but one of reconciliation was favored. The Saxon theologians considered the politics of Zwingli no less detestable than his theology. The failure of Marburg afforded the Lutherans an opportunity to test their approach

to resolving the conflict. The Emperor's summons of a Diet to Augsburg suggested that this opportunity was forthcoming.

### *Augsburg, 1530*

The Emperor's summons had been astoundingly conciliatory. Concerned about the restoration of religious concord, both for the sake
of religion and of political stability, Charles had agreed to 'hear,
understand, and consider everybody's opinion in love and grace.'
He had offered his assistance 'to consolidate all opinions to one
Christian truth and to remove everything which is not properly interpreted on either side.'[16] Charles meant what he said. While he
resolutely opposed the Lutheran 'heresy,' he felt kinship with the
kind of reform advocated by Erasmus. For a short while a conciliatory atmosphere prevailed. During the discussion of the agenda
the Protestants successfully demanded that the religious problem
be considered before the discussion of Turkish aid. This was an astute move, for a Protestant refusal to supply aid against the Turks, if
the religious problem was not settled satisfactorily, hung like a cloud
over the Diet and reminded the Emperor to be realistic in his religious policies and plans.

The Emperor's willingness to 'hear everyone's opinion' suggested
the formulation of a Protestant 'opinion.' In a way this was the
'hearing' that the adherents of the new faith had asked for ever since
1521. Saxony, the most prominent Lutheran territory, naturally took
the initiative. Since no systematic delineation of the Protestant faith
existed, Philipp Melanchthon drafted a statement of faith on his way
to Augsburg. There he wrote a second draft, but after seeing Johann
Eck's collection of 404 heretical propositions, culled from the writings of the reformers, he realized that a more comprehensive confession was necessary. By the middle of June he had completed his
work.

This Augsburg Confession, the *Confessio Augustana*, has come
to be considered the classic theological statement of Lutheranism.[17]
This is ironic, for Melanchthon's intent was quite different. He
wished to underscore the agreement with the Catholic tradition
rather than to stress particular Lutheran emphases, so much so that
he ended the first section of the Confession with the sentence *tota
dissensio es de paucis quibusdam abusibus.* Twenty-one *Articuli
fidei praecipui* (special articles of faith) discussed such basic theological points as God, original sin, christology, justification, and the

ministry. The formulations were both far-reaching and evasive. Thus the first article rejected the errors of Manicheans and Arians, hardly pressing issues, while the fourth had only a terse sentence concerning justification: 'We cannot be justified before God by our power, merits, or works, but are freely justified through Christ by faith.' Article 10, on Communion, was equally brief. The second section dealt with abuses and new ecclesiastical practices, such as Communion under both kinds, celibacy, Mass, monastic vows, etc. The polemical stance of the Augsburg Confession did not concern the theological divergence between the old and the new faith; its argument was that the major differences consisted in 'externals'— the communion cup for the laity, clerical celibacy, etc. If Melanchthon was representative of Protestant sentiment, the Confession showed that on the Protestant side the attitudes had not yet become hardened beyond repair.

The question was how the Emperor would respond to the statement. Three possibilities seemed to exist: arbitration, a council, and the use of force. Charles favored arbitration and asked for a Catholic response to the Augsburg Confession. The Catholic theologians hesitated, since they saw no need to reiterate the Catholic faith. Eventually, they produced a lengthy indictment of the Protestant position. The Emperor found the document 'confused, disorderly, violent, injurious, and hardheaded,' and demanded its revision. This task produced the *Confutatio*, completed early in August. The signatories of the Augsburg Confession were told to accept it and return to the Catholic Church. Otherwise, Charles added, he would act as became his position as guardian of the Church.

The draft of the decree declared the Augsburg Confession refuted by the *Confutatio* and gave the Protestants until April 15 of the next year to return to the Catholic Church. Until that time the recess of the recent Diet at Speyer was to be observed. A general council, to be convened within a year, would consider ecclesiastical reform.[18] The tenor of the draft was conciliatory. The reasons were obvious: lacking strong support from Rome for a council the Emperor realized that he could hardly be successful in his efforts. Moreover, he was politician enough to recognize (as did the Protestants themselves) that he depended on Protestant support for any military action against the Turks.

The Protestant Estates rejected the draft, which on November 19 1530, became the formal Recess of the Diet. By that time, however, the Diet was a rump gathering comprised of the Emperor and the Catholic Estates. Twice, in a little over a year, the efforts to bring the adherents of the new faith back to the Catholic Church had proved unsuccessful. The Protestants had a breathing spell of less than 6 months. Then the showdown would come.

At Augsburg took place the first full-fledged effort to achieve a theological conciliation of the two sides. The uniqueness of the effort lay in the fact that its driving force was neither the Catholic Church nor the Protestant bodies, both of which appeared resigned to the split, but the political authorities. This situation was to become typical for the next two decades. Naturally, this was a formidable handicap. The absence of official religious endorsement circumscribed the maneuverability and raised the specter of official disavowal.

The Emperor had been the crucial figure. Some of his Erasmian advisers had made him open to the need for reform, but in part his pursuit of a policy of religious conciliation had to do with politics. He wanted religious peace in order to have the political stability that he considered indispensable for safety against the Turks and for freedom toward France. In short, it was not Charles, the son of the Catholic Church, but Charles the Emperor who doggedly, if sporadically, pursued conciliation.

The presence of other factions at Augsburg made for a complicated situation. The Protestants were divided. Only the Lutherans had subscribed to the Augsburg Confession, for the unresolved differences concerning the Lord's Supper kept several South German cities and the Swiss from their endorsement. Four of the South German cities submitted a confession of their own, the *Confessio Tetrapolitana*, as did Zwingli, who composed a *Fidei Ratio*. Neither of the two was officially recognized by the Emperor.

Then there was the difference in temperament among those at Augsburg. For example, since Luther could not be present, Philipp Melanchthon served as theological spokesman for the Lutheran cause. He was anything but an aggressive spokesman, more a reed waving in the wind than a bulwark of the faith. When the Augsburg Confession was publicly presented, he wept bitterly: he felt that the unity of Christendom depended on the success of his effort and he was overwhelmed by fear of a permanent schism. And yet it was not really fear that motivated him, but concern for the future of Christendom. Melanchthon was willing to confine the existing disagreements to 'abuses' only and not go into any basic assertion of the faith. If Melanchthon was irenic, his Catholic colleagues (if such be the proper word) were uncompromising and aggressive. Johann Eck was there, a bit older now, but the years had neither mellowed his temperament nor softened his theology. Johann Cochläus and Wimpina, the other eminent Catholic divines, were of like disposition. Among the political figures the situation was the reverse. Philip of Hesse aggressively told the Emperor that he had no right to commandeer his conscience and generally gave little evidence of a conciliatory spirit. Most of the other Protestant rulers shared this sentiment. They were men accustomed to the hard realities of negotiation and confrontation, and may even have perceived the impossibility of reconciliation.

In a way, the issue at Augsburg had been whether the disagreement between the two sides pertained to substantive theological issues or merely to the correction of abuses. Opinions differed. At one point, only the issues of the Communion cup and of clerical celibacy were unresolved, and today we know that Rome was conciliatory in these matters, a fact known too late at Augsburg. Eventually, the negotiations failed over questions of 'ecclesiastical abuse,' while the discussion of doctrine brought concord. And it was the gloomy fact of failure that was to overshadow the subsequent course of events.

Augsburg revealed an ambiguous situation, more hopeful than some had dreamed, more discouraging than others had feared. There had been more than merely a discussion concerning the execution of the Edict of Worms, such as had characterized the two previous Diets. There had actually been a semblance of a theological discussion, an indication that the situation was flexible after all. But the discussion had ended in failure, and this bitter fact overshadowed everything. The Protestants had presented a picture of utter division: not only were there Lutherans, Zwinglians, and those traveling the narrow road between these two, but there were also those of irenic and of not so irenic temperament. The latter distinction could also be found among the Catholics. In short, there could be little reason for optimism when the Diet adjourned, even if the inescapable fact remained unspoken: the Catholic Church had already rendered the verdict. The stipulation of the decree seemed thus both prudent and unavoidable.

## The League of Schmalkald

For the Protestants the Diet created a perturbing situation. The Emperor seemed determined to use force against them after the expiration of the period of grace, and this danger prompted a determined reaction on their part. Philip of Hesse had hardly returned home from Augsburg when he invited the Saxon Elector to discuss with him the possibility of an alliance. Few in Saxony questioned the political advisability of such a move, but the theologians raised a problem of a different sort: was it legitimate to oppose the Emperor? After an initial period of reluctance Luther affirmed the right of resistance against the Emperor. He had been influenced by Landgrave Philip, who had pointed out the difference in the constitutional status of the Emperor and the territorial rulers: the former was elected and had specific obligations and responsibilities; the latter had inherited their offices. The argument was that any resistance of territorial rulers against the Emperor emanated from the exercise of their own authority.

With the theological scruples out of the way, the Saxon Elector invited the signatories of the Augsburg Confession to a meeting at Schmalkald in December 1530. Landgrave Philip, Duke Ernst of Braunschweig, and Margrave George of Brandenburg, together with the representatives of Nuremberg, Ulm, Strassburg, and Reutlingen were present. Agreement was quickly reached on the matter of mutual defense in case of an attack for religious reasons, and the draft of a formal alliance was drawn. Eventually, Saxony, the dukes of Braunschweig, Hesse, Anhalt, Mansfeld, and 11 South German cities, including Ulm, Strassburg, Constance, and Reutlingen, joined the alliance. The formal documents of the League of Schmalkald were signed February 27 1531.[19] The constitution of the League was approved 2 years later. Thus culminated a development that had begun in 1526, when questions concerning military action for or against the new faith had first arisen and 'alliance' had become part of the nomenclature of the Reformation.

The League of Schmalkald was a defensive alliance to protect the signatories if attacked on account of religious reasons. It was a heterogeneous combination of political power, and even though Saxony was, on the face of things, the most powerful partner, the real leadership lay with Hesse and Strassburg. The constitution of the League provided for a common treasury for military defense, for military aid, for a military force of 12,000 men, and for a council of war. But there was no common purpose. The painful bickering of the territories revealed the extent of the political disintegration of the Empire, since even the common religious profession did not result in common political action. Despite this shortcoming, however, the League constituted a major factor in German politics no less than religion for over a decade. Its formation proved fateful, since it took the religious controversy even more explicitly into the political realm. After the formation of the League the alternative to conciliation seemed to be force.

Then came April 15 1531. It was a day very much like any other and the reason lay with the Emperor, who was unable to let deeds follow his words. In less than 6 months the political situation had changed so drastically that Charles had no choice but to pretend that the date had never been mentioned. Seldom was there a figure beset by more trying obstacles. Charles V was like a juggler with more balls in motion than he could handle. Wherever he looked, in the spring of 1531, he faced problems: the reluctance of the pope to convene a council; the obstinacy of the Protestants; the Turkish threat; the uncertainty of relations with France. Pope Clement's promise to convene a council formed a major element in the Emperor's plans to solve the religious problem. Yet it increasingly became obvious that this promise was hardly worth the paper on which it was written. A council was as far off as ever. The Turkish situation remained precarious, especially since rumors about an imminent Turkish attack upon Vienna were circulating. As long as the need for territorial support against the Turks persisted, Charles could ill afford to alienate the Protestants.

Moreover, the formation of the League of Schmalkald had altered the political picture. It showed, as did the Saxon Elector's refusal to concur with Ferdinand's election to the Roman kingship, that the Protestants were committed and determined. Charles's most prudent policy might have been to grant the Protestants coexistence; this was indeed suggested to him by Cardinal Loaysa, who told him that his difficulties were insurmountable and that he should 'accept the heretics and have them be subject to your brother as the Bohemians are.' A fateful suggestion—the acceptance of religious diversity for the sake of political unity. Even though beset with a multitude of problems, Charles would have none of this. He expressed his willingness to recognize the status quo, if the Protestants would aid him against the Turks and acknowledge Ferdinand's election as Roman King. He still held two cards, and either might yet prove to be a trump: a peace with the Turks would free his hands for a firm policy toward the Protestants, while a peace with the Protestants would enable him to pursue an aggressive policy against the Turks.

Then Charles was reminded that his best friends were his greatest enemies. In the fall of 1531 his brother Ferdinand attacked Hungary, a private tour de force against the town of Ofen and John Zapolya, the leader of the Hungarian magnates, who had sought the Hungarian throne after the catastrophe of Mohacs. Ferdinand's move was intended to give him control of a strategic area and the prestige of military victory. It was unsuccessful and only increased the tensions between Suleiman II and the West. Suleiman was aware of Charles's determination to fight the Turks as soon as the opportunity presented itself, but he also knew that the religious turmoil in Germany tied Charles's hands. He thought that the opportune hour had struck. On April 26 1532, his trumpets sounded and a mighty military force marched westward. In June the Turks crossed the Hungarian border.

A Diet had convened at Regensburg a few days before Suleiman began his campaign, and for the first time in a decade the religious problem was not paramount in the deliberations. The eminent issue was the Turkish threat. The Emperor hoped to obtain aid from the Estates beyond what they had granted at Augsburg. The Protestants were willing to contribute, but demanded substantial concessions: the revision of the Augsburg decree toleration, and the annulment of Ferdinand's election. Had the Emperor received strong support from the Catholic Estates, Protestant aid would have been unnecessary. But the Catholics insisted on a strict enforcement of the Augsburg decree, and at the same time refused to contribute aid against the Turks. As far as they were concerned the Turkish threat was not very real. They demanded that the Emperor set a good example by supplying troops of his own and argued that Ferdinand's attack upon Ofen gave them little confidence in the ability of the Hapsburgs to handle the admittedly precarious situation.

Negotiations at Regensburg therefore quickly reached a stalemate. The real site of action was Schweinfurt and Nuremberg, where talks were held between the representatives of the Emperor and the League of Schmalkald. At issue were the Protestant demand for a religious peace and the Emperor's request for aid against the Turks. Several months of negotiations brought no tangible agreement, until the Protestant position became more flexible and consisted mainly in the assurance of toleration and the suspension of religious litigation before the *Reichskammergericht*, the imperial supreme court, until the time of a general council. The possibility of a Turkish attack still called forth common solidarity. Luther admonished the Estates to harmony in such troubled times and, according to an interesting (if erroneous) tradition, intended the first stanza of *A Mighty Fortress Is Our God* to be a battle song against the Turks.

In the end the Protestants granted their support and the Emperor promised what they had asked for: toleration until a council could be held and the suspension of religious litigation before the *Reichskammergericht*. The agreement is known as the *Nürnberger Anstand*, or 'Peace of Nuremberg.' Clearly, it was a major achievement for the Protestants, the first move away from the policy of a rigid enforcement of the Edict of Worms. The Peace had been prompted by the precarious political situation; it was conceded by the Emperor to be a legal move (which had no bearing, of course, on the theological assessment of the existing differences), and it was meant to be only temporary. Still, the time during which the execution of the Edict of Worms had a certain inevitability had passed. A new development had begun.

The formal decree of the Diet at Regensburg propounded a different version of the matter, for the Catholic majority of the Estates was determined to have its way and was unwilling to make any concessions to the Protestants. The Emperor faced the uncomfortable alternative of siding with this majority, accentuating thereby the religious split and making common action against the Turks impossible, or of making concessions to the Protestants and thereby alienating the Catholics. The decree embodied the sentiment of the Catholic majority, which only acknowledged, without obligation, the agreement reached at Nuremberg.

The decree also emphasized the urgent need for a council, and requested that a council convene within 6 months. Should this not be possible, the Diet should gather to deal with the religious issues. Since nothing was said about the decree of Augsburg, it formally remained in force. This constituted an ambiguous situation, for the provisions of Augsburg and Nuremberg could hardly be reconciled.

After the adjournment of the Diet the forces of the Empire proceeded to Vienna to meet the Turks. The Emperor, barely recovered from serious illness, yearned to follow the troops and lead them into battle. He dreamed of a victory by which his name would be forever remembered. 'Should I be defeated,' he said, 'I will leave a noble name behind me in the world and enter into paradise; should I be victorious, I will not only have a merit before God, but would also possibly restore the ancient boundaries of the Empire and obtain immortal glory.'[20] But Charles was thwarted in his aspirations. The Turks were dangerously close to Vienna, but a small fortress in western Hungary, Güns, resisted their atracks for 21 days, and this bold defense sapped the strength of the Turkish onslaught. When Charles reached Vienna, no battles were to be fought and no victories could be attained.

Had he then returned to Germany, events would have taken a

different course, though it must remain a moot question which policy Charles would have pursued. He made his way to Italy instead. There was a good reason. In Germany a truce prevailed, an uneasy one, to be sure, but one that had temporarily calmed the situation. The Turks had been repelled and the relations with France were tolerable. The major issue still unresolved was the religious one, and Charles gave it priority. He knew that short of the use of force against the Protestants the only hope was a council. Since the pope was the key to the convening of a council, Charles hoped to persuade him to action. 'I met with His Holiness,' he wrote in his memoirs, 'but without the full success I had anticipated.' His verdict is true, even though the meeting at Bologna in February 1533 was amicable and papal cooperation disarming. Pope and Emperor agreed on the need for a council and pledged themselves to secure the cooperation of France and the German Protestants. The pope also voiced support for further action against the Turks and assured the Emperor that the English King's divorce proceedings would be decided according to Canon Law.

On the face of things Charles had been successful. The future was to show, however, that no council was to meet during Pope Clement's pontificate. Thus the Emperor's seeming hour of triumph was really one of tragedy.

### Political Crisis in Switzerland

Meanwhile, events in Switzerland had precipitated an ominous showdown. The ecclesiastical changes effected in Zurich in 1525 had brought a Catholic reaction: the Catholic cantons had demanded that the Edict of Worms be administered throughout Switzerland and sought, moreover, the involvement of Austria in Swiss affairs. They threatened that deeds would promptly follow their words.

It was at that time that Zwingli drafted a detailed battle plan for Zurich in case of a Catholic attack.[21] Fervent concern for the preservation of ecclesiastical change (and also for Zurich autonomy) prompted the man of the cloth to write about soldiers, guns, and battles rather than the things of God. The opening words of Zwingli's plan were 'In the name of God'[22]—a telling indication of the interweaving of sword and Bible, of political and religious concerns. Ten years earlier Zwingli had been an Erasmian pacifist and had demanded withdrawal from international power politics; now he sought involvement. The change was fundamental. The Gospel had become something to be defended.

Zwingli's competent strategic plan remained theory, for Swiss fratricidal war was a recourse neither side was as yet willing to face. Moreover, the extensive efforts of Zurich to secure allies and establish a balance of power in Switzerland were successful in December 1527, when it was able to conclude an alliance with Constance. The city of Berne became Protestant and other places showed Protestant leanings, among them Glarus, Appenzell, Graubünden, and Basel.

The Catholic cantons countered by strengthening their political position. In April 1529, they concluded a Christian Alliance, *Christliche Vereinigung*, with Austria. The political situation in the Swiss Confederation deteriorated steadily since the unity of the land was disrupted. Both sides shrank from armed conflict, but their language was euphemistically evasive. Zwingli asserted with strikingly timeless words that 'the peace so eagerly sought by some is war, and not peace; and the war, for which we so eagerly prepare ourselves, is peace, and not war.'[23] On the other side, Thomas Murner stated that 'we should like to keep peace, but the new faith will not leave itself and others in peace.'[24]

Several events in the spring of 1529 increased the tensions. One was the secularization of the monastery of St. Gall, undertaken with Zurich support. It was a blatant demonstration of power politics, indeed the expression of imperialistic tendencies on the part of Zurich. Then in May the authorities of the Catholic canton of Schwyz arrested and burned Jakob Kaiser, a Protestant minister. The following month Zurich declared war on the five Catholic cantons. Zwingli drafted another battle plan and accompanied the Zurich soldiers to the field as chaplain. 'The bell has been cast,' he wrote, 'and soon we shall toll it. We will soon explain our faith with long spears and halberds if they so wish it.'[25]

Last-minute peace talks were successful and no shot was fired. A truce was concluded and soon thereafter a peace, known as the first Peace of Kappel.[26] Its provisions were a compromise between the two sides: the Christian Alliance was dissolved, but the proclamation of the new faith in the five Catholic cantons was not allowed. 'No one should be forced on account of the Word of God,' a neat Protestant phrase that here, for a change, worked to the advantage of the Catholics.

Zwingli was unhappy with the development. Nonetheless, Berne, Constance, Basel, St. Gall, Mühlhausen, and Biel united with Zurich in the *Christliche Burgrecht*, an alliance to defend the 'Gospel.' Schaffhausen and Glarus also were Protestant. But the future seemed dark. The quick formation of political alliances indicated that ecclesiastical change was intimately tied to political considerations. And no one seemed to perceive this more incisively than Zwingli, who frantically sought to broaden the political strength of the Swiss Protestants. He envisioned a European-wide anti-Hapsburg alliance. His persistent effort to reach a theological understanding with Wittenberg concerning Communion was influenced by his political plans. He was convinced that only a politics of strength safeguarded the new faith.

But the Colloquy of Marburg brought no agreement (for theological reasons) and marked a signal failure of Zwingli's political plans. A second failure came within less than a year when the negotiations at the Diet at Augsburg ostensibly excluded Zwingli and his followers from any participation. Zwingli's statement of faith, the *Fidei Christianae Ratio*, was not even officially recognized by the Emperor. Afterward Zwingli had to stand at the sidelines while the League of Schmalkald was formed in Germany. Zurich was able to conclude an alliance with Constance, Strassburg, and Hesse, but this tie was hardly worth the paper on which it was written.

The showdown in Switzerland came quickly. The tensions between the Catholic cantons and Zurich, eased by the Peace of Kappel, took a turn for the worse. Zwingli was persuaded that only war could resolve the issues, and in April 1531 he asked for a declaration of war against the Catholic cantons. His proposal received no support. Within a month, however, an economic blockade was inaugurated against the Catholic cantons to deprive them of essential goods and thereby force them to submission.

In August a fiery comet was seen in the sky over Zurich and people pondered its significance, as 16th-century man always did when confronted with unusual natural phenomena. Queried as to its meaning, Zwingli ominously replied that 'many a man of honor, including myself, will be paying dearly.'[27] Two months later his prophecy had become reality, for he himself lay dead on the battlefield. War had finally come in October, declared by the five Catholic cantons, which were determined to throw off the choking economic blockade. Zurich was ill-prepared. The city had more than 12,000 men of conscription age, yet on the day of battle a mere 700 constituted its fighting force, together with 1,200 advance troops. There were no horses to pull the artillery, and both the morale and the pay of the soldiers were at a low. Twenty-one mobilizations between

1524 and 1531 had boomeranged, rather like the shepherd boy's cries of 'Wolf, wolf' in Aesop's fable.

On the morning of October 11 1531, the Zurich forces went into battle. Among them was Huldrych Zwingli, who accompanied the troops with sword and Bible. In the afternoon the soldiers reached Kappel, 10 miles south of Zurich. Two years earlier both sides had met near this village, but then a truce had been arranged. This time the situation was different. The skirmish began. Twice the Zurich forces were able to repulse the enemy; then they were overrun. Zwingli, who probably fought in the brunt of the battle, was mortally wounded. 'What is it? The body they may kill, but not the soul,' reportedly were his last words.[28] Catholic soldiers discovered him on the battlefield, quartered his body and burned it to ashes—the punishment of the day for a man who was thought both a traitor and a heretic.

By the middle of November peace negotiations were in progress and toward the end of the month peace returned again to the Swiss Confederation. This second Peace of Kappel provided that the individual cantons could determine the religious faith within their boundaries. The further expansion of Protestantism, however, was prohibited. The new faith was recognized in Zurich and the other Protestant cantons, but it was destined to remain a minority religion within the Swiss Confederation. On the face of things nothing dramatic had happened. The new faith had found legal acceptance almost a quarter of a century before such an accommodation was reached in Germany. But the dream of a Swiss Confederation, united in the new evangelical faith, had died, like Zwingli, on the battlefield of Kappel.

Yet something had happened. After the theologians had failed to persuade one another, the parties had marched to the battlefield, there to resolve their theological conflict. The Roman adage spoke of war as *ultima ratio regum*—the final reasoning of kings. The battle of Kappel offered eloquent proof that in the 16th century war could also be the final reasoning of theologians, or, to vary Clausewitz's famous definition, the 'continuation of theological controversy by other means.'

And Europe had watched with eagerness.

### A New Church Emerges

By the early 1530s the ecclesiastical controversy had reached the point where an element of permanence increasingly characterized the scene. No matter what the professed commitments of the Protestant reformers concerning the unity of the Church, the harsh realities of life spoke a language of their own: sermons had to be preached, ministers educated, and congregations organized. In short, a new Church had to be conceived, nurtured, and exposed to the biting winds of life. This was the eminent task of Protestant churchmen in the 1530s and 1540s, the time when elsewhere the issues of reconciliation or recognition were being fought with determination and bitterness.

The formation of Protestant churches was a slow and haphazard process that suggests that the Protestant break with the Catholic Church was not understood as an inevitable parting of the ways. Two separate developments characterized the emergence of Protestant churches, the one chronologically following the other.

The first of these consisted in the abolition of such traditional ecclesiastical practices as were considered unbiblical. This happened at all places of reform agitation. Such change and denunciation of 'false religion' was not meant as a permanent break, but as modifications that the Church at large might either condone or even follow. Those who first undertook the changes in ecclesiastical practice in Wittenberg, Zurich, or Strassburg did not think that they had burned their bridges behind them.

The second development did assume, however, that the break was permanent or that for practical purposes one may as well proceed as if it were. This meant more comprehensive and far-reaching changes and entailed the establishment of new organizational structures, in short, the formation of new churches. Whereas certain external changes were undertaken with relative speed, alterations in temperament were surprisingly long in coming. The process of Protestantization covered the better part of the century.

At the beginning stood the acceptance of the Reformation in a given territory. Obviously, this acceptance did not mean radical discontinuity. After all, the people were the same as were, by and large, the ministers. Even if a sizable segment of the people was alienated from the Catholic Church and supported the new faith, a great many others did not. The clerics in Hesse or Saxony in 1527 were those who had exercised the ministerial functions 2 or 3 years earlier. Of their number not all embraced the Protestant faith. A goodly number surely continued to proclaim Catholic notions as they always had. A visitation undertaken in Saxony in 1526 revealed that only 10 out of 35 ministers possessed what was considered an adequate understanding of the Gospel; one of these was given to drink and thus hardly a persuasive protagonist of the new faith. Such Catholic orientation continued for many years—at least underneath the surface. As late as 1539, the reformer Justus Jonas complained that many ministers were still Catholic at heart and 'only for the sake of stipend and income talk differently.'

The acceptance of the Reformation, or the introduction of the Reformation, was a legal fact and meant the official endorsement of certain changes in ecclesiastical practice. This official step came as the response to popular agitation or was undertaken unilaterally by the ruler. The latter was as possible as the former; obviously, the introduction of the Reformation must not be identified with an expression of popular sentiment.

The specific realities subsumed under the official step differed from place to place. The introduction of the new faith could mean nothing more than the discontinuation of the Mass or the introduction of Communion under both kinds or the closing of monasteries or the rejection of episcopal or papal jurisdiction. It could mean also the formal theological delineation of the new faith. Obviously, the significance of the change differed in each instance. Once the change had been undertaken, however, certain consequences followed. Ecclesiastical life had to adjust to its new form.

Three specific tasks were involved. One pertained to the local congregation, its organizational structure and form of worship, which had to be 'reformed.' A second aspect was the restructuring of the many social functions, such as the care for the poor, which the Church had carried out in the past. And finally there was the matter of the broader organizational pattern of the Church. In Germany the question of the form of the local congregation was greatly influenced by Luther's nonchalance in this respect. He actually wrote several orders of worship, but his *Deutsche Messe und Ordnung Gottesdiensts* (German Mass and Order of Service) of 1526 asserted bluntly that 'in sum and substance this order and all others are to be used in such a way that, if there is abuse, they are promptly abolished and a new one put in its place.'[29] Luther sought to emphasize the centrality of the local congregation in ordering its life, from the selection of the minister to the form of the service. He had expressed this notion in his 1523 treatise *Dass eine christliche Versammlung oder Gemeinde Recht und Macht habe, alle Lehre zu urteilen*[30] (That a Christian Congregation or Gathering Has the Right and Authority to Judge All Teaching). When a fellow reformer proposed an evangelical council to bring about ecclesiastical

uniformity among those adhering to the new faith, Luther retorted
that such uniformity was neither necessary nor advisable. He was
persuaded that structures and forms would issue spontaneously and
creatively from the local congregation. In a few instances this
actually was the case: Thomas Müntzer wrote an order of worship
for Alstedt, and Johann Lang one for Erfurt. But most congregations simply did not have the brilliant minister necessary.

Some of the pressing problems could not be solved on the local
level. This fact inevitably placed the governmental authorities in the
key position, for they alone could assume such broad responsibilities. This development led to the formation of the 'territorial
church-regiment.' This meant that governmental authority super-
vised the external ecclesiastical affairs, the training of the clergy,
their remuneration, the supervision of the faithful. Luther conceded
the ruler's role in ecclesiastical affairs only with great reluctance.
His preface to the *Unterricht der Visitatoren an die Pfarrherren* (Instruction of the Visitors for the Clergy) of 1527 indicated that he
had given up the idea of effecting the building of a new Church by
way of a spontaneous evolution of forms, structures, and patterns.
The territorial Church was to be built with the help of the ruler.
The rationale was the emergency situation. 'Even though your elec-
toral highness has not been commanded to teach or to rule in
spiritual matters,' Luther wrote, 'you are responsible as temporal
authority to prevent discord, rebellion, and insurrection among the
people.'[31] Luther distinguished between the proper function of
governmental authority and responsibilities required under special
circumstances. He argued that such special circumstances existed.
In any case, his exhortation was gratuitous and, if anything, showed
the clash between theological reflection and political realities. By
that time the political authorities were already exercising a considerable role in ecclesiastical affairs, from the inspection of the
clergy to the disposition of church property and its use for educational or charitable purposes. And this situation continued and was,
moreover, duplicated elsewhere in Europe. Thus, the Saxon visita-
tions were undertaken by commissions comprised of theologians
and governmental officials. The former examined the religious and
theological aspects of a parish, while the latter assessed the legal and
economic state of affairs. This cooperation proved to be typical for
Lutheranism in Germany. Theologians and lawyers sat together on
the so-called consistory, the agency administering the churches
under the supervision of the territorial ruler. Strictly speaking, only
organizational matters were under the aegis of governmental

authority, while theological and religious affairs remained the prerogative of the theologians. But the line was thin and often the ruler usurped more rights and prerogatives than were his. The Visitation Articles of 1529 were unilaterally introduced in Saxony by the Elector; only the Wittenberg faculty were consulted.

The laity generally had no voice in ecclesiastical affairs in the territories. Only in Hesse, where the organizational structure was less bureaucratic than elsewhere, was there a measure of congregational participation. The towns, on the other hand, with their unique constitutional characteristics, were different. Not only did their limited geographic confines simplify the situation. Also, since the city councils were representative bodies, a greater measure of popular representation in ecclesiastical affairs prevailed.

An interesting proposal concerning a new church came from Hesse. In October 1526 Landgrave Philip convened his 'subjects of the spiritual and temporal estate' to a 'synod' at Homberg. In attendance were ministers, nobility, and municipal officials. The gathering was neither a political nor an ecclesiastical meeting. In a way, it was a convocation where clergy and laymen deliberated about the future of the Church. One outcome of the deliberations was the drafting of the *Reformatio ecclesiarum Hassiae*, or Homberg Church Order. Landgrave Philip asked Luther for his evaluation and, much to his surprise, the Wittenberg Reformer advised against its introduction. The grounds of Luther's opposition were not completely clear, though he seems to have basically objected to the idealized picture of the Church delineated. In any case, Luther's word meant the failure of the *Reformatio*, which did not gain practical significance.

The *Reformatio* declared the Scriptures as sole norm for ecclesiastical practices. Obligatory confession and fasts were abolished, as was the 'superstitious benediction' of bread, wine, salt, and water. The *Reformatio* also instructed about proper worship and the proper celebration of the Sacraments. The most significant provision, however, came in the last chapters, which advocated a 'congregation of the faithful' composed of those who had separated themselves 'from the false brethren.' 'The faithful' were to announce their separation publicly and exercise authority in the congregation with respect to the election of the ministers and the practice of church discipline. This provision implied the discontinuation of the notion of the *corpus christianum*, the one Christian body, and the division of the faithful into the serious and not so serious ones.

Alongside the institutional side of Protestantism stood its embodiment in flesh and blood—the Protestant ministers. Not all of them were men of achievement, and Protestantism no less than Catholicism had its share of men for whom spiritual commitment was as much a mystery as theological competence. The evidence is extensive. Philipp Melanchthon told about a minister who, when asked if he taught the Decalogue, answered that he had not as yet been able to purchase the book. In addition to the lack of competence and commitment there were also lapses of demeanor.

Not all Protestant ministers lived lives of sterling quality. In 1541 the Hessian superintendents requested Landgrave Philip for a radical cure of clerical immoderation: 'Whereas there is much complaint about clergy who cause considerable offense by their immoderate drinking and other vices and yet remain unpunished as well as unchanged, we recommend that a jail be established in the monastery of Spisskoppel and the unrepentant clergy be given the option of either leaving their parishes or being confined in that jail for a certain length of time with water and bread to bring about their correction.'

If there were shortcomings among the Protestant clergy, there were also many dedicated and competent ministers who carried out their responsibilities with proficiency and conscientiousness. They translated Protestant theory into practice, for they were the field officers of the Reformation. They proclaimed the new evangel, nurtured their congregations, dealt with the political authorities; in sum, they added religious vitality to theological pronouncements. Though Protestantism had espoused the notion of the priesthood of all believers, in practice it became a *Pastorenkirche*, a Church guided by the clergy.

The task of the ministers was to preach and administer the Sacraments. Little difference with Catholicism existed with respect to the celebration of the Sacraments, except it tended to become less and less frequent. The emphasis upon preaching altered traditional precedent and placed a heavy responsibility upon the minister. There had been a good deal of preaching before the Reformation (that there was none is one of the sterotyped Protestant misconcepions), but the sermon had not occupied as important a place as subsequently among the Protestants. The Protestant service consisted of the reading of scriptural passages, the Lord's Prayer or the Decalogue, and always a sermon. This stress on preaching was easier said than done, and it speaks for Luther's practical sense that as early as 1522 he had published a church-postill to provide examples of scriptural preaching. Within his lifetime this 'Wartburg Postill' saw almost 30 editions, obvious proof of its usefulness. The sermons of the postill were to be used by the ministers as an aid in the preparation of their own homiletical exercises or as their 'own' sermons.

Luther's publication set the tone for a whole new genre of religious books that were gladly, and openly, used. The zeal for the Gospel was seemingly more important than questions of authorship. Thus, the words of Luther or Melanchthon were heard from many a Protestant pulpit in the 16th century, even though Luther never darkened the door of that church and the name of Melanchthon was never heard. Probably the people were better off for such plagiarism of their own ministers.

One of the characteristics of the internal history of Protestantism was the determined effort made to provide adequate training for future ministers. This was a universal concern which expressed itself in the stress on education, the founding of universities and academies in Marburg, Geneva, Zurich, and many other places. With passing time, university studies became virtually mandatory for future ministers and by the second half of the century the economic situation of the clergy had at long last improved, even though it remained shamefully low.

## Continued Protestant Expansion

For 9 long years, from 1532 to 1541, Charles V was absent from Germany, and during this time Protestantism formalized its achievements and consolidated its hold. What would have been the course of ecclesiastical events in Germany if the Emperor had been present? One wonders. As matters stood, the continued expansion and consolidation of the Protestant faith were inevitable.

To be sure, the time of Protestant *Sturm und Drang* was over. The religious exuberance of the early years of the Reformation had been replaced by theological sophistication. But the list of territories and cities that embraced the Protestant faith during the 1530s is long and impressive: Württemberg, Pommern, Mecklenburg, Dinkelsbühl, Hannover, Nassau, Bremen, Osnabrück, and many others, especially in North Germany. These ecclesiastical transformations did not happen overnight, were long in coming, and were, as often as not, merely the formalization of a state of affairs which had prevailed for some time. Many territories and cities had bided their time in view of the uncertainty of the decrees of 1529 and

1530, which had made a public acceptance of the new faith unwise.

At stake was not so much the dynamic acceptance of Protestant tenets on the part of the people (though such undoubtedly continued as before), but a change in the formal ecclesiastical structure—the repudiation of episcopal jurisdiction, the dissolution of the monasteries, the secularization of ecclesiastical property, the discontinuation of the Mass, the introduction of what was called 'evangelical preaching.' These formal changes could now be undertaken, for the existence of the League of Schmalkald meant that any use of force on the part of the Emperor would be met by force. Moreover, the Peace of Nuremberg seemed to offer toleration. At long last, the formal acceptance of Protestantism no longer entailed ominous legal and political consequences; quite the contrary, there could be distinct advantages to such an ecclesiastical change. A new kind of Protestantism emerged from these achievements—self-conscious, political, institutional. Its spokesmen were the councillors of the League of Schmalkald; its expression was the church orders in the towns and territories that gave permanent form to the new ecclesiastical life.

This expansion of Protestantism created problems. The new Protestant territories naturally demanded that the provisions of the Peace of Nuremberg should also be applied to them. The Catholics disagreed, holding that the Peace applied only to those territories that had been Protestant in 1532. The *Kammergericht* followed a staunchly Catholic line and kept the Protestants in legal trouble. The matter was hardly serious, but it proved a constant irritant as far as the Protestants were concerned.

Then, in the late 1530s, the atmosphere in Germany appeared to undergo a change, and conciliation seemed, once again, the primary concern of the two parties. Charles V had really never given up hope that rapprochement might be possible, and on the Protestant side Martin Bucer's conciliatory efforts were persistent. In addition to such theological temperament there was a political factor. The formation of the Catholic League of Frankfurt, actually an unimportant grouping of Catholic territories, caused the League of Schmalkald to think that war was imminent. Under such circumstances the offer of Elector Joachim II of Brandenburg, himself an irenic Erasmian, to mediate in the religious controversy found receptive ears. This led to extensive negotiations between the League and King Ferdinand, representing his brother, which lasted for the better part of the fall of 1538. The Protestants were stiff-necked and demanded a permanent peace and the cessation of all religious litigation before the *Kammergericht*. This, of course, would have amounted to the consolidation of the status quo along lines favoring the Protestants, and Ferdinand was unwilling to concede so much. Pope Paul III, unhappy with developments beyond his control, advised the termination of the negotiations and Aleander, the papal legate, suggested that the Emperor appear in Germany with Italian and Spanish troops. But the Emperor was not yet ready for such a drastic course of action and dispatched Johann von Weeze, the exiled archbishop of Lund, to try anew to negotiate with the Protestants.

An agreement was reached on April 19 1539. This *Frankfurter Anstand*, or Peace of Frankfurt, provided that the adherents of the Augsburg Confession, including those who had subscribed after the Peace of Nuremberg, were guaranteed freedom from attack for 15 months, possibly until the next Diet. During this time all ecclesiastical cases before the *Kammergericht* were to be suspended. The Protestants agreed not to resort to arms and to meet shortly in order to reach a favorable decision concerning Turkish aid. Last, but not least, the agreement stipulated that a theological colloquy should be held to explore the possibility of conciliation.

The Emperor, at first rather cool to the idea of a colloquy at that time, was forced by the precarious international situation to agree. Henry VIII's matrimonial advances to Anne of Cleves, a niece of Elector John Frederick of Saxony, raised the possibility of an affiliation of England with the League of Schmalkald. At the same time, France and Denmark were negotiating with the League, which threatened to become a formidable entente of European dimension. To make matters worse, Charles's truce with the Turks was to terminate on July 1 1540. Under these circumstances the Emperor could hardly afford to alienate the Protestants.

A pause for reflection is here in order, lest the dramatic nature of the situation be obscured. After more than 20 years of bitter theological controversy and the formal condemnation of Luther's teaching by the Catholic Church, the hope for an amicable resolution of the religious conflict had not subsided. In both theological camps were men who thought it possible to achieve conciliation. The problem was, of course, that the ensuing colloquies did not take place under the aegis of the Church and thus lacked authority and ecclesiastical stature. Agreement, even had it been reached, would have amounted to very little. Would Zurich, Geneva, England, or Sweden have concurred, not to speak of *all* German Protestants? The only indisputable consequence of a successful colloquy would have been a different psychological atmosphere. Such.

F

however, would have been an eminent accomplishment, indeed.

Of course, not all was pristine purity at Hagenau, Worms, or Regensburg. Over the colloquies hovered a peculiar mixture of political and religious considerations, and the former may even have been more important than the latter. The Emperor considered religious concord in Germany to be of utmost importance for his political plans, though at the same time his understanding of his imperial responsibility as the arbiter of Christendom was an important factor in his thinking. And the Curia was an uneasy bystander. The possibility of an agreement over the religious questions without curial participation was real.

The first colloquy convened at Hagenau in the summer of 1540, but the participants could not even agree on the formulation of an agenda, a somewhat discouraging beginning for the effort to achieve conciliation. The second colloquy got under way at Worms in November, and this time, after lengthy debates on procedural questions, theological questions were indeed discussed. Surprisingly the discussion of original sin brought agreement. And behind closed doors secret conversations were held between Martin Bucer and Johann Gropper, both men of irenic temperament and thus congenial choices to pursue conciliation. The extent of agreement reached was surprising, though the consultation of various Protestant rulers brought only lukewarm reactions. After the modest success at Worms, it was planned to continue the talks at the forthcoming diet to be held at Regensburg, this time in the Emperor's presence.

Into this situation burst an embarrassing scandal involving the political bulwark of Protestantism in Germany, Landgrave Philip of Hesse. The scandal, a macabre interlude in the theological and political course of Reformation events, was Philip's bigamy. Philip's *mariage de convenance* to Duke George's daughter Christina was an amorous failure. He was chronically unfaithful, though always plagued by religious scruples. His sister suggested a permanent extramarital arrangement, and, as matters turned out, Philip did not need to look far for the proper person—Margarete von der Saale, an attractive lady-in-waiting of his sister. But her mother insisted on marriage and this obviously meant complications, for divorce was out of the question, as were those means that, under certain conditions, Canon Law offered. The Protestants had denounced Canon Law as sophistical; events were to show that their own cure was hardly superior. Luther and the other members of the Wittenberg faculty were asked for their opinion. They signed a memorandum which distinguished between general law and special dispensation: monogamy was general law, confirmed by Christ and practice in the Church. The precedent of the Old Testament, however, allowed for a second marriage as special dispensation. Such a dispensation was applicable in Philip's case in light of his burdened conscience, though the second marriage had to be secret as a dispensation *in foro Dei* (in sight of God).[32] Philip accepted the advice and his marriage took place in March 1540. The new bridegroom sent Luther a cask of wine and a letter which informed him that his new wife was a relative of Luther's wife Cathy. Luther was unimpressed, perhaps even embarrassed, and burned the letter.

Before too long rumor concerning this marriage was making the rounds, and such unexpected publicity put Philip in a precarious position. When he sought Luther's permission to publish the Wittenberg memorandum, Luther refused and reiterated his position: a private confessional counsel had been given and was not to be made public, in keeping with medieval confessional practice. At this point, at least, Luther showed himself a good Catholic. The new advice from Wittenberg was that Philip should deny everything; Luther suggested a 'strong Christian lie.'[33] Philip now found that to lie was sinful and he would have none of it. He complained bitterly about the secrecy of the theologians: 'If the matter can be defended in one's conscience before the almighty, eternal and immortal God, what matter then the cursed, sodomite, usurious and drunken world?'[34]

Did the Wittenberg theologians sell out for nontheological considerations? This conclusion seems almost inevitable, for there can be little doubt but that Philip's political stature had something to do with the advice he received. Had he been a man-on-the-street, the Wittenberg divines surely would have been less accommodating. The theologians, however, acknowledged an ambiguous point of Biblical teaching, which seemed to allow the exceptional concession of a multiple marriage.

Once the matter had come to light, the situation was delicate. The *Constitutio Criminalis Carolina*, which the German Estates had approved at Regensburg in 1532, provided the death penalty for bigamy. Philip thought he had no other choice but to seek the Emperor's pardon. In June 1541 the two reached a secret agreement. Philip agreed not to enter into an alliance with foreign powers, nor to support the admission of the Duke of Cleves to the League of Schmalkald. In return he received the Emperor's pardon for any transgressions against 'imperial law and order, publicly or privately committed until this day.'[35] One qualification in the Emperor's pardon had ominous forebodings: an exception was stated in case 'a war be waged concerning religion against all Protestants.'

The Emperor clearly had been the victor. He had successfully paralyzed the League of Schmalkald and had been able to do so with Philip's unwitting assistance. Theretofore, Philip's involvement in the Reformation had been characterized by the conviction that religion and politics were inextricably linked and that the way to safeguard religion was to pursue a policy of political and military strength. His secret agreement with the Emperor showed that he was his own worst pupil, when he comforted himself that his concessions pertained only to the political realm and not to matters of faith.

At that time a military resolution of the religious conflict must have been already on Charles's mind, though at the Diet at Regensburg, in the spring of 1541, conciliation dominated. Charles was the heart of the conciliatory effort, even though the theologians—Melanchthon, Pistorious, and Bucer on the Protestant side; Eck, Gropper and Pflug on the Catholic one—ostensibly stood in the center. The basis of the colloquy was the secret agreement reached at Worms, now introduced, under somewhat mysterious circumstances, as the *Regensburg Book*.[36] Its affirmations were broad and contained the proper sprinkling of Biblical and patristic references, and thus seemed to promise a resolution of the disagreements.

Agreement was indeed reached on several points, including justification. Though broadly formulated, the theological substance of that agreement was the notion of double righteousness, *justitia imputata* and *justitia inhaerens*, the one freely given, God's declaration of acceptance, the other found in man, based on love infused into man's heart, and leading to the fulfillment of the law. Thus justification is by faith *and* by works, by grace and deeds of love. 'Therefore it is living faith which in Christ attains mercy and believes that the righteousness of Christ is imputed him through grace. At the same time such faith receives the assurance of the Holy Spirit and of love.'[37]

This was enormously significant. For more than two decades justification had been the cause of heated disagreement, but at Regensburg both sides found it possible to agree to a common formulation. The initial reaction was one of rejoicing. The Emperor remarked that 'God has been pleased to enlighten' the participants, a statement which by implication spoke negatively about the general inspiration of theologians. Calvin found the agreement evasive, but accepted it, as did a number of other Protestant theologians. But

then the wind shifted. From Wittenberg, Luther resounded negatively about the 'vast and patched thing,' and even Melanchthon, on
second thought, found the article a 'hyena and Talmud.'[38] Cardinal
Contarini, who had stressed the Catholic character of the agreement,
discovered that the consistory did not agree with him.[39] These negative voices turned out to be decisive, especially since the ongoing
negotiations soon reached an *impasse*. In May the Emperor asked
the participants to provide him with a summary statement. He received two, since no agreement had been possible concerning most
articles. The notable exception was justification. The situation was
hopelessly chaotic, for there were really four factions—the die-hard
Catholics and Protestants as well as the conciliatory theologians
from the two sides. The specter of a threefold division, Catholics,
Protestants, and those accepting mediation, hung over the Diet and
indicated that anything less than an enthusiastic and full agreement
was bound to lead to disaster.

In June the Emperor submitted this meager 'result' to the
Estates. The Catholics formally rejected whatever agreement had
been reached and the Protestants followed suit. The hope, now faint,
now optimistic, that the schism between the two sides might be
healed had gone—vanished, as one observer sadly remarked, 'even
as smoke.'[40] Hopelessness and confusion carried the day.

The decree of the Diet expressed once again the hope for a council and provided that a Diet or national council should convene if
no general council was possible. The Protestants were told to accept
the articles on which agreement had been reached. The Peace of
Nuremberg was to continue until the next Diet.

The failure had been, above all, the Emperor's. But he had little
time to ponder his failure, for fire had broken out in other parts of
his imperial realm. Francis I declared war against Charles, the fourth
such exercise between the two monarchs. Francis thought he had
chosen a perfect time and splendid circumstances. The theater of
operations was the Low Countries, which were attacked from three
sides—by the French from the south, by the Duke of Cleves from the
east, and by the Danish navy from the north.

Charles's sister Maria, the regent of Holland, put up a gallant
fight, courageously marshaled the defenses of the land, negotiated a
treaty with England, and increasingly tipped the scales in the Emperor's favor. When Charles threw his forces against the Duke of
Cleves, victory came quickly. In the treaty of Venlo of September
6, 1543, the Duke agreed to the end of ecclesiastical reform in his
territory. Actually, this latter point was a minor provision, but the

consequences were enormous, since the strength of Catholicism in northwest Germany was consolidated.

## The Road to War

'This experience opened the Emperor's eyes and convinced him that it was not only not impossible, but indeed very easy, to subdue such insolence by force—if done at the proper time and with the necessary means.'[41] These words were Charles's own, after the military campaign had ended in amazing and speedy success. From then onward Charles waited for 'the proper time' and the 'necessary means' to wage war against the Protestants. The failure of the negotiations at Regensburg had convinced him that, as matters stood, no theological compromise was possible. Since the Protestants were recalcitrant, only force remained, and Charles was prepared to solve the religious problem in Germany by force.

Early in 1544 a Diet convened at Speyer. For a change, the religious question was not on the agenda, only the equally perennial problem of Turkish aid and—something new—the Emperor's request for support for his war against France. Surprisingly, even the Protestants were willing to supply this aid, an impressive manifestation of German unity against France. In return for their contribution, the Protestants received the assurance that until a general council, or the next Diet, no Estate would wage war against another. The Emperor then turned once again to France. Though his forces penetrated deep into the country, the outcome of the engagement was indecisive. The peace of Crépy, September 14 1544, which ended Charles's war against Francis, strengthened the Emperor's position without weakening that of Francis. The formal provisions of the peace were overshadowed by an agreement concluded secretly five days later. The two rulers agreed to enforce the decisions of the forthcoming council, and Francis offered Charles his military support for the submission of the German Protestants.

Slowly, the figures in the Emperor's game were falling into place. By making peace with Francis the Emperor had eliminated one important obstacle. In May 1544, he undertook successful negotiations for a truce with the Turks. Afterward only the pope stood in the Emperor's way of settling the German religious problem. Pope and Emperor viewed one another with distrust, but since the conciliation between France and the Emperor had created a new situation for the papacy, Paul III accepted Charles's hand of peace.

A Diet, meeting at Worms early in 1545, ostensibly pursued possible avenues of religious conciliation. Behind the scene, however, the Emperor held negotiations with papal representatives to secure support for the proposed military showdown. The papal response was enthusiastic. The Recess of the Diet voiced regret over the impossibility of conciliation and announced that another theological colloquy was to try its hand at the chase that made squaring a circle child's play.

After some delays, this colloquy got under way at Regensburg in January 1546. An air of futility hung over the venture, for the Emperor was not serious and the Protestants hardly optimistic. Still, the two sides went through the routine of attempting to settle their differences. Bucer once again spoke for the Protestants. There had been some difficulty in finding Catholic participants, but finally Johann Cochläus, together with three lesser-known theologians, agreed to represent the Catholic side. All of them were staunch Catholics and thus different in temperament from the irenic men who had been at Regensburg in 1541. Differences concerning the agenda occupied most attention. Bucer seemed the only one who had not lost his enthusiasm, and he seriously undertook an exposition of the Protestant view of justification. When the Protestants refused to agree to complete secrecy, the colloquy was suspended.

While Catholics and Protestants sought to find the more perfect way, Martin Luther died. There is a bit of irony in that his death came while Bucer expounded the doctrine of justification at Regensburg. The day was February 18 1546, and the place, by a strange coincidence, Eisleben, where he had been born 62 years earlier. An errand of Christian love had taken him there to mediate—successfully, as it turned out—in a feud between the Counts of Mansfield.

With age, Luther had become a bit more insolent and argumentative, but his warmth never left him. His very last piece of writing, found after his death, provides a fitting epitaph to his life: 'No one can understand Virgil's *Bucolics* and *Georgics* unless he was, for five years, a shepherd or a farmer. No one understands Cicero's letters, I suppose, unless he occupied an eminent public office for 20 years. No one can understand the Scriptures sufficiently unless he guided the church with the prophets for a hundred years. There is something exceedingly wonderful about John the Baptist, Christ, and the Apostles. Do not manipulate his divine Aeneas, but venerate its footsteps. We are beggars, this is true.'

Thus the last words of Martin Luther, theologian, reformer, and

Christian, were a statement of his faith. Luther witnessed the full consequences of his work, and it surely must have been to him both blessing and curse. The former because his conviction about his faith became ever more definite as the years passed, the latter because he had to experience that frailty forever accompanies spirituality and that the Protestant Churches were not exempt from that historical pattern which weaves threads of strength and of weakness into one fabric.

The Diet itself opened at Regensburg in June, and for a while the situation was what it had been for as long as any one could remember. The imperial proposition spoke of the need for religious peace, but Catholics and Protestants disgreed about almost everything. The prospect seemed to be another stalemate, as had happened so many times in the past. There were also perturbing rumors about the Emperor's armaments, and by the middle of the month the Protestants boldly asked Charles for an explanation of his activities. The answer they received was worthy of the Delphic oracle, for the Emperor informed them that he meant to deal with disobedient Estates as became the authority of his imperial office. This left the question begging and the Protestants persistently asked for his definition of 'disobedient.' This time the answer was clear. Disobedient were those, the Emperor stated, who under the pretense of religion disregarded law and order. The handwriting was on the wall.

On July 20 Charles pronounced the ban over Philip of Hesse and John Frederick of Saxony, the two bulwarks of the League of Schmalkald. This meant war. On the face of things Charles had as good a *raison de guerre* as he could desire. His ban said nothing about religion and cited three violations of law and order, one of which, the *affaire Pack*, dated back to the late 1520s. The major charge pertained to the feud of Philip and John Frederick with Duke Heinrich of Braunschweig over the city of Goslav, a complex situation in which Philip and John Frederick used a semblance of legal justification for a blunt exhibition of power politics against Braunschweig.

But this was only a pretense for the Emperor, who thought of the war as being fought for the cause of religion. Yet the matter was not quite that simple, for some of his allies were Protestants to whom he had guaranteed the retention of the ecclesiastical status quo until the time of a council. Thus, full suppression of Protestantism could not have been his immediate goal. That it was his final goal, however, is clear. Charles was engaging in the kind of temporizing in which he had become an expert. He hoped to defeat the major

Protestant territories first, and later deal with those Protestants who were his allies.

His first task, all the same, was to start at the beginning.

## The War

Once war had been declared the League of Schmalkald moved with astonishing dispatch, mobilized its troops, and agreed on the general conduct of the war. Only the theologians, who believed that a defensive war alone was legitimate, dragged their feet and advised against precipitate action.

Action commenced slowly. For several months no outright fighting occurred, only insignificant skirmishes here and there. In the late summer of 1546 both sides seemed unsure as to the course of action. In the case of the Emperor, this was an expression of his vacillating temperament; among the League of Schmalkald it was the result of incompetent leadership. Either side could then have scored a decisive victory, especially the Protestants. Their earlier blunders, their naïveté concerning the Emperor's intention, even their internal squabbles, could have been things of the past. The prize was to be had for the asking.

Indeed, for a short while the League seemed to have the upper hand, since the Emperor, after having procrastinated so long, had started the war at the wrong time. Most of his troops were in Holland and the papal forces remained in Italy. Without difficulty, Sebastian Schertlin, the seasoned Protestant commander-in-chief, led the Schmalkaldian army to Bavaria, which, if invaded, would have deprived Charles of his German base of operations and kept the papal forces from crossing the Alps. But the council of the League of Schmalkald kept Schertlin closer to home. A bird in the hand—the defense of its own territories in the north—seemed better than two in the bush—the possible defeat of the enemy in the south. But with the Schmalkaldians out of the way, the Emperor had little difficulty in consolidating his military strength for the decisive showdown. The merger of the forces of the Emperor and the pope altered the balance of power.

Nothing dramatic happened in the fall, except that both sides committed blunders that kept them from attaining victory. But since both engaged in this gratuitous exercise, the outcome left matters where they had been at the beginning. In November the League began to be weakened by an acute financial crisis, and before the month was over its forces were compelled to retreat from South Germany. By that time a new element had entered the picture. Swayed by the Emperor's promise of the Saxon electorship, Duke Maurice of (Albertine) Saxony had allied with the Emperor and, together with King Ferdinand, made ready to attack Saxony.

The winter months passed without decisive military developments. The Emperor was in control of South Germany and one Protestant territory and city after the other surrendered, asking the Emperor's mercy. Charles showed himself a harsh and uncompromising victor. Soon the picture changed. In January 1547 the pope announced the withdrawal of his troops from Germany, and two months later he approved (or instigated) the transfer of the council to Bologna. Charles was furious, especially since the pope had been less than discreet about the details of his treaty with the Emperor, stipulating that 'Protestants and Schmalkaldians' were to be subjected, if necessary by force, to the true religion and to obedience to the pope. Since some Protestants were in the Emperor's phalanx, they were hardly pleased to hear about the true purpose of the matter to which they were lending their hands.

At this juncture the two friends turned into enemies. In a way, Emperor and pope had not really been friends. Both had viewed one another with ill-concealed distrust, annoyance, and even anger. The pope, for one, could not but consider the Emperor's various ecclesiastical involvements (aside from that of using force for the unconditional suppression of the heretics) as intrusion, while the Emperor was dismayed over the seeming papal indifference with regard to the resolution of the conflict in Germany. Charles's decision to go to war had brought the two parties together—but only for a painfully brief time.

One major area of disagreement (or misunderstanding) was the recently convened general council. After many years of striving and futile efforts, Pope Paul III had at long last succeeded in convening a council at Trent in December 1545. And the Emperor, who for almost decades had pleaded for such a gathering, found himself in the very paradoxical situation of having to acknowledge that at this particular juncture he had no use for it—especially if its pronouncements and decrees were to enunciate an uncompromising Catholic position.

And as Charles V saw it, the council fathers at Trent were precisely prepared to do just that. While the disagreement concerning the agenda was resolved with a compromise which stipulated that doctrine and reform were to be considered simultaneously, the fact of the matter was that the council defined several important doctrinal issues—on tradition, original sin, and justification—within a very short time. This meant that the council had, virtually overnight, accentuated and formalized the existing doctrinal differences between Protestants and the Catholic Church—and this at the time when Charles undertook to put his sophisticated scheme into action: first to subject most of the Protestants militarily by force, and then to bring them to a voluntary return to the Catholic fold by a mediating formula and the assurance of ecclesiastical reform. The last thing Charles wanted in 1546 was the formalization of ecclesiastical and theological differences.

The differences of opinion came to the fore all too quickly. In January 1547 Pope Paul announced the withdrawal of his troops from Germany (at that time the war had not as yet been decided), and two months later he either instigated or tolerated (the sources are enigmatic) the transfer of the council from Trent to Bologna. This move was certain to aggravate the situation in Germany even further, for Bologna was situated in papal territory and the Protestant charge that the council was not free, but controlled by the Pope, would undoubtedly be multiplied.

When hostilities were resumed in the early spring of 1547, an indecisive state of affairs continued. Late in March, Charles moved northward to join the forces of Maurice and Ferdinand. On April 23 he reached Mühlberg and had come within a stone's throw of the Saxon soldiers. Since the waters of the Elbe flowed majestically between the two armies, the Saxon Elector John Frederick thought himself safe. He had miscalculated, however, the protection of the river. Charles was determined to cross the Elbe at all costs, and in a war council he overcame the opposition of his generals.

It was a Sunday—and afterward people recalled that it had been *Misericordia Domini*, an apt commentary, by the ancient liturgical tradition of Christendom, on the events of the day. Fog hung over the landscape when the first of the Emperor's soldiers reached the river. The Saxon Elector was attending church and the news that enemy soldiers had been seen on the other side of the Elbe disturbed him little. His plan was to move northward. Since he thought the Elbe to be an insurmountable obstacle, he saw no reason to leave church or forego a leisurely breakfast. Artillery that might have blocked the enemy's crossing moved away from the river.

Was the river really impassable, as John Frederick assumed? He was woefully mistaken. A few days before, his soldiers had confiscated two horses from a peasant who took revenge by showing the

Spaniards a passage across the river. Suddenly the enemy was upon the Saxons and wild fighting began; the Saxons sought their salvation in flight and John Frederick was taken prisoner.

The rest is a tale quickly told. The fortunes of war brought an important Protestant victory near Drakenburg in May 1547, but the tide could not be stemmed. In June Landgrave Philip of Hesse surrendered to the Emperor, which meant that for all practical purposes the military power of the League of Schmalkald had been broken. A few North German cities continued their resistance, notably Magdeburg, fortified by strong walls and the presence of two theologians—Amsdorf and Flacius. The Emperor realized that trying to subdue these cities was like biting into granite, and in the larger course of events their resistance made little difference. He clearly was the victor of the war. His position in Germany was stronger than ever, but hardly what it had to be in order to solve the religious and political problems at hand. The religious problem required the full support of the papacy, and the political problem the continuation of the anti-Schmalkald coalition. As Charles made his way to Augsburg in July 1547, to hold a Diet that would deal with the situation created by his military victory, he surely must have pondered the chances of his success.

### Uneasy Peace and Final Decision

Two concerns were on the Emperor's mind at Augsburg: the solution of the religious problem and a change in the political structure of the Empire. Charles was persuaded that his victory over the Schmalkaldians had put him into a position to do both. He was mistaken. Politically, Charles sought to strengthen imperial power in Germany; he hoped to do this by means of an association of the territories that would redistribute the power in favor of the Emperor.

Negotiations concerning the Emperor's proposal had begun in February 1547, but there had been little progress. Moreover, relations between the Emperor and the pope had deteriorated steadily. Charles demanded from the pope the return of the council to Trent, while the pope asked that the Estates accept the decisions of the council. The Estates agreed to do this in November, but then the pope declared that the decision to return to Trent was up to the fathers at Bologna. In January 1548 Charles tired of this diplomatic tug-of-war and protested solemnly against the transfer of the council. France once again was prepared to go to war against Charles and the situation was as complicated as it had always been; Charles could hardly do more than move deliberately and bide his time. As far as the religious problem was concerned, the only feasible choice was to steer a middle course and thereby suspend the real decision until the convening of a council that met his approval.

By February 1548 the failure of the proposal had become obvious. In light of the balance of power in the Empire, it may have been a hopeless venture from the very beginning. But Charles had also been too impatient. No matter how powerful, he was still by no means the undisputed master of Germany. Had he made haste more slowly, content to achieve his goal of a *Bund*, or league, through evolution, the outcome might have been different.

One wonders why Charles did not decree the immediate restitution of Catholicism in Germany. Such would have been the most natural solution, though also the most difficult one. The Emperor's Protestant allies would hardly have liked such a procedure, for, after all, the official *raison d'être* for the war against the League of Schmalkald had been political.

The tenor of the proposed solution was Catholic, even though the section on justification used Protestant terminology to express Catholic sentiment. The section on the Mass, too, sought to accommodate Protestant feelings by describing the Mass only as a recollection of Christ's sacrifice. The Communion cup was temporarily allowed, as was clerical marriage. The other provisions of the 26-article document followed by and large a Catholic line, though the Emperor wanted it to be a mediating proposal—not Protestant, to be sure, but also by no means fully Catholic. When the document was made public in March 1548 opposition came from both sides. The Catholics objected that concessions had been made to the Protestants and denounced the Emperor for having usurped ecclesiastical prerogatives. Moreover, they bluntly refused to be included in the provisions of the document, since as Catholics they had no need to modify their faith. Only the pope had the authority to alter their religion. The Protestants, on the other hand, were displeased with the evident Catholic orientation of the document.

The Protestants were told to accept the document, the Catholics exhorted to stay true to the old faith. After three decades of controversy the end seemed to have come. Maurice of Saxony asserted that he could not accept the document without first consulting his clergy and his Estates. But those who lacked his political power could hardly do other than accept the dictum.

On June 30 1548, the so-called Interim, or, as its official title had it, 'Declaration How Religion is to be Observed in the Empire until the Convening of a General Council' (*Erklärung, wie es der Religion halber im Heiligen Reich bis zum Austrag des gemeinen Concilii gehalten werden soll*) became law, though it applied only to Protestants.[42] At the same time, the Emperor issued a *Formula Reformationis* for the reform of Catholic life. The death warrant for German Protestantism seemed to have been delivered.

But the Interim turned out to be a failure. Since it was the Emperor's last attempt to settle the religious problem in Germany, its failure meant his decisive defeat. The opposition came from all sides. There was no support from the pope, little from his allies, and militant opposition from the Protestants. Some of the opposition clearly was politically motivated, and in some instances there may have been economic considerations. Charles's sister Mary, the regent of the Low Countries, counseled her brother not to be too strict with the heretics, since this might take the trade to Hamburg rather than to Antwerp. But the straw that broke the camel's back was the Protestant resistance.

One of Luther's young disciples, Matthias Flacius, carried the banner of the opposition. He had studied at Basel and Tübingen and had come to Wittenberg to hear Luther. This brought him a 'conversion,' or, as he himself put it: 'I recognized the teaching of the gospel not only through reading or casual reflection, but through my own experience.' When the Interim came, Flacius was persuaded that it was the hour of decision.

The Protestant theologians did their share in opposing the Interim, those 'minor' reformers who had faithfully labored in their communities to introduce and consolidate the Reformation—Johann Brenz, Martin Frecht, Ambrosius Blaurer, Martin Bucer, Andreas Osiander, and all the rest. To their names should be added a host of simple ministers, whose identities have long been forgotten, but whose resolute opposition brought failure to the Interim. Their stand was impressive and their steadfastness inspired the people. If evidence is sought for the hold of the new religious ideas upon the people, this is it. The intensity of the opposition against the Interim, when the rulers were quiet and some of the eminent Protestant theologians accommodating, shows the strength of the Protestant faith in Germany.

The same story unfolded everywhere—reluctance, dragging of feet, outright opposition, and, only in the end, the acceptance of the inevitable. Even then it was an external acceptance, for below the surface the opposition continued. Part of the difficulty was the sheer impossibility of finding clerics in the land—Protestant or Catholic—who were willing to exercise their ecclesiastical functions in accord with the provisions of the Interim.

It was a spattered picture. Here resolute opposition, there unwilling acceptance. Here seeming success, there blatant failure. Before the lasting vigor of the religious resistance could be measured, the course of political events all too speedily provided the final answer to the question of the success of the Emperor's solution of the religious problem.

In March 1550 Charles V convened a Diet to meet at Augsburg. A changed Emperor gathered in the South German city whose name ranks so prominently in the history of the German Reformation. Three years before Titian had been sent to paint the victorious Emperor and he depicted the victor of Mühlberg—high on a horse, clad in shining armor, a lancet in his right hand, confident and determined. In 1550 Titian painted the Emperor again, but this time the setting was different. It was the Last Judgment, in which the Emperor appeared as one of the many who stood before the throne of judgment. The difference between the paintings is telling. Then the pride of the victor, resolutely determined to impose his will upon the conquered; now the awareness of failure and a growing disposition to turn to spiritual concerns.

The imperial proposition made much of the papal willingness to reconvene the council at Trent and decried the widespread disregard of the Interim and its provisions for ecclesiastical reform. The decree of the Diet of February 14 1551, ordered the continued administration of the Interim, but agreed that the objections against it would be considered at a future date. The decree also instructed the Estates to attend the forthcoming sessions of the Council of Trent.

On the face of things the Diet had followed the Emperor's wishes. But far more serious problems remained unsolved. The Emperor's obvious intent to suppress Protestantism had alienated his own Protestant allies and angered his old Protestant foes. And his intent to restructure the relationship between Emperor and territorial rulers had precipitated even more difficulties. In 1550 three Protestant territories had explored means to protect their faith and had also sought contact with France. Since France had concluded peace with England at about that time, the specter of French intervention in German affairs seemed real.

It was Maurice of Saxony who crystallized the latent opposition against the Emperor. Formally a Protestant, Maurice had fought in the War of Schmalkald on the side of the Emperor (a fact which earned him the uncomplimentary title 'Judas of Meissen'). This would indicate that religion was hardly a serious matter for Maurice, and indeed it was not. He was not unreligious, but his policies were prompted by considerations of *realpolitik* rather than any commitment to his interpretation of the Gospel. Not too long after the adjournment of the Diet of Augsburg, Maurice had rallied several Protestant territories into an alliance directed against the Emperor. This venture, known also as the *Fürstenrevolution*, saved the stature of Protestantism in Germany.

The resistance of the Protestant territories against the Interim might have led, as Augsburg 1550 anticipated, to some sort of modification of the Emperor's policy. As matters stood, however, the saviour of German Protestantism was Elector Maurice and his princely confreres, few of them concerned about religion. The bonds of alliances and the tensions of opposition were oriented by other considerations. Strong religious sentiment continued to prevail on both sides, but the great issues of the day were of a different character: the territorial rulers were concerned about their own regional interests.

In March 1552 Charles asked his brother Ferdinand to enter into negotiations with these rulers, but indicated that there were to be neither religious concessions nor any acknowledgment of the need for political reforms in Germany. It was hardly a basis conducive for fruitful negotiations, which promptly failed. Maurice demanded mainly a permanent religious peace, with full recognition of Protestantism. This demand ran counter to everything the Emperor stood for and, understandably, Ferdinand objected.

Despite this initial failure, the talks were soon resumed at Passau. In the end, persistence paid, for an agreement was reached. The situation in Germany was such that the political power of German Protestantism was increasingly impressive. No help had come from the council of the Church, which had aggravated, rather than eased, the tensions between Protestants and Catholics. Something had to be done about the religious situation in Germany unless armed conflict was to be renewed. And since Charles was once again at war with France, trouble with the Protestants was an alternative he could ill afford. The agreement reached at Passau stipulated that no Estate should be attacked for religious reasons and that the next Diet would attempt a conciliation between the two religious parties. Maurice had demanded permanent peace and on the face of things he had not received it. Since the agreement stipulated that if no definite settlement was reached at the next Diet the peace should be extended, an element of permanence was present after all.

Any agreement had to be approved by the Emperor and by the rulers allied with Maurice. Initially both were hesitant. Charles did not want to acknowledge the failure of the religious policy which he had pursued since 1521. Ferdinand pleaded with him, reminded him of the chaos in Germany, pointed out the threat of the Turks— but without avail. Maurice had similar difficulties, but early in August the Hessian Landgrave William approved the agreement and this broke the ice, for in the middle of the month the Emperor, too, set his signature to the document. 'Solely the consideration of your peculiar situation, your realm, and your lands, have prompted me to do so,' he told his brother.[43] His heart clearly was not in it. For all practical purposes Passau was the last step of the long way which had begun in April 1521, when the young Emperor, exuberant in his Catholic faith, had demanded that the professor from Wittenberg be condemned.

In practice, some Protestants were little willing to tolerate 'papal abuses' in their territories, even as the Catholics refused toleration for Protestants—a telling illustration, one suspects, that the shoe fitted the same foot and that double standards could be found on both sides. But more than a theological principle was at stake. The new faith was firmly established in Protestant territories, with little Catholic sentiment remaining, whereas in places still Catholic considerable agitation for Protestantism existed which, if officially condoned, might lead to ecclesiastical change.

After almost 30 years of extemporization, the situation in Germany demanded a definitive solution. The Emperor's military tour de force against the Schmalkaldians had ended in failure. At Passau the Protestants had demanded a formal recognition of their faith, and their voices had not subsided. But the Emperor was as yet unwilling to concede defeat, though he did convene a Diet to be held at Augsburg and asked Ferdinand to represent him there. 'Do not look for any other reason,' he wrote his brother, 'it is only the religious question concerning which I have insurmountable objections.'[44] Ferdinand should only approve such decisions as he could accept in good conscience. (Later Charles protested 'against everything that would offend, hurt, weaken or endanger our true old Christian and Catholic religion,' and subsequently he refused to offer an opinion about the negotiations.) If the Emperor was thus absent from Augsburg, so was the papacy. Cardinal Morone had been named papal legate to the Diet, but within a week of his arrival he was forced to return to Rome to participate in the conclave for the election of a new pope. Since the new pope, Marcellus II, succumbed within eight weeks, another conclave was necessary. This meant Morone's extended absence from Augsburg and thus no strong representation of papal interests there.

The contested issues during the negotiations at Augsburg were many, though one stood out—the permanence of the settlement. The two other important questions had to do with ecclesiastical jurisdiction and Church property. The Catholics could neither acknowledge the abrogation of the former nor the secularization of the latter without surrendering important affirmations of their faith. The Protestants, on the other hand, were certain to see the acknowledgment of ecclesiastical jurisdiction as the retention of ecclesiastical authority contrary to that of the ruler. And ecclesiastical property had been used in Protestant territories for the support of education and religion, with no funds available for its restitution. The Protestants accordingly demanded the acceptance of the secularizations.

On September 25 the estates agreed to 'a permanent peace'— permanent, that is, unless a future council would bring conciliation.[45] The basic provision of the peace was the right of the territorial rulers to determine the official religion within their territories. Just before the end of the century the famous phrase *cuius regio, eius et religio* was coined to describe the significance of the provision. Subjects disagreeing with the accepted religion of their territory had the right to emigrate. The so-called *reservatum ecclesiasticum* provided that the religious change of any ecclesiastical ruler after 1552 (in other words, the acceptance of Protestantism by a ruler who exercised political authority by virtue of his ecclesiastical office) was 'personal' conversion only, which would not affect the ecclesiastical and political status of that territory.

The Protestants had yielded at this point, but they were paid well for their concession. All ecclesiastical changes, including the secularization of church lands, up to 1552 were formalized, and the 'spiritual jurisdiction' in Protestant territories was 'suspended' until a future conciliation. No bishop could claim this 'jurisdiction' in Protestant areas.

Few happenings of Reformation history were more significant than the decree promulgated on September 25 1555. All the flowery oratory of the occasion could not obscure the fact that the tedious negotiations, the inevitable compromise, and stubborn determination had produced a haphazard document. One wonders, however, if there existed any other alternative. In theory, of course, there were many, but they had all been tried and been found wanting. Only the permanent recognition of Lutheranism remained. Under the circumstances nothing else was possible, since neither of the two religious factions was politically strong enough to force its will upon the other. The actual course of negotiations might have been different here and there, but new successes for one side would doubtless have been coupled with new concessions, and in the main the outcome would have been the same.

The peace established the legal recognition of Lutheranism and thereby the religious division of Germany. For 63 years—until the Thirty Years' War in 1618—peace would prevail in Germany, and even when war came, it had other and perhaps more pertinent causes. Germany was spared, therefore, the kind of religious-political turmoil that would characterize the situation in France or Holland, since here the legal problem of the coexistence of two religions had been solved more than a half century earlier. Some problems remained. One was the provision that 'all others, who do not subscribe to said two religions, shall not be referred to in this Peace and completely omitted.' These others were the Protestant sectarians, notably the Anabaptists, the Zwinglians, and the Calvinists. Practically, the provision was unimportant, since the 'sacramentists, Anabaptists, and other despicable sects' were not numerous and possessed little, if any, political stature. Moreover, events showed that Calvinism was not kept from its aggressive expansion in the second half of the century. The significance of the provision lay rather in its assumption that only two religious factions were politically respectable.

Full religious freedom had not been achieved even for Lutherans and Catholics. Only the territorial ruler had this privilege; his subjects had to accept his ecclesiastical decision or pack their belongings and emigrate. Accordingly, German ecclesiastical life developed along territorial lines, even as did the political life of the Empire. There was deep significance that both pope and Emperor were absent from the deliberations at Augsburg. Karl Brandi was prompted to call this 'the most perfect expression for the dawn of a new era.' Both had lost their ability to influence the course of action in Germany. On paper the traditional concepts of universal Church, Emperor, and pope were still invoked, but obviously they had lost much of their meaning. The territorial ruler assumed a new responsibility —politically autocratic and ecclesiastically important, *summus episcopus* in Lutheran territories.

A few weeks after the adjournment of the Diet came the real

climax. On October 25 Emperor Charles announced his abdication at Brussels. On that occasion he reviewed his life—from the day, 40 years earlier, on which he had been declared of age—his successes and his failures, lamented his failing health and the absence of peace. Stark symbolism lay in Charles's selection of his birthplace as the site for his abdication. He had returned to the beginning.

The following August, Charles left Brussels for Spain. Toward the end of November, he saw for the first time the palatial house built for him adjacent to the monastery of San Jeronimo de Yuste, not far from Madrid. He had come home. For little more than a year, from February 1557 to September 21 1558, he lived there. He had reached the end of the road and found solace only in his religion and in the things of the world to come. To be sure, his life at San Yuste was by no means ascetically simple. He had attendants, counselors, cooks, physicians, and all the rest, but these made little difference to a man who had already departed from the turbulence of the world.

There are many legends about Charles's sojourn at Yuste—that he occupied himself with synchronizing his many clocks or that he ordered his own Requiem Mass to be celebrated in his presence. No legend is ever without some substance, and though not fully accurate these stories may convey something of his temper and despondency at the time. Tired of life, Charles turned to things celestial. In his final weeks he often sat in front of Titian's monumental canvas *Gloria*, which depicted mankind appearing before the judgment seat of God. Titian had included Charles and his late wife in the huge throng—Charles's head bare of the imperial crown—and perhaps Charles pondered, while looking at the canvas, how he would answer on the judgement day. On September 21 1558, Charles died. In his last hour the Archbishop of Toledo gave him a crucifix and reminded him of Jesus' death as the source of grace.

The life of Charles V was inextricably linked with the course of the Reformation. With uncanny irony the years of his public activities paralleled those of the German Reformation: in 1519, when he was elected Emperor, the case of Martin Luther became an *affaire d'état*, and in 1555 his abdication came in the wake of the recognition of Lutheranism in Germany. But more was involved than chronological proximity. Charles exemplified par excellence the intimate interaction of religion and politics that characterized so much of the Reformation era. He was both a Catholic and the German Emperor and he thought, following the ideas of his chancellor, Gattinara, that these two functions could be in perfect harmony. But they could not, and this was Charles's tragedy. Had he been less of a dreamer of noble dreams and aspirations, less of a devout Catholic, less of a disciple of Charlemagne—he might have been more a man of action. As matters went, Charles was a failure at what mattered most to him—perhaps all the more blatant a failure because he lived in an age so rich in achievements.

# CHAPTER SIX

# The Spread of the Reformation in England

King Henry VIII towers over the history of the English Reformation exactly as Holbein's famous painting shows him—bold and confident, determined and resolute. The Reformation is unthinkable without the King. Thomas More had once counseled Thomas Cromwell to tell Henry always 'what he ought to doo, but never what he is able to doo; so shall you shewe your selfe a true, faithfull servaunt and a right worthy Counsailour; for if a Lyon knew his owne strength, harde were it for anye man to rule him.'[1] The advice was gratuitous. Henry did know his own strength and events in England derived their momentum from this fact.

The Reformation in England followed the pattern of that elsewhere in Europe: theological revolution, reformative zeal, and organizational consolidation by the strong hand of the ruler. The uniqueness of the English situation lay in Henry's conservative theological temper, which under ordinary circumstances would hardly have disposed him to any kind of ecclesiastical change. Quite the contrary, by temperament and previous record he seemed predestined to excel all other sovereigns in his jealous zeal for the Catholic faith. Yet it was to end differently. Henry occupied the central place in the ecclesiastical changes in England. In a way, however, this was not unusual.

Elsewhere in Europe the rulers also determined the course of ecclesiastical change. England added only a quantitative distinction to a general practice, and to the untrained eye there is little difference between Henry's role in England and, say, that of Gustavus Vasa in Sweden. When an English cleric later in the century chose to explain the Lord's Prayer by noting that 'it comes from our Lord, the King,' his exegetical ignorance yielded a deep insight into the facts of life.[2]

But would the King's ecclesiastical maneuvering have been possible without a congenial religious atmosphere? What is more, was not this atmosphere influenced by the religious upheaval on the Continent? The answer must be in the affirmative and thus two factors, in addition to the heavy hand of the King, must be cited as important elements: the religious ferment in the land and the Continental precedent. But these factors would not have prevailed against the King. Nowhere in Europe did a permanent religious settlement take place against the will of the ruler, and one must be skeptical if such would have been possible in England.

Not much needs to be said about the state of the English Church before the Reformation, for conditions there generally conformed to the European pattern—the ambiguous mixture of spiritual vitality and ecclesiastical abuse that constituted basically a stable situation, but potentially lent itself to easy exploitation. Only in two respects were there unique characteristics. While the English people were not any more worldly than their Continental counterparts, they seemed to have been a bit more heretical. England did have a long tradition of heresy. Periodically the records of pre-Reformation times tell about apprehensions of Lollard heretics, and from the last decade of the 15th century onward the incidence of Lollardy increases. John Foxe, the martyrologist, spoke of the 'secret multitude of true professors' and the comment has been made that Foxe's account is incomplete rather than incorrect.[3] Though the actual extent of Lollard survival may have been limited, an atmosphere of antiRoman dissent was not alien to England.

## The Reformation under Henry VIII

The first official recognition of Lutheran ideas came from none other than the King himself. Henry had read Luther's treatise *The Babylonian Captivity of the Church* with indignation and, amateur theologian that he was, he published a reply, *Assertio Septem Sacramentorum* (Assertion of the Seven Sacraments), which, while hardly one of the eminent publications of the 16th century, was a competent treatment of the traditional Catholic doctrine. In September 1521 a special copy was presented to the pope, who expressed his admiration for the King's erudition and one month later conferred the title *Defensor Fidei*—'Defender of the Faith'—upon Henry.

The King's noble efforts notwithstanding, the incidence of Lutheran ideas became more numerous in subsequent years. There was the so-called Society of Christian Brethren, a somewhat enigmatic enterprise, which sought to distribute religious books, even heretical ones. Whether this meant the conscious colportage of Lutheran ideas is another question. At Cambridge a group of young dons met at the White Horse Inn—on the face of things a harmless discussion circle on matters of current theological interest. Little is known about this group—the only source is a brief passage in Foxe's *Actes and Monuments*—and those historians who have discussed it have used imagination rather than evidence by listing those then in Cambridge whom they would have expected to attend.[4] Men such as Barnes, Gardiner, Fox, Heath, Lambert, Latimer, Ridley, Shaxton, and Tyndale may have been among those attending. If so, the group included future heretics and ecclesiastics, future bishops and martyrs. Not all of them became reformers, and at the time they probably were more excited by Erasmus than by Luther, though soon the group was tellingly dubbed 'Germany.' Then, as always, it was chic to discuss the latest in theological fashion.

Leader of the group—this much we do know—was Robert Barnes, who in 1526 was cited to appear before Cardinal Wolsey, chided for preaching 'before the butchers of Cambridge' and holding to erroneous doctrine. Barnes preferred to recant his view that the Church should not hold temporal possessions, that the bishops were successors of Judas Iscariot, and that the Church sold spiritual offerings as the peasants sold cows and oxen. But Barnes continued on his way, characterized by cocksureness and Lutheran ideas, until at long last he departed for the Continent.

Also in 1526 Tyndale's English translation of the New Testament, printed at Cologne and Worms, found its way across the Channel. The connection between this publication and the spread of Protestantism in England may seem nebulous, for on the face of things the vernacular Scriptures could hardly be labeled a heretical document. Yet in England, even as on the Continent, the awareness of the damages caused by the vernacular Scriptures in the hands of the Protestants led to their denunciation. The attitude was justified, for Tyndale offered more than a translation: preface, notes, and marginal annotations were extensive—and they were pure Lutheranism. Though Tyndale borrowed heavily from Luther and was, perhaps, his greatest popularizer in England, he was by no means a slavish follower. His theology to the end remained open to new ideas and insights, as witnessed by his *Parable of the Wicked Mammon* and *Obedience of a Christian Man*, of 1528, and the *Practice of the Prelates*, of 1530.

If the survival of Lollard heresy was one unique feature of the English scene, the influence of Erasmian humanism was another. Humanism stood in more than chronological proximity to the Reformation, and the line between the humanist critique of ecclesiastical abuse (real or imagined) and the Protestant repudiation of Catholic religion was as thin as a razor's edge. Many contemporaries never perceived the difference. But the fact of the matter is that in England (as elsewhere) humanism supplied both defenders and opponents of the Catholic Church, an indication that its theological propensity was ambiguous. Some, like Stephen Gardiner or Thomas More, criticized the Church until they realized that they were only adding fuel to the fire of the heretics. Then they stiffened in their attitude, became unwilling to acknowledge any ecclesiastical shortcoming, and were indisposed to explore new ways of theological reflection. Others, like Robert Barnes or John Hooper, increasingly turned into ardent Protestants.

The religious scene in England in the 1520s was in lively and exciting ferment. Its ingredients were essentially three—Lollardy, Erasmian humanism, and the new theology coming from Germany. There were forebodings that religious life in England might undergo turbulence, if not change. The chronicler may be spared, however, from offering a conjecture whether these forebodings would have become reality, since all of a sudden a new element of far-reaching repercussions entered the scene.

On June 22 1527 King Henry VIII informed his wife that they were not truly husband and wife and could not continue to live together. Since the two had been married for 17 years, this was astounding news for Catherine of Aragon. Thus began Henry's quest for a 'divorce' which was to overshadow, for the next half decade, the foreign and domestic affairs of England and eventually lead to the cutting off of the English Church from its Roman matrix.

Catherine had come to England in 1501 to be betrothed to Henry's elder brother Arthur. Political considerations had prompted the match and since these persisted after Arthur's unexpected demise, Henry was called upon to take his brother's place. But Canon Law forbade marriage with the widow of one's brother, though it was possible (under stringent conditions) to receive a papal dispensation. Such a dispensation was indeed received, the impediment of affinity existing between Henry and Catherine removed, and the marriage performed.

After almost two decades Henry began to have doubts about the legitimacy of the dispensation (and thereby also his marriage). What prompted this insight at that particular time is difficult to say, and one can only offer conjectures. The absence of a male heir may have set him pondering and became undoubtedly a factor of major importance. Catherine had become pregnant eight times during the first ten years of her marriage, but only one child, Mary, had survived infancy. In the end neither Henry's vow to lead a crusade against the Turks nor the counsel of Spanish physicians was able to alter the inevitable. There was no male heir. As matters stood, the succession would fall on Mary, and Henry surely shuddered at that thought.

Henry claimed that the study of Scripture had convinced him that he was under a divine curse for having violated the law of God. 'My conscience was incontinentlie accombred, vexed, and disquieted,' he said, 'whereby I thought myselfe to be greatlie in danger of Gods indignation. Which appeared to be (as me seemed) the rather, for that he sent vs no issues male: and all such issues male as my said wife had by me, died incontinent after they came into the world, so that I doubted the great displeasure of God in that behalfe.'[5] A literal reading of Lev 20.21 ('And if a man shall take his brother's wife, it is an unclean thing: he hath uncovered his brother's nakedness; they shall be childless') seemed to him to suggest that he was under a divine curse.

Another version was offered by Reginald Pole, who charged that Henry's 'passions for a girl' had been the reason.[6] The 'girl' was young and vivacious Anne Boleyn. The Venetian ambassador reported that 'Madam is not one of the handsomest women in the world,' and, judging from her portrait, Anne indeed was no beauty. But love makes one blind; Henry fell madly in love with her but she kept him at arm's length. Surely in the beginning Henry had no idea of the interminable complications facing his amorous fancies. He confidently thought that the Church would grant his request for an annulment of his marriage with Catherine. After all, he could point to his services to the Church which had earned him the title of 'defender of the faith.'

But there were complications. Henry's argumentation ran counter to the consensus of a formidable array of canonists who claimed that, given certain conditions, a dispensation to marry one's brother's widow was altogether proper and did not conflict with either natural or divine law. While the details of the argumentation were exceedingly intricate, Henry's case was by no means unique (how could it be, with generations of canonists exploring every minute aspect of marriage law?) and a forceful consensus stood against him. The papal dispensation properly removed the impediment of 'affinity' and possibly that of 'public honesty.' Whatever peripheral ambiguities there may have been—as, for example, whether the marriage between Arthur and Catherine had been actually consummated—were summarily removed by a second dispensation, discovered in the course of the 'divorce' proceedings. Henry's case, already weak on account of the tradition of Canon Law, was made even weaker by the political situation. Almost simultaneously with Henry's dramatic announcement to his wife, the troops of Charles V conquered Rome, making Pope Clement VII virtually a prisoner. Charles, as nephew of Catherine of Aragon, was interested in the divorce case and used every conceivable pressure to have the decision go in Catherine's favor. This put Clement VII in a difficult position, which was worsened by his characteristic slowness in making decisions. 'I have never seen him so slow,' wrote Stephen Gardiner[7] and Henry's 'great matter' provided Clement with a splendid opportunity to demonstrate his tendency to procrastinate. The pope must have thought that by making haste slowly he could resolve the difficulty, though he surely entertained little doubt about its seriousness. There is no evidence that he was ever willing to make an uncanonical decision, even though Charles and Henry, each in his own way, exerted pressure. Clement thought that if the decision were postponed long enough the matter would, somehow or other, resolve itself. Little did he know the King's dynastic concern and his passion.

The first stage in the proceedings was dominated by Cardinal Wolsey who thought, perhaps too self-confidently, that Henry's request would encounter no complications in Rome. When he realized that it did, he sought to force a decision in Henry's favor. The only concession he got, however, was that Cardinal Campeggio came to England in 1528 to try the case together with him. He did not know that Campeggio had instructions not to pronounce a sentence without further word from Rome.

After a year or so, Henry realized that he could expect no help from Rome. This meant failure for the man who had pursued his policy. In October 1529, Wolsey was indicted for violation of the statutes of *praemunire*. Eight days later he lost the chancellorship, to be succeeded by Thomas More, very much against the long-

standing practice that the chancellor be a bishop. Since More opposed the King's 'divorce' he received the concession not to be involved. Thereby the King's highest official remained aloof from the
major political issue of the day.

Parliament, which had not met for years, convened in November 1529. The business at hand seemed routine, though several bills
dealt with ecclesiastical matters and were bluntly anticlerical in tone.
Probate fees of mortuaries were restricted and pluralities of benefices
were prohibited, as were all efforts to secure papal dispensations for
such pluralities. This last provision was the most crucial stipulation
of the Pluralities Act, since it placed an English statute over papal
prerogatives. The language of the Act was cautious, for only the
effort to obtain a dispensation was prohibited and nothing was said
about papal authority as such.

By that time another development was in the making. In 1529
Thomas Cranmer, a Cambridge don, suggested that the real issue of
the 'divorce' was theological: not the canonists and scholastics of
bygone centuries mattered, but the teaching of Scripture. The theological consensus of the universities was all the King needed to set
aside the edict of the papacy. The suggestion fell on fertile ground.

A grandiose canvass of the citadels of higher learning began.
Oxford and Cambridge were sounded out first and the situation
there proved paradigmatic of things elsewhere. There was no clear-
cut position and, accordingly, the confusion of the academicians had
to be resolved by governmental intimidation. As a rule the opinion
of a university was dependent on its geographic location: Spanish
universities decided in favor of the papal dispensation and French
seats of higher learning against it. In the end the results were impressive, but inconclusive. Henry could comfort himself that formidable opinion favored his 'divorce,' but the sentiment was by no
means incontrovertible. Moreover, the opinions were but scraps of
paper and of little practical import in a world of hard realities.

And so more time passed since the King had first voiced his
pangs of conscience. He had engaged in legal maneuvering, had
pleaded and pressured, but without avail. Henry surely realized that
the means utilized thus far had proved unsuccessful. There was a
deadlock, and he probably had no clear notion as to how to break it.

In December 1530 the attorney general filed charges against the
English clergy. The nature of the charges is not exactly clear—
whether it was mere complicity with Wolsey for having accepted his
legatine authority or a general violation of the *praemunire* statutes.
The clergy were stunned, but in convocation they quickly regained

their equilibrium: 'subsidies' of £100,000 were offered by the province of Canterbury and of £18,840 by the province of York as grants to the King in gratitude for his defense of the faith. In plain language, these grants were meant as bribes. Henry needed the money, but he wanted more: he informed the clergy that they had to acknowledge their guilt and at the same time the King's position as 'protector and only supreme head of the English Church and Clergy.' John Fisher, Bishop of Rochester, suggested the insertion of the phrase 'so far as the law of Christ allows,' and this was the way it was accepted by a convocation.[8]

This acknowledgment of royal headship was revolutionary. In view of the increasing royal control of ecclesiastical affairs throughout the 15th century, it may not have been particularly dramatic. Still, it was more than the extension of existing trends. The clerical protest against the clause indicated the drastic nature of the innovation. There is evidence of Henry's preoccupation with ecclesiastical affairs during that time, of a growing awareness on his part of the nature of true royal authority. Possibly, the Henrician Caesaropapism developed during this time parallel to but quite distinct from the quest for the 'divorce.' There was talk, startlingly new, about the ancient privileges of the English Church or about the true nature of Henry's 'imperial' office as it related to the Church. But for the time being, there was only talk, nothing more.

The years between 1529 and 1532 were a time of transition, when the tools for a revolutionary change in policy were very much present, but Henry—a staunch, if conventional Catholic—grappled for traditional means of resolving the deadlock over the 'divorce.' Even an indefatigable optimist had to admit in 1531 that the King was not any closer to his goal than he had been in 1527. Time was running short and Henry grew impatient. The final effort to cajole the papacy—at its weakest point, namely, money—came early in 1532, when Parliament passed the Conditional Restraint of Annates which prohibited the payment of annates to Rome. This bill had rough sailing in Parliament, telling evidence of the papal loyalties of Englishmen. Henry meant to tighten the financial screw and deprive the pope of his English revenue. For the time being, however, there was only a threat; the execution of the bill was left to the King's discretion. The lesson was to be unmistakable: no divorce, no money.

In March the Commons presented a supplication to the King which had all the appearances of a grievous sigh of a people oppressed by the Church. The 12 complaints included both the sublime and the ridiculous—that minors were given benefices and that there were too many holy days, especially at the harvest time, 'upon which many great, abominable, and execrable vices, idle and wanton sports be used and exercised.' The heart of the matter was stated at the beginning: the clergy make laws, the King was told, 'without your knowledge or most royal assent,' none of which were 'declared unto them in the English tongue.'[9]

After initial hesitancy and reluctance, the clergy submitted to the King, though it must be noted that only a rump portion of the Southern Convocation did so: 'Having our special trust and confidence in your most excellent wisdom, your princely goodness and fervent zeal to the promotion of God's honor and Christian religion, and also in your learning, far exceeding, in our judgment, the learning of all other kings and princes,' the clergy agreed to obtain royal assent for all new constitutions, canons, and ordinances.[10] The following day Thomas More, pleading ill health, resigned from his office as chancellor. Something dramatic had happened. Chapuys, the Spanish ambassador, reported that there was 'a new papacy made here.' The clergy were now inferior to shoemakers, he said, for these could at least make their own statutes.[11]

Henry needed someone to carry out the policy, and Thomas Cromwell was the man. He had been Wolsey's secretary and, somewhat unexpectedly, had weathered the fall of his master. After attracting the King's attention, he was for 10 years or so his right-hand man. Recent research has convincingly demonstrated that Cromwell possessed the genius of mind and the singularity of purpose that enabled him to be the eminent figure of the 1530s. He stepped into a vacuum and he filled it splendidly. His counsel to Henry was that as sovereign of an 'empire' he possessed supreme authority in both Church and state. Early 16th-century England brought the clash between two concepts of governments, the one medieval, characterized by ultimate ecclesiastical supremacy over kings, and the other modern, characterized by the supremacy of the positive law of the state over any claims of the law of nature, God, or the Church. Cromwell proved to be the capable proponent of the latter view, seeing in Parliament the physical manifestation of the nation in action and realizing the possibilities which this offered. Quickly it became evident that the wind was blowing from a new direction. Henry's patience had been exhausted, a fact that was made all the more palatable by the presence of a scheme that offered a solution. Those who had ominously prophesied that it would be all over with the pope's authority in England if the King's request were denied could comfort one another with the accuracy of their prediction.

Parliament, after some formidable opposition, erected the hurdle to keep Catherine from appealing to Rome. The Restraint of Appeals prohibited, with allusions to historical precedent, any appeal abroad by declaring England to be an 'empire' whose King could adjudge all spiritual and temporal matters in his realm.[12] Cromwell was the architect of this statute and its godfather Marsiglio of Padua, whose *Defensor Pacis* offered philosophical support. Practically, the Restraint kept the 'King's great matter' in England; theoretically, it culminated the delineation of a new concept of government. A perfunctory trial, presided over by Cranmer, declared the marriage between Henry and Catherine invalid. A week later Anne Boleyn was crowned Queen of England.

The preoccupation with the 'King's great matter' and the introduction of ecclesiastical change by parliamentary statute must not lead to the assumption that the English scene was bereft of theologians and theological reflection. Such was not the case. Neither the pursuit of the 'great matter' nor the parliamentary fiat would have been possible without a concomitant religious restlessness and anti-Roman agitation. England had its reformers—men who had accepted the new interpretation of the Christian Gospel and propagated it in print. One need not bestow undue creativity and brilliance on these men, or suggest that they played the crucial role in the course of events. But they brought about religious ferment, and thus theirs was an indispensable role in the English Reformation.

Initially their message consisted in a vague echo of Lutheran commonplaces, of those sweeping assertions that reformers everywhere propounded with disarming self-confidence and naïveté: the stress on Scripture and salvation by faith, the rejection of works-righteousness and human traditions. Afterward came a more sophisticated delineation of the new theology, though the King's own conservative temper—dramatically illustrated by the Six Articles of 1539—always tended to keep matters in check.

First in importance was the English translation of the New Testament. Such translations were actually not new in England, though William Tyndale's work was epoch-making. The irony of the matter was that the vernacular Bible, surely a non-partisan document, esteemed by Catholics no less than Protestants, should have become a piece of Protestant propaganda. This was the case, however, and one suspects that the stench of Lollard heresy may have played its part in this respect. John Foxe's *Book of Martyrs* relates many instances where the common people's facility with the Scriptures was uncommonly profound and extensive. Literacy was amazingly high in England and books could be widely read. At the very least, the dissemination of the vernacular Scriptures reduced the willingness to listen to official ecclesiastical pronouncements and confirmed the religious autonomy of the individual. People, even common people, could take the Bible into their hands and decide as to which side was right or wrong in the theological controversy. They may have been mistaken in their conclusions and since they lacked theological training one suspects that they often were. But their lack of training did not keep them from adding their marginalia to the Sacred Writ. Vice was turned into virtue in this regard, for the Protestants argued that it was basically erroneous to hold that Scripture could not be understood by simple men and women, for the teachings of Jesus were utterly simple.

Alongside the vernacular Bible stood a host of other publications. Tyndale is a good illustration even in this respect, for he translated not only the New Testament but also wrote several theological tracts, notably the *Parable of the Wicked Mammon* and the *Obedience of a Christian Man*. His denunciation of Rome was vitriolic: 'that great idol, the whore of Babylon, antichrist of Rome, whom they call the pope.'[13] At the same time he glowingly expounded the Protestant notion of righteousness of faith: 'Faith bringeth pardon and forgiveness freely purchased by Christ's blood.'[14]

He had many comrades in arms. John Frith published *A pistle to the Christian reader: the revelation of antichrist* (1529) and *A letter unto the faithful followers of Christ's Gospel* (1532). George Joye wrote an *Answer to Ashwell* in 1531, a discussion of justification by faith. From the pen of William Barlow came *A dyaloge descrybyng the orygynall ground of these Lutheran faceyons* (1531) and William Roy published *A Proper dyaloge, betwene a gentillman and an husband man* in 1530.

All in all, some 40 Protestant books were published between 1525 and 1533. While this figure is too modest to warrant the assertion of a widespread impact, it is sufficient to suggest an intrusion of the new theological currents into the country. There is no evidence that these theological writers decisively influenced the religious atmosphere. But the English religious scene was more turbulent then than it had been 10 or 15 years earlier, and this without any direct relationship to the King's 'great matter.'

Certain parallels existed between the English development and that on the Continent. In both instances there was a religious agitation and in both instances the goal was to reorient religion along lines congenial to the new interpretation of the Gospel. In England, even as on the Continent, the official climate was none too friendly with regard to these efforts. Tyndale felt it advisable to leave for the safety of the Continent, as did George Joye and Robert Barnes. John Frith was burned at Smithfield in 1533.

The parliamentary promulgation of the notion of royal supremacy introduced a new element into the picture, inasmuch as the new 'doctrine' called for theological exposition. Alongside Stephen Gardiner's *De vera obedientia*, the most eminent specimen of its kind, were also the proverbial lesser lights: Edward Foxe's *De vera differentia regiae potestatis et ecclesiasticae*, Richard Sampson's *Oratio*.[15] The godfather of these attempts was Marsiglio of Padua and his *Defender of the Peace*.

What F. L. Baumer has called the 'cult of authority' of Henry VIII found here its poignant expression and extension. Gardiner's comment that God 'hath set princes, whom, as representatives of his Image unto men, he would have to be reputed in the supreme and most high room, and to excel among all other human creatures'[16] was consistently, if not persuasively, unfolded for the spiritual as well as the temporal realm.

The King's break with Rome naturally called for theological support. From 1534 on, antiRoman propaganda was not only tolerated but actively encouraged. And even printing history was thereby influenced. Theretofore the Protestant tracts had been printed on the Continent and were smuggled to England; now they could actually be printed in England. A tract entitled *Of the olde god and the new*, probably by Miles Coverdale, was prohibited at its first publication in 1529—and officially endorsed five years later! Thomas Cromwell stood behind this propaganda effort, and he did his work well. Protestant propaganda moved freely, though an element of precariousness continued to be present. Henry wanted antipapal propaganda and support for the notion of royal supremacy. At the same time, however, he was staunchly Catholic in his theological orientation and the outright propagation of salvation by faith or of a nonCatholic understanding of the Sacraments was to him an abomination and he would have none of it. Robert Barnes, John Lambert, and William Tyndale were but three of the victims of the conservative King.

To propound theological notions in Henrician England after the break with Rome was rather like walking a tightrope. The argument had to be both antipapal and proCatholic, thus exhibiting a combination of ingredients that required an exquisite measure of theo-

G

logical balance on the part of the author. Still, a multitude of writings—several hundred theological books, devotional tracts, primers, plays, and poems—issued from the printing presses during the last dozen years of Henry's rule. There can be little doubt that the tenets of the Protestant Reformation were widely expounded.

Since the King himself seemed unsure of the direction of his ecclesiastical policy, official encouragement (or repudiation) of specific theological positions remained haphazard. Indeed, for a while the key word was ambiguity—as the subsequent sequence of official documents, from the *Bishops' Book* to the Six Articles and the *King's Book*, made abundantly clear. England steered a middle course between the Scylla of Henry's staunch Catholicism and the Charybdis of the repudiation of Rome.

One religious option of the time seemed to supply this strange mixture up to a point: the thought of Erasmus. There can be little doubt that the great humanist made an impact on the English scene after the break with Rome. While the official endorsement of Erasmianism did not come until 1547 with the stipulation of the Injunctions of that year that the clergy should study the Gospel Paraphrases of Erasmus, the informal influence was felt long before then. Several of his treatises had been published in England in the early 1530s, notably his *Exhortation to the Diligent Study of the Holy Scripture*, of 1529, which subsequently was included in Tyndale's 1536 edition of the New Testament.

In a variety of ways the Erasmian program of religious renewal seemed congenial to England. The repudiation of formal religiosity, such as veneration of saints and relics, the rejection of pilgrimages, indeed, of all forms of so-called 'superstition,' the stress on a moral and ethically oriented understanding of the Gospel—all these emphases seemed to be congenial to the ecclesiastical program favored by the King, especially since a basically Catholic orientation overshadowed it all. But, while there may have even been support in high places, such as Thomas Cromwell and Catherine Parr, one must not describe the character of Henrician religion as Erasmian. This it may have been in part, albeit only in part.

When harvest time came to England in 1534 ecclesiastical life was what it always had been. The familiar prayers were offered, the traditional services performed, the Catholic faith expounded and confessed. Something was different, though. The bond that united the English Church with Rome had been cut. The repudiation of papal jurisdiction meant that ecclesiastical authority had to be newly defined. Several parliamentary statutes passed in 1534 sought to do so. The Ecclesiastical Appointment Act dealt with the filling of ecclesiastical appointments; the Dispensation Act placed all authority for dispensations with the Archbishop of Canterbury; the Act of Submission of the Clergy transformed into statute the earlier acknowledgment of convocation not to legislate without the King's consent; the First Act of Succession vested the English crown in the issue of Henry and Anne and thereby bestowed parliamentary sanction on the King's divorce; the Supremacy Act transformed the acknowledgment of convocation that the King was the supreme head of the Church into a parliamentary statute; the Treasons Act, finally, made it a criminal offense to question the King's titles or to suggest that he was a heretic.

If the various ingredients in the English religious scene in the early 1530s are obvious enough, their relative importance in the precipitation of ecclesiastical change is enigmatic. Traditionally the King's 'divorce' has been singled out as the factor of primary importance, which suggests that Henry's determination to free himself from Catherine of Aragon at all costs brought the breach with Rome. One can also cite the religious ferment in England (either of indigenous origin or an importation from abroad) and argue that the Henrician Reformation by statute constituted only the legal foil for profound religious changes. Or there is the possibility of asserting the priority of constitutional considerations, in the sense that the King developed a growing awareness of the proper scope of the royal office, an awareness that increasingly entailed the notion that kingship included authority over Church as well as state.

The best way to characterize the situation is to stress the interplay of these factors. All of them were present, of course, and their collective presence, their mutual forcing as well as thwarting of the course of events, made for the actual course of events in England. Had not all of them been present, there would undoubtedly have been individual expressions: a confrontation between King and pope, resolved amicably; religious agitation, but no outright introduction of the Protestant faith; a quest for a 'divorce,' but a shying away from final consequences.

If any of these factors was decisive, then it was the 'divorce' which alone provided the element of urgency and seemingly inescapable pertinence. That Henry did not enjoy the full prerogatives of kingship could be pondered and then forgotten; that some reform was called for in England was likewise a matter that could be ignored. Only the absence of a male heir was a cruel reality which assumed, with each passing day, greater urgency and relevance.

Most Englishmen proved to be the King's loyal subjects in the religious change, a good preparation for the even more drastic alterations to come in the future. Whether of high or low estate, of clerical or lay persuasion, they chose to travel the path of least resistance. Their reason was—as Bishop Bonner tellingly confessed—plain fear, 'for otherwise there would have been no way but one.'[17] Since it was a lonely way, only a few traveled it. But two of the most famous Englishmen were among them: Thomas More and John Fisher, arrested for their refusal to render the oath prescribed in the Act of Succession. They were brought to trial in June 1535, and charged that in violation of the Treasons Act they had maliciously denied the King the title of supreme head of the Church. Both were sentenced to death, both victims of obvious miscarriages of justice.

Europe was shocked. Erasmus wrote a poem in More's memory and told a friend, 'In the death of More I feel as if I had died myself.'[18] More himself put it this way: 'I am the King's true faithful subject . . . and I pray for his highness, and all his, and all the realm. I do nobody no harm, I saw none harm, I think none harm, but wish everybody good. And if this be not enough to keep a man alive, in good faith I long not to live.'[19]

It is not clear what goal Henry perceived for his religious changes. His own theological orientation was Catholic. Indeed, the Act of Restraint of Annates, of 1534, stated explicitly that neither King nor people intended 'to decline or vary from the congregation of Christ's Church in any things concerning the very articles of the Catholic faith of Christendom.'[20] Still, the introduction of royal supremacy was bound to have theological ramifications, not only marital ones for Henry.

## The Dissolution of the Monasteries

With the execution of Fisher, More, and the small company of Catholic martyrs, the curtain fell on the first act of the Reformation in England. It could have been the last. Though theological ambiguities existed, further religious changes were not inevitable, and the general pattern of ecclesiastical life might have continued. But there was a second act, even more spectacular than the first, prompting Nicholas Harpsfield to reflect that the King could no more keep from further changes 'than it is possible for a man to roll a millstone from the top of a high hill and afterward to stay it in the midst of its course.' By parliamentary fiat the English monasteries were dissolved.

Henry's financial problem was a major cause. The cost of government had risen substantially during his rule due to several factors, not the least of which was his extravagant involvement in European power politics. The Restraint of Annates had diverted into the royal exchequer moneys that had theretofore gone to Rome, but this was only a drop in the bucket. More was to be had from the Church for the asking, especially from the monasteries, which possessed over half of the wealth of the Church. A simple statistic reveals the relationship of monastic wealth to the King's pecuniary troubles: at the end of Henry's reign the annual rental value of the monastic lands was more than double the annual expenditures of government. The confiscation of monastic wealth promised to end the financial embarrassment of the government. Cromwell's scheme was to use the property for a permanent endowment for the crown. And there were additional benefits. While most of the monasteries were loyal, potentially they were propaganda centers for the Catholic faith. To close them was an act of prudence.

In the summer and fall of 1535 Cromwell undertook a visitation of the monasteries. When the work had been completed, the visitors produced a report which depicted the monasteries as iniquitous dens of vice, corruption and superstition. The King himself appeared before Parliament to relate the sorry tale, and his performance must have been impressive. Hugh Latimer recalled many years later that 'when their enormities were first in Parliament house, they were so great and abominable that there was nothing but down with them.'[21] The King sought to persuade Parliament that the monasteries were wealthier than necessary and that many no longer served a proper spiritual purpose.

To disentangle fact and fiction in the report of the visitors is impossible, though there seems little doubt that English monastic life was hardly blooming with spiritual vitality in the fourth decade of the 16th century. But this did not make the monasteries dens of iniquity, as the report charged. In all likelihood, most monasteries were pursuing their functions in about the way they had for some time.

Early in 1536 Parliament passed the Act for the Dissolution of the Lesser Monasteries, which were those with an annual income of less than £200. Not the number of the religious in a house, nor even specific monasteries, but the 'clear yearly value of two hundred pounds' marked the dividing line between those houses 'wherein (thanks be to God) religion is right well kept and observed' and those abounding in 'manifest sin, vicious, carnal and abominable living.'[22] The Act provided that the property of the monasteries was to go to the King; actually quite a few of them obtained exemptions. The religious had the choice of transferring to larger monasteries, serving as secular clergy, or giving up their clerical vocation. The number of those who received a dispensation to leave their monastic profession was great. In 1539 the larger monasteries were dissolved, though some of these had voluntarily done so already. One year later, English monasticism ceased to exist.

The impact of the dissolution was far-reaching. An institution that had been at the heart of English religion for centuries ceased to exist. Thousands of monks and nuns (slightly over 9,000) became homeless and without vocation. Enormous wealth changed hands. The composition of the House of Lords was altered by the disappearance of the abbots. And there were social and economic consequences, since the monasteries had provided, especially in less populous places, lodging for the traveler and alms for the poor. On the other hand, there was a profit to learning, since some monastic funds, at least, were used for educational purposes, such as the endowment of professorships and the establishment of cathedral schools. In any case, Cromwell's scheme to keep the monastic lands in the hands of the crown did not materialize, for pressing fiscal needs (caused by the wars against France and Scotland) forced their sale. And, above all, the dissolution precipitated a turbulent uprising.

The summer of 1536 had brought much rain in England and an age disposed to regard anything unusual as an ominous forboding of the future promptly offered its interpretation: the word was that the rains were God's vengeance for the execution of More, Fisher, and the other martyrs. The first month would be 'rainy and full wet, next month death, and the third month war.' True enough, an uprising occurred in the North, beginning in Lincoln in October. It was quickly subdued, but others occurred in places many miles apart.

There were differences between the various uprisings. In Lincoln the townspeople were the banner-bearers, in York the gentry. The grievances were a motley assortment of economic, social, and religious concerns. The common motif—with the exception of the uprising in Cumberland and Westmorland—was an indignation over the recent religious changes in the land: the royal supremacy, the new bishops, the dissolution of the monasteries. Thus, 24 articles, drawn up at Pontefract in December 1536, demanded that the heresies of Luther, Wyclif, Huss, Melanchthon, and others be suppressed, and 'the supremacy of the Church touching *cura animarum* to be reserved to the See of Rome.'[23]

The uprising in Yorkshire, under the leadership of Robert Aske, constituted the most serious threat to the crown. The throng of rebels was impressive. When they gathered outside York in October, there were 20,000 of them, including over 4,000 horsemen. Hull fell to them as did the fortress of Pontefract.

The King moved with dispatch, but the forces he put into the field were not the equal of the rebels. Toward the end of October the two armies had moved within fighting distance. Had the rebels struck against the King's poorly organized army, they would have carried the day. But Aske was not a rebel at heart. He only wanted the redress of certain grievances of which he thought the King himself innocent. By making vague promises Henry swayed him. Aske tore off the rebels' badge and asserted that henceforth he would only wear the badge of the King. The Duke of Norfolk, recalled from retirement to command the King's forces, had little difficulty in quelling the uprising. Wherever he went he left behind him hanging and executions—including Robert Aske—as a mute, yet eloquent, warning against 'shameful insurrection and unnatural rebellion.'[24] Thus the uprising came to naught. By matching shrewdness with dishonesty, Henry survived the most serious crisis of his rule.

The northern uprisings revealed the extent of discontent in the land. It was not only that the King had broken with Rome. There was more to arouse discontent and prompt restlessness among the people. Catherine of Aragon had been a popular queen and her shoddy dismissal in favor of a 'fair wench' hardly endeared Henry to the people. Then there was the trial of Fisher and More, other executions, the attack on the property of the Church, the uprisings and their ruthless suppression. Indeed, there was not much that looked encouraging, though conversely the King had reason to breathe more easily. Most of the clouds had, at long last, disappeared from the horizon: the international situation was tolerable and, after 10 years of marital complications, Henry had a male heir. In October 1537 his new wife, Jane Seymour, gave birth by Caesarian section to a boy. Jane died 12 days after the delivery, restoring Henry to the enviable status of Europe's most eligible suitor.

The task of guiding the new Church in England was Thomas Cromwell's. As the royal viceregent he looked after ecclesiastical affairs and demonstrated his administrative competence. At the same

time he showed himself a skillful proponent of the King's ecclesiastical cause by launching an extensive propaganda effort. He was
joined by Thomas Cranmer the new Archbishop of Canterbury.
But the King was never far away. He was erratic and unpredictable,
his interest in matters theological oscillated between active interest
and nonchalance. Cromwell was so efficient because his policies
agreed with those of the King.

It is telling that the initial official statements concerning
ecclesiastical policy (aside from the cluster of acts promulgated in
1533 and 1534), the First and Second Royal Injunctions, were doc-
trinally vague and addressed themselves primarily to matters pertaining to the broader social involvements of the Church, which was
conceived as the eminent bond of the body politic, the assurance of
public order and morality.

In July 1536 Convocation had accepted the so-called Ten
Articles.[25] Initially drafted by the King, the Articles stated 'what all
bishops and preachers should instruct and teach our people.' Their
compass was comprehensive: the Creed, Communion, Baptism,
Penance, justification, images, saints, and rites and ceremonies. The
Articles were a skillful exercise in ambiguous phraseology which
allowed a Catholic no less than a Protestant interpretation. Undoubtedly the Articles sought to steer a middle course between
affirming the King's conservative propensity and accommodating
the League of Schmalkald. Only three Sacraments (Baptism,
Penance, Communion) were recognized; the Scriptures and the three
ancient creeds were declared the norm of faith; the superstitious use
of images, saints, and ceremonies was condemned. At the same time,
the theological substance of the Articles tended to be Catholic.
Auricular confession was required in the Sacrament of Penance and
the article of justification noted the need for 'perfect faith and
charity' for the 'attaining of the same justification.' Henry was negotiating with the League of Schmalkald at the time and found such
an approach useful.

Within a month Cromwell modified the theological ambivalence
of the Articles with Injunctions that offered instructions as to how
the ministers should edify their people.[26] The clergy were to set forth
the Articles and explain the usurped power of the Bishop of Rome.
Instructions concerning the proper understanding of saints and pilgrimages were to be given, for the people 'shall please God more by
the true exercising of their bodily labors, travail or occupation, and
providing for their families, than if they went about to the said pilgrimages.' The Lord's Prayer, the Apostles' Creed, and the Ten

Commandments were to be taught in English, and the clergy were exhorted to study the Scriptures rather than the interiors of alehouses or the subtleties of card playing.

In August 1537 came the publication of *The Godly and Pious Institution of a Christian Man*, a handbook on Christian belief. Since it was the outgrowth of lengthy discussions among the bishops, it is also known as the *Bishops' Book*.[27] The *Institution of a Christian Man* consisted of an exposition of the Apostles' Creed, the Commandments, the Sacraments, and the Lord's Prayer. Its orientation was conservative. Though a distinction was made between Sacraments instituted by Christ and holy and godly signs, all the traditional seven were expounded. The four Sacraments not recognized by Protestants (Confirmation, Matrimony, Holy Orders, and Extreme Unction) were declared to be 'of such antiquity, of such excellence, yea, and of such efficaciousness, too, that many graces follow all those persons that reverently' receive them. The exposition of justification allowed a Catholic as well as a Protestant interpretation.

Both the conservatives and the liberals among the bishops signed the Institution, an indication that both sides could interpret it in their own way. Aside from its evasive theological stance, the document was characterized by its submissive references to the King. Whenever the subject matter suggested even a tenuous reference to royal authority, the bishops wasted no time making it. Henry had actually covered the draft with a host of corrections which he passed on to Cranmer, who discarded his customary submissiveness and voiced disagreement with quite a few of these changes. The section on Baptism had stated that man was justified 'not for the worthiness of any merit or work done by the penitent, but for the only merits of the blood and passion of our Saviour Jesus Christ.' The King's insertion proposed 'not *only* for the worthiness . . . but *chiefly* for the merits' . . . and thus made for a conservative statement. Cranmer objected and argued 'that certain it is, that our election cometh only and wholly of the benefit and grace of God.'[28]

In September 1538 the second Royal Injunctions were issued.[29] Again, the outright doctrinal references were scant, and the practical exhortations conveyed a Protestant temper. The ministers were exhorted to declare 'the very gospel of Christ' and to prompt the people to works 'of charity, mercy and faith, specially prescribed and commanded in Scripture,' and not to 'works devised by men's phantasies beside Scripture.' Examples of such 'phantasies' were 'wandering to pilgrimages, offering of money, candles or tapers to images or relics, or kissing or licking the same, saying over a number of beads, not understood or minded on.' At the same time the clergy were instructed to examine the people every Lent in the Lord's Prayer and the Apostles' Creed and threaten them with the denial of Communion if they lacked sufficient knowledge.

Of far-reaching import was the stipulation that 'the very lively word of God' which everyone must 'embrace, believe, and follow, if he look to be saved,' should be read and, moreover, 'one book of the whole Bible of the largest volume, in England,' put into all parish churches. This was a new development. A few years earlier Henry had issued a proclamation which had denounced 'the divulging of this Scripture at this time in English tongue,' insisting that it would be more to 'further confusion and destruction than the edification of their souls.' By 1538 the situation was different, and the influence of the Protestant gospellers was evident.

This stipulation of the Injunctions called for an official version of the English Bible. Cromwell decided to bring out one and entrusted Miles Coverdale with the task. Coverdale, who had published an English Bible in 1535, might be called *un terrible simplificateur*, for he knew no Hebrew and only little Greek, and simply translated from German and Latin. And what he could not get from Luther's translation or the Zurich Froschauer version, he lifted out of Tyndale. He was neither a Biblical scholar nor even a translator, but a gifted stylist who knew how to turn a smooth phrase. The result of his efforts was the so-called 'Great Bible,' first published in April 1539 and republished six more times before the end of 1541.

The title page pompously stated that it was 'the Byble in Englyshe of the largest and greatest volume,' and the ornamentative woodcut placed the King in that gloriously prominent center place theretofore reserved in similar title-pages for God, who found a place, a small place, near the top of the page. The practical problems thwarting the use of the English Bible were many. The price of a copy was high and literacy necessary to make use of it. The provision that the Bible was to be put into all parish churches overcame the practical difficulties. Moreover, readers often read aloud to non-readers.

The publication was revolutionary. The Bible became the cornerstone of the religious edifice. A Reformation principle found vivid expression, as did the sentiment of the Christian humanists who yearned for the revival of Biblical studies. English history, not to speak of ecclesiastical history, was profoundly influenced by the vernacular Bible. The Puritan dissent later on in the century would have been quite impossible without it.

### The End of an Era

In 1539 Parliament passed the Six Articles Act, the 'whip with six strings,' as Protestants called it. The theological ambiguities of the Ten Articles and the *Bishops' Book* were dramatically removed. As matters stood, neither the 'gospellers' nor the conservatives were content and the pendulum had to swing one way or the other. It swung in the conservative direction, influenced by the King's own religious temperament and, perhaps, by his awareness that the country still preferred it that way. The six points of doctrine (transubstantiation, communion under both kinds, celibacy, vows of chastity, private Masses, and auricular confession) affirmed by the Act expressed traditional Catholic sentiment.[30]

There is no reason to speak of a conservative reaction during the last eight years or so of Henry's reign. Naturally, the Six Articles proved a profound shock to the gospellers in England and their comrades in arms on the Continent; all their hopes and aspirations seemed to have come abruptly to naught. Even Cranmer felt sufficiently frightened to return to a state of practical celibacy by sending his wife back to her native Germany. And the close chronological connection between the promulgation of the Six Articles and Cromwell's fall and Barnes's execution suggested that these events were parts of a comprehensive plot to eradicate Protestantism in England.

One doubts if Henry intended such a reversal of his ecclesiastical policy. Probably he had become concerned about the all-too-formidable barrage of Protestant propaganda and teaching. Good Catholic that he was, he could not but view this development with dismay. The Six Articles were meant to stabilize the religious situation in England on the basis of the status quo. They were to be an amber light for all would-be reformers. No additional measures of antiProtestant suppression followed. Above all, the ferocious penalties (the denial of transubstantiation or marriage on the part of one who had vowed chastity entailed the death penalty) of the Act were hardly applied. Thus the bark proved much worse than the bite. Henry sought to halt 'creeping' Protestantism. And the evidence suggests that temporarily at least he accomplished his goal.

Almost to a day a full year passed between the promulgation of the Six Articles Act and Cromwell's fall, yet during the greater part of that year Cromwell's position seemed safe and secure. The vice-regent fell because his conservative foes of long standing, notably the Duke of Norfolk and Stephen Gardiner, had been able to persuade the King of his responsibility for the illfated royal marriage with Anne of Cleves, that nonentity on the pages of Tudor history. A court camarilla that despised him, as did Norfolk, because he was an upstart without noble birth, and that detested him, as did Gardiner, because he favored Protestant ideas, abruptly gained the King's ear and brought about his fall. Soon after Cromwell's death the King gave evidence of remorse, indicating his awareness that he had lost the most faithful and the most competent servant he ever had. But neither remorse nor sadness could undo what had been done. And, as Henry was soon to realize, even the charming and alluring diversion of his fifth wife, Catherine Howard, who was some thirty years younger than he, brought no lasting answer.

'I crye for mercye, mercye, mercye,' Cromwell had written to the King.[31] But without having been heard—one of the witnesses at his trial was Richard Riche, who had already distinguished himself by perjurious service for the King in More's trial—he was condemned. John Foxe, the martyrologist, called him a 'valiant soldier and captain of Christ' and provided a moving, though apocryphal, account of Cromwell's last moment: 'He patiently suffered the stroke of the axe, by a ragged butcherly miser, which very ungodly performed the office.'[32] In his last words Cromwell protested his orthodoxy and offered a prayer for the King.

The irony of the occasion was that on the day of Barnes's execution two other Protestant sympathizers were burned, and three priests—Thomas Abel, Richard Fatherstone, and Edward Powell (who were beatified in 1886)—were hanged, drawn, and quartered for having denied the King's supremacy. 'What a country England was to live in,' a foreign observer remarked, 'when they hanged papists and burned antipapists.'[33] To have executed an equal number of Protestants and of Catholics on a single day may seem to some an undue manifestation of the *via media* Henry was disposed to travel. But neither Cromwell's fall nor Barnes's execution heralded a Catholic reaction. To be sure, Gardiner returned to the council and occupied an influential position, but there was still Cranmer, who exhibited an amazing theological versatility and personal persistence.

During the next years the King carefully mediated between the conservatives and the Protestants, temporarily moving in one direction, but always reverting to the other. The last doctrinal pronounce-ment of the reign, the *Necessary Doctrine and Erudition for Any Christian Man*, came in 1543. It is known as the 'King's Book,' be-cause Henry had not only called for its drafting but also contributed the preface, for him a splendid opportunity to demonstrate his pedestrian theological competence.[34] Theologically it was conserva-tive, though the royal preface did contain a gratuitous blast against the 'pretensed universal primacy' of the pope. Reginald Pole had the book read from the pulpits of Gloucester during Mary's rule, and this is evidence for its theological orientation.

Also in 1543 the authorization to read the Bible was taken from the 'lower sort' and restricted to the upper classes of society. The act that provided for such restriction had the interesting title Act for the Advancement of True Religion (34 and 35 Hen. VIII, c. 1), and the parallel note in the 'King's Book' observed that the reading of the Bible had led some 'to sinister understanding of Scripture, presumption, arrogancy, carnal liberty, and contention.' There were additional religious changes. A revision of service books was ordered in 1543, and a book of homilies was submitted to Convocation but not published. In 1545 a book of vernacular prayers was authorized. That same year an act authorized the King to seize the last bit of ecclesiastical property, the so-called chantries, and to use it to pay for the war with France. Also that year Henry made his last ap-pearance in Parliament. He had words of commendation for his loyal subjects (after all, Parliament had 'nationalized' the chantry endowments), but also biting criticism: 'Charity and concord is not amongst you, but discord and dissensions beareth rule in every place.' The King quoted Paul and laid it on the line: 'One calleth the other Heretic and Anabaptist, and he calleth him again, Papist, Hypocrite and Pharisee. . . . Thus all men almost be in variety and discord and few or none preach truly and sincerely the word of God, according as they ought to do. You of the temporality be not clean and unspotted of malice and envy, for you rail on bishops, speak slanderously of priests, and rebuke and taunt preachers.'[35]

What occupied Henry's mind during those last months of his life when sickness increasingly burdened his worn-out body is im-possible to know. Perhaps he was concerned to ward off a possible attack of Charles V upon England upon the successful conclusion of the military conflict with the League of Schmalkald. Perhaps he intended a full introduction of Protestantism in the land, such as John Foxe suggested when he wrote that 'most certain it is and to be signified to all posterity, that his full purpose was to have repurged the state of the Church.'[36] On the other hand, it is well possible that Henry thought that his hybrid of ecclesiastical complexities, which produced shaking of heads on the part of everyone except Henry himself, could survive and was a stable creature. Perhaps he saw the answer precisely in the continuation of the Henrician formula; after all, he was always a bit self-confident and vain, and an astute statesman.

The strange composition of the proposed council of regency for his minor son complicates matters, though the most obvious explanation is surely that Henry was concerned to thwart a return to Rome—in which event his son, Edward, would have been considered a bastard and the Tudor dynasty conceivably removed from the English throne. To allow the Protestants to triumph would, however, have been squarely against Henry's own theological temper.

In any case, Henry took the secret with him into his grave. What is more, from his grave he could well ponder that one cannot rule from that place. The two tutors of his sons (who had been conscientious humanists) turned into ardent Protestants and, most importantly, one member of the council of regency so forcefully asserted himself within a few weeks that he became the dominating figure.

In the early morning hours of January 28 1547, the King died. His last request had been to see Thomas Cranmer. When the archbishop arrived he found the King in the throes of death. The King stretched out his hand and for the last time the two men, so unlike in character, locked their hands. Cranmer asked the King for a sign of his trust in Christ, and with one last thrust of his ebbing strength the King pressed his hand.[37]

So died a strange man. Few men in the 16th century pursued policies more erratic and bizarre, more brilliant and disgusting. Tellingly, one of the foreign ambassadors had once called him 'an old fox.'[38] And yet, when the lord chancellor announced his death to Parliament, there were tears in his eyes.

### The Edwardian Revolution

'The trumpets sounded with great melody and courage to the comfort of all them that were present.' So the chronicler reported the scene at the King's passing. Henry's nine-year-old son, Edward, ascended the throne, the sixth English king to bear the name. He was a handsome youth, with an angular face that resembled his mother's.

His *Literary Remains* show that he was intelligent and devout, a bit perplexed about what was going on about him, yet anxious to learn.

The change in England's rule could not have been more dramatic. The crown passed from a strong and autocratic ruler to a child, and power in the land to a group of councillors, sixteen in number, designated as Council of Regency. Henry had provided for equality on this Council, but the Duke of Somerset promptly saw to his own appointment as Lord Protector and within two months the Council had been transformed into an advisory group for Somerset. The people called Somerset the 'good duke' and he was indeed a conscientious, intelligent, and able figure. But the country was beset by more problems than he could handle—a precarious financial situation, restlessness among the peasants, uncertainty about religion. To solve them all required more ability and luck than Somerset could muster.

With respect to the religious problem the continuation of Henry's policy suggested itself as the best solution. Somerset indeed professed to this approach when he announced that 'he would suffer no innovations in religion during the king's mastery's young age.'[39] But Protestant sentiment was widespread and Henry's powerful personality no longer kept matters in check. A host of would-be reformers who had lived an uneasy truce between outer conformity and inner persuasion during the Henrician rule advocated substantial religious change. On the Council the sentiment was divided between Protestants and Henrician Catholics, but Somerset's own religious conviction swung the pendulum in the Protestant direction.

In July 1547 a book of homilies was issued, entitled *Certain Sermons or Homilies Appointed by the King's Majesty to be declared and read by all parsons, vicars, and curates,* every Sunday. Cranmer had contributed the homily on salvation and it gave the book an unmistakable Protestant ring. By and large the homilies were moralistic in tone and inveighed heavily against 'the fear of death,' 'whoredom and adultery,' 'strife and contention,' and stressed 'the reading of Holy Scripture' and 'good works.' The Injunctions which ordered the use of the homilies provided that the clergy were to obtain within three months 'the New Testament both in Latin and in English, with the Paraphrase upon the same of Erasmus.'[40]

Parliament met in November 1547 and repealed the Six Articles Act, the statutes against heretics and Lollards, and removed all restrictions on the printing and reading of Scripture. Catholics, theretofore under the threat of the Treason Act, and Protestants, theretofore under the threat of the acts against heretics, could breathe more easily. Aside from testifying to Somerset's own religious perspective this parliamentary move may be interpreted as an effort to still the waves of religious excitement. For such had indeed reached England and it was obvious that the country was ready to discuss the issues that had perturbed the Continent for three decades. Richard Smith, professor at Oxford, reflected that 'the nation was everywhere afflicted with so great miseries, shaken with so many differences of sects, tossed with so many waves of divers opinions, as scarcely any country ever before was.'[41] The point was well taken, for the easing of legal restrictions unleashed a flood of Protestant propaganda.

The focal point of the doctrinal agitation was Communion. On this issue a variety of concerns came to the fore—the repudiation of the notion of the reenactment of Christ's sacrifice on the Cross in the Mass, the demand for the reception of both elements and for alternate interpretations of the nature of Christ's presence in the elements other than transubstantiation.

An 'Order of Communion' was issued in March 1548. Its stipulations were somewhat vague. Thus, Communion under both kinds was suggested, but not made obligatory. Of greater importance was the insertion of English prayers in the divine service. Subsequently a commission, with Cranmer and other 'bishops and learned men,' was appointed to draft a new liturgy. In January 1549 Parliament discussed the proposal of the Committee, approved it and ordered its introduction. *The booke of the common prayer and administration of the Sacraments*, as its title read, was introduced by the body politic without approval of a convocation.

The *Book of Common Prayer* is one of the famous documents of the English tongue. One reason lies in its beautiful form. While its theology is often ambiguous, the polish of its prose has rarely been matched. In the *Book of Common Prayer*, spanning centuries and oceans, the ancient saying *lex orandi, lex credendi*—the law of prayer is the law of faith—has found expression. The cadences of its prayers have expressed the piety of the Anglican tradition and indeed of English-speaking Protestantism.

The sources of the *Book of Common Prayer* were several and heterogeneous: the Sarum Breviary, from Salisbury; the divine office of Francisco de Quinonez, the great liturgical genius of the early 16th century; several Continental Protestant church orders. But the whole is greater than its parts. The several sources were fused into a creative unity. While the medieval tradition provided the basic outline, everything smacking of Catholicism was omitted

—exorcism in Baptism, the use of incense and holy water in burial, the consecration of the oil for the anointing of the sick. A few traditional practices were continued, such as the prayer for the dead and Extreme Unction. The most distinct changes were made with respect to Communion. The prayer of consecration was followed by a general confession, to be offered by one of the communicants. All references to the sacrifice of the Mass were omitted. The words of the *Book of Common Prayer* were in the vernacular. People could speak them and listen to them. The mystery of the ancient office, spoken in Latin, disappeared and the translucency of the vernacular took its place.

The Act of Uniformity which introduced the *Book of Common Prayer* prohibited the use of other forms of worship: this was the extent of religious conformity imposed. At issue was public worship and only the clergy were held responsible for compliance. No effort was made to establish conformity of belief, to require attendance at worship, to supervise the lives of the faithful—or not so faithful. Catholic worship was abolished, but within the framework of the *Book of Common Prayer* various theological interpretations were possible. Somerset, whose imprint on the course of ecclesiastical events was obvious, was a latitudinarian at heart and he found a kindred soul in Cranmer. And there were others, such as William Turner, who argued in their pamphlets that diversity of theological views need not entail persecution.

Still, the Act may have precipitated an uprising, the deeper causes of which reached back into the early part of the century. Prices had risen drastically; according to some observers they trebled in the first half of the century. Population had increased much faster than did productivity, and this, too, constituted a problem. One problem was the so-called enclosures, a result of the effort on the part of landlords to deprive tenants of their land and convert it into sheep pasture—English wool was a highly sought commodity in Europe.

Social reformers, the so-called 'Commonwealth Men,' were propounding their remedies concerning the alleviation of social ills. Though in actual fact the sheep enclosures were quite insignificant, except in the midlands, the noise made by the pamphleteers drowned out the economic realities. People thought this to be a problem, and their sentiment made all the difference. Hugh Latimer, John Hales, and Thomas Smith were the outstanding representatives, and the eminent document was the *Discourse of the Common Weal of this Realm of England*. Somerset appointed several commissions to investigate the compliance with various acts regulating enclosures, but nothing came of these.

This was the setting for several uprisings, in Devon and Cornwall in the West and in Norfolk in the East, that occurred in the summer of 1549. In Devon the insurrection followed on the heels of the introduction of the *Book of Common Prayer*. The demands of the rebels, formulated in 15 articles, revealed a curious mixture of economic and religious concerns; yet the basic grievance was religious. The Mass was to be reinstituted; the Six Articles were to be restored, as was the use of Latin in Scripture and the divine service. Cornishmen, so it was argued, could not understand English any better than Latin.

In Devon and Cornwall it was a conservative rebellion, in economics as well as in theology, whereas the uprising in Norfolk in September, under the leadership of Robert Kett, conformed to the pattern of the German Peasants' War: social and economic demands were clothed in the new religious slogans. The Norfolk rebels used the *Book of Common Prayer* in their services. The religious sentiment in Robert Kett's 29-point petition—akin to the German Twelve Articles of 1525—pertained more to the place of the Church in society than to theology proper: the ownership of land, the education of youth, the integrity of the village priest.

Within weeks of the suppression of the rebellion Somerset was arrested and sent to the Tower by order of the Council. Thereby the first phase of Edwardian rule came to an end, and the scene began to be dominated by John Dudley, Earl of Warwick, the main instigator of Somerset's fall. Dudley was an egotistical opportunist, willing to engage in whatever intrigue seemed most advantageous to him. His father had been beheaded by Henry VIII for conspiracy: the son may have been predisposed to walk the path of intrigue and scheming. In all probability Dudley was without religious conviction, though before his death on the scaffold he confessed that he had always been a Catholic, a surprising statement from the lips of a man who led England onto a distinct Protestant course. He had greatly profited from the religious change and its revocation would have had disadvantageous consequences for him. Moreover, he was a man greedy for power, and he may have sensed that only the consolidation of Protestantism would thwart Mary's accession to the throne. Religious policy in England became pronouncedly Protestant. The new bishops—Nicholas Ridley in London, John Hooper in Gloucester, and Miles Coverdale in Exeter—were avant-garde reformers. Tunstall and Heath, the outspoken conservative bishops, were deprived of their sees. Even Cranmer, up to that time a rather moderate Protestant, began to move to a more aggressive position. To what extent he was responsible for a revision of the *Book of Common Prayer* is uncertain. At any rate, in March 1552 the second Act of Uniformity was passed by Parliament, which ordered the introduction of a new prayer book. The new edition had commendable words for the old, calling it 'agreeable to the Word of God and the primitive Church,' but here obviously the left hand (the preface) did not know what the right (the book itself) was doing, for the changes, particularly in the section on Communion, were drastic. The terms 'Mass' and 'altar' were no longer used. In the first prayer book the minister, in distributing the elements, said: 'The body of our Lord Jesus Christ which was given for thee preserve thy body and soul into everlasting life.' The second prayer book replaced this with the following: 'Take and eat this in remembrance that Christ died for thee and feed on him in thy heart by faith with thanksgiving.' The emphasis was on 'remembrance.' With this new book the English Church was as distinctly Protestant as it ever was to be, especially since Catholic vestments were also forbidden.

After the new prayer book had been approved and was already in print, John Knox, the Scottish reformer, arrived on the scene and complicated matters. Knox had come to England in 1549 and was temperamentally unable to accept the book as Biblical: to kneel when receiving the Sacrament, as the prayer book enjoined, was for him idolatry. He was able to arouse the conscience of the young King in this matter, but the problem was that the book was in press. The Solomonic solution was to add an appendix, the so-called 'Black Rubric,' which explained that kneeling did not mean adoration but gratitude. Since Christ, and thus his body, was at the right hand of the Father, he could not be adored in the elements. The 'Black Rubric' safeguarded tender consciences as well as theological integrity.

The new prayer book did not lend itself to the same breadth of interpretation as the first one, but the atmosphere of tolerance in England was retained. The second Act of Uniformity which introduced the book was stricter than the first, but it was still sufficiently vague to let matters stand where they had been three years earlier. Church attendance was enjoined upon the people *expressis verbis*, since many people 'following their own sensuality, and living either without knowledge or due fear of God, do willfully and damnably' refuse to attend divine worship.[42] This, however, was the extent of religious regimentation.

Cranmer's other work of importance and permanence was the Forty-two Articles, which in their printed form claimed to have been 'agreed on by the Bishoppes, and other learned menne in the Synode at London,' a misleading statement, for the authorization came from the King, whose mandate of June 9 1553, a few weeks before his death, made subscription mandatory for the clergy and those seeking university degrees. Theologically the Articles were conservatively Protestant. The Lutheran Augsburg Confession, with its stress on the early tradition of the Church, was the obvious paradigm. Even Article 17, on predestination, with its seemingly 'Calvinist' sentiment, can be explained from a Lutheran perspective, for the Article merely asserted that God had chosen to redeem some men through Christ, and considered the human side of election as Luther would have put it. The eucharistic teaching of Article 29 was vague, though it was clearly closer to Zurich than to Wittenberg. Repudiating the theological left (the Anabaptists) and right (Catholics) the Articles sought to steer a middle course.

Practically, the Articles attained no immediate significance. The monarch who succeeded to the throne was of a vastly different theological propensity and categorically dismissed them. But the Articles survived the Marian Restoration and, molded into the Thirty-nine Articles in 1563, have remained the theological foundation of Anglicanism to this day.

After six years of Edwardian rule, Protestantism was firmly embedded in England. Some of this had been accomplished by the foreign divines, notably Martin Bucer, but there were many native reformers to spread the Protestant evangel where it counted most— among the people. From 1548 on, a flood of Protestant writings rolled over the English countryside. Some writers, such as Peter Moone or John Ramsey, were obscure and hardly brilliant. Others, like Hugh Latimer or Richard Cox, were respectable as well as profound. They wrote both distinctly theological tracts and devotional works such as Hugh Latimer's famous *Sermons on the Plough*. These writings increased the Protestant faith in the land.

On July 6 1553 King Edward, the 'godly and virtuous imp,' died. For four days his demise was kept secret while Dudley desperately plotted to influence the course of events. Next in line of succession stood Edward's stepsister, Mary, who would have spelled disaster for the ambitious Dudley. His solution was to eliminate both Mary and her stepsister, Elizabeth, from succession (they could be labeled bastard children) and name the children of Frances Brandon, a niece of the late King, as rightful successors. This in turn placed

Jane Grey next in line. On his deathbed Edward had agreed to this scheme, and four days after his death Jane was proclaimed queen. But the very next day Mary asserted her own rights to the crown, and within another two days Dudley's house of cards had tumbled. He had failed to arrest Mary, who was welcomed by the people with spontaneous and enthusiastic support. The Protestant divines at Cambridge had offered fervent prayers for Dudley's success, but no divine intervention came forth—unless, that is, Mary's spectacular success be so considered.

## The Marian Reaction

What Henry VIII had so desperately striven to avoid, even to the point of sacrificing communion with Rome, occurred in July 1553, when a woman ascended the English throne. It was as if that unfailingly and arrogantly self-confident King had only been teased with his son Edward. Mary Tudor was 37 years of age when she received the royal crown, and those years had left their imprint upon her. Her father had once boasted *ista puella nunquam plorat* (this girl never cries),[48] a most telling characterization of his daughter. Though by nature gentle and simple, Mary possessed harsh features that were the result of experience. Rejected by her father and mistreated by her brother and his Council, hers had been an unhappy life, which found comfort only in religion. Naturally, this was the religion of her mother—Catholicism. This was her life, and little else mattered. Mary had stood aloof from the English scene for more than two decades and did not comprehend that the religious changes undertaken by her father and brother had become accepted by the people. She was mistaken when she took the wave of popular enthusiasm as an approval of her Catholic faith.

Mary ascended the English throne at a time when tranquility had to be restored. Had she risen to the call of the hour she would have become a great ruler. But history has given her the ugly name of 'Bloody Mary.' This is ironic, since Mary possessed deep piety, personal integrity, and noble ideals—an uncommon accumulation of qualities for a Tudor. But epitaphs are written, for better or for worse, by posterity, and in this instance posterity appeared on the scene all too quickly. Had Mary lived as long as her sister Elizabeth, English religious history might have taken a different turn. Everywhere the will of the ruler succeeded, if given time, in determining the religious sentiment of the people. Mary undoubtedly could have done the same. This is not to underestimate the impact of Protestantism in the land, but generalizes what is a standard characteristic of the Reformation in Europe: only by attaining political control could Protestantism score permanent success. The trouble with Mary's rule was, above all, neither her religion nor anything else but its brevity. Five short years could not assure the advent of a lasting Catholic era in England.

Still, Mary committed more than her share of blunders. She was unable to translate her noble qualities into action that would be congenial to the English people. Her attitude was almost that of a surgeon performing an operation, determined to bring about improvement. The English people had forsaken the Catholic faith, and she was going to rectify this evil. This was her foremost task, even though her initial statements on religion showed a magnanimity rather uncommon in the 16th century. She was going to leave each one free as to the religion he would follow, she said. She must have thought that the English people would quickly return to the Catholic faith; the few who did not could be ignored.

Mary mistook the English temper. As soon as she recognized this, the situation changed. Several of the 'Protestant' bishops were deprived of their sees and some were arrested. The adamant Protestants emigrated to the Continent, about 800 in all, many of them able and important figures, later known as the 'Marian Exiles.'

Parliament met in October 1553 and passed several bills of repeal pertaining to ecclesiastical legislation. The act which had annulled Henry's marriage with Catherine was rescinded, as were the new definitions of heresy promulgated under Edward. According to the latest version of the law of the land, Mary was the legitimate offspring of a proper marriage. Later Parliament repealed several other statutes which pertained to the prayer book, the prohibition of the Mass, the marriage of the clergy, and episcopal appointments. Mary's intention clearly was to take the country back to 1529. There was considerable resistance in Parliament to the changes— one-quarter to one-third of the members dissented—surely a telling evidence for the extent of Protestant sentiment among its members. At the touchy matter of the restoration of papal supremacy Parliament balked outright, and there was also strong indication that the restitution of monastic property would run into trouble.

Not all Englishmen were willing to accept the reversal of ecclesiastical policy. Wales, Warwickshire, Kent, Devon, Leicestershire were restless and threatened to rise in rebellion, but only the situation in Kent constituted a danger to the crown. Led by Sir

Thomas Wyatt, an uprising occurred there. Initially the rebels were successful and marched on London. The Queen had been told to leave the city, but in a dramatic appearance before the mayor and aldermen she told them that she would stay. She did have the stuff of courage. London did not fall—and neither did Mary and her throne. Wyatt was captured and the Queen's vengeance fell upon him and the other leaders of the conspiracy.

The thorny matter of the re-establishment of the Catholic faith in England remained unresolved. Mary still bore the title of 'Supreme Head of the Church,' even though in practice she used the nondescript 'etc.' in its stead. The lands of the Church continued to be in illegal hands and the pope's sentence against England still stood. Upon Mary's succession, Pope Julius III had appointed Reginald Pole as legate to England to bring about reconciliation. When he finally arrived in England in November 1554, he proved to be a tough customer, for he insisted on the restitution of the Church lands. This would have meant far-reaching repercussions, since the lands had often changed hands and the question as to who should make restitution defied an easy practical solution.

The touchy problem of Church lands constituted the main stumbling block in the return to the religion of the Fathers. Once it had been made clear that the formal restitution of Catholicism did not mean the forceful reassignment of these lands to the Catholic Church, no formidable resistance remained. As soon as the present owners of the Church lands realized that their property would remain untouched, they saw no reason why they could not condone and passively accept the changes. After having experienced no less than four changes in the official religion of the land (including the two undertaken under Edward), the English people had tired of the religious controversy and theological squabble, and were willing to accommodate themselves to any policy. The most adamant Protestant partisans were on the Continent: this fact had some bearing on the ease with which Mary's ecclesiastical changes were accepted in England; it meant, moreover, that a body of men of ardent religious conviction was absent from England. Of equal importance was the nature of Marian Catholicism, or, to put it differently, the difference between the formal restoration of the Catholic religion and a genuine interest in things Catholic on the part of the people. The former came easily enough. The latter proved to be an impossibility. Mary Tudor had remained aloof from the impressive process of Catholic revitalization and renewal that had been taking place on the Continent for some time. Hers was still the strong but quiescent

Catholicism of the early decades of the century. Nothing illustrates her ecclesiastical temperament better than the fact that she failed to avail herself of the most dynamic force Catholicism had then to offer—the newly founded Society of Jesus.

In addition, there were the disagreements between Pope Paul IV and Cardinal Pole (and the Queen)—another instance of the pathetic fact that the proponents of the old faith frequently were unable to pursue a common cause. Rounding out the picture are the anti-Spanish sentiment in England and the drastic weakening of episcopal ranks during the last twelve months of Mary's reign. English Catholicism in 1558 hardly possessed the inner vitality to withstand any attacks.

Parliament considered reconciliation with Rome toward the end of November. On the last day of that month came the moment for which Mary had been waiting for over 20 years. Speaking through the voice of Parliament, the English people declared themselves 'very sorry and repentant of the schism and disobedience committed in this realm.'[44] England, after a lapse of two decades, was Catholic again. The genuine religious sentiment was something else again. The Venetian ambassador reported that there were three factions: Catholic, Protestant, and 'the third is a neuter, being indifferent.' Parliament passed several bills to provide the legal basis for the religious restoration. The ancient law against heresy was revived, and in January 1555 all of Henry VIII's ecclesiastical legislation—from the Statute of Appeals to the last Supremacy Act—was repealed, while explicit provisions for the protection of the holders of Church lands were made.

At that time the persecution of the religious dissenters began, and it did not terminate until four years later when Mary's reign itself came to an end. The instigator was the Queen herself, who must have thought she did penance for the heresy of her father and brother. She showed herself thereby a true child of the age, for religious diversity was, for 16th-century man, a pill too bitter to swallow. Diversity seemed to entail the disruption of order which was feared as much as the possibility that the dissenter might infect others with his heretical venom. Since criminal law was severe, and capital punishment an all-too-common matter, the Marian persecutions were in a way neither particularly unique nor ruthless. The number of victims was less than 300, but the psychological impact of the systematic effort was substantial in a country that for more than two decades had experienced gradual alienation from Catholicism.

And the pen of John Foxe added a spectacular glow to the persecution and the martyrs. Foxe would not have been so successful, however, if his work had not spoken to the sentiment of the people. He was far away on the Continent when it all happened, but with indefatigable exuberance he went about collecting his material. Published first in Latin at Basel in 1559, his story appeared in an expanded English version four years later. The title of Foxe's work set the tone for its content, for no cool and neutral report of fact was it meant to be, but a passionate defense of a great cause: *Actes and Monuments of These Latter and Perillous Dayes, touching matters of the Church, wherein are comprehended and described the great persecutions and horrible troubles that have bene wrought and practised by the Romishe Prelates.* In the preface came the inevitable apology to the reader who might feel—together with the author, so we are assured—that in light of the 'infinite multitude' of books another publication may be 'superfluous and needeles.' Foxe's implication was, of course, that it was not superfluous, for he meant not merely to tell a story but score a point. He did not mean to be a historian. He was little concerned, for example, about the details of the 'King's great matter,' but lengthily narrated how it led to the spread of the Gospel. As in the case of other 16th-century martyrologists, Foxe's credibility has been questioned, though recent research has vindicated his judicious and accurate handling of the facts.

For several hundred years the *Book of Martyrs*, as Foxe's book is commonly known, was a second Bible for the English people, frequently chained beside the Great Bible in English parish churches. Such fame was hardly only theological. The content of the *Book of Martyrs* made it fascinating both for those who sought spiritual edification and for those who wanted to be taken to the dungeons and have chills up and down their spines—reading about martyrs writing in their own blood on the walls of their jails, or about persecutors with 'monstrous making and misshapen fashion of feet and toes.'

The Marian persecution hardly endeared the Catholic faith to the English people, who were shocked by the harsh suppression of a religious sentiment on the part of those who themselves had shared it a few years earlier. The country was perturbed by the burnings and there was public sympathy for the victims. The most illustrious victim of the persecution was Thomas Cranmer, who on Mary's succession had been deposed as Archbishop of Canterbury. When he was brought to trial, he first confessed to his Protestant convictions boldly. But he soon wavered. A brief recantation which acknowledged the pope to be the head of the Church of England 'so far as the laws of God and the laws and customs of this realm will permit' marked the beginning, and five additional and far-reaching recantations followed. The last one confessed that he had misused his office and authority, that he had exceeded Saul in malice and wickedness, that he was a blasphemer, a persecutor, and contumelious.[45]

The chronicler will never know Cranmer's turmoil while his hand wrote those words. Was he sincere? Did he grasp the straw to save his life? Cranmer had been catapulted to prominence against his desire. At his trial he recalled that upon receiving word of his nomination to the archbishopric he delayed his return to England for weeks, hoping that the King would forget about him. Henry did not, Cranmer became archbishop, and rose to be the King's trusted ecclesiastical advisor. Cranmer was a scrupulous scholar, ever willing to follow new insights and suggestions. He was persuaded that by divine ordination a sovereign exercised authority in the external affairs of the Church and that the people were called upon to render obedience. When Mary ascended the throne and demanded his obedience, he found himself on the horns of a dilemma, created by his temperament and theological perspective—his willingness to change and to be submissive.

On the day of his execution, however, he spoke differently. Every man hoped to give an exhortation at the time of his death, he remarked, and this he wanted to do: 'I come to the great thing that troubleth my conscience more than any other thing that I ever said or did in my life, the setting abroad of writings contrary to the truth.' He renounced everything which he had written since his degradation: 'And foreasmuch as my hand offended in writing contrary to my heart, therefore my hand shall first be punished. For if I may come to the fire, it shall be first burned.'[46]

It matters little that Cranmer was Protestant and his judges Catholic. If the ecclesiastical labels had been reversed—as they were at other places and at other times during that eventful century—the story would have the same meaning. The lesson of the religious persecutions of the 16th century is not only that men then killed for religion as men today kill for political or social ideals but that, in the end, man's spirit does prevail.

Matthew Parker, Archbishop of Canterbury under Queen Elizabeth, offered the most incisive commentary on Cranmer. In the margin of *Bishop Cranmer's Recantacyons* he wrote two words—not of condemnation but of explanation: *homines sumus*—'we are all human beings.' Thomas Cranmer, man of high achievements and distressing shortcomings, serves as a reminder that history is not only made by heroes and saints but by human beings, simple and complicated, courageous and weak.

The Marian persecution did not extinguish Protestant sentiment in England. Some Protestant congregations, notably the one in London, went underground but continued their corporate life. Foxe's *Book of Martyrs* contains striking accounts of Protestant activity during the years of Mary's reign. Protestant leaders who had not gone into exile pursued a life of study without surrendering their Protestant convictions.

Perhaps the country was holding its breath. The North was generally conservative and thus more congenial to the Catholic religion, but even there minor annoyances—about married clergy or monastic lands—cropped up with almost predictable regularity. In short, the English people went about their daily chores and showed no enthusiasm for the old religion. There were few zealous Catholics in the land, no eloquent Catholic pamphleteers, no gifted Catholic preachers. The Catholic faith was imposed from the top, and this was bound to be a failure.

In November 1558 after long delays and great reluctance, Mary consented to name Elizabeth as her successor, provided her step-sister would agree to maintain the Catholic religion and pay her debts. Mary had formally accepted the Catholic faith. An air of resignation overcame her and her mind seemed somewhere else. A few days before her death she remarked 'what good dreams she had, seeing many little children like angels play before her, singing pleasing notes.' In the early morning hours of November 17 1558, Mary died and 43 years of an unhappy life came to an end. Later that same day her chief advisor, Cardinal Pole, also passed away, as if one star had governed both their destinies or as if the one was not to face the future without the other.

A little over five years had passed since Mary had come to London. The cheers which then had greeted her had faded and the joyful brightness of that August morning had given way to the dreary cold of November. At Mary's death the English people shed few tears to grace her departure. And this was a telling verdict. She had ventured to accomplish great things *ad majorem dei gloriam* and, outwardly, she had accomplished them. But her zeal had proved a poor guide in the affairs of state; she had pushed too hard too fast. Perhaps this was due to her dogmatic zeal, perhaps to her awareness that she was living on borrowed time and what was to be done had to be done quickly. At the end, at any rate, stood failure in her

religious policy, for even though the Catholic faith had been formally restored in England, the heart of the people had not been
won.

In history the seal of success is the permanence of accomplishment, even as the seal of failure is repudiation. Did Mary Tudor
ever ponder that her stepsister Elizabeth might repudiate what she
herself stood for? Were it not for the sad fact that she committed
the blunder of making martyrs, her name would be written, as has
been remarked, as on water.

### The Elizabethan Settlement

The ruler who succeeded to the English throne in November 1558
was again a woman—Mary's stepsister Elizabeth, 25 years of age,
tall, full of poise, with reddish hair, not particularly attractive,
though with striking eyes. Rather like her stepsister, Elizabeth had
had a trying youth. At her birth there had been the disappointment
over her sex. Soon thereafter her mother had lost the King's favor,
and Elizabeth lived to experience the consequences of being considered a bastard. Her stepsister Mary had despaired over a similar
experience. But not so Elizabeth. She learned the art of diplomacy
—a bitter process, to be sure—but one that enabled her to rule England superbly for some 45 years. When she died England was all the
more powerful for her reign. 'I pray God save her Grace, long to
reign over us, to the glory of God,' a contemporary had written when
she came to the throne.[47] And so she did. During her reign England
rose to be the first power in Europe.

The foremost problem facing the new Queen was what to do
about religion. When Edwin Sandys wrote to Heinrich Bullinger in
Zurich upon Pole's death, 'We have nothing to fear . . . for dead men
do not bite,' he expressed the sentiment of the gospellers, who felt
the time ripe for a change.[48] Whatever religious conviction Elizabeth
may have held, in 1558 she acted as a good Protestant, though perhaps due more to circumstances than to personal conviction. As a
daughter of Anne Boleyn she was, of course, illegitimate in the eyes
of the Catholic Church, and at the news of her succession Pope Paul
IV plainly expressed himself along such lines. She would hardly embrace the religion that so labeled her. And what began as political
expedience may well have settled as personal habit, though the
Queen never became a Protestant zealot. Scholars disagree about her
religiosity, some seeing her as a bulwark of the Protestant faith,

while others suggest that she was what the French called a *politique*, an Englishwoman first and a religious partisan second. The evidence is inconclusive. Elizabeth kissed the Bible in public, but she was a good actress and may well have done this for the gallery.

She spoke highly of the Augsburg Confession, and a charmingly simple verse, perhaps apocryphal, expressed her view of the Lord's Supper: [49]

> 'Twas God the word that spake it,
> He took the Bread and brake it;
> And what the word did make it,
> That I believe and take it.

Evidently she did have some religious opinions, for at the execution of Mary Queen of Scots she told Parliament, 'When first I took the scepter, I was not unmindful of God the Giver, and therefore began my reign with his service and the religion I had been born in, bred in, and I trust shall die in.'[50]

If Elizabeth's personal circumstances, her background and religious convictions, were one factor in disposing her to venture yet another alteration of the official ecclesiastical state of affairs, the temper of the English people undoubtedly was another. The inner fiber of Catholicism in England had been damaged beyond repair. For almost a generation England had not really known the traditional faith (excepting, of course, the five years of Marian rule) and dynamic Catholic leadership was absent. No enthusiastic and youthful proponents of the old faith had come to the fore during the five years of restored Catholicism.

The slight likelihood of a continuation of Catholicism as the official religion left the question as to the specific nature of the change altogether open. Elizabeth, in other words, had the option of moving into one of several directions. She changed the official religion of England for the fourth time in 30 years. At the beginning she could hardly do anything else but reverse the religious policy of her stepsister, but this need not have meant more than the return to the religion of her father's reign. To do more was hazardous and she must have known it. Elizabeth told the Spanish ambassador that she wanted to restore religion as her father left it. The leaders of the Church were solidly Catholic and the international situation, in light of the ongoing war against France, was precarious. The ardent Protestants were abroad, and even though the English people were weary of the religious persecution under Mary, Catholicism continued strong. The settlement she eventually chose was neither the only nor indeed the self-evident one. The perpetuation of the kind of settlement wrought by her stepbrother was by no means inevitable. What Elizabeth herself wanted seems clear, namely, a settlement at once limited and conservative, one that would have allowed her to make further changes (of whatever quality) at a later date. The meager evidence also indicates what the Commons wanted, namely, the comprehensive reestablishment of Protestantism. Accordingly, demand stood against demand. The outcome was a compromise, where neither got all it wanted, but more than the other side originally was willing to concede.

At first the new Queen made haste slowly. She prohibited any changes in the order of worship, and the list of her titles in the first state document had an enigmatic 'etc.' at the place where both her father and brother had used the title of 'Supreme Head of the Church.'

Toward the end of January, Parliament met. A bill was introduced to 'restore the supremacy of the Church of England, etc. to the Crown.' The evidence concerning this bill and what happened in Parliament is embarrassingly enigmatic. Obviously the supremacy was to be reintroduced. But what else? Elizabeth seemingly was content to let the details of a religious settlement rest until a later time. Such a circumspect policy would have allowed her to settle the political problems before the religious ones.

When the Protestant Commons received this bill they decided to take advantage of it, adding enough Protestant riders to make it a comprehensive instrument for religious change. The more conservative Lords changed the bill back into its original form, whereupon the Commons diplomatically passed the bill which shortly before they had so drastically revised. Simultaneously, however, they approved a bill which reestablished Protestant worship. Thus the Commons had made their sentiment plain. They wanted more than the supremacy and the possibility of additional changes in the future: they wanted the introduction of Protestantism right then and there.

On Wednesday of Holy Week, March 22 1559, both Houses of Parliament had passed the original bill, which needed the Queen's assent to become law. Elizabeth had every intention of giving this assent, but then changed her mind. Parliament, instead of being dissolved, was only adjourned until after Easter. What had happened? The Queen had been informed of the peace concluded at Cateau Cambrésis between France, Spain, and England. The international situation had cleared and Elizabeth could face the domestic issues without regard to possible complications abroad.

Moreover, Elizabeth may have realized that there was no likelihood that Catholics would agree to any change, no matter how conservative. The Convocation of Canterbury had voiced a strong protest against the proposed bill, a noteworthy departure from 30 years of ecclesiastical silence and all-too-willing concurrence with royal decrees. The leaders of the Church would not fall in line. The Queen was clearly caught in a dilemma: the Catholic hierarchy was intransigent, unwilling to accept the supremacy. The Protestants in the Commons were adamant. In the end Elizabeth found it the lesser evil to move into the Protestant direction.

Upon reconvening, Parliament began its consideration of two new bills, one dealing with supremacy, the other with uniformity. The bishops put up formidable resistance—the Bishop of Chester asserting that the faith must depend on more than the whims of Parliament—but in the end both houses approved both measures.

In substance, the Act of Supremacy undid Mary's repeal of Henry VIII's ecclesiastical legislation: the Act of Annates, the Statute of Appeals, the Consecration of Bishops, and the Submission of the Clergy. In addition, Mary's submission to Rome also was rescinded. For the second time within 30 years England had cut its ties with Rome and the Church in England was, once again, the Church of England. The clock had been set back to 1547, though there were a few additional changes. The Queen was not designated 'supreme head' of the Church, but its 'supreme governor.' Surely, more than semantic subtlety was involved here. Elizabeth was not the self-styled and self-confident theologian her father had yearned to be. She was a partner of Parliament and her 'governorship' was indirect at best. The new title lacked the theological significance of the old one, and, as it turned out, both theory and practice of Elizabeth's rule were different. The Act of Supremacy also redefined heresy, or rather it repealed, to speak more exactly, Mary's Act which had revived the old heresy laws. The Act made Scripture, the decrees of the councils of Nicaea, Constantinople, Ephesus, and Chalcedon, and Parliament acting with the consent of the Convocation, the basis on which heresy was to be judged.

The Act of Uniformity reintroduced the second Edwardian Act of Uniformity which had accompanied the prayer book of 1552. A few changes were made in the prayer book. In the litany the minister's petition, 'From the tyranny of the Bishop of Rome and all his detestable enormities' was omitted and the 'Black Rubric,' the unauthorized marginalia of 1552, disappeared. The most spectacular change, however, concerned the Lord's Supper and consisted in the juxtaposition of the words of distribution of the 1549 and 1552 editions. Theologically, this meant a compromise between the Lutheran view of the real presence and the Zwinglian view of a spiritual presence in Communion.

It is not known if Elizabeth thought the settlement permanent. But, while its coming into being was the result of accident and compromise, it early began to be seen as a profound and wise act. Through the centuries the settlement has shown an amazing ability to be many things to many men, admixing Protestant substance with Catholic principle. Indeed, the Anglican settlement delivered what some of the early Continental reformers had promised: a reformation only of the recent and blatant errors of the Church.

With the statutory settlement of religion out of the way, the theological definition of the Elizabethan Church remained as the major unresolved issue. Reformation England virtually had a tradition of theological nonchalance: Henry VIII had waited until 1539 before promulgating the Six Articles and Edward until 1553 before issuing the Forty-two Articles. The new Archbishop of Canterbury, Matthew Parker, evidently thought a doctrinal clarification a necessary part of the settlement and drafted Eleven Articles in 1559.[51] He circulated them among the clergy, but his theologically general statement lacked official endorsement from either Parliament or Convocation and could lay claim only to the distinction that it had been published by the Queen's printer.

More influential (and more substantial) than Parker's quasi-official tour de force was the treatise of John Jewel entitled *Apologia ecclesiae anglicanae*, which was published in 1562 and came out in an English translation (*An Apologie or answere in defence of the Churche of Englande*) two years later. The concern of the learned and irenic book was to show that Scripture, the Fathers, and the early Church agreed with the teaching of the English Church. What was taught in England was not new, but ancient and thus truly Catholic. 'We are come,' wrote Jewel, 'as near as we possibly could, to the church of the apostles and of the old catholic bishops and fathers, which church we know hath hitherunto been sound and perfect and . . . a pure virgin, spotted as yet with no idolatry nor with any foul or shameful fault; and have directed according to their customs and ordinances not only our doctrine but also the sacraments and the form of common prayer.'[52]

Jewel's was a personal statement only. Convocation addressed itself to the problem in 1563 and came forth with a revision of Cranmer's Forty-two Articles. After extended discussion seven of these (those dealing with grace, blasphemy against the Holy Spirit, the keeping of the Law, and with four ancient heresies) were omitted, the wording of some of the remaining ones was changed, four new articles (on the Holy Spirit, good works, 'the wicked which do not eat the body of Christ in the use of the Lord's Supper,' and Communion under both kinds) were added, to bring this theological revision to the so-called Thirty-nine Articles.

Theologically the new Articles were evasive. On their surface they seemed to propound a moderate Protestantism, though last century John Henry Newman thought it possible to give them a Catholic interpretation. The concern of the framers of the document was to invoke the teaching of the early Church, repeating in a way what Philipp Melanchthon had intended with his Augsburg Confession of 1530. One can see connections between these two documents, though at one crucial point, that of Communion, the Thirty-nine Articles (Articles XXVIII and XXIX) propounded a view that had been bitterly repudiated by Luther: 'The Body of Christ is given, taken, and eaten, in the Supper, only after an heavenly and spiritual manner.'

Parliament approved the Articles in 1566, but Elizabeth declined to give her assent. She soothingly asserted that the Articles contained the faith 'she doth openly profess' but added that she could not approve them because she disliked their form.[53] Obviously, she had more than stylistic scruples. Her official approval would have formalized the theological character of the settlement of religion in England and she was concerned about possible international repercussions.

Formal approval did not come until 1571.[54] By then the settlement had for all practical purposes become permanent, and the papal bull of excommunication at long last (in February 1570) was hurled against Elizabeth. The ways of Rome and Canterbury had definitely parted.

Additional obstacles had to be overcome before ecclesiastical life in England returned to relative normality. At Mary's death five bishoprics had been vacant. Cardinal Pole's death added a sixth, and by the end of the year there were actually ten. Once the problem of maintaining the apostolic succession had been solved with the help of Henrician and Edwardian bishops, the vacant sees were filled with Protestant émigrés from the Continent and divines who had escaped the Marian persecution in England. The appointments were

H

made slowly while the income from the sees was, as John Jewel wrote, 'gloriously swelling the exchequer.'[55] While generalizations are difficult, one is inclined to suggest that most of the new bishops were more staunchly Protestant than either the settlement or the Queen.

The task of guiding the religious settlement between the Scylla and Charybdis of determined and moderate Protestantism was difficult. No sooner had the settlement been concluded than it began to be vigorously assailed. It survived because that was what the Queen wanted, and also because of its own remarkable inner strength.

### The Puritan Dissent

The most persistent attack upon the Elizabethan settlement came from the so-called Puritans, and we must pause to speak of their principles as well as of their history. 'The hotter sort of protestants are called puritans,' was the simple verdict of one contemporary.[56] One might call the Puritans the 'reformers of the Reformation,' for they were persuaded that to realize the Biblical ideal, the Reformation (in this instance the settlement) had to be reformed. The Puritan William Fuller pointedly wrote to the Queen 'but halflie by your Majesty hath God bene honoured, his Church reformed and established.'[57] These desired reforms pertained either to matters of practical churchmanship or to theological issues, even though the practical issues entailed theological presuppositions. On the surface, however, the controversy between the Puritans and their opponents seemed to be about embarrassing trifles.

Much has been written on the question of the Puritan temperament, but the matter remains elusive. In a way, 'Puritan' sentiment is timeless, the rigorous insistence on a 'purified' Church, divested of additions and unbiblical impurities. That one of the medieval heretical movements should have used the very name ('Cathari') is surely telling. William Haller's comment that it is difficult to say who was the first and who may prove to be the last Puritan underscores this point.[58] The historian, at any rate, must be careful to distinguish between 'Puritanism' as it emerged in the second half of the 16th century and 'Puritanism' as it characterized the English scene in the 17th century. The former, which will presently be described, was devoid not only of the sectarian propensity (the 16th-century Puritan did not think of leaving the official Church; he wanted to reform it), but it was also without that kind of sour-faced drabness and dedication to the proposition that anything enjoy-able is sinful which the historian of the 17th-century scene so ubiquitously encounters. This introspective sensitivity is well illus-trated by these random entries from the diary of Samuel Ward—a roll call of such shortcomings as 'my immoderate laughter in the Hall att actes at 9 aclock'; 'my immoderate eating of walnutes and cheese after supper, wherby I did distemper my body'; 'my con-fused lecture which I red to my auditores'; 'my want of meditation of Cyrist when I ly downe to sleep.'[59]

Then there is the matter of Puritan origins. Many suggestions have been made—the Lollard heritage, the influence of the vernacu-lar Scriptures, or the general revival of learning. There is also the influence of the Continental Reformation, particularly of the Cal-vinist variety. The best explanation would take all these factors into consideration and conclude that indigenous (and timeless) sentiment was strengthened by Continental influence.

The significance of this Continental-Calvinist tradition must not be overlooked. Many of the Marian exiles, who had preferred a resi-dence abroad to the hazards of England, had encountered a different manner of religious reform than that which they had known in their native land—resolute, comprehensive, dynamic. And there was also a theological setting that demanded their admiration. Both the faith and the life of the Church had been reformed, and the result seemed impressive. Actually, the Marian exiles had become bitterly divided over the question whether the second prayer book did express Bib-lical religion or not. Some of the exiles had openly broken with the prayer book since in their view it contained too many Catholic rem-nants.

These tensions were brought back to England with the return of the exiles, not the moderate ones, of course—those who had used the prayer book in their services abroad—but the adamant ones, such as the followers of John Knox, who on their return found a settle-ment promulgated which was based upon the prayer book. Their opposition was emphatic.

Thus the Elizabethan settlement of religion stands at the be-ginning of Puritanism, since dissatisfaction with it evoked dissent. Those who later became known as 'Puritans' argued that too many vestiges of popery remained in the English Church, and they would have none of it. Impatiently they sought further change. The range of dissatisfaction during the next few years was wide: the prayer book of 1549 was the basis of the settlement; the higher clergy lived in pomp and circumstance; wafers were used in communion; the host was elevated; the service was ritualistic and assigned an inferior place to the sermon; saints' days were observed, and so forth. The list is almost endless. If a common denominator could be established, one's understanding of the sources of Puritanism would be much better. In part, at least, the first Puritan dissent was a reaction to the lukewarmness of those who approved the settlement.

The Puritan debate engrossed England for the better part of a century, attesting, if nothing else, to the measure of religious freedom prevailing there. By and large the Puritan dissenters were able to keep their heads on their shoulders and their pamphlets on the printing presses, though neither task was particularly easy. In all this, one needs to keep in mind that in its initial thrust Puritanism was a clerical movement, spearheaded by the exiles who had returned to England upon Elizabeth's succession. Naturally, there was support among the laity, especially the nobility; the persistent agitation in the Commons for further ecclesiastical change and the establishment of numerous lectureships of Puritan tendency makes this obvious. Still, the preponderance of the clergy and, more importantly, of clerical issues must be noted. The controversy over vestments and polity would exercise (or excite) especially the men of the cloth.

The first clash occurred over ministerial vestments. The Royal Injunctions of 1559 had stipulated the wearing of 'seemly habits, garments, and such square caps' for the clergy.[60] Those who saw such vestments as unbiblical abomination protested. Vestments were a natural point of controversy, for the daily officiating of the clergy formed an ostensible thorn in the flesh of those who abhorred everything that smacked of papal religion. Thomas Sampson wrote, 'What hope is there of any good when our party are disposed to look for religion in these dumb remnants of idolatry?'[61] The need for additional ecclesiastical change seemed nowhere more urgent than here.

By the end of 1564 the antivestments cause had its spokesmen: Thomas Sampson and Laurence Humphrey, both from Oxford. Their opponent was Archbishop Parker, who thought that the two academicians could be silenced by theological colloquies. In January 1565 Elizabeth charged him to take firm measures against such 'dissension or variety' as might 'impair, deface and disturb Christian charity, unity, and concord.'[62] Parker, who may have even had a hand in drafting the Queen's charge, wrote several articles which were to achieve the desired conformity among the clergy and issued them in March 1566 under his own name. These *Advertisements* indicated, among other things, the proper 'apparel for persons ecclesiastical'; they prescribed an oath for the clergy, exacting the surely laudable promise to read one chapter from the Old and the New Testament daily, and demanded conformity to the vestment provision of the document.[63]

The dissenters were unwilling to yield. Disturbances of worship services occurred and a literary controversy began. A host of pamphlets issued from the printing presses, often distinguished more by zealous devotion than by incisive argumentation. The author of *A briefe discourse against the outwarde apparell and Ministring Garmentes of the Popishe Church*, for example, thought that the issue lent intself to poetic consideration: [64]

> The Popes attyre, whereof I talke,
> I know to be but vaine:
> Wherefore some men that wittie are,
> to reade mee will disdaine.
> But I woulde wishe that such men shoulde,
> with judgment reade me twise:
> And marke how great an evill it is,
> Gods Preachers to disguise.

The parting of the ways came quickly. In April 1566 Archbishop Parker noted that some 'do profess openly, that they will neither communicate nor come in the church where either the surplice or the cap is, and so I know it is practiced.'[65] In August, Bishop Grindal wrote to Switzerland that there was talk of withdrawal and the establishment of private meetings. In June 1567 came the first actual evidence, when a clandestine gathering of disgruntled souls was uncovered in London. Several of the leaders received a night's lodging in the London jail and were examined the next day by Bishop Grindal. They admitted their opposition to the 'idolatrous, popish and offensive' vestments and asserted that there was no scriptural support for this practice.

Soon there was additional evidence that separatist conventicles were forming at other places in England. Naturally, this development raises the question whether permanent separation was intended. Probably not, though it was natural that the dissenters would seek out one another's company and strengthen their conviction. They hoped for a change of sentiment on the part of their opponents. The Puritans were persuaded that the religious settlement of 1559 was not definitive but could—and would—be changed and modified. This was their hope.

The tensions persisted. In 1572 the simmering fire burst anew into flames. In June appeared *An Admonition to the Parliament*, a devastating catch-all of assorted antisettlement polemic.[66] Not much of the polemic was new, not all was profound, but everything was advanced with a cocksure conviction that acknowledged no contrary argument. Two young London clergymen—youth was as much a common denominator of Puritan sentiment as was the desire to 'purify' the Church, a fact explicitly acknowledged by John Strype's book on Whitgift—named John Field and Thomas Wilcox had collaborated on this *Admonition*. They asked that ministers be 'called' by the congregation, that all ministers be equal, and the 'titles, livings, and offices, by Antichrist devised,' such as archbishop, bishop, and dean, be abolished. The Church should be governed by a simple ministry of ministers, elders, and deacons.

Puritan discontent thus received a new focus—the episcopal form of Church government. At the same time a new leader appeared, Thomas Cartwright, Professor of Divinity at Cambridge. In the spring of 1570 he lectured on the Book of Acts and, measured by this Biblical standard, he found the ecclesiastical practice in England sorely wanting. His proposals were that the offices of archbishop and bishop should be abolished; that deacons and bishops should direct a congregation, the former caring for the physical and the latter for the spiritual needs; that a minister should be assigned to a certain congregation which would elect him.

Cartwright was blamed for the authorship of *An Admonition to the Parliament*, and he promptly became embroiled in a bitter literary feud with John Whitgift, Professor of Divinity at Cambridge. At issue was the principle of scriptural interpretation. Cartwright argued that no practice ought to be allowed in the Church unless there was a scriptural statement permitting it, while Whitgift asserted that Scripture allowed for freedom: 'I find not one certain and perfect kind of government prescribed or commanded in the scriptures to the church of Christ.'[67]

When Matthew Parker died in 1575, he was succeeded by Edmund Grindal, a competent and efficient churchman, and—a committed Protestant. He had been influenced by Martin Bucer, was a figure of international renown, and basically thought the settlement of 1559 open to modification. Promptly he ran into difficulties with the Queen, who sought to have things her way by interfering directly in ecclesiastical affairs. Grindal reacted with vehemence, if lacking etiquette, in language the Queen had never heard before—and was not to hear again: 'I am forced, with all humility, and yet plainly, to profess, that I cannot with safe conscience, and without the offence of the majesty of God, give my assent. . . . Bear with me, I beseech you, Madam, if I choose rather to offend your earthly majesty than to offend against the heavenly majesty of God. And although ye are a mighty prince, yet remember that He which dwelleth in Heaven is mightier.'[68] He was suspended from office from 1577 until his death in 1583.

Grindal's main shortcoming was that he thought the settlement of 1559 not sacrosanct and open to modification. His successor was John Whitgift. If his opponents stood for 'purity' in the Church, he stood for 'discipline.' He was an antiPuritan if anyone was, but at the same time he was a staunch Calvinist; to be the latter seemingly did not exclude being the former. His literary battle with his Cambridge colleague Cartwright had shown him to be a theologian of some stature, and his conduct of ecclesiastical affairs at Worcester, where he had been bishop, revealed his administrative abilities.

Once appointed to the archiepiscopal office, he lost no time to still the waves of ecclesiastical discontent. A set of articles was drawn up as the instrument with which to achieve uniformity. These articles stated that Parker's unsuccessful *Advertisements* were in agreement with the Word of God—for the Puritans a most offensive assertion. Accordingly, the Puritan divines refused to subscribe to the articles. Suppression of Puritan sentiment became more emphatic, and suspensions of nonconforming ministers more frequent. The Puritans countered by organizing 'classes' for fellowship and prayer.

Deep in his heart the Puritan thought that he could somehow or other persuade the Church of England to revise the settlement of 1559 and accept the pattern which he considered Biblical. But as the years passed and this thought became increasingly an illusion, men appeared on the scene who were ready to separate from the Church. Robert Browne, 'dissent incarnate' as he had been called, illustrated the kind of soul-searching and meandering vacillation that characterized those who made the radical break. Twice arrested for nonconformity, he finally crossed the Channel to Holland with a group of faithful followers. Here he published in 1582 his famous pamphlet— *A Treatise of Reformation without tarying for anie, and of the wickedness of those Preachers which will not reforme till the Magistrate commande or compell them.* His thesis was simple. The Church of England was so corrupt and unbiblical that true believers had no choice but to go their own way, 'be they never so few.' Browne de-

nounced the ministers of the English Church as 'dumbe dogges, des-
troiers and mutherers of soules,' indeed, as 'pope's bastards,' and
he joined in the denunciation of the polity and the discipline of the
Anglican Church.

At this time Richard Bancroft, later Archbishop of Canterbury,
came onto the scene. He was a competent ecclesiastic, a skillful theologian, a good administrator, an eloquent preacher who applied his
talents to the suppression of the Puritan party. He also was a man of
no compromise who felt that concessions were neither necessary
nor Biblical. In a famous sermon, preached in February 1589, at
'Paules Crosse,' his repudiation of Puritanism reached its climax.
He asserted that the episcopal system had been used by the Church
from the very beginning.

There was no need to change the English Church, for it is the
'Church which maintaineth without error the faith of Christ . . .
which holdeth up the true doctrine of the Gospel in matters necessary to salvation and preacheth the same.' How 'verie strange,' Bancroft observed, that 'Christ should erect a forme of government for
the ruling of his church' and yet not have it practiced for 1,500
years. Bancroft left little doubt about his belief in the 'old and
present Apostolicall forme of Church-government under her excellent Majestie, by Archbishops or Arch-builders, and Bishops, practiced in the Apostles times.'[69]

The ecclesiastical climate in England became increasingly severe.
In 1593 Penry, Greenwood and Barrow, three adamant Puritans,
were hanged for sedition. That same year the Queen issued an Act
to retain the Queen's subjects in obedience. To attend meetings of
'conventicles' was declared incompatible with the affirmation of the
Queen's supremacy. Offenders were given a period of grace in which
to conform; if they refused, they had to abjure the realm.

About the same time, in 1594, began to appear the most profound apologetic for the Elizabethan settlement, Richard Hooker's
eight books of the *Laws of Ecclesiastical Polity*. The work almost
did not see the printer's ink for lack of interest. It was a voluminous
venture that the 40-year-old divine proposed, and it took considerable effort to get it printed and many years to sell. Puritan writings
occupied the day and the cadences of Hooker's Elizabethan prose
were as difficult to fathom as they were beautiful to read. In 1592 a
publisher pointedly rejected Hooker's work, but two years later the
first four books of the *Laws of Ecclesiastical Polity* appeared.

The first of these books is unquestionably the most famous, for in
it Hooker formulated, in graphic color and grandiose sweep, his

basic assumptions, which were at once Aristotelian and Thomistic: the rationality of God and man, the intrinsic importance and centrality of law, natural and revealed. Against the Puritan assertion that divine law was revealed only in Scripture, Hooker argued that reason, too, is from God and must be used to discern God's will. In the second book came the repudiation of the Puritan assertion that Scripture contained all that is necessary for a religious life. Against this scriptural exclusivism Hooker posited the need for additional authorities—tradition and the Church, wherever Scripture was indifferent or obscure. Hooker argued that the Anglican Church was the perfect expression of such reasonable authority. His remaining books argued against those who assert 'that our form of church-polity is corrupted with popish orders, rites and ceremones'; 'that touching the several public duties of Christian religion, there is amongst us much superstition retained in them'; 'that our laws are corrupt and repugnant to the laws of God'; 'that there ought not to be in the church, bishops'; 'that to no civil prince or governor there may be given such power of ecclesiastical dominion.'

Hooker, a modest and devout man, was an exponent of the tradition of a theologian such as Thomas Aquinas, that affirmed the continuity between man *and* God, the divine *and* the human, not in order to play out one against the other, but in order to make God the more exalted. Hooker put it this way: 'God being the author of nature, her voice is but his instrument.' The genius of the work was the use of the heritage of medieval scholasticism: the *Laws* are only 'by accident a piece of Protestant literature.'

Hooker's work was the most profound exposition of the Anglican way, but it failed to persuade the Puritan protagonists. This was the case not because they were beyond persuasion—though this may have been true—but because what he called peripheral they called fundamental and where he insisted that the Scriptures were silent they argued on behalf of explicit scriptural citations. Hooker's argument accentuated rather than breached the gap between the Anglicans and the Puritans. Indeed, the incisiveness of his work altered the structure of Anglicanism. Theretofore it had been catholic, even subsuming the Puritan dissenters. From then on it became exclusive, making the Puritans very much aware that there was for them no place in the Anglican inn.

## The Catholic Reaction

The story of the Elizabethan settlement is not complete without a reference to the Catholic reaction, for the Anglican *via media* was assailed from the Catholic right no less than from the Puritan left. In some ways this Catholic challenge was more formidable, for, in contrast to the Puritan attack, it had political overtones and international ramifications—though how much was a contested question.

The reaction of the Marian Church to the settlement had been determined. With astounding unanimity the bishops had refused to consider any change, thereby forcing Elizabeth in a way into the Protestant ranks. Shrewdly, Elizabeth pursued a policy which rendered this episcopal protest ineffective. She allowed the bishops neither to remain in office nor to become martyrs. They were simply replaced, and thus English Catholics were leaderless. The Uniformity Act provided fines for nonattendance at church, but this proved no serious problem. The Catholics who could afford it paid their fines, while others sat through the official services reading their 'popish Latin primers.'

During the early years of Elizabeth, English Catholics had a good chance to live their religion inwardly without being molested. Clandestine priests provided, especially to the nobility, the necessary priestly services. The number of committed Catholics was not large and probably dwindled considerably during the first decade of Elizabeth's rule. More important was the temperament of these English Catholics. Obviously, they regretted the settlement, prayed for a change, but otherwise were content to let things run their course. As long as Parliament did not prescribe conformity of belief, they saw no reason to react. The Northern Uprising of 1569 does not disprove this point, for it was neither very popular nor very religious. The attitude of the Catholics was understandable. More than three decades had passed since the country had been Catholic for any length of time, and only those in their late forties and above could recall those days. What is more, they had not been particularly dynamic days for the Catholic Church either. And the five years of Marian rule had been all too brief to reverse the trend. In short, indigenous Catholicism was bound to lead a quiet and unobtrusive existence.

Elsewhere in Europe, however, Catholicism was of a new and dynamic temper, exemplified by the Council of Trent and the Jesuits as well as a resurgence of spirituality. A new type of Catholic of English background but molded on the Continent was unwilling to write off England to heretics and schismatics. The leader of these Englishmen was William Allen. Even as the 'Marian exiles' had not forgotten their native land, never failing to hope and pray for a change, so did William Allen, after his departure in 1559, never cease to remember England. To return England to the Catholic fold was his life's purpose. He founded a seminary at Douay, in the Low Countries, in 1568 to train Catholic missionaries for England.

> We recall the mournful contrast that obtains at home: the utter desolation of all things sacred which there exists; our country, once so famed for its religion and holy before God, now void of all religion; our friends and kinfolk, all our dear ones and countless souls besides, perishing in schism and godlessness; every jail and dungeon filled to overflowing, not with thieves and villains, but with Christ's priests and servants, nay with our parents and kinsmen.[70]

From the seventies onward, Catholic priests and missionaries began to arrive in England, all in all 400 of them by the end of the century. They entered England in disguise, moved secretly from place to place, celebrated Masses and catechized, constantly dreading apprehension. They were a new breed of priests, and had their equals existed two generations earlier, perhaps no history of Protestant success in England would need to be written. They came armed with pamphlets combatting the Anglican Church and, before long, they also had an English translation of Scripture, the so-called 'Douay Bible'—not because they really believed in a vernacular Bible, but because it was clearly an important propaganda weapon.

Several acts of Parliament sought to keep the activities of the Catholic missionaries under control. One act against 'divers persons called or professed Jesuits, seminary priests and other priests' of 1585 provided the penalties of 'high treason' for any priest, and in 1593 all Catholics were placed under close surveillance. Many priests were apprehended and almost 200 paid the supreme penalty for their devotion. Most were nameless men whose deaths history has forgotten, though at the time several martyrologies, in spirit very much akin to those celebrating Protestant martyrs and issuing from Protestant presses, were published. A few are recalled by the Catholic Church, men such as Cuthbert Mayne, or Edmund Campion (beatified in 1886). It was Campion who on the scaffold voiced the Catholic assertion that if he stood condemned so did all of England for centuries, ever since the Christian Gospel had found its way to the land. And as regards their intention, he asserted, 'we travelled only for souls, we touched neither state nor policy.'

The point was well taken. But there was another side to the matter, expressed by the bull *Regnans in Excelsis*, of 1570, which had not only excommunicated Queen Elizabeth but had called upon all Englishmen to refuse obedience to her as an usurper of the throne. Practically this pronouncement had no significance (hardly any Englishmen knew about the bull), but once known it did confront Catholics in England with the unhappy alternative of being disloyal either to their religion or their Queen.

What were the intentions of the priests who slipped into England under the cover of darkness and false identities? Were their purposes only religious and devotional? Or were they part of a scheme to overthrow Elizabeth and her government? There is no doubt that the English government thought so. William Cecil, the lord treasurer, and Francis Walsingham, the secretary of state, saw a disloyal Catholic behind every bush, and Walsingham, in particular, designed a grandiose spy network to unearth every last bit of evidence, engaging in practices which, in his own calmer moments, he surely despised. But he was persuaded that the danger was real—the danger not of a vital Catholic faith, but of treason against the realm.

The priests, in turn, protested their political innocence. They could do so all the more since a papal brief from Gregory XIII had assured English Catholics that they might lawfully obey the Queen, a point William Allen vigorously stressed in his *A True, Sincere and Modest Defense of English Catholics*, of 1584. Things were a bit more complicated, however. Neither Allen nor any other of the Catholic publicists left any doubt that basically the ecclesiastical censure was valid. Once the day of its execution dawned with the help of King Philip II, the situation was different. There is no war 'so just or honorable, be it civil or foreign,' Allen wrote, 'as that which is waged for religion; we say for the true, ancient, Catholic, Roman religion.'[71]

In 1588 Allen published a vituperative pamphlet entitled *An Admonition to the Nobility and People of England concerning the Present Warres*. The argument was rather routine: Elizabeth was an illegitimate usurper of the English throne and the people owed her neither obedience nor allegiance. Indeed, when the hour of judgment struck with the invasion of England by the forces of righteousness, the English people had an obligation to rise against the 'Jezebel' on the English throne, that 'incestuous bastard,' that 'infamous, depraved, accursed, excommunicate heretic,' and save themselves, their children and children's children from eternal damnation.

But Allen did more than offer theoretical reflections on how loyal Catholics should face their heretical Queen; he also engaged actively in numerous plots to depose Elizabeth or invade England, more spurred on by his unbounded enthusiasm than by realistic appraisals of the situation. His memoranda went to Spain, the Vatican, France. One note submitted in 1576 suggested that 'some Englishmen, men of trust and prudence, chiefly priests, who will cross over into England secretly from Flanders, and covertly prepare certain gentlemen in England, useful in this affair, whose names, of course, will only be given them by word of mouth.'[72]

William Allen and his associates thus combined a religious and a political program, the reestablishment of Catholicism in England and the deposition of Elizabeth. The former was primary, but there can be little doubt that Allen realized the indispensable corollary of the latter. Intriguingly, the situation facing Allen was identical with that faced by Protestants elsewhere in Europe. A change in the religious orientation of a country could only be achieved through a change in its political structure. Elizabeth's steadfast pursuit of an antiCatholic ecclesiastical program meant there was no possibility of converting her. The use of force was the only answer.

That this Catholic political threat was ever serious may be doubted. Political dissension and dissatisfaction could hardly be incited from abroad without indigenous support. English Catholics were lukewarm in their religion and loyal subjects in their citizenship. The irony was that abroad different assessments of the English situation made the rounds, optimistic ones, as a matter of fact, that suggested that most Englishmen were Catholic at heart—if not most of them, then at least one-third. Had the landing of the Duke of Parma with the help of the Spanish Armada ever materialized that famous summer of 1588, the true state of affairs might have emerged, that is, to what extent Catholic Englishmen would have rallied to the Spanish Catholic side. As matters stand, however, history does not reveal its alternatives and the historian is left without the answer.

# CHAPTER SEVEN

# The European Dimension

The Protestant Reformation was a phenomenon of European dimension, a fact which attests its vitality and underscores its historic significance. This European Reformation had two distinct aspects. To begin with, there was the religious component. People throughout Europe heard, read, and accepted a new interpretation of the Gospel. They broke with the Catholic Church and formed (or sought to form) new congregations of their own. They developed new religious styles of life, with their own hymns, forms of worship, and literature. In the end, these Protestant congregations either were able to consolidate (as, for example, in Holland) or they succumbed, for one reason or another, to the use of force against them. Success or failure, theirs always was the gripping story of a religious movement seeking to assert itself in a hostile environment.

The Reformation could also mean something else, for there was the kind of political involvement of religion which had already developed in Germany, that ambiguously religious world of diets, councillors, edicts, and ecclesiastical litigation, which concerned itself with the legal recognition or rejection of the new faith. This was the world of power politics, alliances, intrigues, conspiracies, even war. Here the cause of religious change and renewal intersected the *haute monde* of diplomacy, and religion became a part of political history.

Obviously, these two aspects were interrelated—or one at least hopes that they were—though they must be distinguished. They were not necessarily the two sides of the same coin, for one could well be divorced from the other: the Anabaptists illustrate the exclusive preoccupation with religion and Gustavus Vasa of Sweden the pre-

224

occupation with politics. Most of the time, however, the Reformation was both, an indication of its vitality and its ambiguity. It affected virtually all European countries, from Scandinavia to Italy, from Spain to Poland. While by no means equally successful everywhere, the Protestant message touched them all. Only two countries escaped the turbulence of the Protestant message, Ireland and Spain, both of them nestled along the perimeter of Europe, far from the cradle of the new faith. There is evidence of a few Protestant congregations in Spain, but generally the new religion had little impact in that country. The political authorities were all-too-determined to crush deviate religious sentiment. In the case of Ireland the stubborn opposition against anything English may have been a factor.

Several general observations may be made about the expansion of the new theology from Germany to other lands. They presuppose that the Reformation in Europe is to be traced to Luther's proclamation, an assumption by no means universally accepted in scholarship. With respect to England scholars have minimized outside influence and stressed the indigenous elements of reform. And the same has been argued for France, where the reformative efforts of Bishop Briçonnet at Meaux have been cited as the beginnings of ecclesiastical reform in that country. This perspective would see the Reformation in Europe as the simultaneous expressions of reformative change, precipitated by the general state of ecclesiastical affairs in the early 16th century.

One fallacy of this approach is that it all too easily identifies reform and Reformation. While there may have been instances in which concern for reform was an important factor, the real aim of the Protestant Reformation was surely not so much 'reform' as 're-interpretation' of the Gospel, and it was characterized before long by an inimical stance toward the Catholic Church. The Reformation may have built on earlier expressions of reform sentiment, exemplified by Colet in England, or Lefèvre and Briçonnet in France. In the final analysis, however, the Reformation introduced an element of discontinuity into these efforts and nothing illustrates this better than the fact that most of these 'reformers,' such as Erasmus, Lefèvre, or Briçonnet, never joined the Protestant cause.

Still, even a negative conclusion concerning the dependence of the Reformation in Europe on Germany and Martin Luther will need to acknowledge that Luther's ideas made their way from Germany to the four corners of Europe. His name became a household word even in France and England and Sweden. Such was made possible through a number of ways. There was a heavy flow of traffic between

Germany and the rest of Europe which enabled the man in Oxford to know what was happening at Basel, and informed the cleric at Strassburg about developments at Wittenberg. Of considerable importance was the correspondence between academicians in which the communication of scholarly news was often an important content: in March 1518 Erasmus, for example, sent Thomas More a copy of Luther's *Ninety-five Theses*, and in April 1519 he wrote John Fisher about the Wittenberg professor.

News and ideas were taken abroad by men who traveled more or less professionally across borders. Foremost, of course, were the merchants, concerning whose role the English scene offers particularly conclusive evidence. Then there were the students, especially those returning home from Germany. They brought the news, in some instances as mere reporters, in others, however, as partisans of the new faith. The printers must also be mentioned, for economic interest or conviction (or both) made them send abroad the pamphlets propounding the new faith.

There is evidence for the colportage of Luther's books outside Germany. Zwingli propagated their distribution in Switzerland, Erasmus said that they were read in the Low Countries, and in England they were publicly burned. In February 1519 the Basel printer Froben shipped 600 copies of Luther's tracts to Spain and France, a business and religious enterprise of major proportions. About that time a student at Paris wrote that Luther's writings were received 'quite openly' and Luther himself declared that his tracts were read by the doctors of the Sorbonne.

Since Luther's tracts were read in France or England, one is inclined to assume a situation similar to that in Germany existed in those countries. However, there were incisive differences. To begin with, only the basic notions of Luther could be communicated abroad. Most of his early writings, though addressed to specific issues, were general in nature and did not express a specific 'Lutheran' propensity. During the early years of the Reformation, Luther did not publish any direct exposition of his understanding of justification, and of his views on the Lord's Supper only the basic outline—the repudiation of Catholic sacramentalism—was clear. The label 'Lutheran,' so freely placed upon the proponents of the new theology, was in a sense misleading. 'Lutheran' was only the affirmation of the primacy of Scripture in the formulation of religious truth, the repudiation of the primacy of the pope and the Church, and the minimal value placed on external rites and observances.

Secondly, Luther's tracts had to be in Latin in order to break the linguistic barrier between Germany and Europe. The German writings were useless and only his Latin ones afforded a possibility of communication. This meant, of course, that Luther's message underwent an important modification. In Germany Luther had been able to speak directly to the common people. He had done so successfully, as the number of reprints of his vernacular tracts shows: the 18 reprints of his tract on the Lord's Prayer, the 19 of the tract on *Christian Liberty*. Such direct communication was impossible for linguistic reasons elsewhere in Europe; accordingly, the popular response to the Lutheran proclamation found in Germany could not materialize in other countries. Only in Germany could there be a popular movement. The transmission of Luther's ideas abroad had to focus on essentials and on catchy slogans—Scripture versus man-made traditions, salvation by grace versus salvation by works.

Despite this handicap, the new theology found active propagators on native soil. Its spread was not dependent upon outside literary influence but could utilize the efforts of indigenous colporteurs who shared the characteristic of youth and Erasmian propensity, men such as Bilney, Tyndale, Barnes, Biros, Wishart, or Petri. Some of them, as, for example, Olavus Petri of Sweden, had actually been in Germany and savored the new theology first hand. Others, like William Tyndale of England, traveled there after their 'conversion.' All of them were little known at the time and certainly no part of what might be called the academic or ecclesiastical 'establishment.' In short, these European reformers exhibited the same characteristics as their German colleagues.

Each country had such native reformers, men who ventured to proclaim the new theology and did so initially against great odds and at great personal danger. Several paid for their faith with their lives and thereby showed the intensity of their commitment: the first Protestant martyrs—two men burned at Brussels in 1523—came not from Germany, but from a place to which the new faith had been imported. The native reformers assured the spread of the Protestant faith in their lands, since their efforts transformed the ideas from abroad into a message congenial to the new environment.

The propagation of the new theology took the form of an amalgamation of basic notions of Luther's theology with elements from the native reformers. This synthesis explains the immense variety of theological emphases that characterized the scene, making the Reformation in Hungary different from that in Sweden or Poland. One would hardly have expected these reformers to have adopted all of Luther's thought, especially since the 'Lutheran' notions reaching them were, as already noted, so general as to require further delineation. Moreover, the men who carried the Protestant message forward in the various countries had pondered theological issues before they encountered Luther. While this encounter proved to be of considerable importance in their theological development, it could not do away completely with the theological background already present. Luther was only one of several factors in their development.

The transmission of Luther's ideas was thus twofold, direct and indirect. The former occurred through his writings as these were read in the various European countries, while the latter took place through the native reformers. If the one was pure, but vague, Lutheranism, the other was a mixture of several elements.

An additional consideration pertains to the chronological divergence between the Reformation in Germany and that elsewhere in Europe. In Germany the movement reached its climax by the end of the 1520s, at a time when the European Reformation was only slowly getting under way. One might almost say that the German Reformation ended before the European Reformation began. This time lag had two significant ramifications. For one, it meant that the defenders of the ecclesiastical status quo had what might be considered an advance warning. The defenses could be strengthened and the counterattack launched. The kind of *blitz* so devastatingly successful in Germany was impossible elsewhere in Europe.

The time lag between Germany and Europe also helps to explain the important modification of the new theology from what might be described as a vague Lutheranism to a distinct Calvinism. The fact of the matter is that, while the Reformation in Germany was eminently Lutheran, in Europe it was Calvinist. Did this mean that Calvin's thought was more persuasive or that Luther's was too Teutonic? An explanation seems needed and the discrepancy in time between the two Reformations affords an initial clue. At the time Protestantism vied for acceptance in Scotland, England, the Low Countries, or France, Calvinism was the ascending star in the firmament of the Reformation, while Lutheranism was beset by vehement internal strife.

The Protestant goal was to spread the new Gospel; it was as simple as that. The Protestants were convinced that they possessed the authentic understanding of the nature of Biblical religion. They sought to share it with others and were willing to die for it. The

Reformation of the 16th century is not understandable without this centrifugal tendency and evangelistic impulse.

But the Protestants sought more than that. They wanted the right to live their faith, to worship publicly without legal restriction. Indeed, they strove for the official acceptance of their faith. And such was a legal matter, to be decided by the governmental authorities. Naturally, therefore, the Protestant quest was to obtain a favorable governmental decision. In many instances they were successful: in numerous German territories, in Sweden, in England. In other places they made a persistent effort to sway the ruler's sentiment, notably in France, where Zwingli and Calvin exerted their influence on Francis I to accept the Protestant faith. As matters turned out, they were unsuccessful but this very failure prompted another approach in the quest for legal recognition. And this was to affiliate with the political power in the land in order to force the ruler's hand. In France, Scotland, Poland, and the Low Countries, the Protestants sought to achieve the goal of legal acceptance of the Protestant faith by allying with the nobility against the ruler. The specific situation differed from country to country, not only with respect to the ultimate outcome of the struggle, but also with respect to its basic characteristics. In France, for example, the Catholic cause, and thus the opposition to the Protestant efforts, was advocated not by the King but by a faction of the nobility. Accordingly, the struggle was between rival factions, with the King occupying an uneasy and helpless position between them. In both Scotland and the Low Countries another variant can be observed. There the rulers were foreign, and the struggle against them took the form of opposing foreign influence. But whatever the specific situation, the Protestant cause became embroiled in a complex political picture and ceased to be a purely religious phenomenon. Since the Protestant goal was political—the legal recognition of Protestantism—this development is hardly surprising.

We now turn to enlarge the geographic scope and consider further points of the compass. Four countries will be singled out and this for the reason that events there seemed to have been more significant than those in other places. While separate sections will be devoted to particular countries, the course of events in France, Sweden, Scotland, and Poland will be viewed synoptically. Each of these countries, of course, had its own particular Reformation history, each its particular story of Protestant success or failure. These histories have been variously written. To relegate them to collective existence is not to minimize their importance, but to assure that the multiplicity of events does not obscure the common lines of development.

The compass to be covered is admittedly extensive. Accordingly, the task is frustrating, for to recount the events of decades on a few dozen pages means to slide from generalization to generalization. An apology is in order for such brevity which frankly grows out of the conclusion that, while important in their own right, the histories of the Reformation in these countries are primarily significant for their paradigmatic confirmation of general trends of the period. One wonders if the extension of our purview to additional countries would alter our conclusions. Probably not. The countries chosen for a closer scrutiny constituted the eminent places of reformatory agitation. Denmark, Hungary, or the Netherlands would have added further names, dates, and theological insights, but contributed little new to the understanding of the nature of ecclesiastical change in the 16th century.

The course of events in the four countries chosen followed some marked parallels, while it was characterized at the same time by significant differences. It is our contention that parallels and differences afford a notion as to the success (or failure) of the Protestant quest for recognition.

## France

The story of the Reformation in France can be told in several ways —as the account of a religious movement or of the struggle between competing factions for political power, of the influx of Lutheran ideas into the country or the eventual emergence of Calvinism as the eminent Protestant faction. It is always the same historical reality, of course, though differing emphases will open different perspectives.

This study will show how the Protestant movement became involved in a fierce political power struggle. It took the better part of the entire century to demonstrate that Protestantism could not be victorious in France and the stations along the way were marked by persecution, wars, and bloodshed. The historian, who occasionally, at least, is wiser than were the contemporaries, can see the options clearly enunciated at the beginning. Given a saturation of the land with Protestant ideas, the task was to convert the monarch to the new faith; it was as simple, or as difficult, as that. Aside from the possibility that the ruler experienced a religious conversion, as variously happened in Germany, the *raison d'être* for a change of ecclesiastical loyalties might have been the existence of tangible advantages—the case of Henry VIII being the spectacular, if unsavory, illustration. But in France no obvious political (or personal) advantages of this sort existed. A unique relationship prevailed between the Church and the crown. The Pragmatic Sanction of Bourges, promulgated in 1438, had established several important ecclesiastical privileges of the crown. It caused a running battle between crown and papacy which was not resolved until the Fifth Lateran Council, when it finally was declared null and void. But this was a Pyrrhic victory since a concordat, concluded at the same time, granted to the crown virtually the same rights enjoyed before, including the right to nominate bishops, abbots, and priors. In short, the French King possessed extensive power in ecclesiastical affairs. Since this meant, among other things, considerable revenue, he could hardly be lured to break with Rome for the mundane reasons important elsewhere in Europe.

The alternative facing the Protestants was, accordingly, to force the King to undertake ecclesiastical change on account of the widespread expression of such sentiment among the people—and the Protestants tried to do precisely that. Zwingli dedicated one of his major works to Francis, and Calvin followed suit with the dedication of the *Institutes* to the King. Or the Protestants sought to bring about (as a minimum program) the legal acceptance of Protestant worship in the land: *le vray office de roy estoit de vacquer à la cognoissance de tels différends.*[1] Even if not often so consciously formulated, such considerations undoubtedly were present.

There was yet another possibility, and that was for the Protestants to seek a change through political means, by using force or by using a political issue. In the end this is what happened, though it took several decades for such determination and the political issue to appear. Eventually, the course of ecclesiastical change became embedded in political developments. The cause of religion was thus conjoined to the cause of politics, and the proponents of the one saw advantages in taking up the other: the Protestants saw their cause strengthened by political power, while those concerned with political issues took up the cause of religion for the advantages it would bring.

The first phase of the French Reformation was characterized by the influx of Lutheran ideas into the country. The simplest explanation of its origins is to see it as the extension of Luther's proclamation. An impressive phalanx of French scholars has dissented from this view, arguing that there existed an independent reform move-

ment in France before Luther, evidenced by the widespread propagation of the Bible toward the end of the 15th century and the reforming attitudes of Marguerite d'Angoulème and Jacques Lefèvre
d'Etaples.

The problem resolves itself with a definition of the term 'Reformation,' which obviously can be applied to a variety of reform
efforts in the late 15th and early 16th centuries. The term can be
restricted, however, to the doctrinal and ecclesiastical reorientation
which had the break with Rome as its most dramatic corollary. In
this latter sense it is impossible to speak of an autonomous French
Reformation. However much Jacques Lefèvre deviated from
medieval scholasticism or however close his Biblical commentaries
came to a view of justification subsequently embraced by Luther and
the reformers, he was not a Protestant. A humanist, Lefèvre was in
many ways critical of the Church, but always its loyal son, a fact
illustrated by his faithful allegiance to the Church after the Lutheran
controversy had begun to divide the people. Doctrinal affirmation
was less important than the ecclesiastical temper.

Thus the Reformation in France had its beginnings when Luther's
writings first found their way into the land. In August 1521 a mandate published *à son de trompe et cri public* confiscated all of
Luther's writings, and in November a royal ordinance prohibited
the publication of all writings 'favoring and defending the books of
Luther.'[2] Luther was grouped with such heretics as Wyclif and Hus,
and his *Babylonian Captivity* was compared to the Koran.
Lutheranism had taken root, though obviously its impact was
limited to the clergy and those who could read Latin; only after
1524 were Luther's works translated into French and vernacular
tracts began to appear.

The defeat of King Francis I at Pavia in 1525 and his subsequent imprisonment by Charles V had repercussions for the
ecclesiastical situation. It seemed necessary to leave no doubt about
the orthodoxy of the French Church to gain the sympathies (and
political support) of the pope, and thereby help effect the release of
the King. The *Parlement* of Paris and the Sorbonne—the one the
political, the other the theological authority—strove to excel one
another in the persecution of Lutheran heretics.

Personally Francis was of a moderate, humanist religious orientation. But he could not afford to be sentimental about the protection
of the religious innovators. Charles V was his arch foe and the support of the papacy indispensable. Francis would probably have supported the side of the Catholic faith even if the international

situation had been different. As matters stood, however, this situation gave him little choice. Politics thus intermingled with religion from the very outset of the religious controversy in France—and in contrast to Sweden or England political prudence suggested the perpetuation of the ecclesiastical status quo.

Francis opposed deviation within the French Church, not only because he wanted to remain in the good graces of the papacy, but also because his fierce struggle with Charles V made a tranquil domestic situation mandatory. His objection was not so much to doctrinal aberration but to the disruption of unity and tranquility. Francis was indisposed to surrender control of the Church for the sake of questionable doctrinal adventures which offered little except risks and pitfalls.

In the early 1530s France was characterized by a steadily increasing influx of Lutheran ideas and by the equally steady assimilation of Lefèvre's humanism by the Lutheran evangel. The government continued to oppose ecclesiastical innovation. Yet its opposition was unsystematic, haphazard, and ineffective.

Two harmless events precipitated the showdown between the new faith and the old Church. One was the speech of a distinguished academician, the other a handbill posted on the door of the King's bedroom. The consequences in both instances were far-reaching.

The oratorical feat came on All Saints' Day, 1533, with a speech of Nicolas Cop, rector of the University of Paris. It was a mélange of Erasmus, Lefèvre, and Luther, theologically quite harmless, yet startling, for it was propounded on an official occasion and given the aura of academic approval. Loyal Catholics were in an uproar and demanded action against Cop, who unceremoniously fled to Switzerland. Afterward Francis I enjoined the *Parlement* of Paris to suppress the Lutheran heresy. The next 12 months passed with numerous arrests, convictions, and deaths; France increasingly proved an inclement climate for the new faith.

In October 1534 came the second event, the posting of handbills at Paris and various other places throughout the country, including the door of the King's own bedroom at the royal castle at Amboise. The author of this ingenious Protestant propaganda effort was one Antoine Marcourt, who considered the Mass to be the abomination of abominations, 'through which the world, unless God has mercy, will be completely devastated, destroyed, ruined.'[8]

Marcourt's move was understandable, but hardly prudent. Since the handbills had been posted at several places at the same time, an organized group was thought to stand behind the coup, to demonstrate the strength of the new faith. The King had to ponder the disquieting thought that the religious innovators had been able to reach the door of his own bedroom. More was at issue than theological deviation, for the fear that Protestants tended to disrupt law and order, despite Protestant remonstrances, haunted the authorities. One does well to remember that at the very time the handbills were posted the Anabaptists at Münster gave a frightful demonstration of such disruption.

Francis was determined to act. Within a month seven persons had been sent to the stake. A stern mandate ordered full censorship. Perhaps the King meant to do no more than teach the Protestants a lesson. His political ties with the League of Schmalkald, as well as his own temperament, kept him from drastic measures. In July 1535 he signed the mandate of Coucy, which freed the imprisoned Protestants and allowed Protestant refugees to return to France—the amnesty, incidentally, which gave John Calvin the opportunity to return to his native land for the final time. During the next two years Francis was preoccupied with foreign affairs but afterward he had the opportunity to deal with domestic affairs. In 1539 and 1540 he issued additional mandates against the Protestant heretics and thenceforth the suppression of heresy became an affair of state.

On July 1 1542, a royal order prohibited the sale and reading of several Protestant books, including one entitled *l'Institution chrétienne*—a French translation of Calvin's *Institutes*.[4] This was Calvin's entrance upon the French Reformation. A new element was thereby introduced into the French scene, and during the next several years the new faith in the land underwent a metamorphosis. What theretofore had been vaguely 'Protestant' (always referred to as 'Lutheran') became distinctly Calvinist. This change is understandable in light of the theological developments in Germany and Switzerland. Lutheranism did not have the ability to undertake an aggressive colportage of its ideas. The War of Schmalkald, the heated controversy over the Interim, and the ensuing theological quarrels brought its involvement in a struggle for its very life as well as its theological identity. Geneva and Calvin, on the other hand, were unperturbed by armed conflict or theological dispute. Moreover, Geneva was strategically located with respect to France, and Calvin, himself a Frenchman, was not a detached bystander viewing a strange land and an alien people: this was his native land, these his fellow countrymen.

With the death of Francis I in 1547 and the succession of Henry II the effort at suppression continued with even greater determination and ruthlessness. Henry resolutely opposed the French Protestants. He possessed little of his father's empathy for a humanist religion—and he was deeply persuaded that Protestantism constituted a mortal danger for the realm. One of his first measures was to establish a new judiciary body, the *chambre ardente* (fire court), which was entrusted with the function 'to counter the blasphemous and heretical disturbers of the peace and tranquility of this most Christian kingdom.'[5] In the two years of its existence, from December 1547 to January 1550, it rendered over 500 verdicts, most of them death sentences.

In 1551 Henry issued the Edict of Chateaubriand, which sought to render the existing provisions for the persecution of heretics more effective. The Edict spoke of the 'common malady of this contagious pestilence which has infected many noble towns,' and its 46 articles outlined the judicial treatment of heretics. Once more persecution was intensified, yet success failed to grace the efforts. Some of those who had earlier advocated severity against the Protestant heretics began to have second thoughts. What was to be done if the persecution did not accomplish its goal? Was it possible to continue the policy of persecution indefinitely? If not, what kind of rapprochement was possible between the Protestants and the King? Emperor Charles V was facing the same questions in Germany, answering them with the Peace of Augsburg. But the German situation was different, for there the new faith had attained political stature and the Peace of Augsburg was not so much a religious conciliation as a political truce.

Henry was unwilling to forsake his grim determination to free his land from the heretical pestilence. Still, he realized his problems: his foreign policy was bankrupt and his dream of conquests abroad, especially in Italy, had not materialized. Governmental finances were in a desperate state and the army was not equipped to launch a major attack upon Spain. The outgrowth of his awareness was the treaty of Cateau-Cambrésis, signed in April 1559, and ending half a century of intermittent Spanish-French conflict.

A few months later, on July 10 1559, the King died unexpectedly. The French Protestants uttered words of relief upon hearing this, for a ruthless enemy of their cause was gone. The 12 years of his reign had been a constant and unyielding effort to crush the Protestant sentiment. The heir to the throne was Francis II, 15 years of age, hardly capable of leading the affairs of state. Was a regency necessary? This question should have been explored, but it was hardly discussed, for Cardinal Guise summarily took over the reins of government. Guise's maneuver evoked the protest of the noble family of the Bourbons, who argued that, since the King was a minor, a council of regency should be formed.

This constitutional situation was to have profound repercussions for French Protestantism. There were religious overtones to the tensions between the Bourbons and the Guises: the former sympathized with the Protestants, while the latter advocated a policy of suppression. Thus, a religious note indirectly impinged on the constitutional problem. The French Protestants were drawn into the controversy. They supported the Bourbon claims to the regency and argued that the Guises were usurpers from abroad—most of the Guise lands were in Lorraine—and had to be resisted. The theological rationale for this attitude came from Calvin's doctrine of the right of resistance of the *magistrats inférieurs*, which held that the *princes du sang* (the higher nobility) had the right to oppose the unconstitutional moves of the Guises in order to reestablish the constitutional government in France. A victory of Antoine of Navarre over the Guises promised toleration for the Protestants.

During this time there also appeared among the French Protestants the question of whether to resort to arms against the tyrant. This was the notion of revolution, which from then until the end of the century became a major element in the history of the French Reformation. Was this a departure from previous views or the proper extension of Calvin's ideas? The truth lies in the middle. Still, the face of French Protestantism changed after Henry II. Theretofore, the adherents of the new faith had been committed to a religious cause. They had risked their lives to read the forbidden Protestant books or to attend the worship of the Protestant congregations. This changed and French Protestantism increasingly found its adherents among men who had other than religious reasons to follow its banner. Nobles flocked to its ranks. Political parties emerged. Prior to 1559 Protestants tended to be martyrs; after 1559 they were revolutionaries.

The setting of this change was important. A constitutional question was perturbing the country and the charge of usurpation of legal rights was raised. Opposition to the Guises could be justified on constitutional grounds—and this political decision could be supported by religious argumentation. French Protestantism did not change its political ethics in a vacuum but in a legal context.

Religiously, the future seemed favorable for the Protestants. In May 1560 a new mandate allowed personal freedom of religion but prohibited public assemblies. Two persons were responsible for this change of policy: Catherine de Medici, wife of Henry II, and Michel de L'Hôpital. Catherine was not deeply interested in the religious questions which perturbed the time. Niece of Pope Clement VII, she was no doubt a great woman, though she was neither very pious nor very learned, nor even very principled. But she was an astute politician. She also possessed a good deal of feminine charm that brought success where a man might have failed. Her imprint on events in France was profound, and such could hardly have been possible without genius on her part. Her motivation was the concern for her children.

Michel de L'Hôpital was the new chancellor. He was a man of ability and talents, but hardly of greatness. Catholics had stereotyped contempt for him, Protestants reserved awe. He is said to have been part of the growing faction of the 'politique,' comprised of moderate adherents of both religious groupings, who were persuaded that the country needed, above all, a strong monarchy to end the religious strife. L'Hôpital would have betrayed his insight and he relegated religion to an inferior place. But his religion was neither staunchly Catholic nor aggressively Protestant; it was of that evasive, yet powerful, version propagated by Erasmus. It consisted of simple precepts and essentially was a way of life. L'Hôpital thought that this religion was the answer to the religious problem facing France. He was persuaded that the use of force against the heretics was bound to be unsuccessful, and that the Catholic Church should concern herself with the Calvinist charges and answer them. His goal was irenic concord.

The King's unexpected death changed the political picture overnight. His successor was Charles IX, the second son of Henry II, 11 years of age. This time there was no question that a regent was needed. This should have been the moment for Antoine of Navarre to assert his rights as *prince du sang* and claim the office of regent, but he yielded to Catherine de Medici, who assumed the regency. Thereby the die had been cast. Antoine's failure to claim the regency meant that a major chance to introduce the Reformation by governmental fiat had been lost.

Catherine had a notion as to how the religious problem could be solved. Convinced of the strength of Protestantism—perhaps it was her fatal error to have overestimated that strength—she sensed the futility of continued persecution and thought it possible to clear the air with a truce. Afterward a council, either national or general, might effect conciliation. In short, hers was the program of de L'Hôpital and exemplified the same weakness. The Catholics were hardly receptive to such a course of action and neither were the Calvinists. Catherine might have learned a lesson from the futile efforts of Emperor Charles V, whose mediating policy also had satisfied neither side. The weakness of her policy was the inability to rally supporters; its strength was an astute understanding of the realities of the situation. The country could not be pacified with a substantial segment of the populace in opposition, and Catherine realized this better than anyone else.

In January 1562 Catherine issued the Edict of St. Germain, which permitted the Protestants to hold worship services outside fortified cities. This was an epoch-making concession. After almost 40 years of struggles and persecution, the French Protestants received the right to public worship. The tradition of only one religion in the realm was broken. No longer was it possible to speak of *une foi, une loi, un roi*, since two faiths were officially recognized, though how long this arrangement was to last was another question. The preface spoke of 'reunion and return to one fold, which is all that we desire,' which might suggest that the Edict was to be temporary. Be that as it may, the French crown was willing to consider a temporary suspension of the traditional notion of the *corpus christianum*, the society where Church and state were one. And this was truly revolutionary.[6]

But this turn of events did not herald the resolution of the controversy. Indeed, for the remainder of the century the French countryside was filled with the sounds of battle and the sights of destruction. The Wars of Religion began at that time and lasted intermittently until the Edict of Nantes was issued in 1598. After theological arguments no longer persuaded and diplomacy no longer restrained, the battlefield was to render the final verdict. Such had been the development in most places where the Protestant faith had sought legal recognition—in Switzerland, Germany, the Low Countries, Scotland. France followed such precedent, though there the conflict lasted longer and was more catastrophic than anywhere else. Moreover, in France religion constituted only the veneer in those wars: men exploited the sacred in order to pursue the profane. To be sure, the lines were always neatly drawn, with Catholics on one side and Protestants on the other. But often neither Catholics nor Protestants were really concerned about religion. Other considerations impinged upon the action and made lip service to one brand of religion both easy and prudent.

In a real sense the war was caused by the failure of the crown to assert itself against the two religious factions. Catherine's program was one of conciliation, but she had found no response in the realm. The Protestants thought themselves too strong and the Catholics too challenged to enter upon the path of compromise. For a while Catherine had been able to keep the two parties in check, but that time had passed. The outbreak of hostilities was by no means deliberate, determined, or planned. Indeed, the transition from peace to war was surprisingly smooth, and the country found itself involved in a fratricidal conflict before this was realized. Voices of warning, particularly from Geneva, had gone unheeded. Calvin had written that 'the first drop of blood shed by our men will cause streams of blood which will flood all of Europe.'[7] But he had little influence over the French Protestants, no matter how numerous and intense his pleas.

The Peace of Amboise, in March 1563, terminated the first round of hostilities but hardly cooled tempers and left the Protestants dissatisfied. Initially, Condé, their leader, had demanded the reinstatement of the Edict of St. Germain, but the Protestant nobility, rather unconcerned about those not of noble rank, failed to support him. Accordingly, the Peace granted religious freedom only to the nobility, which was allowed to hold worship in its castles. Commoners were allowed to worship at one place in each bailiwick, though outside the town. No Protestant worship was allowed in Paris.

The Peace was a step backward compared with the more liberal provisions of the Edict of St. Germain. The war had shown most Frenchmen still to be good Catholics, or, to put the matter in a slightly more dramatic way, a great many Frenchmen turned Catholic again upon seeing the ruthless Protestants in action. Before the war, Calvin had warned his French compatriots lest their impatience bring the Protestant cause to naught. He was not mistaken.

By that time French Calvinism had achieved organizational consolidation and theological identity. The heterogeneous background of Protestantism in France meant that there had prevailed considerable diversity and no clear delineation of its faith. Doctrinal uncertainty prevailed, as expressed in a debate on predestination at Poitiers in 1558, which Calvin sought to settle from a distance with epistolary admonitions. Increasingly, the need for a statement of faith was felt, and a meeting of French Protestants in Paris in May 1559 tackled the problem. More than 50 elders and ministers from churches all over France were present 'within sight of the stakes.' Francis de Morel, minister of the Parisian congregation, served as moderator.

Two items dominated the agenda: the drafting of a confession of faith—*confession de foy*—and a church order—*discipline écclésias-tique*. The confession, which has been called the 'purest expression of the Calvinist understanding of Scripture,'[8] had been supplied in its first draft by Calvin, who did not hide his displeasure over the French desire for a formulation of the faith. He felt that the discussion about a confessional statement might produce tensions within the Church.

The heart of the confession was the affirmation of righteousness by faith. The need for works resulting from this righteousness was stressed, and the typically Calvinist understanding of man's nature and divine predestination received its proper delineation. The confession recognized the Sacraments of Baptism and Communion. Concerning the latter it stated, 'through the secret and incomprehensible power of his Spirit, he nourishes and vivifies us through the substance of his body and blood.' It is a mystery that surpasses 'the measure of our senses and the order of nature' and 'is only to be comprehended by faith.'[9]

The confession also spelled out the structure of the local congregation. Article 29 asserted that the 'true church must be ruled according to the order which our Lord Jesus Christ has instituted.' Parallel to the Genevan *ordonnances écclésiastiques* of 1541, the confession provided for three offices in the Church: ministers, elders, and deacons. This structure was declared as 'sacred and inviolable,' to be maintained even if the magistracy and its laws should oppose it.

The church order, in turn, regulated the outer structure of the congregations. The minister was to be selected by a county synod. The elders and deacons were elected by the deacons and elders themselves. In contrast to the practice at Geneva, the French church order, dealing with a much larger situation, left less room for the democratic involvement of the congregation in the determination of its affairs. The document was aristocratic in character and a self-perpetuating consistory appeared as the powerful body. Provincial synods were to convene at least once a year, and a national synod, comprised of two ministers and two elders from the 15 or so provincial synods, was to represent the Church in the whole country. There were also stringent provisions about church discipline, worldly attire, improper dances and books, but, in the absence of governmental support (as was the case in Geneva), the nature of church discipline had to be spiritual.

In addition to its theology and organizational structure, French Protestantism also created its own ethos. Nothing could be more misleading than the assumption that the French Protestants were pre-occupied with political affairs and paid little attention to the things of the spirit. Calvin had helped to form this ethos, which afterward developed in its own way. The elements were boldness, determination, exuberance. Seeing the world as the scene of a struggle between God and Satan, the French Protestants knew themselves on the side of God, which was victorious no matter what the outward appearance of things. Thus Calvin wrote these words to five Protestants languishing in a prison at Lyons: 'We cannot be frustrated of the hope which we have in him and in his holy promises. You have always been settled on that sure foundation, even when it seemed as though you might be helped by men, and that we too thought so. Whatever prospect of escape you may have had by human means your eyes have never been dazzled so as to divert your heart and trust.'[10]

But a high price had to be paid: the history of the French Reformation was accompanied by the suffering of Protestants from the time of the inception of the movement to the end of the century. Of course, religious persecution was a standard ingredient of the Age of the Reformation; still, the suffering of the French Protestants deserves a special note. At some places, Protestants and Catholics held to some sort of gentleman's agreement with respect to one another. France was the country where the Catholic authorities faced not merely sporadic expression of Protestant sentiment, but a powerful movement. Every effort was made to crush it.

The number of victims was high—higher than that of any other group in the 16th century, though the contemporary chroniclers may have been too involved or careless when it came to putting down figures; numbers made little difference. What is important is that such persecution helped mold the temper of French Protestantism.

All martyrs seal their conviction with death, but they do so in different ways. Indignation, boldness, rejoicing, humility, can find expression in a man's last hour. The French martyrs were bold. They were *milites Christi*, soldiers of Christ, and their last hour was a time neither of humility nor rejoicing over the communion with God which was to be theirs. They vehemently indicted their accusers. The outward expression of this mood was that the French martyrs often went to their execution singing. The five students of Lyons who suffered death in 1553 sang a Psalm on the way to the place of execution; many others did the same.

French Protestantism was a singing Church. Clement Marot, an Erasmian humanist, who frowned upon the factions dividing

Christendom and preferred to be known as 'a Christian,' provided the hymns. Somewhat accidentally at first, he had tried his hand at translating the Psalms. A first group of 13 Psalms was published at Strassburg in 1539, and three years later came an edition of 30. Melodies of sundry origins were added to his words. The hymns were sung in prisons and at the stake no less than in services of worship. Their texts were paraphrases of the Biblical passages and their music, often in a minor key, forceful and exuberant. This was the heartbeat of French Protestantism.

Finally, a word must be said about the political reflections of the French Protestants. Influenced by a variety of sources, including, of course, John Calvin, but molded by the sequence of political events from the constitutional crisis of 1559 to the Massacre of St. Bartholomew in 1572, the thinking of French Protestants underwent a change. There had been a few impatient ones all along who groaned under the oppressive persecution and longed to repay in kind, taking to force to obtain the victory of their Gospel. But most of the Protestants were moderate, influenced by Calvin, who incessantly counseled that God had called them to patience and suffering rather than the use of force. He rejected those who, as he put it, sought *mundum instanto convertere*. But the continuous persecution, the constitutional crisis, and especially the Massacre of St. Bartholomew reoriented the Protestant attitude toward the crown. Theretofore, French Protestants had emphasized their loyalty toward authority. The new pamphlets argued a different case, even as many hardly espoused religious concerns. Sharply antiroyalist in tone, they saw royal power not as absolute, but as dependent upon legitimate use. Francis Hotman's *De furoribus gallicis*, of 1573, was an account of the Massacre and a vehement indictment of the crown. His *Franco–Gallia*, of that same year, showed that in the past the people had exercised sovereignty and that the absolute exercise of royal power was a recent development. An anonymous work, *A Defense of Liberty Against Tyrants*, of 1577, attributed to Philip du Plessis Mornay, may have been the most influential pamphlet. Its theme was the proper attitude toward authority. Did the orders of a sovereign have to be carried out, even if they were contrary to the law of God? Was resistance against a sovereign permissible? The tract asserted that the *officiarii regni* (officials of the realm) had the right and the responsibility to resist a king who violated the law of God. Kings were not above the people: 'Seeing that the people choose and establish their kings, it follows that the whole body of the people is above the king, for it is a thing most evident, that he who is established by another, is accounted under him who has established him.'[11] A tract entitled *Du droits des Magistrats sur les sujets*, by Theodore Beza, argued that an unfaithful king had to be removed from office, and another tract, *La France—Turquie*, compared Charles II and the Turkish sultan.

In 1584 the country, already beset by constitutional woes, was faced with a new issue: the problem of the successor to Henry III, who was childless and (after the death of his younger brother) the last of the Valois. Next in line stood Henry of Navarre who, as leader of the Protestants, was bitterly opposed by all Catholics. This gloomy prospect rallied the Catholics. The Catholic League allied itself with Philip II, while Pope Sixtus V excommunicated Henry of Navarre and deprived him of all claims to the French crown. Still, the last of the seven Wars of Religion in France which broke out in 1585 demonstrated the confusion of religion and politics in the land. Henry III increasingly resented the power and influence of the Guises—so much so that he instigated the assassination of Duke Henry of Guise and Cardinal Louis of Guise in December 1588. The following summer a rabid Catholic sought revenge by assassinating the King.

On his deathbed Henry asked the army to swear the oath of obedience to Henry of Navarre as his successor who took the appelation of Henry IV. With Henry of Navarre the French Reformation and the Wars of Religion reached their end. Though a Protestant and a leader of the Protestants, Henry was hardly a religious person. Beyond the routine of religious exercises, especially before and after battles, he gave no evidence of religious conviction, except a coolness—of all things considering his leadership of the French Protestants—toward a rigorous Calvinism. Had he lived in Geneva, his problems with the consistory there would have been unending; he was hardly a model Calvinist. His goal was to be a Frenchman, and his conversion to Catholicism was less a traitorous default of the Protestant faith (to which he never really held) than a wise political move.

In July 1593 Henry abjured his Protestant beliefs and professed the Catholic faith, uttering, according to tradition, 'Paris is well worth a mass.' The point, if authentic, was well taken. Paris was the citadel of Catholicism and Henry could never hope to rule the city as a heretic. And Paris was France. He realized that only as a Catholic could he unite the country. Decades of indecisive civil war were ample evidence. Henry's acceptance of Catholicism did not change the political picture overnight. A long struggle was necessary

I

before he finally controlled the country. His conversion brought the more moderate Catholics into his camp, even as it freed the country from the oppressive threat of war with Spain. An astute use of force, persuasion, and money brought the nobility to his side. The Protestants, though shocked by his ecclesiastical turnabout, remained his loyal subjects, and the antiroyalist sentiment which had become so widespread among them during the days of Charles IX and Henry III disappeared.

On April 13 1598, the King took the decisive step of settling the religious problem by promulgating the Edict of Nantes, the last one of a long list of edicts and mandates, begun with the Edict of Chateaubriand in 1551. Within certain limitations, the Edict granted freedom of worship to the Protestants.[12] They were allowed to worship in places where they had done so in 1596 and 1597; elsewhere, Protestant worship was restricted to one place in a bailiwick. Paris continued to be prohibited to Protestants, as were episcopal and archiepiscopal seats. The Edict decreed the full equality of Protestants in governmental offices, and guaranteed them one hundred places of safety for a period of eight years. This last provision seems particularly noteworthy since it revealed the peculiar character of the Edict: though issued by the King, it was essentially a contract between two political powers.

The Edict marked the end of the Reformation in France. For the first time the notion of religious freedom was embodied in a document of state. The principle of the *corpus christianum*, of whatever ecclesiastical coloring, was repudiated. It was a departure from more than a thousand years of Western history, during which a citizen had been, by the fact of his citizenship, a Christian of the kind prescribed by his sovereign. The Edict of Nantes ended this, heralding a development that was to encompass, as the centuries passed, all of Europe. In Germany such toleration came after the end of the Thirty Years' War, in England after the Glorious Revolution —while in France, herald and forerunner of this development, the revolutionary beginnings were subsequently reversed. In 1629 the political and military provisions of the Edict of Nantes were rescinded, and in 1685, three years before the Toleration Edict in England, Louis XIV revoked the religious provisions. The notion of national unity, even in religion, was to be once more victorious.

At the time of the Edict of Nantes, the Protestants comprised about one-tenth of the population, a figure which shows they could hardly force their will upon the land. The Edict gave them the maximum that could be attained under the circumstances. Still, France had come a long way since that day in August 1523, when the *Parlement* of Paris and the theological faculty of the university there had joined hands to suppress the ideas of Luther. The ensuing 75 years had brought the failure of those efforts, and the Edict of Nantes safeguarded the accomplishments of Protestantism in France. Yet Protestantism had failed in its foremost goal—to convert the entire country. That the decisive battles, theological as well as military, were fought in the second half of the century, when a revived Catholicism had replaced the weariness of an earlier generation, undoubtedly was an important factor. Accordingly, the Protestant slogans had to be theological, and could not avail themselves of the potent religious exuberance characteristic of Germany in the 1520s. But above all, the explanation must point to political factors, and especially the monarchs. Here might have been the cause to rally widespread support, but it simply did not come forth. Without the benefit of religious enthusiasm and a real political issue, Protestantism was not strong enough to win, even though it eventually became involved in political strife.

## Sweden

In Scandinavia the Reformation expanded and consolidated in a unique fashion. There at the outset of the century the Church was lively and no popular criticism was voiced. The Renaissance prelate, the immoral monk, or the absentee bishop was an unknown figure. The monasteries were centers of authentic spirituality and important places of learning.

Surprisingly, it was in Sweden that the ecclesiastical transformation was most comprehensive. Hardly anywhere else was the Reformation as successful. There it succeeded in achieving quickly what elsewhere came only after tense and tedious development. The explanation is to be sought neither in the bankruptcy of the old Church nor in the forcefulness of the Protestant proclamation.

The incumbent on the throne of the Union of Kalmar, which comprised all of Scandinavia, at the outbreak of the Reformation was Christian II, one of the most remarkable rulers of the century. A contemporary said of him that he had 'the face of an Italian,' and this observation reflected on his temper as well. Christian was a typical Renaissance ruler, literate, learned, cultured, but ruthless and egotistical. He opposed the higher clergy and nobility, though it is hard to say if he was guided by a progressive temper or by absolutist tendencies. One of his main political goals was to bring Sweden into closer submission to Denmark. In so doing he favored and supported the pro-Danish faction in Sweden, represented by the Archbishop of Uppsala, Gustav Trolle, who for reasons partly personal was bitterly feuding with Sten Sture, the administrator, or *rigsforstander*, in Sweden. In 1517 the Swedish estates, convened by Sture, deposed the Archbishop. His influence in Rome, however, caused Sweden to be placed under interdict and brought about Sture's excommunication.

Christian collected arms and men, and in January 1520, invaded Sweden under the pretense of defending the Church. Sture was defeated. Magnanimously announcing an amnesty for those who had fought against him, Christian invited the nobles of the realm to Stockholm to join him in the coronation festivities. Unsuspecting, they came, but a scheme, arranged between Christian and Trolle, brought their downfall. The archbishop announced that the royal pardon had not affected the ecclesiastical censure and requested Christian to punish the nobles on behalf of the Church. Christian complied. Over 600 nobles and clergy were executed.

This 'Massacre,' or 'Blood Bath,' of Stockholm was to have serious repercussions. For one, the Church, in the person of Archbishop Trolle, had become intimately involved in the political strife besetting the country and had done so on the side of those whose interests seemed to be foreign rather than Swedish. Such a turn of events was bound to isolate the Church. Moreover, the political picture changed quickly, despite the seemingly fatal blow to Swedish leadership. Christian seemed to have scored a decisive victory, but it proved to be short-lived. Gustavus Eriksson Vasa, scion of the Sture family, began to garner the support of the remaining nobility and the peasants, and set out to throw off the Danish yoke. His first success came in 1521 with the defeat of Archbishop Trolle and two years later he was in control of most of the country. That same year Christian II himself was deposed in Denmark, whereupon Stockholm surrendered and Gustavus was elected King of Sweden and Finland. From then on Denmark and Sweden went their separate ways.

At his election Gustavus gave the customary assurances about maintaining the 'privileges, persons and possessions of the holy Church,' but there was a hollow ring about this assurance, since this Church had sided with his political opponents. A pressing issue was posed by vacancies in most of the existing episcopal sees.

In the spring of 1523 the King nominated the papal nuncio John

Magnus, a conscientious but weak figure, as Archbishop of Uppsala. In addition, four other bishops were nominated, loyal Catholics, but politically on Gustavus's side. In September he requested the papal confirmation of these nominations, asking, at the same time, for the suspension of the payment of the annates. The country was too destitute to pay and would pledge 'greater obedience' in other matters.[13] But Pope Adrian continued to support Archbishop Trolle and, moreover, appointed a foreigner to one of the vacant sees. Gustavus found that appointment unacceptable and threatened that, if necessary, he would procure the confirmation of his bishops 'from the only and high priest, Jesus Christ.'[14] The threat was obvious, yet Adrian's successor, Clement VII, showed himself unwilling to engage in this kind of ecclesiastical blackmail. He confirmed only one of the royal candidates and turned down the request for the suspension of the annates. This was virtually the last communication between Rome and Sweden.

In Sweden the initial phase of what might receive the label 'Reformation' entailed nothing more than the repudiation of the papal authority, which took place against the backdrop of a steady spread of Lutheran ideas. Laurentius Andreae, Archdeacon at Strengnäs, illustrated the new theological orientation in 1524, when he asserted that the Church was the communion of believers and not of prelates. If this smacked of Lutheran heresy, Andreae added, those who so argued should first check if their own teaching was scriptural.[15]

Andreae became an advisor to the King—he had been appointed the King's secretary and chancellor in 1523—and he established himself as a staunch partisan of the new faith. An astute politician in addition to being a competent theologian, he persuaded the King that the acceptance of the Lutheran faith offered benefits without liabilities. A sure indication of a new direction came in January 1525, with the promulgation of a mandate which stipulated that the income of the Church was to go to the King. One month later, Olavus Petri, a minister in Stockholm and perhaps the foremost theological exponent of Protestantism in the land, married. And Gustavus in turn urged the translation of the Bible into the vernacular. Nothing came of this project, however, and part of the reason was that the translation assignments were handed out rather thoughtlessly and incited little enthusiasm on the part of the proposed participants.

In 1526, the first Protestant tract in Swedish appeared. Entitled *A Useful Teaching*, it came from the pen of Petri, who had derived a good deal of his material from Luther. That same year a Swedish New Testament was published, in all likelihood also Petri's work.

During the next two years Petri continued to publish prolifically and thereby laid the foundation for Protestant literature in Sweden.[16]

A blacksmith's son, Petri had attended the University at Wittenberg between 1512 and 1518.[17] Those years surely must have left their imprint upon him, even though the details of the influence remain enigmatic. Upon his return to Sweden, he quickly became a preacher of renown. His subsequent involvement as the great popularizer of the tenets of the Reformation in the ecclesiastical transformation in Sweden was substantial and significant. In 1530 he published a catechism and one year later a Swedish order of worship. His thought was not original and his theology hardly brilliant. With the exception of his *Een liten boock om sacramenten* (Little Book Concerning the Sacraments), his writings were practical in orientation, often mere translations from Luther and other German Protestant theologians. He was more concerned with reforming the religion of the people than with delineating a theology. He was, in the pulpit as well as in his pamphlets, a preacher.

The country meanwhile continued in a state of crisis. Gustavus was hard pressed by his foreign creditors, yet he had no money and new taxes were out of the question. Convening a diet at Vesterås in 1527, he confronted the assembled estates with the news that the country was at the verge of bankruptcy. This was hardly novel; what was new, however, was the insistence that the solution lay in the confiscation of the property of the Church. One of the bishops retorted that to touch the property of the Church was to touch the authority of the pope. Gustavus seemed impressed by the argument and told the estates that under the circumstances it would be best for him to abdicate. He 'would move on his way,' he said, 'never to return to this unreasonable, perverted, and ungrateful fatherland.'

After some hesitation the estates agreed that they had nothing to lose from the King's proposed action—nothing, that is, except their faith—and everything to gain. Gustavus waited until he had been implored three times not to abdicate before he agreed to change his decision. The recess of the Diet handed the episcopal castles and lay-fiefs over to the King, who, in effect, was given the authority to decide what the needs of the Church were.[18] Moreover, all ecclesiastics were placed under the authority of civil courts for civil offenses. The 'pure Word of God should be preached' and the Scriptures read in churches and schools.[19] Together with the recess an *ordinantia* was issued which spelled out the relationship between the spiritual and the temporal realm. The existing structure of the Church was retained, though episcopal jurisdiction and the authority of the bishops were restricted and replaced by that of the King. The bishops, who had put up a valiant resistance, in the end acknowledged the King's authority.

The Diet of Vesterås was the beginning of the Swedish Reformation.[20] Royal authority in ecclesiastical affairs was strengthened and the ties with Rome were broken. Otherwise, however, ecclesiastical life in Sweden was hardly altered. The bishops continued their episcopal functions even as the clergy continued their accustomed round of activities; only the stipulation of the *ordinantia* that the Word of God be preached introduced a new, if vague, element into the situation. The Roman orientation of the Swedish Church was repudiated, as were the legal prerogatives which the Church had theretofore enjoyed. But the new Church could not have been labeled Protestant, and many years were to pass before that could be said. All the same, a beginning had been made. The obvious parallel of the Swedish events with the maneuvering of Henry VIII in England comes to mind, for in both instances the sovereign acted in response to a specific need against the backdrop of the existing Protestant sentiment.

The royal usurpation of ecclesiastical power and property had evoked hardly any repercussions, Gustavus's position was stable, and his decision to be crowned was the outward expression of this consolidation of power. A few days before his coronation, in 1528, Petrus Magni, the Bishop of Vesterås, the only bishop confirmed by Pope Clement VII in 1524, ordained three bishops and this provided for formal apostolic succession.[21] Since he was not a Protestant, he had the three episcopal candidates assure him, perhaps somewhat gratuitously, that they would seek papal confirmation at the earliest opportunity.[22]

A synod at Örebro, in 1529, undertook additional ecclesiastical changes. The chief spokesman was Laurentius Andreae, who proposed several innovations, such as Communion under both kinds. A number of anti-Catholic proposals dealing with education, liturgy, and polity were passed. The clergy were exhorted 'to proclaim, propagate and advance the Word of God'; holy days were restricted, and papal jurisdiction over the bishops was rejected.[23]

In a way, the synod of Örebro propounded a *via media*, and thus neither the committed Protestants nor the adamant Catholics were happy about the outcome. The former resigned themselves to verbal antics—Olavus Petri was insulted in the streets of Stockholm for having betrayed the Gospel—and the latter moved to action. In the south of the country, in Smaland, a rebellion broke out over discontent with the King's ecclesiastical policy. Gustavus was charged with having allowed the Lutheran heresy to enter the land, having usurped the property of the Church, and having altered its traditional and honorable customs. In the face of this danger Gustavus persuaded, promised, cajoled, bribed, and succeeded in containing the rebellion to a small area, where it quickly collapsed. He argued that no new religious teaching had been introduced in the country. If ecclesiastical property had been confiscated, then this was done in accord with the provisions of the Diet of Vesterås. Gustavus asserted that he could not keep priests from marrying if such was not prohibited by the Word of God, and if unchristian books had been published in the realm no one had been forced to read them. The royal argumentation seemed plausible.

From then on Protestantism had smooth sailing in Sweden, always, of course, under royal aegis. The four bishoprics vacant in 1529 were filled with men of Erasmian leanings who were Catholic rather than Protestant. Since the Swedish Church continued in a state of theological limbo, such a choice was not completely untenable. The Archbishopric of Uppsala, vacant since 1521, was another matter—both embarrassing and important—for the position was too crucial to fall to someone not in sympathy with the Protestant cause. But the King made haste slowly. He wanted neither a strong man who might effectively oppose his policies nor a committed Protestant who might pursue a staunchly anti-Catholic policy. Gustavus's thinking was influenced, no doubt, by the international situation at the time, especially Charles V's evident determination to subdue the German Protestants by force. The formation of the League of Schmalkald early in 1531 removed these clouds from the political horizon. In August and September 1531 a gathering of the Swedish bishops brought the election of Laurentius Petri, a brother of Olavus, to the archbishopric. His Protestant conviction was beyond doubt.

Needless to say, there was no curial confirmation, and this caused no little anxiety on the part of some of the bishops. Two of them secretly notarized their objections against their participation in the consecration and renewed their allegiance to the Roman Church. Practically, however, such clandestine opposition had no significance, and Laurentius was consecrated, the rite being performed by duly ordained bishops.

The consecration of a Protestant archbishop marked the end of what might be called the first phase of the Swedish Reformation. A number of external changes had taken place, though neither the theological clarification of the new Church nor the acceptance of the new teaching by the people was anywhere in sight. Additional reforms were decreed during the following years, such as the partial translation of the Mass into Swedish, the abolition of clerical celibacy, and the publication of a Swedish Old Testament. Ecclesiastical policy in the 1530s was aimless; since Gustavus possessed little religious concern, and had largely achieved what he desired, namely, more power and money, this was an understandable characteristic. Below the surface simmered tensions between the King and those guiding ecclesiastical affairs. Gustavus drained the financial resources of the Church to the utmost and at the same time he chided it for its failure to provide for education and a literate ministry.

A visitation in 1540 surveyed the religious state of affairs and also provided new revenue in the form of precious metals for the King, who claimed that such utensils as ornate chalices were no longer needed by the churches. At the same time, a *conservator* was appointed for each province to supervise ecclesiastical affairs. While the details of this administrative restructuring of the Swedish Church are not overly important, the further loss of independent authority on the part of the Church was crucial. In 1541 a Swedish translation of the Bible appeared. In itself this hardly was a Protestant feat but, given the times, it was a further stimulus in the move away from Rome. The godfather of the translation was Luther, and the titlepage of the publication was disarmingly frank about the work's indebtedness to Luther's translation. That same year a Swedish Mass was introduced.

Then popular discontent erupted into the open. The changes in the land had been extensive. A strong sovereign had accumulated increasing power, leaving the nobility without its traditional freedom. And the common people were no less resentful about the religious changes. Their way of life had become different. The King's representatives pried into their affairs, levied new taxes, issued decrees, and changed their religion. A visitation in 1541 had brought further confiscation of ecclesiastical property and stirred up renewed resentment. A rebellion broke out in May 1542, and for awhile the King's throne tumbled. But the rebel leader, a peasant by the name of Nils Dacke, was no match for the King. Though the hostilities lasted for well over a year, Gustavus emerged as victor and afterward his position was stronger than ever. He lost little time to prove this point. A Diet of Västerås in 1544 issued several reform measures which purged the Swedish Church of additional vestiges of Catholic practice. The preaching of the 'Word of God' was enjoined, pilgrimages were forbidden, as were the worship of saints, private Masses, and images.[24] The estates pledged to be the King's loyal subjects, and the King promised to rule justly.

The ecclesiastical reforms of 1544 marked, in a real sense, the end of the Reformation in Sweden. Hardly any additional changes of substance were made in the future, even though Gustavus left no stone unturned to wrest more and more power from the Church.[25] The King's policy was oppressively obvious, and several bishops decided to face the consequences and resigned their episcopal responsibilities. In 1560 only Archbishop Laurentius Petri was left to consecrate new bishops and thus formally perpetuate the apostolic succession. Gustavus was hardly concerned about this subtle point of theological doctrine, particularly since the German Protestant rulers provided ample evidence that the apostolic episcopacy was not germane to the Protestant faith.

The ecclesiastical transformation in Sweden had been smooth and undramatic. There was no drastic change, no sudden upheaval. Catholicism had faded away. The monasteries were not forcibly closed down, as had been the case in England. Deprived of their economic base, they decreased in significance until they disappeared. Church services were in the vernacular, but they closely followed the Catholic practice. No new theological statement was adopted by the Swedish Church.

In 1560 Gustavus was succeeded by his son Eric, the 14th monarch to carry the name. He was as capable and brilliant as his father, but lacked the mental equilibrium that distinguishes the genius from the insane. After nine stormy years the nobles decided that they had had enough, and deposed him. Next in line of succession was Gustavus's second son, John III. He was hardly a rousing improvement over Eric, but his reign showed some ostensible political success. A Protestant of the kind officially recognized in Sweden, John had ambitions to resolve the religious disagreement between the two sides. An amateur theologian of sorts, he drafted a church order in 1575, the *Nova Ordinantia*, and a liturgy two years later, the *Liturgia Svecanae Ecclesiae*. Confidently, he felt he had cut the Gordian knot of the religious controversy. The liturgy, known as the 'Red Book' for its reddish-brown parchment cover, followed the Roman Missal and had a definite Catholic flavor. The clergy objected to the Book, as did the nobility, but the King persisted in advocating its use. At the same time he secretly dispatched an emissary to Rome to establish contacts with the Curia, asking specifically that Communion under both kinds, a married clergy, and the vernacular Mass be allowed in Sweden.[26] In all likelihood Pope Gregory XIII never intended to grant these requests—he had earlier turned down the Swedish Queen's request for Communion under both kinds—but the King's attitude opened vistas of restoring Sweden to the Catholic Church. Gregory dispatched Antonio Possevino, secretary to the General of Jesuits, as papal nuncio to Sweden.[27] Possevino arrived in December 1577, and at once set out to convert the King to the Catholic faith. Since John had a high opinion of his theological erudition, this was no easy task. After several months Possevino's persuasiveness began to wear down the King, who declared himself ready to accept the Tridentine confession of faith. He attended Mass, exclaiming—according to one contemporary—'I embrace the Catholic Church forever.'

If he actually said those words, he defined 'forever' in a strikingly new way. The formal acceptance of Catholicism in Sweden was made dependent on the papal response to John's earlier requests. And this response was negative. Since John was too sagacious a politician not to know that Catholicism without these concessions was impossible in Sweden, the papal refusal to accede to the requests meant the end of Catholic restoration.

John died in 1592 and was succeeded by his son Sigismund, who in 1587 had already been elected to the Polish throne. This succession implied a political program bound to be rejected by the Swedish nobility. That Sigismund was a Catholic (and had an adamant Catholic wife) did not help matters, as it allowed political and religious sentiment to coalesce into opposition. Charles, the late King's brother, led the opposition. The controversy over the introduction of John's liturgy had left the Swedish Church divided and theologically confounded. Charles realized that only a united Church could successfully oppose Sigismund's efforts to restore Catholicism in the land. In March 1593, he convened a meeting at Uppsala, mainly attended by the clergy, but also by members of the council and nobility. This gathering denounced the liturgy of John III, the 'cause and root of many disorders,' for its 'superstition,' declared the Bible the sole authority of faith, and asserted that the three ancient Creeds, together with the Augsburg Confession, were its proper interpretation. At the same time, teachings of Zwingli and Calvin were condemned. Other provisions prohibited worship services not in conformity with the accepted faith, and demanded the reestablishment of the University of Uppsala for the education of the Swedish clergy. Sigismund was to accept these stipulations as a prerequisite for his coronation.

The *Uppsala Möte*, as this gathering is known, was the most significant event in the history of the Swedish Church during the 16th century. 'Sweden is become one man, and we have all one Lord and one God,' the chairman of the gathering reportedly exclaimed. The period of doctrinal uncertainty, prevailing since the ties with Rome had been severed, ended. The Swedish Church was Lutheran—vaguely Lutheran, to be sure, for Lutheranism in Germany had long found the Augsburg Confession insufficient to define its theology. In Sweden this Confession seemed adequate to give identity to the Swedish Church.

Sigismund was still in Poland when the news of this *fait accompli* reached him. He refused to give his approval and on reaching Stockholm in September 1593, he had Catholic services held in contradiction of the provisions of the *Uppsala Möte*. On the day of his coronation he formally accepted the provisions, though in a secret protestation to Rome he stated that he had made the concession under duress and would not feel bound to honor it once he exercised full control in the country.

Soon political issues added to the religious discontent. Sigismund violated his coronation agreement by appointing deputies for the provinces directly responsible to him rather than to the council. A meeting of the Swedish Diet at Söderkoping in 1595 agreed that Charles should act as regent during the King's absence. Moreover, direct communications between the King and the provincial deputies were prohibited. Catholic priests were expelled from the country and the Mass was no longer allowed to be celebrated. Clearly, a political crisis had been precipitated—Swedish fear of Polish influence in the land—to which a religious issue, the imposition of Catholicism, could easily be attached.

Thereby the victory of Lutheranism in Sweden was made final. It came at a time when the fortunes of Protestantism elsewhere in Europe were precarious and the Counter-Reformation was prying piece after piece from the Protestant edifice. Sweden, quite the contrary, was a shining light on the Protestant horizon.

### Scotland

In Scotland the Lollard tradition provided the same semi-indigenous backdrop as it did for the ecclesiastical change in England. Although its impact upon Scotland has not been thoroughly explored, Lollardy had surely survived into the 16th century in Scotland. The principal cause of the ensuing religious ferment, nonetheless, was Luther, whose writings were disseminated in Scotland as they were elsewhere in Europe.

In the mid-twenties one Patrick Hamilton appeared on the scene and proclaimed the Lutheran evangel. He had been abroad on the Continent to study and had there encountered the wave of enthusiasm for Luther's proclamation. When he returned to Scotland, he forcefully preached the new Gospel according to Wittenberg. With 'Master Patrick Hamilton,' so John Knox wrote in his *History of the Reformation in Scotland*, 'our history doth begin.'[28] Hamilton penned a little treatise, written in Latin and translated into English under the title *Dyvers Frutful Gatheringes of Scrypture concernying Fayth and Workes*. It is known as *Patrick's Places* and was an impressive exposition of the Protestant faith. Hamilton wrote that faith makes 'God and man friends,' or that 'the faith of Christ is to believe in him; that is, to believe his word and to believe that he will keep thee in all thy need and deliver thee from evil.'[29]

Convicted of heresy, Hamilton was executed in February 1528. John Knox recorded the details of the execution, and recalled Hamilton's gesture to his servant, to whom he gave his clothes: 'These will not profit in the fire; they will profit thee. After this, of me thou can receive no commodity, except the example of my death which, I pray thee, bear in mind; for albeit it be bitter to the flesh, and fearful before men, yet it is the entrance unto eternal life, which none shall possess that denies Christ Jesus before this wicked generation.' Knox added that in 'St. Andrews, yea, almost within the whole realm (who heard of that fact), there was none found who began not to inquire: Wherefore was Master Patrick Hamilton burned?' Knox also reported that Cardinal Beaton was told 'if you will burn them, let them be burnt in deep cellars, for the reek of Patrick Hamilton has infected as many as it blew upon.'[30]

But some 18 years passed before another prominent Protestant reformer appeared on the scene—George Wishart, still in his thirties, 'comely of personage.' He had studied at St. Andrews, probably had seen Patrick Hamilton's burning, and subsequently had become a parish priest. His Protestant convictions forced him to flee to England, then to the Continent. By 1543 he was back in his native land and the following year he began to proclaim the Protestant message.

His return to Scotland had been prompted as much by political reasons as by his zeal to spread the new evangel. The death of King James V in 1542 found Scotland in a deep crisis. The country had suffered a disastrous defeat in battle at the hands of the English and the future was uncertain. After the King's death, Cardinal Beaton produced a document to show that James had named him regent for his infant son. At once the document was labeled a forgery by the nobility. In January 1544 the estates named the Earl of Arran regent; Beaton was arrested as conspirator against the realm. Parliament confirmed Arran's appointment and at the same time authorized the use of the vernacular Bible. Arran had Protestant leanings and favored close ties with England. In the end Beaton emerged victorious in the struggle. The ties with England—in the form of a marriage treaty between Mary Stuart and Edward—were voided, the alliance with France was renewed, and Beaton was made chancellor. The English party had been defeated.

In this setting George Wishart proclaimed the Protestant Gospel. The political situation meant that his proclamation strengthened the pro-English party. In March 1546 he was burned as a heretic.

Before too many weeks had passed a group of Scottish noblemen provided a sequel to the execution by assassinating Cardinal Beaton. Their chaplain was John Knox, who thus made his entrance into the spotlight of history. Samuel Johnson called him one of the 'ruffians' of the Reformation, and, true enough, there was a kind of uncouthness about him which prompted a recent biographer to speak of him as the 'thundering Scot.'[31] An eloquent tribute was a word uttered at Knox's grave: 'Here lies one who neither flattered nor feared any flesh.'[32]

One cannot speak about the Reformation in Scotland without John Knox. That God had chosen him to proclaim his message constituted the very marrow of Knox's life. Had there been no Calvin in the 16th century to stress the profundity of God's election, John Knox would have taken his place, for the conviction of God's omnipotent rule was real and deep for him. In his *History* Knox related how he was asked, while serving on a French galley, if he thought 'that ever they should be delivered,' and he recorded his classic answer: 'God would deliver them from that bondage, to his glory, even in this life.'[33]

Knox's association with the conspirators took him for almost two years to a French galley—a long time, rowing endlessly across the North Sea, between Scotland and France, and France and Scotland. In later years Knox rarely spoke about his experience, but when he did his words abounded in pangs of sorrow. 'I knaw how hard the battell is betuix the Spreit and the Flesche, under the heavie cross of affliction,' he remarked at one time, 'whair no warldly defence, but present death dois appeir. I knaw the grudgeing and murmuring complaynts of the flesche; I knaw the angir, wraith and indignation, which it conceiveth aganis God, calling all his promisis in doubt, and being ready everie hour utterlie to fall frome God.'[34]

When he was released, early in 1549, Knox became the minister at Berwick, an English town near the Scottish border. It was a rough place, unruly and chaotic, full of homeless men, refugees, mercenaries, and others attracted like magnets to such situations. It was an arduous assignment, but Knox was persuaded that he handled it well: 'God so blessed my weak labours that in Berwick (where commonly before there used to be slaughter by reason of quarrels that used to arise amongst soldiers), there was as great quietness all the time that I remained there as there is this day in Edinburgh.'[35] Afterward followed a lengthy sojourn on the Continent, part of which was at Geneva. There he saw a Church truly reformed both in faith and in life, an experience which prompted the famous and exuberant eulogy that Geneva was 'the maist perfyt school of Chryst that ever was in the erth since the dayis of the Apostillis; in other places, I confess Chryst to be trewlie preachit; but maneris and religioun so sinceirlie reformat, I have not yit sene in any uther place.'[36]

In the meantime the situation in Scotland itself deteriorated steadily. Politically, the country was badly divided between the regent Mary of Lorraine, who pursued a pro-French policy, and the Scottish nobility, who favored close ties with England. The marriage treaty between Edward and Mary's daughter, Mary Stuart, concluded in 1543, had long been voided and had been replaced by a new treaty with the French dauphin Francis. French influence was increasingly felt in Scotland. The marriage between Mary and Francis in 1558 seemingly made the fateful ties with France insoluble. Again, the Catholic orientation of the ruler made the converging of political and religious considerations impossible: those who desired political change naturally saw the cause of the new faith as an obvious handmaid.

On December 3 1557 a group of Scottish Protestant noblemen signed a covenant which began with these words: 'We, perceiving how Satan, in his members, the Antichrists of our time, cruelly doth rage, seeking to overthrow and to destroy the evangel of Christ and his Congregation, ought, according to our bounden duty, to strive in our Master's cause even unto death.' The document challenged the clergy to promote 'the most blessed Word of God' and pledged to defend these ministers, 'the whole Congregation of Christ and every member thereof at our whole powers and waring of our lives, against

Satan and all wicked power that does intend tyranny or trouble against the aforesaid Congregation.'[37]

In 1558 Knox intervened in the political struggle. He published a vehement little pamphlet entitled *The First Blast of the Trumpet against the Monstrous Regiment of Women*.[38] Knox primarily sought to address himself to the regent Mary and his point was simple: Mary should abstain from idolatry and convert herself to the true Biblical religion. This was Knox's message on other occasions; this was his message now. But those who wanted to read more than a simple evangelistic exhortation could find something else in the tract: Knox asserted that a ruler who persecuted true religion (as did Mary) could not legitimately claim the loyalty of her subjects. 'If any man be affraid to violat the oth of obedience which they have made to such monsters, let them be most assuredly persuaded, that as the beginning of their othes, proceding from ignorance, was sinne, so is the obstinate purpose to kepe the same nothing but plaine rebellion against God.'[39] Protestant sentiment intensified.

Again religion and politics intertwined. The Peace of Cateau-Cambrésis of April 1559 freed France to strengthen its preoccupation with Scotland. Confident of French support, the regent had issued in February a proclamation which made any violation of ecclesiastical regulations—such as eating meat during Lent—punishable by death. Moreover, Protestant clerics were outlawed. Obviously the regent was forcing a showdown.

Then, in May, John Knox returned to Scotland. More than a man had returned: Knox was a symbol of a cause. At Perth, he preached a fiery sermon in the morning, and when a priest tried to say Mass in the afternoon—and boxed a man's ear who spoke out against it—the storm broke. By evening the 'rascal multitude' had stripped the town of everything that to them suggested idolatry.[40]

Scotland soon was at the brink of civil war. The Protestant nobility peacefully occupied Edinburgh and took hold of most of the country. Still, the outcome of their confrontation with the Queen Regent depended upon the success of either side to get reinforcements from England or France. In July the Protestant lords appealed to Elizabeth for help. She saw the dangers of a French-dominated Scotland, though she also realized the risk of a break with France.

After some hesitancy, the English Government provided financial assistance to the Protestants. Then French troops arrived in Scotland and promptly the Protestants demanded that the regent send them back. The regent refused and the Protestant lords formally deposed her in October.

The new year brought England's naval intervention, and in February a treaty was concluded between England and the Protestant lords. Afterward English troops crossed the border and, together with the Protestants, began a siege of Leith. France, the only hope of the Queen Regent, was beset by internal difficulties and was, moreover, threatened by a Spain that was unwilling to condone French imperialism in Scotland.

On June 10 the Queen Regent died. Mary of Guise had tried valiantly to maintain order in the country and to thwart the advance of Protestantism. Her qualifications had been impressive and admirable, but she had failed. Her pro-French policies had alienated the nobles. In July both England and France agreed to withdraw their troops from Scotland. Parliament was to meet in August. Governmental authority was exercised by a council on which the nobility had a majority. The sentiment in the land and the withdrawal of French troops raised Protestant hopes.

When Parliament met in August, a petition was drafted in which the Protestant divines were asked 'to draw, in playne and severall heidis, the summe of that Doctrine, quilk they wald menteyne, and wald desyre that present Parliament to establische, as hailsome, trew, and onlie necessari to be believit, and to be resavit [received] within that Realme.'[41] On August 17 Parliament adopted a confession drawn up by Knox and his ministerial colleagues; a few days later several statutes were passed against the Mass and papal jurisdiction. Merely the celebration of the Mass was prohibited, nothing more. The political situation did not lend itself to the imposition of ecclesiastical uniformity or the deprivation of the bishops. The Scottish Reformation shows that even prudent political circumstances needed formidable popular sentiment.

The chronicler must not overemphasize the events of 1560. Parliament had not been authorized to deal with the religious question, and not until 1567 did the crown finally give legal sanction to the new Church. For seven years there was, as one of the Protestant leaders remarked, 'nothing of our religion established, neither by law nor parliament.'[42] The assertion that the decision of Parliament in 1560 made Scotland Protestant begs the question as to precisely how this occurred. What happened in 1560 was simply that a new Church was recognized, while the structure of the old Church was left intact. While 1558 and 1559 had been a rather tumultuous time —Archbishop Parker prayed in England, 'God keep us from such a

visitation as Knox hath attempted in Scotland, the people to be or-
derers of things'[43]—the establishment of Protestantism took place
quietly.

The atmosphere in Scotland was one of continuity and gradual
change, taking place in a setting of civil strife. Monasteries were not
forcibly dissolved in Scotland. Nor did there take place, at least for
several years, the deprivation of those religious who decided to remain Catholic. There were no imprisonments or executions in the
Scottish Reformation.

Afterward Knox and several other ministers went to work on a
church order. The result was the so-called *Book of Discipline*, presented to Parliament in January 1561.[44] The *Book* was a comprehensive effort to order the life of both the Church and society at large.
On certain points—such as the Sacraments—the book was refresh-
ingly simple; on others, it was concerned with tedious detail—such
as its stipulations with respect to the widows of clergymen, or the administrative structure of the three universities, including professorial
salaries (the professor of philosophy received £100, the professor of
medicine and law £133, the theologians £200). There were serious
discrepancies of emphasis in the *Book of Discipline*. While the procedure of electing superintendents was dealt with in great detail,
hardly anything was said about their functions. Such unevenness
was unintentional, for the book did not benefit from careful revision
but was speedily adopted.

The *Book of Discipline* outlined ways of altering the financial
structure of the Church, and also ecclesiastical discipline, so dear to
Calvinists. An interesting distinction was made between 'crimes
capital'—such as blasphemy, adultery, murder, etc., which do not
fall 'under the censure of the Church' since they are to be 'punished
by the civil sword'—and 'drunkenness, excess (be it in apparel or be
it in eating and drinking), fornication, etc.'[45] Another feature was the
office of superintendent, who, for all practical purposes, performed
the functions of a bishop: he was addressed as 'my lord superintendent' instead of 'my lord bishop' and his emoluments were in keeping with the episcopal precedent.

The preceding paragraph has already noted the Calvinist character of Scottish Protestantism. There are several reasons, not the least
of which is to be sought in the theological orientation of John Knox
himself, who may well be called one of Calvin's most enthusiastic
disciples in the 16th century. His exuberant comment about Geneva
—'the most perfect school of Christ since the days of the Apostles'—
is well known and often quoted. There were certain modifications

of the Genevan practice (the office of superintendent was one of these), but theologically Scotland followed the lines set forth by Calvin.

One final distinction must be duly recorded. The legalization of the Calvinist faith in Scotland marked the first (and last) instance of a formal establishment of Calvinism anywhere in Europe. The movement was formidable in many places—the Netherlands, France, Hungary—but only in Scotland did it score success.


## Poland

In Poland there prevailed an atmosphere of relative toleration which made the religious spectrum far more checkered than any-where else in the West. Whereas in Germany or France one faith dominated and fenced off its competitors, greater diversity prevailed in the East. This made Lutherans, Calvinists, Anabaptists, Bohe-mian Brethren, and even Antitrinitarians more or less equal part-ners in the attempt to proselytize the land. Thus Poland was a religiously pluralistic society where—in contrast to the countries in the West—the arm of government was not used to establish a nor-mative religious tradition. The consequences were twofold. This situation created an atmosphere of mutual affinity—what we might well call ecumenical temperament. The Consensus of Sandomiersz, of 1570, was of this a most eloquent expression.[46] On the other hand, the absence of a strong, single, Protestant grouping made the country an obvious target for the Counter-Reformation. The varieties of Protestantism were a major argument in the Catholic polemic, which insisted that truth was one and Protestantism, variously divided, could not be truth. The Catholic efforts were successful, and Poland reaffirmed its ties with the Catholic fold. Thus the story ended about where it had begun, and since success is for most historians—as for the capitalist entrepreneur—the criterion of selection, the history of the Reformation in Poland seems to offer little excitement.

In Poland the Reformation failed after almost succeeding. The early spread of Protestant ideas, unsupported by governmental edict, was as successful as anywhere else in Europe—evidence of the per-suasiveness of the new theology. Then came the collapse, not so quickly as a house of cards, but just as irretrievable. Since there was no determined persecution, such collapse of Protestantism is doubly noteworthy. It attests that neither the religious commitment of the Protestants nor their political strength was formidable enough to force the lasting recognition of their religion. Had the Protestants been able to entice the King to their side, the story would have ended differently. But this was not the case. Nor was the Protestant nobility, the lower *szlachta* and the higher magnates, willing to oppose the King. They possessed the power they wanted and had little political reason to support the cause of religion.

The initial form of Protestantism reaching Poland was Lutheranism.[47] From the 1540s on Calvinism made its appearance, and subsequently it emerged as the principal form of Protestantism in the country. Such Calvinist prominence is not surprising, and one need not consider such considerations as the Polish antipathy toward Germany, the Germanic character of Luther's message, or the congeniality of the more democratic form of the Calvinist Church government for the temper of the Polish nobility. The simple fact is, as has been observed elsewhere in this study, that Calvinism was the aggressive form of Protestantism at the time, and Calvin the shining star on the Reformation firmament. The acceptance of Calvinism was a natural phenomenon.[48]

When King Sigismund I died in 1548, the presence of Protestant ideas in Poland had reached the point where the political authorities had to make a decision as to how to deal with the movement. The new King, Sigismund August, leaned toward Protestantism. He was devout, concerned about reform, and enlightened about ecclesiastical dogma. He had followed the theological controversy with unusual interest, and even corresponded with Melanchthon and Calvin, who twice challenged him to introduce the Gospel in Poland. But the hopes were premature, for Sigismund remained a faithful son of the Catholic Church. Perhaps he was a true Catholic at heart, or he may have realized that Protestantism was not strong enough in the land to allow him to become a Protestant.

Important was the Protestant orientation of the *szlachta*, the lower nobility. At diets in 1547 and 1548 the *szlachta* demanded that the Word of God be preached freely. While they were unsuccessful in their effort, the vigor of their demand was indicative of the atmosphere in Poland. Indeed, even the Catholic hierarchy lent support, albeit indirectly, to the Protestant cause by advocating ecclesiastical reform in ways hardly compatible with Catholic principles. Some demanded that the clergy might marry and others sought the Communion cup for the laity. One cleric, Stanislaus Orzechowski, denounced clerical celibacy in several tracts and then married. In April 1551, he was excommunicated and his property confiscated, whereupon he argued that at his ordination he had not been asked to render the vow of celibacy, and he appealed to the nobility for help. The *szlachta* made his cause their own. They took the case to the Diet and declared themselves unwilling to discuss political matters unless this usurpation of clerical authority was condemned. Eventually, the bishops agreed to a suspension of ecclesiastical jurisdiction for a period of one year.

During the next years the Protestants consolidated their success, established an organizational structure of their Church, and continued to exert political pressure to secure the legal recognition of their faith. At a diet in 1555 they hoped to achieve this formal recognition. At that time negotiations were taking place at Augsburg, which were to give religious freedom to the German Protestants, and the Polish Protestants were determined to attain the same. They demanded religious liberty. The bishops voiced their opposition, though further negotiations brought an agreement about the convening of a national synod and the suspension of ecclesiastical jurisdiction until that time.

The King set out to obtain papal approval for such a national synod, at the same time requesting a married clergy, the vernacular Mass, and Communion under both kinds. The response of the Curia was negative. This response, together with the dispatch of a papal legate to Poland, may have caused the King to have second thoughts about the Protestant demands: in 1557 he prohibited any further expansion of Protestant worship. His order, however, was one thing; its implementation another. At diets in 1562 and 1563 the *szlachta* demanded a permanent end to ecclesiastical jurisdiction. The King allowed no member of the nobility to be tried by an ecclesiastical court without a prior conviction by a secular court. Most of the ecclesiastical litigation came to a standstill, but there was no formal statement, a fact which allowed the King in 1564 to announce that his decision did not intend to curtail the traditional rights of the clergy. That same year he accepted the decrees and canons of the Council of Trent—but in 1565 the Diet of Piotrków declared all decisions of ecclesiastical courts null and void. This meant a victory for Protestantism. The situation continued ambiguous, since religious freedom was essentially restricted to the nobility.

The decision of 1565 allowed an unmolested life for Protestantism for several years. It was firmly established and its Lutheran, Calvinist, Bohemian, and Antitrinitarian branches took on distinct organizational forms. Printing presses poured out Protestant propaganda, the desire for Protestant literature was widespread. In 1563 a Polish Bible had appeared, though this time the Protestants had been beaten to their favorite project by the Catholics: two years earlier the Catholics had published a Polish translation of their own.

About the strength of Protestantism guesses only are possible. In 1569 almost half of the upper house of the Polish Diet (comprised of the higher nobility), excluding the bishops, was Protestant. No comparable figures are available for the lower house, the Chamber of Representatives, though one may assume on the basis of the action taken at several diets that a majority was strongly Protestant.

The death of Sigismund August in July 1572 confronted Poland with the problem of its dynastic future, since the King had been the last of the Jagiellon dynasty. From then on the Polish kingship became an elective office, dominated and manipulated by the nobility, which was little willing to burden itself with the luxury of a strong monarch. During the deliberations following the King's death the Diet agreed to legalize Protestantism. The Confederation of Warsaw of January 28 1573, granted religious freedom to Protestants but used nomenclature that was vague so as to raise doubts if the Antitrinitarians were also included in the provision. The Confederation also failed to state if the Protestants were assured only personal religious freedom, or if legal recognition was given to their public worship.

The successful candidate for the Polish throne was Henry of Valois, whose willingness to accept the Confederation had a great deal to do with his election. His reign in Poland was short-lived, however, and after a brief interregnum Stefan Batory was elected King and ruled until 1586. His religious policy was ambivalent but generally favored Catholicism. His successor, Sigismund III, whose rule extended for almost half a century, until 1632, pursued a determinedly Catholic policy. When he died, Poland was once again a Catholic country.

Even as the spread of Protestantism, this revitalization of Catholicism took place without any aggressively active involvement of the King. Batory had been fond of the Jesuits and favored them in a variety of ways; Sigismund III was a devout Catholic. Yet neither Batory nor Sigismund openly persecuted the Protestants. Protestantism just faded away, sapped of its inner vitality and strength.

What were the reasons? The answer is difficult. For one, Polish Protestantism was never a popular movement and always remained restricted to the nobility. But the absence of popular support alone was not fatal to the Protestant cause. There were other factors, which proved to be decisive.[49] The Catholic Church was too strong

—not so much religiously, but with respect to the power of the hierarchy which had political influence, was supported by the King, and withstood the initial Protestant assault without noticeable defections from its ranks. Most importantly, however, the political base of Protestantism was not broad enough. The towns might have provided strength for the Reformation, but they possessed no political voice and, therefore, their religious sympathies could find no political expression. And the Polish kings never wavered in their Catholic loyalty. Protestant sentiment remained restricted to the magnates and the *szlachta*, whose attitude thus became crucial for the cause of the Reformation. If either defected, Protestantism was lost in Poland. And such a defection did indeed occur. But even more important was the fact that Protestant sentiment was never sufficiently strong even among the nobility. Since there was little political gain for the nobility in accepting Protestantism, their response to the religious issue was solely governed by religious considerations. They preferred to remain Catholic. In Poland politics and the Reformation never coalesced.

Until the 18th century, Protestants were legally protected in Poland. Even though life was made difficult for them, they continued to exist—with the exception of the Antitrinitarians, who were refused the Christian appellation and were expelled in the 17th century. Religiously speaking, Poland passed beyond the Reformation era in a strangely ambivalent state. Catholicism and Protestantism coexisted, the one vigorous, the other listless. The Reformation in Poland failed because Protestantism was unable to make its political case.

## Conclusion

In the end, the attempt at ecclesiastical transformation was successful in two of the four countries examined, while the outcome in the other two remained in doubt for a long time. Naturally, the historian wonders if any generalizations emerge from this fact. The two countries that turned Protestant (Sweden and Scotland) were situated in northern Europe, and it is tempting, though admittedly unscholarly, to see some sort of pattern in this fact, especially since this corresponds to the pattern discernible in Europe at large. Nor is it really helpful to consider the timing of ecclesiastical change: Sweden turned Protestant in the 1520s, while Scotland did so in 1560. One can only say that the two countries in which the outcome of the religious controversy was still undecided in 1560 eventually remained Catholic. This may be mere happenstance—or evidence for a significant turn of events.

The introductory pages of this chapter suggested the eminent role of politics in the cause of ecclesiastical change. This concluding assessment must now seek to summarize the evidence. With one exception, each of the four countries examined in this chapter was characterized by the presence of more or less serious political problems. The issue of religious change did not confront a stable society, but one experiencing political turbulence independent of the challenge posed by the Protestant Reformation. The four societies may have experienced religious problems as well; though such was the case, the relevance of this fact for the ecclesiastical course of events was limited. The same must be said with regard to the social or economic conditions. Their impact on the religious transformation was indirect at best.

The Protestants' quest was for more than a 'platonic' propagation of their interpretation of the Christian faith. After the initial uncertainty had passed, the Protestants wanted the Catholic Church replaced by their own—or, if this was impossible, at least the legal recognition of their faith and its public expression. The matter of reformation assumed a definite legal quality which made the political involvement inevitable.

A further word must be said about the nature of the political problem to which we alluded. Three countries experienced different kinds of problems and, in a way, Poland did not experience any whatsoever. This fact, too, had its peculiar repercussions.

In Sweden the issue was posed by the recently won independence from Denmark and by the financial needs of the crown. Gustavus Vasa found himself in dire financial distress, and the wealth of the Church seemed likely to end his worries. Moreover, the Church had been an active participant (and even partisan) in the struggle between Sweden and Denmark—and, unfortunately, had been on the losing side. The fact that no theological changes or liturgical modifications were undertaken in Sweden on the heels of the confiscation of ecclesiastical property and the royal usurpation of ecclesiastical prerogatives would support the contention, already repeatedly made, that the initial intent of the reformers was by no means to cut the ties with Rome. Gustavus Vasa's primary concern was to remedy his fiscal distress and, at the same time, make sure that the Swedish Church was beyond the slightest suspicion of disloyalty. There was little theological agitation and the ecclesiastical transformation effected by the King was smooth and almost painless. The theological clarification of the meaning of the change came only several decades later.

France and Scotland, in turn, experienced a different political problem. In these countries the attempt at ecclesiastical change had initially failed, but continued Protestant agitation characterized the scene for decades. Politically, both countries saw competing factions strive for power in the land. In Scotland the contest was between the nobility and the Queen Regent, though underneath lurked the resentment of Scotsmen against foreign (French) influence. In France the controversy was, at least from the late 1550s onward, between competing factions of the nobility. The King stood in the middle, without the ability (or the power) to prevent the two factions from dragging the country into war and bloodshed.

These political tensions in Scotland and France existed independent of the religious turbulence and the efforts at ecclesiastical transformation. Indeed, they were prior in time and weightier in substance. They had a bearing on the cause of the Reformation since it quickly became obvious that a religious meaning could easily be attached to the existing political issues. This was the case for several reasons. The proponents of the political status quo favored the Catholic faith. This was true in the case of the Queen Regent in Scotland and the King in France. Such Catholic sentiment prompted them to suppress the incipient manifestations of Protestantism, which thereby became alienated from them. This, in turn, made it easy and prudent for Protestants to support those in political opposition to the status quo, since precisely this political opposition seemed to assure the realization of their own religious and ecclesiastical goals.

But if those concerned about religious change aligned themselves with a political faction because they saw advantages to their own religious cause, those primarily concerned about politics could similarly discern the advantage of supporting the religious claims of the Protestants, inasmuch as this assured them additional political strength. Thus, there were obvious advantages on both sides. Those interested in political change benefited from the support of those who desired change in religion—and vice versa.

The Protestants did not thereby introduce a political component into their quest for the true Gospel, for such a component had been present ever since the Reformation had begun. In light of the intimate relationship of Church and state, this had been an inescapable development. The Protestants were refused the right to public worship; it was inevitable that they would seek political means to attain this legal goal.

This takes us to Poland. On the face of things, events in France and in Poland did not differ in their final outcome: in the end both countries withstood the Protestant challenge and remained within the Catholic fold. But an important difference existed with respect to the intensity of turmoil that accompanied the period of Protestant agitation. France suffered immense bloodshed and bitter civil war, while Poland escaped such a turn of events. The reason for this must not be sought, however, in the areas of religious commitment or numerical strength of the Protestants. Rather, it lay with those indigenous political issues that were present in one country and absent in the other.

Poland did not have the kind of political issue that, in one way or another, perturbed not only France and Scotland, but Sweden, England, and even Germany as well. The Protestant nobility in Poland might have forced an issue at the death of Sigismund II, when the Jagiellon dynasty ended and the election of a Protestant king was a possibility, however remote. But apart from the desire of the Protestant nobility to have a Protestant king, there was no compelling reason to make such a move. Traditional prerogatives or constitutional liberties were not endangered—and the country would have been thrown, as was France, into a civil strife for no obvious reason.

It should be noted that the development sketched and the comparisons drawn pertain only to considerations external and empirical. They say nothing about the profundity of the message or the persuasiveness of the claims. Nor do they speak of the intensity of spirituality and piety that did (or did not) characterize the inner history of Protestantism (or Catholicism) in these countries. We have commented on matters pertaining to legal recognition and political treaties. While this is not the only history the chronicler of the Reformation can write, it is the one that relates how inner faith and conviction became embedded in the harsh realities of power politics.

That politics and religion should have been so intimately connected in the Reformation so that man's spiritual aspirations were seldom free from entanglement in things utterly mundane was the legacy of medieval civilization to the 16th century. Whatever its shortcomings, and there were many, this fact meant that the Reformation was able to exert its influence upon the ongoing history of Western civilization.

# CHAPTER EIGHT

# The Catholic Reaction

For Catholic Christendom the turbulent 16th century was no less important than for the emerging Protestant churches. It was at once the hour of its greatest crisis and of its greatest triumph. Perhaps the latter would not have been possible without the former; there are times in history when a high price must be paid for profound achievement.

About the depth and profundity of the crisis there can be little doubt. Never before had the Catholic Church been confronted with such a formidable desertion, never before with such flagrant disregard of her principles. The seamless robe of the Church was torn apart—and the one Church became a wistful dream. In former days Catholics viewed the Reformation mainly with disgust and anger. But there is also, and always has been, an element of sadness when recalling how in the 16th century man after man, priest after priest, country after country, renounced the Catholic faith which they had pledged to uphold; how statues and shrines, revered for centuries, were removed from churches; how spiritual endowments that had comforted men's souls were abolished; how monasteries, in which men strove to live piously, were deserted. Some of the losses were, to be sure, countered, and when the Reformation era had passed, the Catholic Church—what was left of it—was assuredly stronger, more vital and aggressive than it had been when it all started. But even as the destroyed shrines could not be restored, so were heresy, apostasy, and the rejection of papal authority irreparable.

Thomas More compared the Catholic Church to the land against which the sea will never prevail. But there was no way for the

269

Church to mend its seams completely, no matter what its renewed splendor, vigor, and spirituality.

Protestants have remarked, rather exuberantly, that Catholicism became a Church again through the Reformation. Properly understood, this remark has much in its favor, for even though there were varied Catholic efforts at spiritual renewal quite independent of the challenge of the Protestant Reformation, the fact remains that the Reformation intensified the sense of urgency with which new efforts at deepened spirituality (often copied from Protestants) were undertaken. There is no telling what might have been had there been no Reformation, for history, it is said, does not reveal its alternatives. As matters stand, the impact of the Reformation upon Catholicism, directly and indirectly, was strong and formidable indeed.

Historical parlance has used the term 'Counter-Reformation' to describe Catholic history in the 16th century, stressing the reaction against the Protestant Reformation as its dominant theme. The difficulty with this term is, however, that it overlooks all those developments and events in the course of the 16th century which had little, if anything, to do with the Protestant challenge. Accordingly, some scholars have preferred as an alternate term, 'Catholic Reform and Counter-Reformation,' to emphasize the dual characteristic of 16th-century Catholic life, its indigenous self-renewal, and its reaction against the Protestant Reformation. While it is a bit clumsy and raises the question of chronological priority, it is useful and deserves general acceptance.

The purpose here is not, however, to unfold the full panorama of Catholic history in the 16th century. This would be an assignment of major proportions and should not be relegated to a few incidental remarks in one chapter out of many. The concern now will be those facets and developments that have to do with the relation between Catholicism and the emerging Protestant tradition, with the way the Reformation became a part of Catholic history and the Catholic Church reacted to the Protestant challenge. Thus, neither the label 'Catholic Reform' nor that of 'Counter-Reformation' is fully adequate.

One may conveniently begin by recalling the assertion made earlier concerning the nature of the Reformation—that it was a spontaneous movement of elementary religious forces that sought to replace a sophisticated Church and religion with a handful of simple affirmations. Its cause was not the state of the Church but the thought of Martin Luther. It was characterized, from the beginning, by the intrusion of nontheological factors into what might have been a purely academic debate. Thus an unexpectedly sharp tone characterized the ensuing controversy, which was incisively influenced, within a matter of two years, by the formal ecclesiastical verdict against Luther.

From the vantage point of the Catholic Church, and especially the Curia, the situation was difficult. Neither the nature of the information about Luther reaching Rome nor the disposition of the officials entrusted with the examination of his teaching (such as Sylvester Prierias) allowed a full and comprehensive assessment of the matter. Considerations of European politics (the election of a new German Emperor upon the death of Maximilian I) preoccupied the Curia for almost a year and afterwards made it difficult to make up this deficiency. And the aggressively persistent presence of Johann Eck continued to pour oil on the fire until, in June 1520, he reached his goal.

In short, the course of curial action was hardly surprising, and, given the situation, it could not have been otherwise. Yet a different and very perceptive comment on the matter had earlier come from none other than Pope Leo X. It was a squabble among monks, he had remarked. One suspects that this was not meant as a positive statement but it expressed, however unwittingly, the observation that what was taking place in Germany required as little official curial action as did a thousand other 'monkish squabbles.' With all his congeniality, his preoccupation with art and learning in Rome, even his view of the papacy as a temporal monarchy, Leo's initial remark was more astute than most that were made afterward.

In the great debate that followed, largely after rather than before Luther's excommunication, the Catholic Church found itself at a decided disadvantage, if for no other reason than that the offensive was on the other side and those on the defensive are always at a disadvantage. It is the dissenter who propounds novel and startling ideas, requiring the defender of the status quo to reiterate what has been said and written a thousand times before. Henry VIII's *Assertio Septem Sacramentorum*, a spirited defense of the sacramental teaching of the Catholic Church, is a good case in point. If it was a mediocre work, as most later commentators seem to think, then this explains why it was well-nigh impossible for Henry to say anything strikingly new on a subject that had already been discussed *ad infinitum*.

An additional disadvantage must be noted. The stress of controversy has a way of calling forth extreme statements which, in a more relaxed and circumspect atmosphere, would probably not be made. Not surprisingly, in the Reformation controversy the Catholic protagonists were driven to all sorts of dubious pronouncements. Perhaps they did not fully fathom the authentic Catholic position, as has been suggested. More likely, however, the high tension of the polemical atmosphere misled them. They were inclined to degrade Scripture, denounce its use in the vernacular, reject the need for reform—precisely because their Protestant antagonists so emphatically affirmed all that. But in so doing, they unduly narrowed the Catholic position (which, for example, in principle had never been against a vernacular Scripture), lost many friends, and influenced few people. And the matter of ecclesiastical reform accentuated graphically the two horns of the dilemma. If the need for reform was conceded, such an admission was water on the mill of the Lutherans, who could boast, as indeed they did after Pope Adrian VI's famous confession of 1523, that this proved what they had been saying all along. If, on the other hand, Catholics denied the need for reform, they were likely to be chided for being dishonest in the face of seemingly indisputable evidence. Earlier in this study, the attempt was made to show that the state of the Church on the eve of the Reformation was relatively stable and that the actual abuses (as well as the popular demand to remove them) were few and far between. The Catholic dilemma was obvious.

Of even greater importance was the lingering uncertainty as to the nature of the whole controversy. There was no end to persuasive or even prophetic pronouncements, but here, as always, too many cooks spoiled the broth: the multitude of suggestions was bewildering. Some thought that at issue were certain ecclesiastical abuses which needed only to be corrected to restore blessed tranquility. Others pointed to theological disagreements, but precisely what these were remained astoundingly enigmatic and uncertain. The bull *Exsurge Domine* seemed to suggest that Luther's errors pertained mainly to the doctrines of indulgences and penance; Erasmus singled out questions of anthropology as the crucial point; Melanchthon was persuaded at Augsburg in 1530 that conciliation would be possible if the Communion cup were offered to the laity and priests be allowed to marry. Luther declared that the controversy was about the proper understanding of Christ; and somewhere along the line the concept of justification—later to be labeled the *articulus stadentis et cadentis ecclesiae*—crept into the picture. In short, the suggestions were many and the confusion was great.

It is hardly surprising, therefore, that the controversy remained inconclusive, not, of course, in terms of the official posture of the Catholic Church which was clear ever since the bull *Exsurge Domine*, but in terms of full clarity about the nature of the controversy. The tons and tons of paper used in battle made this a grandiose free-for-all, with subsequent generations of scholars assuredly knowing the time and the issues far better than did the contemporaries. This abundance of riches, it seems, explains the situation far better than any peculiarities of Catholic theology in the early 16th century.

Indeed, such was the burden (or curse) of all Catholic apologetes in the early years of the Reformation, of theologians like Johann Eck, Thomas Murner, Johann Cochlaeus, Thomas More, and others. Naturally, these men differed in theological insight, religious acumen, and literary gifts; some arguing more incisively than others, some enjoying greater popularity. But, above all, they all shared a formidable disadvantage. They had to defend the status quo, reiterate the position that had been known for years and hardly allowed room for creative restatement. Moreover, they had to counter bold and sweeping generalizations, for in a way the reformers were the kind of *terribles simplificateurs* whose imprint on the course of history Jacob Burckhardt so resoundingly bewailed. In short, the handicap was formidable and the obstacles virtually insurmountable.

The situation changed only after the mood of desperation (and righteous indignation) had given way to a calmer reflection on the nature of the situation. Then, and only then, did Catholic writers— Peter Canisius is one of the eminent illustrations—adapt their ways. They supported the vernacular Scriptures, wrote popular catechisms, and denounced the life and thought of the new churches. They had enough empirical evidence before their own eyes to garner a most devastating polemic.

In this Babel of voices two recurrent themes were heard again and again from the lips of Catholics: the call for reform and for a council. In both matters, as in all other Catholic affairs in the 16th century, the key lay in the papal office. The popes of the time of the Reformation labored under the handicap of the immediate past. The Renaissance popes, from Nicholas V to Julius II, had been concerned (successfully, as it turned out) to transform Rome, the center of religion, into a glorious center of art and culture. They had also engaged in Italian power politics, seeking to preserve the integrity of the Papal States against the aggressive encroachment from other Italian states. When, in the course of the 16th century, the character of the popes changed, it was difficult to turn over a new leaf from one pope to the next. Only slowly did the popes become concerned with more distinctly ecclesiastical matters and preoccupations. Even then they were caught in the fierce struggle between France and Spain as though between two millstones. Since ecclesiastical pronouncements and policies invariably entailed political ramifications (which were promptly contested by one side or the other), there was no easy way to proceed. Thus the relatively simple matter of Henry VIII's 'divorce' from Catherine of Aragon became at once involved in European power politics, and Pope Clement VII, called upon to rule on the canonical regularity of the marriage, was faced with the task of squaring the circle. Or, take the proposal for a general council, which was as vehemently rejected by Francis I as it was advocated by Charles V, both guided greatly by political considerations: the situation was indeed difficult.

The seven popes in the half century between 1513 and 1565, from Leo X to Pius IV, personally were upright men; indeed, some, such as Adrian VI, were deeply spiritual. The tragedy was that they viewed the crisis besetting the Church differently, and undertook to prescribe different remedies. The brevity of papal reigns was here undoubtedly a factor of considerable importance. These seven popes ruled, on the average, for about seven years, all too brief a time to initiate, undertake, and carry out policies. Omitting the two lengthy papal rules, those of Clement VII (1523–1534) and of Paul III (1534–1549), the tenure of their predecessors and successors shrinks even more. If we remember that Charles V ruled the German Empire for almost a half century, and that England had only four sovereigns during the entire century, the discrepancy becomes even more obvious.

The rule of Leo X, during which the Reformation erupted, may have been handicapped by his easy-going and somewhat secular disposition. Far more consequential, however, were other factors: the inadequate awareness of the true nature of the controversy across the Alps, and the feeling of accomplishment after the adjournment of the Fifth Lateran Council which had promulgated a great number of reform measures and had reached a rapprochement with the French crown. The house had been set in order. It seems futile to ask if the reform decrees of the Lateran Council lacked seriousness of purpose or were haphazard. The main problem was that this legislation never had a chance. No sooner had the Council adjourned than the Lutheran affair began to excite people with different issues and challenges. The Council was rather like a fruit that ripened out of season: it sought to achieve its goals in terms of one epoch, but it was judged by another.

The election, in January 1522, of Adrian VI was a compromise, the last effort before the cardinals agreed not to agree. Adrian was a devout and spiritually minded man who saw the reform of the Church and especially of the Curia, as the eminent goal of his pontifical rule. But he was alien to the workings of the Curia, an inept administrator, suspicious of his advisors, and all these made for the futility of his efforts. Above all, there was the exceeding brevity of his rule; Adrian died less than two years after his election. He had not had sufficient time to undertake his policies. Thus success, as well as failure, was not to be his. His epitaph aptly quoted one of his own sentences: 'Alas, how much depend the efforts of even the best of men on the time.'[1]

The papal brief which the legate Chieregati read to the German estates in Nuremberg in January 1523 indicated the lines of Adrian's program. The frank confession that shortcomings in the Curia and the Church were, in part, responsible for the religious controversy was accompanied by an emphatic repudiation of the Lutheran heresy and the pledge to undertake reform. Adrian thought the religious issue closed by Luther's condemnation. A vigorous attempt at ecclesiastical reform must have seemed to him the means to reduce the restlessness and rebellion against the Church.

The 11 years of the pontificate of Clement VII brought little change, prompting Leopold von Ranke, who was otherwise not easily given to dramatic pronouncements, to call Clement 'the most catastrophic pope ever to occupy the throne of St. Peter.' In part this unfavorable verdict had its cause in Clement's temperamental inability to make decisions, though it might be more appropriate to say that he sought to postpone making decisions as long as he knew that they were bound to be catastrophic. Far more important, however, was the fact that Clement faced virtually insurmountable political complications. The struggle between France and Spain reached the Holy City in 1527, with the spectacular *sacco di Roma*, and made Clement temporarily a prisoner of the Emperor. The divorce of Henry VIII put him in a position where any decision, no matter what, was bound to have fateful political as well as ecclesiastical consequences. No wonder that Clement sought to postpone the showdown. That he allowed the decision to be against Henry (it surely was the more catastrophic choice) speaks for his integrity, since the weight of Canon Law determined his decision. And if all these were not sufficient problems, the persistent resistance of

K

Francis I against a general council made such a council an impossibility, even if Clement had wanted one, which he did not.

So little, if anything, happened during Clement's pontificate—no general council, no officially sponsored reform. England deserted the Catholic ranks, as did Sweden and a great part of Germany. But these facts tend to be misleading. That both England and Sweden turned Protestant could have been halted neither by a council nor by ecclesiastical reform. Only in Germany might the situation have been different, though even there the number of those who cited theological disagreements rather than practical abuse as the issues at stake (which made conciliation almost impossible) was on the increase.

Under Paul III, who succeeded Clement in 1534, the various streams of Catholic vitality burst out into the open, rather like flowers after a sunny spring day. The 15 years or so of Paul's pontificate marked the turning point of Catholic history in the 16th century. His personal background, prior to his ordination, had been checkered and he always remained a devoted patron of the arts (he commissioned Michelangelo to paint the Last Judgment and the ceiling of the Sistine Chapel). He raised two of his grandsons to the cardinalate alongside such eminent men as Reginald Pole, Pietro Carafa, John Fisher, and Gasparo Contarini. His pontificate was not without its shadows, but this is less significant than the fact that under him the Catholic Church made a comprehensive effort to regain both its vitality and its self-confidence.

This last facet was particularly important. To be sure, under Paul's pontificate the notion of 'reform' was officially accepted by the papacy and this proved vastly consequential. Of even greater significance was the recapturing of the vision of the triumphant Church, the regaining of self-confidence, which in later years, as is well known, found such splendid expression in the spirit of the Baroque.

There was vitality in the Church before Paul—the work of individual bishops, the Oratory of the Divine Love together with its monastic offspring, the Theatines. Under Paul III the many little springs became a mighty river. In 1535 the Regulars of St. Paul, or Barnabites, were approved and one year later the Capuchins. In 1540 came the approval of the Somaschi and of the Society of Jesus. Somehow or other, the Jesuits and their founder, St. Ignatius of Loyola, were to overshadow most other expressions of the resurging Catholic spirituality in the 16th century, but it is needful to recall that they were but a small part of a much larger picture. Indeed, their real impact on the Church at large did not come until many decades later. At mid-century the Jesuits were only a handful of men and their vision one of dedication, zeal, and obedience.

Initially, Ignatius and his companions had to endure a good deal of opposition and persecution from high and low places, an indication that not all of the Church was ready for new and exciting ways to foster spirituality and serve the Church. Ignatius, rather like Luther, had experienced a spiritual crisis, but in contrast to the German reformer he had found the answer in the bosom of the Church. Thus, he symbolizes that the Catholic Church did possess the vitality and spirituality needed in the early 16th century: the story of Martin Luther will always need to be juxtaposed with that of Ignatius of Loyola.

And something else. The story of Ignatius was the story of a man committed to serving his Church and his God. From all indications, the existence and spread of the Protestant heresy played only a minor role in this resolve. Undoubtedly, he was made aware of it during his Parisian student days, but by that time his spiritual commitment had already been made. Ignatius of Loyola would have walked his path of devotion even if the world had never heard of Martin Luther and the other reformers. He symbolized indigenous Catholic reform in the 16th century and illustrated, at the same time, how these reform impulses could be turned to combat the Protestant Reformation. Before too long, the Jesuits turned their attention to the suppression of heresy and speedily became the most formidable expression of the so-called Counter-Reformation.

It was during the first part of the pontificate of Paul III that the Catholic Church gave a spectacular demonstration of its ability to face even uncomfortable facts. Pope Paul had appointed a reform commission in 1535 and another one the following year. Early in 1537 a report was presented—the famous *Consilium de emendanda ecclesiae*,[2] one of the outstanding Catholic documents of the sixteenth century. This *Consilium* had devastatingly harsh words for the Curia, harsh words also for the conduct of ecclesiastical affairs. At the same time it suggested a number of realistic reform proposals, such as proper procedures for granting benefices or dispensations.

In a way, the *Consilium* was an unexciting assessment of the ecclesiastical state of affairs. It was candid about the abuses existing in the Church and realistic about the means of improvement. But there was no electrifying pathos, no revolutionary appeal. It is doubtful, however, if such would have been even possible, for the correction of abuse tends always to be unexciting and pedestrian.

More important was the philosophy of the *Consilium*. At issue were the purification and vitalization of the Catholic Church. The Protestant challenge was peripheral; 'emendment' was an intraCatholic matter that could be pursued without engaging in theological discourse or dialogue with Protestantism. By the same token, the *Consilium* intimated that theological clarification was even peripheral for the Catholic Church itself. The document seemed to assume that nothing needed to be said about the doctrine of the Church, for the improvement of its life was crucial. This attitude related both the ongoing religious controversy and the vitalization of the Church to the removal of abuse and corruption.

Whatever its orientation or thrust, the document failed to attain practical significance, even though Cardinal Contarini worked hard and fast toward that goal. All efforts became lost in the quicksand of complex issues and considerations, even as it became obvious that both those who advocated change and those who resisted it talked against the backdrop of the Protestant challenge, a fact that obviously complicated matters. Contarini declared that nothing could be more beneficial for the Church than curial reform, while others retorted that nothing would be more disastrous since then the Protestant charges would be vindicated, after all. Actual changes were few and far between.

During Paul's pontificate, the Inquisition was centralized in Rome in order to achieve a more effective means of combatting the Protestant heresy.[3] No one was exempt from its scrutiny and examination, neither of high or low estate, and upon conviction only the pope had the right of pardon. The far-reaching jurisdiction of the Inquisition was well taken: the case of Bernardino Ochino, General of the Capuchins, who converted to Protestantism, was signal evidence that heresy was no respecter of persons and, in high places, doubly dangerous.

'Inquisition' is a word that can hardly be mentioned without evoking an emotional response. The mental picture is that of the anonymous informer, the arrest at night, dungeons, torture, auto-dafés. While by no means comparable in severity (and abuse) to its medieval progenitor, the Roman Inquisition of the 16th century did represent a comprehensive and systematic effort to suppress religious dissent. Such, however, was by no means a Catholic prerogative, but was practiced, with grim and humorless determination, by virtually all religious factions. The Roman Inquisition differed in degree rather than in kind.

If the eminent achievement of Paul's reign was the convening of the council at Trent, to be examined presently, his failure was his inability to discern the depth of the Lutheran problem in Germany. Paul was unwilling to join forces with the Emperor and work for the suppression of heresy. He favored religious reform, but was also concerned about Italian political affairs. He thought that he could ill afford to take sides in the conflict between Charles V and Francis I. Neutrality seemed to him the best policy and he pursued it with determination. Politically, this policy had much to commend itself, but religiously it made the suppression of the German Protestants an impossibility, since that depended on close cooperation between Emperor and Pope. Pope Paul never could help seeing in Charles V not only the protector of Catholic Christendom (which he was), but also King of Spain (which he also was). And the political goals inextricably linked with the latter office caused him to be suspicious.

The achievement of Paul III's rule was the convening of the Council of Trent in December 1545. It came after decades of agitation, demands and pleas. 'All the world shouts for a council,' nuncio Aleander had written to Rome in 1521.[4] One suspects his sweeping generalization was here, as elsewhere, a bit overstated. Many people (though not those who really mattered) saw a council as panacea for all ecclesiastical ills, real and imagined. In the beginning of the controversy Luther was one of those who called for a council. After his conversation with Cardinal Cajetan in 1518, he issued an appeal for a council and did so again after having been served the bull *Exsurge Domine*. His *Open Letter to the Christian Nobility* called upon the German nobility to convene a council. Many others felt the same way, even after Luther's excommunication, though not all who did so were concerned about Martin Luther. Many thought that a council would be the best means to achieve the correction of ecclesiastical abuse. In 1523 the German Diet called for a 'free Christian council in Germany' to meet within a year, and in 1524 this demand was repeated, with the provision that if an ecumenical council was impossible, a German national synod should be held. Nothing came of this, for Emperor Charles intervened and prohibited any gathering.

Yet it was Charles who, for the next two decades, pressed most persistently for a general council. His conception of his responsibility as Emeror, his piety, and his political program suggested this course of action. A council would restore concord not only in the Church but also in the empire, and the one was as welcome as the other. This combination of religious and political considerations was precisely the reason for King Francis I's vigorous opposition to a council; he was determined to block any move that would be to Charles's advantage, and the solution of the religious problem in Germany would be exactly that. Thus, the conflict between the two eminent Catholic rulers made a council in the 1520s and early 1530s impossible, even if Clement VII had vigorously pursued a conciliar policy—which he did not. Paul III unsuccessfully strove for over 10 years to convene a council. Within one month of his election he twice affirmed his intention to call one. Of course, Clement had offered similar verbal assurances, but Paul let deeds follow his words. In 1536 he formally convened a council for 1537[5] but five times the facts of political and ecclesiastical life forced a postponement, until finally, in December 1545, the modest number of some 30 bishops and heads of monastic orders opened the 19th ecumenical council of the Church.

This long delay, despite the numerous pleas, had many reasons. The tensions between Spain and France have already been noted; as long as these persisted no council was possible. But there were also specifically ecclesiastical considerations which had to do with the objective of the proposed council. Once convened, what was the council to do? The Protestants had strange notions in this regard, for they demanded that a council, free from papal control and guided only by the Word of God, should undertake a comprehensive review of the teaching of the Church. Such, naturally, was unacceptable to Catholics who, in turn, had the option of seeing a council as a means of resolving the religious conflict or as an intra-Catholic affair. In either case, however, the immediate question was whether a council was really necessary. Not only were there the obvious fears of a resurgence of conciliarism as the result of a council; there were also the facts that Luther's teaching had already been condemned, that the Protestant errors were but old heresies in disguise, and that correction of abuse could be effected without a council. Considerations such as these overshadowed the years between the beginning of the Reformation and the actual convening of the council at Trent.

No sooner had the Council assembled than disagreements concerning the agenda came to the fore. Should ecclesiastical reform or doctrinal clarification be discussed first? There was a new complication. After decades of unceasing pleas for a council, Charles V found that it had convened at a most inopportune time. He was about to wage war against the League of Schmalkald, after which he planned to impose a conciliatory religious solution. (It had to be conciliatory, since some of his allies were themselves Protestant.) A council accentuating the existing differences by a forthright definition of Catholic doctrine was the last thing he wanted.

But this was precisely what the council fathers set out to do. While the disagreement over the agenda had been resolved with a compromise (dogma and reform were to be considered simultaneously), the whole tenor of the first doctrinal decisions of the Council was not so much conciliation with the Protestants as the delineation of a *via media* among conflicting Catholic positions. Thus, ecclesiastical traditions were to be accepted *pari pietatis affectu* with Scripture;[6] justification was declared to be 'making just' of the sinner whose will cooperates with grace (session VI); the traditional teaching on transubstantiation was confirmed (session XIII); as were the sacrificial character of the Mass (session XXII) and the sacramental character of marriage (session XXIV). In addition, a number of reform decrees accompanied the dogmatic decisions of the council fathers—all the way from the establishment of lectureships on Scripture at cathedral churches to regulations concerning the resident obligations of bishops and priests.

Not until the end of 1563 was the work of the Council finally completed. After it had finally convened in 1545, a conflux of factors brought two temporary adjournments, in 1548 (which lasted until 1552), and 1553 (which lasted until 1562). At the time of its final adjournment, the Council had not completed its entire agenda, but the consensus of the fathers and the Curia favored a closing.

It was a different council from what Luther and his fellow Protestants, and even some Catholics, had anticipated or hoped for when the call for a gathering of the universal Church had first been sounded. Reconciliation with the Protestants (if this had ever been the goal) was not achieved. This was as much due to the Protestants as to the council fathers, for the Protestants had impossible notions as to the composition and work of a council. Sole reliance on Scripture as the norm for faith and life (for them a sincere and unobjectionable demand) was bound to evoke Catholic opposition, both because Catholics realized that to them Scripture seemed to teach differently, and also because they could not surrender past papal and conciliar expositions of the faith.

These differences would have been formidable, if insurmountable, at the very outset of the controversy. By 1545 they made conciliation plainly impossible. By then three decades of theological debate had led to an inevitable hardening of positions, and this suggested to the Council not the bridging of the gap as its major task, if such were indeed possible, but the delineation of the proper Catholic position.

The proximity of the colloquies of Worms and Regensburg to the Council of Trent can be considered a confirmation or a rejection of the view just expressed—the former because these colloquies, with their failure, demonstrated that conciliation was impossible despite serious efforts, the latter because as little as four years before the Council there were men of goodwill still convinced that conciliation might be achieved. Be that as it may, one must be careful to argue the inevitability of the course taken by the Council: it was the most obvious, most natural, most promising road taken; hardly, however, the only one.

What was the significance of these two decades of intermittent conciliar activity? The first historian to narrate the history of the Council, Paolo Sarpi, was persuaded that the Council had made the split between the Catholic Church and Protestantism irreparable. Nor had it effected any reform worthy of the name. It had been a stark tragedy, a trick of the papacy to assert its power. One might almost call this the Protestant perspective, for Protestants were convinced that the Council had been dominated by the Curia—contemporaries quipped that the Holy Spirit came to Trent in the pocket of the courier from Rome—and, if measured by the goal of reunion, the Council did indeed fail miserably. The significance of Trent for Protestant history is slight. Only indirectly did the Council also reach Protestant Christendom.

The Council of Trent symbolized the resurgent spirit of Catholicism, the spirit of reform and renewal, of the Theatines and Jesuits, of the Roman Catechism. It did not create that spirit, but became its most dramatic expression and its formal focal point. It signified that the Catholic Church had regained its self-confidence. In the figure of speech used by Reginald Pole, even as Christ had risen after three days, so the Church had done the same. Though it took decades for the new spirit, formalized by the Council of Trent, to manifest itself throughout the Church and in music, art, architecture, the spirit of victorious resurgence was present. The period of the Baroque—the sculptures of Bernini or Puget, the paintings of Rubens or Velásquez—portrayed this spirit in most dramatic fashion. It was a militant and victorious spirit, profoundly aware of its strength and its tradition. Tragically, a disaster was necessary to bring all this about.

---

# CHAPTER NINE

# Concluding Observations

There is no limit to the ways one can consider the Reformation. All the same, in the past one view has clearly dominated: the notion that the Reformation was essentially a religious event. Catholics have seen it as a heretical rebellion against the authority of the Church, led by reformers who were ignorant theologians and immoral men who destroyed the flourishing world of the Middle Ages. Protestants have naturally failed to concur with such sentiment, and their canvas transformed into glowing colors what had been dark and dreary in Catholic perspective. They saw the Reformation not as heresy but as the restoration of the true Gospel; the reformers were not apostates but propagators of the apostolic faith. The Church before the Reformation had been perverted and unspiritual, in dire need of reform and renewal.

## The Nature of the Reformation

Catholic and Protestant historians came to different conclusions concerning the broader significance of the Reformation. The latter saw it as the beginning of the 'modern world' and attributed to it all the blessings of modern civilization, from women's suffrage to indoor plumbing.[1] The former, exemplified by Joseph de Maistre, the eminent political theorist of the early 19th century, found the ills of modern society, from the disrespect for authority to the disregard for religion, the direct result of the Protestant Reformation. Indeed, as far as he was concerned there was little difference between the Reformation and the French Revolution inasmuch as both were rebellions against authority. He detested both.

One need not document the details of these two views. Both the traditional Catholic and the Protestant perspectives combine elements of fact as well as fiction. What is more important is that the sentiment of historians has echoed the assertions of the controversialists in the 16th century. The historiography of the Reformation during the past 300 years is thus an echo of the sentiment in the Reformation era, and a reminder of the heat of the controversy and the intensity of conviction.

The Reformation can be seen as a phase of that quest for reform which accompanied the Church from the eleventh century onward. So understood, the reformers echoed the cry for a reform of the Church *in capite et membris* that was propounded from the councils of Constance and Basel to Nicolaus of Cusa and Erasmus of Rotterdam. They thereby receive an illustrious line of progenitors for which the nomenclature 'pre-reformers' constitutes an interesting description. This makes Luther a sort of 16th-century Hus or Wycliff, with the only distinction being the brilliance of his theological insight or the ripeness of the time.

A variant of this view is to see the Reformation as a reaction—as a 'counter-reformation'—to the theological climate of the 15th century, particularly to the nominalism of such theologians as Gabriel Biel.[2] This nominalism may be viewed either as consistent development of earlier trends or as an extraordinary theological confusion, alien to the authentic spirit of medieval theology. In either case, the Reformation becomes 'counter' movement, an understandable, though in light of its 'heretical' deviation doubly ironic, phenomenon.

Such diversity of opinion makes interpretations of the Reformation difficult. Still, a few tentative observations can be offered. Luther and the other reformers meant their proclamation as a call to authentic Biblical religion. Their concern, despite occasional lapses of tongue and tone, was not practical. The worldly prelate, the power-hungry bishop, the immoral priest (assuming these existed in distressingly large number) were outside their solicitude; the correction of abuses occupied only a peripheral place in their thinking. Episcopal pluralism or clerical simony was detestable, to be sure, but not the main issue. The tracts of the reformers rarely took notice of such practical matters. It took Luther more than a decade of theological strife to recall his practical experiences on his trip to Rome.

The reformers' concern was with what they called the 'Gospel' and its appropriation by the individual—the trusting acceptance of the divine offer of forgiveness despite one's unworthiness. This notion entailed a number of ancillary assertions—such as the sufficiency of Scripture to teach this Gospel, the repudiation of work-righteousness—but basically everything revolved around the Gospel. Indeed, as is so well known, a multitude of Protestant divines devoted their attention to an elaborate (and persuasive) delineation of this Protestant Gospel. The main theological foci were properly noted —the centrality and sufficiency of Scripture, justification, the Sacraments, the Church—and generations of Protestants of all varieties (and Catholics as well) were persuaded that the *raison d'être* for the great schism was to be sought in profound and insurmountable theological differences.

This study has not denied the existence of such disagreements. It has suggested, nevertheless, that a proper historical understanding of the inner momentum of the Reformation would relegate them to a secondary place. To a considerable extent the full theological awareness of the difference, (and their doctrinal delineation) did not come until a relatively late time, when for a cluster of reasons the ways between the old faith and the new had parted. One must also ask if the theological differences were of such fundamental import as to precipitate (or explain) a schism of Western Christendom. After all, one issue that was fundamental, justification, initially was not Catholic dogma but allowed free discussion.

One can understand the nature of the Reformation best by looking at its religious rather than theological emphases. The concern of the reformers was essentially to renew, perhaps to redirect, Christian spirituality, to turn the faithful from reliance on self to reliance on grace, from external routine to inner involvement. Any Catholic could have readily concurred with such goals, as indeed many did in the first few years of the Reformation. To be sure, such religious concerns were oriented by theological presuppositions; our contention is that fundamentally, at least in the beginning, these were not incompatible.

The Protestant Gospel was thus not so much a system of theological loci as a matter of spirituality. It was not so much an adamant call to ecclesiastical revolution as a concern for the entire Church. If these are accurate observations, one has the answer to the question whether the reformers thought their interpretation was diametrically opposed to the teaching of the Catholic Church. Did reformers view their proclamation as inescapably provoking a confrontation? Did they deliberately break with the Church, stubbornly confident that they were on the side of the angels while their Church was in abomin-able error?

Their denunciations leave little doubt but that they did not think this Gospel properly taught in the Catholic Church. Did this mean irreconcilable opposition? The evidence suggests that it did not. This is to say that the reformers did not consider their understanding of the Gospel heretical, but thought that it could be subsumed, somehow or other, under the mantle of a truly Catholic Church.[3] Specifically, the Protestant interpretation might be afforded toleration or it might even receive official endorsement. The reformers preferred the lat-ter, but obviously they were willing to live with the former.

The fact that at the beginning there were no dramatic doctrinal divergences is supported by the observation that, in 1517, the proper understanding of justification, so dear to Luther, was not dogmati-cally defined by the Church, and a great deal of latitude existed with respect to what could be legitimately taught concerning this matter. The various theological attempts at conciliation (such as at Augs-burg in 1530 or at Regensburg in 1541) also indicated that the lines were by no means rigid and that, rightly or wrongly, men who joined irenic disposition and theological competence thought it possible to heal the breach.

But the heat of controversy increasingly called forth emotional words, and the theological pronouncements on the part of the re-formers became more daring, if heretical: witness Luther's 1520 tract *The Babylonian Captivity of the Church* and its blunt repudia-tion of four of the seven traditional Sacraments and the reinterpre-tation of the remaining three. One may see this deteriorating develop-ment as the consistent manifestation of the real theological dif-ferences. One may also attribute it to psychological factors, such as the vehemence of the opponents' polemic, or the nonchalant swift-ness of the official proceedings. The literary controversy was marked on both sides by forceful emotional overtones and a good deal of abusive language: it is ironic that academicians who are considered to be among the most reasonable of men succumbed so easily to emotion.

It is true that when all was said and done Luther and the other reformers failed to exhibit the virtue that eminently characterizes a faithful Catholic: obedience to the Church. And it is equally true that in the moment of disobedience the reformers rejected the notion that the Church is infallible and the pope the vicar of Christ on earth. In so doing they substituted a new view of the Church and a different understanding of authority. They would rather be heretics than be unfaithful to their notion of the Gospel. Accordingly, one may suggest that the real issue at stake was that of authority: the Church or the individual, the pope or conscience. But to suggest this must acknowledge the presence, in the theological struggle, of a facet of incisive importance.

The reformers were persuaded that their views had been rejected out of hand. This sentiment, alongside their conviction that theirs was the true Gospel, explains their adamant obstinacy in the face of ecclesiastical censure and condemnation. The sources show that Luther, for one, outdid himself with expressions of obedience and servility to the Roman see in 1518 and early 1519. In view of this attitude, the charge of a hasty condemnation of Luther is especially serious. If anywhere, the fault of the Catholic Church in the schism we call the Reformation lies here—not in its neglect of reform or in its toleration of abuse, but in its failure to afford the notions of Luther a full hearing. Of this the carelessness with which the bull *Exsurge Domine* quoted Luther is a good illustration. The recent studies of Hans Küng and Otto Pesch suggest that the Reformation view of justification is much closer to the Catholic tradition than has been assumed. The 19th-century Catholic historian Ignaz Döllinger aptly remarked that one need not condemn Luther for a few pages out of a hundred volumes.

Such was the setting that caused the reformers to be dismayed and then turn adamant. The case can be made that they emphasized their insight only after they had become persuaded that they had not been heard. Seen from the vantage point of the eventual outcome, Luther's condemnation was proper. Even if Luther had never taught some of the censured propositions and was all too speedily condemned, there were others that were plainly heretical. The question is, however, if he would have persisted in affirming these had he been given a more sympathetic hearing.

One does well to remember that at the beginning of the Reformation stood an intriguing constellation of forces and developments which influenced the course of events far more than outright theological considerations. The confusion of ecclesiastical and political concerns, the temperament of the protagonists, the bias of the reports reaching Rome, the inaccurate citations from Luther: these, among others, were the ingredients for the bull of excommunication that settled the fate of Western Christendom. Strictly theological issues were present, but in themselves these would have precipitated a different course of events.

This setting throws light on the nature of the impact made by

Luther on his contemporaries. Most of those who thronged to him
and supported his cause did not consider themselves in opposition
to the Roman Church. Even if they were against the clergy or
ecclesiastical prerogatives, they were not really against the Church.
The resolute mood of separation came much later. The Reformation was a filial revolt; in other words, a prodding to get the Church
to undertake certain changes. Dissent and loyalty, defiance and
obedience, combined and explain the popularity of Luther's cause,
even as they explain the subsequent disintegration of Luther's movement which occurred when the Church required submission.

This brings us to a final reason for the schism. There were those
who risked disobedience rather than give up what they had come
to call the Gospel. It is somewhat beside the point, therefore, to
cull from the multitude of medieval theologians those whose views
were akin to Luther's and the other reformers', label them 'pre-
reformers,' and conclude that there was nothing new under the sun.
Undoubtedly, similarities existed. Thus, Jacques Lefèvre's views on
justification may have been identical with those of Luther. But why
did the one remain a faithful Catholic whereas the other was considered a heretic? More must have been at stake than theology.

By the same token, however, defiance and subjectivism alone do
not account fully for the impact of the Reformation. If anything,
they militated against it, for disposition to martyrdom is hardly a
generic human characteristic. And the reformers surely were no exception. The early years of the Reformation were indeed characterized by an exuberant disregard of possible consequences on the
part of the reformers, but during that time these consequences were
not at all obvious. Still, something more than youthful rashness must
have been present. Theology did play an important role, though not
so much with respect to specific doctrines, such as justification or
the Sacraments, but with respect to a comprehensive understanding
of the Christian faith.

### The Consequences of the Reformation

'And all the king's horses and all the king's men . . .' One thinks
of this trivial rhyme when reflecting on the Reformation, for its
most spectacular consequence undoubtedly was the division of
Western Christendom. To be sure, there had been schisms before:
the eminent one between East and West, the modest one between
the Bohemian and the Roman Church, the pathetic one between the

rival factions of Rome and Avignon in the 14th century. But these divisions (not to speak of those created by the heretical splinter groups of the Middle Ages) had hardly entered the consciousness of Western man. At the dawn of the 16th century the Church was one, bedazzling in its complexity and confusing in its structure, yet one in faith. There was no doubt about allegiance to this Church, holy, catholic, and apostolic. And even those who were uneasy about it, as for example the humanists, still remained loyal. But at the twilight of the century everything was different: the unity of Western Christendom had vanished and had become a wistful dream. Christendom in the West was divided—indeed not only into two factions, but into four, even five: Catholics on the one hand, and Lutherans, Calvinists, Anglicans, and Anabaptists on the other. The coexistence of these rival Churches was an uneasy one, since each claimed stubbornly the sole possession of Christian truth and denounced its rivals with vehemence and self-confidence. As a matter of fact, the mutual denunciations between Protestants were hardly less pronounced than those between Catholics and Protestants.

To what extent this diversity of the Christian Church was a nagging or perplexing awareness on the part of the 16th-century man is difficult to say. Within the borders of a country only one Church was officially recognized and, accordingly, a kind of pragmatic, if artificial, uniformity existed. Only France, the Low Countries, Poland, Germany, and England experienced religious diversity, though often of a most bitter kind, and thus evidenced the division of Christian truth in blunt and spectacular fashion. One must keep in mind that whatever ecclesiastical uniformity existed was maintained by an external force, namely, the political authorities. Once this factor was removed (by the self-limitation of the authorities), the full impact of the religious diversity was bound to be felt in a dramatic way. Even in the 16th century, however, the empirical division of Christendom lessened the Christian claims for truth.

On the face of things the division in the West entailed a weakening of the Catholic Church, since the new Protestant churches grew on soil vacated by Catholicism. A glance at the map of Europe in 1600 might convey the conclusion that the Catholic losses were tolerable. Indeed, in the end the desertion from Catholic ranks was less than had been hoped by some and feared by others: Germany, at one time on the verge of embracing the new faith completely, retained a Catholic majority, especially in the South and Northwest; Poland, Hungary, and France, at one time likewise on the way toward Protestantism, eventually declared for the Catholic faith; Italy, Spain, and Ireland escaped the religious turmoil altogether.

To minimize the Catholic losses would be, however, a superficial conclusion. The most populous countries, even as the most powerful ones, were (with the exception of France) Protestant. The political scales increasingly tipped in favor of Protestant Europe— England, Sweden, Prussia were the countries that were to dominate the future world of European diplomacy and politics.

If, as has been noted, the signal consequence of the Reformation was the division of Western Christendom, the significance of the division in Protestant ranks requires further comment. Neither historically nor theologically was there ever a single Reformation; there were several—certainly no less than five, perhaps more. The Protestant Reformation was never a monolithic phenomenon, but always a house divided against itself.

When Bishop Jacques Bossuet wrote his famous history of Protestantism, he gave it the telling title *Histoire des variations des Églises protestantes* (1688). His main argument was that the divisions within Protestantism were the most persuasive proof of its falsehood. Protestantism lacked unity in doctrine—a point well taken. The hopeless and apparently insoluble division called into question the basic Protestant affirmation that Scripture was clear and self-evident, and that men of goodwill could readily agree on its meaning. Luther, who had first voiced such sentiment, was to learn its weakness in his controversy with Zwingli over the interpretation of Communion. His increasingly rigid view of Scriptural interpretation may well have been influenced by his dismay over the inability of men, even of men of goodwill, to agree on the interpretation of Sacred Writ.

Was the basic Protestant assertion mistaken? One cannot answer this question without the realization that through the centuries Christians have been unable to agree completely on the message of Scripture. Thus the history of the Catholic Church is at once the story of the definition of ecclesiastical authority in order to curb the yearning of the faithful to add their marginalia to the Sacred Writ. It is one of the ironies of the Reformation that Luther raised an issue that the Catholic Church had long faced—and long decided. In any case, the inability to read Scripture the same way is not a peculiarly Protestant malaise; the history of the medieval Church—say, for example, with regard to such issues as the immaculate conception or papal infallibility—shows that Catholics are not immune. What made the difference was, of course, the presence of an external authority—the Church—which safeguarded and vouchsafed agreement in essentials. The Reformation, on the other hand, shows that such authority was not completely absent. Indeed, where it was present little diversity prevailed. England under Elizabeth and German Lutheranism toward the end of the century are good cases in point. In both places theological agitation existed, creeds were formulated and revised, but the authority of government kept matters in check and retained uniformity.

None of the new Protestant bodies, once they had established themselves, was truly 'catholic' in the sense that diverse or heterogeneous points of view were subsumed within them. Catholicism, on the other hand, possessed the ability to do precisely that. Moreover, it had the 'escape valve' of monasticism, which allowed those dissatisfied with the standard ecclesiastical practices to go their own way and yet remain within the Church. Such possibility did not exist in any of the Protestant churches, where a break was necessary to assert a different religious or theological position. Also, the mood of separation unmistakably was in the air, and prompted many to leave whatever ecclesiastical body they happened to be associated with (Catholic or Protestant) and venture to start a new one.

Once the ties with Rome had been cut and a new Church had been created—the cases of England, Geneva, and Saxony show that this could be done with greater or lesser dependence on traditional forms —the Protestants found themselves confronted with the need to undertake a pedagogical effort of major proportions. The task was to educate the people.

One must guard against two false impressions. The 16th century was not preoccupied with religion to the point that every last man and woman (and perhaps even child) were obsessed with religious concerns.[4] Obviously, it is risky to generalize about Europe at large, about both major religious factions, or about developments extending over several decades. But the evidence suggests that after an initial period the preoccupation with religion declined in most countries. Many people were only little concerned about the things of the spirit.[5] Of course, such matters as religious conviction and commitment are not empirically demonstrable. But there are some indirect empirical clues, such as the persistent governmental mandates exhorting church attendance, the appalling religious illiteracy, or the pathetic self-indictments of the reformers. All these indicate that in Protestant lands the Kingdom had not come with the Reformation. The quasi-official homily of 'the Place and Time of Prayer,' issued in England in 1574, may be considered a bit of indirect evidence, for it had this to say about the way some people observed Sunday: 'They rest in ungodliness and filthiness, prancing in their pride, pranking and pricking, pointing and painting themselves, to be gorgeous and gay; they rest in excess and superfluity, in gluttony and drunkenness, like rats and swine; they rest in brawling and railing in quarrelling and fighting.'[6]

The hallmark of those unconcerned with religion was that they simply ignored the Church. They pursued their business ventures, circumventing the moral teaching of the Church, and lived their lives unencumbered by ecclesiastical pronouncements. As long as governmental authority continued to enforce ecclesiastical standards, overt violations of these standards were rare. But wherever the atmosphere was lenient, as for example in England, a different situation prevailed. At issue was not so much outright opposition, for such was rare indeed and came, as a matter of fact, mainly from a few religious zealots, such as the Anabaptists or the Puritans, rather than from the indifferent unbeliever. But the anatomical posture, where the head nodded and the heart remained uninvolved, surely was not infrequent, and undoubtedly increased as the level of theological sophistication among the Protestants rose.

A second erroneous impression about religion in the 16th century has to do with the level of religious literacy among the people. There may have been a few laymen who, with nothing at their disposal but a good portion of native intelligence, were able to confound the academic theologians. But these were the exceptions. The mass of the people was illiterate and even good will could rarely overcome this handicap. After all, the ability to read generally is a prerequisite for theological competence.

If such widespread religious illiteracy were not enough of a problem, there was also a good deal of superstition, belief in magic and astrology, which was hardly congenial to an informed understanding of religion. The tolling of bells during thunderstorms, for example, supposedly kept lightning from striking in the hearing range of the bells. Religious ignorance was universal, though more so in the rural areas than in the cities. Of this the church visitation records offer ample evidence. Thus the records of a visitation in Lüneberg in 1568 indicated that the people almost without exception were unwilling to come to the mid-week catechetical instruction. There were blatant misunderstandings about the Decalogue which in one village version was rendered as, 'The first shall have no other goal; the second shall not use the name of God in vain; the third shall keep the sabbath holy.' In a village near Magdeburg only three people of 52 families knew the Lord's Prayer.[7]

Catechetical instruction had been virtually nonexistent before the Reformation and the people were by and large religiously ignorant, a fact explained by the ubiquitous presence of illiteracy rather than any conspiratorial or wicked attempt on the part of the Church to keep the people in darkness. This situation presented formidable problems for the Protestant churches in their educational efforts. Qualified and competent teachers were necessary, indeed, not just a few but one for every parish. Educational literature had to be written. Luther's *Small Catechism*, printed on cardboard to be hung on the walls of living rooms, was one of the earliest attempts to supply this need. Then came a host of similar publications. No less than 200 editions of such catechisms were published in the 16th century.

There were understandable problems, for the people often were neither willing to go through the rigid intellectual exercise nor able to devote the necessary time. In the first few years of the Reformation considerable exuberance had prevailed for things religious; but this had slowly faded, rather like the evening sun. The Lord's Prayer, the Apostles' Creed, and the Decalogue were the mainstays of the instruction—hardly sufficient, one suspects, to express the fullness of the Protestant faith. The visitation records indicate that the Decalogue was as much a mystery as the Trinity for the common people and that the simple recitation of the Apostles' Creed was connected with unsurpassable difficulties—all this the fateful legacy from Catholic days. Nor was the clergy generally better. The famous visitation of the clergy of Gloucester by Bishop Hooper in 1551 revealed appalling clerical ignorance. The men of the cloth hardly knew the basic affirmations of the faith, not to speak of the specific Protestant affirmations. If theological insight was thus restricted, it is not surprising that the ministerial incumbents in England found no reason to protest the ecclesiastical changes of 1547, 1553, or 1558, no matter how theologically incisive. Increasingly, an effort was also made to convey the specific emphases of the particular tradition. While the details of this effort belong to a subsequent epoch of Christian history, its systematic and conscientious pursuit created a distinct confessional identity. The early decades of the Reformation had brought a confessional self-consciousness, though not always a concomitant identity. The new confessional identity entailed a deeper theological understanding, a sharper denunciation of the opponent and a distinct liturgical life.[8]

Obviously, a causal relationship existed between clerical incompetence and popular ignorance. Only as ministerial standards rose in the second half of the 16th century did the general situation improve. More and more Protestant ministers received a university education and attained the formal competence to function as teachers. Still, the lower clergy, such as the village vicar or pastor, continued to find themselves in a difficult economic position with few, if any, financial attractions. Such had been the case before the Reformation, though now the married clergy had significantly larger economic needs. In the 16th century the ministerial profession possessed little social dignity.

The clergy, however, played a crucial role and all religious groupings realized this. The reformers stressed theological education. Wittenberg was a good example, but there were others. Zwingli introduced the so-called 'prophecy' (a kind of theological seminary) in Zurich in 1523. Four years later Landgrave Philip founded a new university at Marburg, where theology was 'queen' among the sciences. Later other centers of ministerial training were established, notably the Genevan Academy, founded by Calvin in 1559. Saxony declared university studies mandatory for future ministers in 1594, a demand which increasingly became general.

From every indication, the picture differed little among Catholics or Protestants. Both were heirs to the same situation, which must not be attributed to any Catholic shortcomings: the fact that even in Protestant regions the problem persisted into the second half of the century should quickly dispel such a notion. To be sure, the Catholic Church had stressed the liturgical life and shown itself slow to undertake the vast catechetical effort, once the invention of printing had made this feasible. But the twin problems of illiteracy and religious apathy were no respecters of ecclesiastical tradition.

Both Catholics and Protestants thus emerged from the Reformation era with a gigantic educational task—to dispel religious ignorance and to further spirituality. The task of dispelling religious ignorance enjoyed an advantage and labored under a handicap, the former because of the increasing stress on public education and widespread literacy, the latter because of the religious apathy that followed the intense preoccupation with religion during the Reformation.

## Reformation and Society

To talk about the significance of the Reformation is, to quote the proverb, to step boldly 'where even angels fear to tread.' Even sophisticated canons of historical research cannot convincingly demonstrate the inevitable generalizations, and an element of doubt will always linger on. The question is whether ideas, specifically religious ideas, can influence political, economic, social or cultural behavior—and if they did so in the 16th century.

The celebrated thesis of the German economist Max Weber on the role of Calvinism in the rise of the spirit of capitalism is a good case in point. Weber argued that certain Calvinist principles had helped create the atmosphere out of which the ethos of modern capitalism emerged. This was a bold postulate which, not unexpectedly, evoked vehement dissent, some based on empirical evidence (that capitalist tendencies can be observed in late 15th-century Italian cities, that some of the thriving economic centers a century later were not Calvinist, that Calvin himself was economically rather conservative); other evidence was dependent on philosophical observations (that religion has had no compelling influence on the political or economic behavior of men).[9] Though reams of paper have been filled, the debate remains inconclusive.

Like any other period the 16th century was characterized by a complex cluster of factors, political, economic, cultural, religious. Short of a rigidly determinist view of history, of whatever variety, it seems most plausible to assume that these factors played different roles of importance at different times. Surely, at certain times religion was influenced by political or cultural factors, while at other times it may have exerted its own influence. The multiplicity of factors will cause the specific role of religion to remain enigmatic.

Politically, the eminent significance of the Reformation was the comprehensive repudiation of ecclesiastical control over the state. The perennial struggle between *imperium* and *sacerdotium*, between political and ecclesiastical authority, so graphically evidenced by Pope Boniface VIII's bull *Unam Sanctam*, was resolved in favor of the former. One might see this as the culmination of a trend extending over the later Middle Ages. But more was at stake, if for no other reason than that the new relationship received a theological rationalization on the part of Protestant divines. Indeed, some of the Protestant political theorists, such as Stephen Gardiner in England, took an opposite position, insisting that the authority of the ruler embraced ecclesiastical matters as well. The most dramatic reversal of the relationship between Church and state occurred in England, where the King's new title 'Supreme Head of the Church' was a spectacular symbol for the change. Later in the century Thomas

Erastus wrote his *Explicatio gravissimae quaestionis* to argue for the complete submission of ecclesiastical affairs under political authority. Indeed, even Catholic practice often conformed to Protestant theory. Little difference existed between Catholic and Protestant countries, a fact partially explained by the importance of the ruler in rejecting or introducing the new faith.

The acquisition of certain ecclesiastical authority on the part of government was only one of several developments that grew out of the religious turbulence of the 16th century. The state was autonomous, not under the jurisdiction of the Church, and at the same time it exercised educational and charitable functions. This meant that the state assumed a direct moral stature which it had theretofore lacked. In a way, it was a matter of taking over responsibilities previously carried out by the Church through endowments and monasteries, perhaps a case of a bad conscience.

The Reformation provided the theoretical justification for this, whether as an ex post facto *pièce justificative* or as a revolutionary innovation need not be of concern here.[10] The fact itself proved to be of immense significance. A new kind of state made its appearance as a consequence of the Reformation. No longer did it wrestle with the Church, for it had acquired the power and prerogatives desired. While the state was still far from secular—religious affairs were important and in all countries an 'established' Church existed—religion was only one facet of many, not unlike trade and commerce.

Even as the proper care of ecclesiastical affairs was seen as the responsibility of the ruler, so loyalty and obedience on the part of the subjects were thought to be an expression of piety, as Stephen Gardiner's tract on *Vera Oboedientia* so tellingly argued. Religion was seen as an immensely cohesive factor in society, its moral handmaid (with the cost to the state very modest). All this can be viewed as the continuation of principles long established, though a new element entered the picture on account of the delineation of the right to rebellion. Among the Calvinists in France and the Low Countries a full-fledged theory of resistance was developed, precipitated by the concrete circumstances which they faced at mid-century. Bitter persecution and an ambiguous constitutional situation made this development almost inevitable, and once the new theories had been propounded they could not be retrieved. The French Monarchomachs Languet, Hotman, Duplessis-Mornay argued the case in an interesting juxtaposition of Biblical and secular argumentation: the 'tyrant' who violated both the law of God and of the land was to be resisted. The argument received theological respectability with the

*Confessio Scotica,* of 1560, which included *tyrannidem opprimere* among the good works of the faithful.[11]

But such was the sentiment of the 'outsider,' regardless of ecclesiastical label. It is telling that during Elizabeth's reign the émigré English Catholics on the Continent developed the same argumentation in favor of rising against an unlawful ruler. Thus, both sides propounded the same startling political theory, though in practice the Protestants, being generally on the receiving end, reflected more on these issues.

Otherwise, the changes in the political realm were few. Religious dissent, if publicly expressed, continued to be unthinkable and was suppressed with varying degrees of sternness or ruthlessness. Neither tolerance nor religious freedom was an entry in the vocabulary of 16th-century man, though generally only the Anabaptists experienced fire and sword, and they suffered the double liability of being suspected revolutionaries and blasphemers. Otherwise, confiscation of property, compulsory emigration, or imprisonment was the more normal legal procedure. Whether these constituted a dramatic advance over previous practice is dubious. All countries, Catholic and Protestant alike, clung to the notion that religious uniformity was indispensable to the tranquility of a political commonwealth. And despite the direct or indirect changes resulting from the Protestant Reformation, the notion of the 'Christian commonwealth' continued. Even the secularized functions assumed by the state, such as education, for example, did not lose their religious ornamentation.

With respect to the economic and social dimensions of society, the Protestant Reformation was indirectly revolutionary and directly conservative. Luther's concept of 'vocation,' which held that all professions and endeavors, no matter how lowly and mundane, had a spiritual blessing, was of immense significance.[12] It made the work of the butcher and baker, if performed in the proper spirit, God-pleasing and thereby undoubtedly released creative and stimulating forces. Of course, there had always been butchers and bakers, and even if one accepts the impact of Luther's notion, one may be entitled to an expression of doubt if sausages and bread were made any tastier, cheaper, or faster by Protestants as the result of this new ethos. Probably not. The difference lies in the fact that this secularization of man's 'vocation' redirected some of the talent that previously had wound up in the ministerial profession and made some men become teachers, lawyers, or doctors who might have turned to the Church in an earlier age. In the early 18th century the English physico-theologian William Derham was to calculate how much manpower had been lost to European society through the monasteries. His point was naïve, but well taken. Instead of disappearing behind the walls of the monasteries, men in Protestant lands strove to live their religious faith in the classroom or the court chamber. To use a modern term, they 'secularized' the Gospel. The impact, while beyond verification, must have been substantial.

On the more explicit level of economic and social considerations, however, the reformers were conservative. Though they differed over what were the mandates of the Gospel for the economic and social realms, they were concerned to explicate these mandates and, moreover, basically express their distrust of the market place. Rather like their scholastic predecessors, the reformers pondered endlessly such problems as the just price, the legitimacy of taking interest, or poverty. They propounded new notions (Calvin, for example, rejected the economic dogma of the Middle Ages that money was sterile), but they sought to influence society by hammering in the rigoristic ethical concepts of the Gospel rather than by offering innovations in economic theory. If Luther and Calvin had had their way, economic life would have continued as before.

The plain fact was that commerce and trade were not any more receptive to Protestant counsel than they had been to Catholic. Indeed, new empirical developments, such as the supplies of silver and spices from the New World, the rise of the chartered trading companies, the geographic discoveries, and increased population, increasingly cast their spell over the economic activities of the 16th century. Actually, little spectacular economic innovation can be discerned in Europe until the early 17th century—and at that time Protestantism, including Calvinism, was playing a different role in the affairs of society.

There may have been some men, even groups of men, whose economic endeavors were influenced, as Max Weber suggested, by their religious ethos, by such virtues, at once religious and economic, as thrift, self-denial, and self-discipline. One surely cannot dismiss Weber's thesis altogether. But many other men pursued their economic endeavors with technical competence rather than religious faith, and the course of the economic development in Western Europe was influenced by facts rather than ethos. The Augustinian theologian Peter of Aragon provided an apt commentary on the whole matter toward the end of the century when he confessed that 'the market place has its own laws.'

The reformers inveighed against sundry social abuses, such as prostitution, excessive drinking, or luxury in dress, as Catholics had done all along. Their vehemence raises the suspicion that they realized the colossus against which they were struggling. Luther (witness his Open Letter to the Christian Nobility) had strong opinions concerning these matters, but argued that the secular authorities (the 'Christian' nobility) should formulate and execute the proper policies in this respect, with the Church providing the ethos to inspire such action. Accordingly, there were few formal ecclesiastical pronouncements from Lutheran bodies, only individual pronouncements or governmental edicts. The number of those was legion. It is hard to say, however, if they were always issued (or received) with the religious ethos Luther desired; certainly they were not always successful.

Among the Calvinists the story was different, for here the moral mandates of the Gospel were seen to be more directly applicable in society. Certain activities, such as dancing or playing cards, were prohibited in Geneva, and in place of the usual tavern Calvin sought to institute (unsuccessfully, as it turned out) a new version in which beverages were weak and theology was strong. Calvinists elsewhere sought to do the same. They relied on governmental mandates but, whenever issued, these were, in contrast to those in Lutheran lands, transparently religious.

One of Luther's propositions condemned in the bull *Exsurge Domine* had been that the authorities should see to the abolition of begging, a sentence taken from his *Sermon von dem Wucher* (Sermon on Usury) of 1519, and echoed in his Open Letter to the Christian Nobility one year later. Though only a peripheral point, Luther (and the other reformers as well) expressed a clear concern over this issue and the need to reassign the traditional functions of the Church in this regard. Accordingly, a universal characteristic of the early efforts at ecclesiastical reconstruction was the drafting of regulations concerning the poor. The first formulations (undertaken in Wittenberg and Leisnig) failed because too much was attempted too fast. But their influence was still far-reaching. In the Ecclesiastical Ordinances of Geneva the care of the poor and indigent was entrusted to the deacon, one of the four offices in the Church. Thereby such care was formally made a responsibility of the Church, a notion characteristic of the entire Calvinist tradition. The care of the poor was institutionalized by the Calvinist Church.

Soon the full dimensions of the problem of poverty became obvious. Luther had thought the ecclesiastical property sufficient for alleviating the plight of the poor, but too many people had their fingers in the pie and too many other purposes strove for support.

Luther had also made many interesting observations about the problem: he had distinguished, for example, between the poor willing and those unwilling to work—but all this fell by the wayside. In due time, government stepped in (witness the Poor Laws under Henry VIII and Elizabeth I) and proceeded according to its own counsel, though this 'market,' too, had its own laws: poverty seemed as firmly entrenched in society as wealth.

One cannot overlook the element of continuity between the late 15th century and 50 or so years later. In the later Middle Ages the municipal authorities had increasingly concerned themselves with the problem of the poor; for example, by appointing wardens to look after them and distribute financial support. Moreover, several of the earliest comprehensive regulations concerning the poor in Germany —issued at Augsburg and Nuremberg in 1522, at Strassburg in 1523 —stand in such close chronological proximity to the beginning of the Reformation that it is impossible to make a valid assertion about possible connections. And it is equally impossible to suggest how this existing trend would have continued in the 16th century had there been no Reformation. It is clear, however, that the Protestant churches paid considerable attention to the problem. Among the Calvinists this took the form of explicitly asserting the responsibility of the Church in this regard, while among the Lutherans this responsibility was to be discharged through a cooperative effort of Church and secular authorities. But even in Lutheran areas the legal provisions promulgated were included in the church orders rather than in purely secular documents.

How much such religious ornamentation influenced actual practice is difficult to say. In places where Calvinist congregations (with their stress upon direct ecclesiastical responsibility) were without governmental support and had to shoulder the responsibilities themselves, practical consequences did issue from religious ethos. For other places, the evidence is more evasive. The fact of the matter was that the Protestant churches did not have the resources to undertake a comprehensive effort at poor relief. Confiscated Catholic Church property was far too meager for any continuing effort.

In short, the theological and religious affirmations of the reformers were many; there can be little doubt about their concern. Indeed, the structures established by the civic communities to deal with this question breathed this new religious ethos. One is inclined to assume that not all of these words of instruction, guidance, and counsel were written as on water but did have some impact on the deeds of men.

With respect to the cultural consequences of the Reformation, the conclusions come more easily since the evidence is more clear cut. Still, a caveat is necessary: whatever consequences can be discerned were indirect ramifications of religious emphases rather than a cultural concern as such. And they were derived from the nature of the Protestant message, which was as demanding as it was simple. Thus, people had to be able to read in order to comprehend for themselves the meaning of Scripture. If the Church was to be a dynamic community of all the faithful, literate men and women were necessary. The consequences of such premises were many. The Scriptures and pamphlets in the vernacular were emphasized, a fact which aided the emergence of vernacular literature in the various countries. By way of contrast one may recall that the humanists had written primarily in Latin.

The concern for public education, first propounded by Luther in 1524, was a corollary. The intent was not so much to further secular education or the liberal arts, but to train informed Christians.[13] Religion and education worked harmoniously together. At the beginning of the religious controversy the Reformation had seemed hostile to education. This was the way Erasmus felt. As late as 1528 he bewailed the matter in a letter: 'Wherever the Lutheran teaching has come to rule, learning is perishing.'[14] In part Erasmus's word of gloom grew out of his yearning for tranquility, which he saw as the indispensable prerequisite for learning. But there was also the seeming anti-intellectualism of the Reformation. Had not Luther's proclamation been a blunt and comprehensive repudiation of traditional learning? Had the reformers not charged that the universities were teaching abominable error, and that the study of Aristotle was despicable? Luther had asserted that the learned theologians and academicians were in error and that it was given to simple and unlearned men to understand the Gospel. Such emphases helped rally the unlearned but literate segments of society behind Luther's cause. And as time passed it became obvious that these emphases entailed considerable pedagogical demands and that, in the final analysis, the lines between the Reformation and education were positive.[15]

Education prior to the Reformation was characterized not so much by quantity as quality; it was, moreover, undertaken by the Church. The reformers argued that the responsibility should be in the hands of the secular authorities. Luther argued the case in his 1524 tract *To the Councillors of all German Cities That They Establish and Maintain Christian Schools*,[16] and this was the way it worked out practically. The confiscated ecclesiastical property of the Catholic Church provided the financial basis for the educational effort, even as in England the chantry endowments funded education.

The contribution of the Reformation to the notion of public education was thus twofold. It consisted in the demand, perpetually put forward, that schools be established and, secondly, in the transfer of educational responsibility from the Church to the state. This did not mean, however, that the Church abdicated its educational involvement. The ties between Church and school remained strong and the Peace of Westphalia of 1648 explicitly stated that schools were 'annexum religionis.'[17] Often the Protestant parson took care of the heavenly alphabet and the worldly one as well.

The reformers echoed the goals of the humanists concerning the content of education.[18] They stressed the study of languages (Latin for clarity of thought, Greek and Hebrew for understanding Scripture) and advocated textual criticism and literary analysis. At the same time they emphasized the value of historical studies. The primary motivation was to provide the basis for theological understanding (along lines congenial to Protestant thought), with the training of teachers, lawyers, and doctors as a corollary concern. Protestant learning enjoyed the advantage of not being unduly restricted by the weight of tradition. It was able to explore new avenues. Above all, scholarly endeavor in Protestant lands could be pursued (in the later part of the 16th and then in the 17th century) without undue ecclesiastical interference or restriction. That the Nuremberg reformer Andreas Osiander contributed a preface to Copernicus's famous work on *The Revolutions of the Heavenly Bodies*, in which he defended the scientist's right to offer hypotheses, is worthy of note in this connection.[19] In part this attitude finds its explanation in the self-confidence of Protestantism, in part by the Protestant conviction that any pursuit of truth would confirm rather than deny religious truth. Even more important, however, may have been a kind of pragmatic self-limitation. Protestantism, after all, was a divided house, and nowhere possessed the universal stature of Catholicism. The condemnation of Galileo by the Saxon consistory would have looked rather foolish and would have been rather ineffectual. In other words, the very division of Protestantism made for its relative congeniality to scientific endeavor.

In the arts Calvinist austerity cast a shadow over whatever artistic exuberance the new faith generated. Any artistic endeavor must be directly related to the liturgical life of the Church to assume an immediate religious dimension. But Calvinist churches were whitewashed and plain, devoid of ornamentation and decorations, the outgrowth of a literal application of the Old Testament proscription of graven images. Wherever this rigid temperament made its appearance—in Zurich, Geneva, or England—treasured works of art were destroyed, while no new creative forces were released. The visitor to English cathedrals, stately and ornate, encounters with painful monotony the destruction wrought by the Edwardian Reformation—from the shrine of St. Thomas à Becket at Canterbury to the decapitated statues of saints at Ely. One must acknowledge these iconoclastic tendencies of the Reformation, remembering that the men with paintbrush and hammer did not look at objects of art, but at idolatry, not at treasures to be esteemed, but at blasphemy to be removed.

In the Lutheran and Anglican traditions no such austere rigidity existed, but then even they had little opportunity to demonstrate their propensity. The Middle Ages had bequeathed magnificent churches to the 16th century and no need existed, therefore, to build new ones and in so doing express the new faith in artistic form.

In the realm of music the Reformation found a splendid expression. This is not surprising, for the liturgical life of the Church allowed a direct application. To be sure, there were exceptions: in Zurich, for example, church music was considered an abomination and worship without congregational singing prevailed until the end of the century. All in all, the Protestant Reformation was a singing movement. It created hymns which turned out to be an important element in its popular success. The Protestant hymn was the expression of the entire congregation (and thereby was related to the musical tradition of St. Ambrose of Milan). At the same time, its lyrics were in the vernacular, which enabled the people to understand what they were singing. The restricted practice of the medieval Church became the widespread rule.

Luther's musical inclinations were here vastly influential. He arranged the publication of a modest German hymnal in 1524, and contributed 24 of the 32 hymns. Other reformers also wrote and composed hymns, at times using popular tunes of the day, at times translating ancient Latin hymns, frequently rendering Psalms into German. The latter form was found particularly attractive since it symbolized the Biblical orientation of the Reformation. This was especially the case among Calvinist congregations. Calvin insisted that only Biblical words could be used in the divine service and the first French Protestant hymnal, of 1539, contained only vernacular 'paraphrases' of the Psalms from the pens of Calvin and Clement Marot.[20] Subsequent hymnals were characterized by the same literal use of the Psalms, by their earthy language, and by melodies derived from the ancient Gregorian chant and from contemporary melodies. The church music of the Calvinist tradition was circumscribed in its form but far-reaching in its appeal.

Strictly speaking, these developments pertained to the life within the Church and cannot really be viewed as cultural consequences of the Reformation. In the secular realm, composers continued to be preoccupied with religious music. The trend toward secular music may have been temporarily halted in the 16th century, a result of the religious orientation of the age. But there was nothing peculiarly confessional in the religious music of the time, except in the formal sense that Catholic composers, such as Palestrina, used for their works the liturgical frame of reference provided by the Mass.

That there were cultural consequences of the Reformation would seem to need little verification. The difficult question pertains to their extent and significance. What can be said is that the Reformation instilled a new ethos into society—the notion of direct, personal responsibility; the concept of personal (and corporate) election; the postulates of discipline, of autonomy of the secular powers. To say this, however, is neither to suggest that such notions were absent before the Reformation nor to argue that the fact of their propagation alone proves their practical influence. Marriage is here a good case in point: one of the emphatic assertions of the reformers had been that marriage was as acceptable a state in the sight of God as celibacy. Marriage was made religiously respectable. Whether these pronouncements, such as those found in Luther's tract *On Marital Life*, made any practical difference, however, is a different question. One suspects that people after the Reformation married for much the same reasons as others had before.

The question of the broad cultural consequences of the Reformation is, in the final analysis, the question of the role of ideas in the affairs of men. Religious ideas were present in the 16th century, forceful, daring, revolutionary ideas, though we do well to remind ourselves that in such interaction of religious ideas and society, the former rarely appeared in pristine form. But they made their impact within the Protestant churches, probably also within the broader realm of society, and thereby may have done their share to help transform Western civilization.

# EPILOGUE

At the end the question remains how the Reformation of the 16th century is to be interpreted. From what has been written on these pages it should be obvious that no answer is considered possible aside from a precise definition of the term 'Reformation.' One must distinguish between the 'Reformation' as an event in the history of Christian thought and piety and the 'Reformation' as a phase in the political history of Europe. E. W. Kohls distinguishes between 'evangelical movement' and 'political Reformation' as phases in the development.[1] With respect to the former, one might argue that it was not so much a theological as a religious phenomenon. Theological differences (or the exaggeration of theological differences) may have caused the separation of the ways; the emergence of a movement, of an impressive phalanx of 'Martinians' was caused by something else. Obviously there was an inescapable backdrop of doctrine and theology, but more important was the desire for a new form of piety. The Reformation was a theological phenomenon only because it was a religious one.

This is also the point of contact with the 'political' Reformation, for the religious movement did not remain confined to the ecclesiastical realm, as did, for example, German Pietism or the Wesleyan movement two centuries later, but assumed a political dimension. In this way the focus changed. At issue was the proper understanding of Christian piety, or the proper interpretation of the Gospel. Also at issue were considerations of public polity—the legal recognition of the Protestant interpretation, the forms of public worship, the secularization of Church property. The dramatis personae were the political authorities, whose religious orientation was quite secondary. Since there were inescapable political conse-

305

quences to the repudiation of Rome (the assumption of greater power over ecclesiastical affairs or the appropriation of ecclesiastical property), the significance of these events for the political history of Europe was immense.

This twofold involvement made the Reformation of the 16th century a unique event in the history of the Christian tradition. It meant a certain complexity, for the Reformation became not only a significant development in the history of Christian thought but also an important phenomenon in political history as well. Thus it means different things to different people.

The Reformation was also a chapter in the ongoing quest for the message and the faith of the New Testament. This was the way the Protestant reformers understood their activity and their theological proclamation. The fact that many of their contemporaries, above all the Catholic Church, failed to concur with such sentiment indicates that the message was not so persuasive or self-evident as the reformers were wont to believe. But the historian must acknowledge their claim and also record the ambiguous response of the contemporaries.

Events in the 16th century mirrored in an intriguing way the course of the Christian faith during its long and eventful history. And this not only with respect to the quest for the true Gospel, but also with respect to the divisions this caused: the condemnations and counter-condemnations hurled from one side to the other; the establishment of orthodoxy and the denunciation of heresy; the presence of personal and emotional factors; the discrepancy between the real and the ideal. The Reformation century brought little that is new in these respects. It echoed timeless themes.

Today some may see the Reformation as an object of antiquarian historical interest—like Alexander's Persian Wars or the agrarian upheavals of the 17th century. Others will view it as far more than that: as an historical episode that has direct bearing on their faith, either by evoking empathy or by calling forth rejection. Both views have something to commend them, and we shall not seek here to resolve the issue.

So much is certain, that today those who hold to the second view have become more respectful towards the other side. Fire and sword have disappeared as the means whereby to score a theological argument, as have the poisonous pen and the slanderous tongue. One suspects, if a sentimental (and unscholarly) word is appropriate in conclusion, that most of the protagonists of the 16th century, were they alive today, would welcome this turn of events.

# NOTES

*Notes to Chapter One*

1.  F. Lau, 'Luthers Eintritt ins Erfurter Augustinerkloster,' *Luther* 27 (1956): 49–70.
2.  Martin Luther, *Werke: Kritische Gesamtausgabe* (Weimar, 1883–), 8: 685. Hereafter cited *D. Martin Luthers Werke*.
3.  *Ibid.*, 50: 657.
4.  E. H. Erikson, *Young Man Luther* (New York, 1958).
5.  *D. Martin Luthers Werke*, 58: 2–3.
6.  *Ibid.* (*Tischreden*), 4: 4414.
7.  A. Zumkeller, 'Martin Luther und sein Orden,' *Analecta Augustiniana* 25 (1962): 254–290.
8.  *D. Martin Luthers Werke*, 38: 143.
9.  *Ibid.*, 56: 258.
10. *Ibid.*, 56: 419.
11. *Ibid.*, 56: 171.
12. *Ibid.*, 56: 272.
13. *Ibid.*, 54: 183–184.
14. K. Aland, *Der Weg zur Reformation: Zeitpunkt und Charakter des reformatorischen Erlebnisses Martin Luthers* (Munich, 1965).
15. H. Denifle, *Die abendländischen Schriftausleger bis Luther über Justitia Dei und Justificatio* (Mainz, 1905); J. Lortz, *Wie kam es zur Reformation?* (3d ed.; Einsiedeln, 1955), pp. 34–43.
16. G. Biel, *Quaestiones de Justificatione* (Tübingen, 1501).
17. See L. Grane, *Contra Gabrielem: Luthers Auseinandersetzung mit Gabriel Biel* (Copenhagen, 1962).
18. *D. Martin Luthers Werke* (*Tischreden*). 2: 2800b.
19. *Ibid.*, 1: 224–228.
20. *Ibid.* (*Briefe*), 1: 111.
21. W. Köhler, *Dokumente zum Ablassstreit von 1517* (2d ed.; Tübingen, 1934), pp. 104–116.

L

22. *D. Martin Luthers Werke*, 1:567.
23. *Ibid.*, 1:234.
24. F. Myconius, *Historia Reformationis* (Leipzig, 1718), 4:23.
25. *D. Martin Luthers Werke*, 1:364.
26. *Ibid.*, 1:530–628.
27. P. Kalkoff, 'Zu Luthers römischen Prozess,' *Zeitschrift für Kirchengeschichte* 25 (1904); 31 (1911); 33 (1912).
28. *D. Martin Luthers Werke*, 2:51.
29. P. Kirn, *Friedrich der Weise und die Kirche* (Leipzig, 1926).
30. C. Henning, *Cajetan und Luther: Ein historischer Beitrag zur Begegnung von Thomismus und Reformation* (Stuttgart, 1966).
31. *D. Martin Luthers Werke (Briefe)*, 1:216.
32. N. Paulus, 'Die Ablassdekretale Leos X. vom Jahre 1518,' *Zeitschrift für katholische Theologie* 37 (1913) :394–400.
33. *D. Martin Luthers Werke*, 9:209.
34. E. Walder, *Kaiser, Reich und Reformation, 1517–1525* (Bern, 1952), pp. 30–33.
35. *D. Martin Luthers Werke*, 6:405.
36. *Bullarium romanum*, ed. F. Caude et al. (Rome, 1845–), 5:748–757. Hereafter cited *BullRom*.
37. H. Roos, 'Die Quellen der Bulle "Exsurge Domine,"' *Theologie in Geschichte und Gegenwart*, ed. J. Auer and H. Volk (Munich, 1957), pp. 909–926.
38. *D. Martin Luthers Werke*, 6:469.
39. *Ibid.*, 6:511.
40. *Ibid.*, 6:512.
41. *Ibid.*, 7:21.
42. *Ibid.*, 7:28.
43. J. Luther, 'Noch einmal Luthers Worte bei der Verbrennung der Bannbulle,' *Archiv für Reformationsgeschichte* 45 (1954):260–265.
44. *BullRom*, 5:761–764.
45. *Deutsche Reichstagsakten, Jüngere Reihe*, vols 1–4 (Munich, 1823–1905), 2:515.
46. *Ibid.*, 2:526.
47. *D. Martin Luthers Werke (Briefe)*, 2:298.
48. E. Kessel, 'Luther vor dem Reichstag in Worms 1521,' *Festgabe für Paul Kirn*, ed. E. Kaufmann (Berlin, 1961), pp. 172–190.
49. *Deutsche Reichstagsakten, Jüngere Reihe*, 2:555.
50. P. Kalkoff, *Die Depeschen des Nuntius Aleander* (Halle, 1886), p. 143.
51. *Deutsche Reichstagsakten, Jüngere Reihe*, 2:595–596.
52. *Ibid.*, 2:654.
53. *D. Martin Luthers Werke (Briefe)*, 2:305.

## Notes to Chapter Two

1. E. Heidrich, *Albrecht Dürers schriftlicher Nachlass* (Berlin, 1908), p. 96.
2. Martin Luther, *Werke: Kritische Gesamtausgabe* (Weimar, 1883–), 8:421. Hereafter cited as *D. Martin Luthers Werke*.
3. *Ibid. (Tischreden)*, 2:1289.
4. *Ibid. (Tischreden)*, 1:146.
5. H. Bluhm, *Martin Luther: Creative Translator* (St. Louis, 1965).
6. H. Bornkamm, *Luther im Spiegel der deutschen Geistesgeschichte* (Heidelberg, 1955), p. 228.
7. *D. Martin Luthers Werke (Deutsche Bibel)*, 7:385.
8. *Ibid.*, 10.3:1–64.
9. *Ibid.*, 6:203.
10. S. R. Cattley and G. Townsend, eds., *The Acts and Monuments of John Foxe*, 8 vols. (London, 1843–49), 3:721.
11. P. Kalkoff, *Die Depeschen des Nuntius Aleander* (Halle, 1886), p. 44.
12. P. Böckmann, 'Der gemeine Mann in den Flugschriften der Reformation,' *Deutsche Vierteljahresschrift für Literaturwissenschaft und Geistesgeschichte* 22 (1944): 186–230.
13. L. v. Muralt, 'Stadtgemeinde und Reformation in der Schweiz,' *Zeitschrift für Schweizer Geschichte* 10 (1930): 349–384.
14. H. Schöffler, *Wirkungen der Reformation* (Frankfurt, 1960), pp. 110–132.
15. *Deutsche Reichstagsakten, Jüngere Reihe*, vols. 1–7 (Munich, 1893–1905), 3:21.
16. *Ibid.*, 3:397.
17. *Ibid.*, 4:604.
18. A. Waas, 'Die grosse Wende im deutschen Bauernkrieg,' *Historische Zeitschrift* 158/159 (1938): 457–491.
19. G. Franz, *Quellen zur Geschichte des Bauernkrieges* (Munich, 1963), pp. 174–179.
20. *D. Martin Luthers Werke*, 18:361.
21. *Ibid.*, 18:319.
22. B. Moeller, 'Die deutschen Humanisten und die Anfänge der Reformation,' *Zeitschrift für Kirchengeschichte* 60 (1959): 46–61.
23. *D. Martin Luthers Werke*, 18:786.
24. D. Erasmus, *Opus Epistolarum Des. Erasmi*, ed. P. S. Allen, (Oxford, 1906–1958) 1167, 1342.
25. Erasmus, *De Libero Arbitrio*, ed. J. v. Walther (Leipzig, 1910), p. 91.
26. *D. Martin Luthers Werke*, 18:709.
27. *Ibid.*, 18:656.
28. Erasmus, *De Libero Arbitrio*, p. 4.
29. *D. Martin Luthers Werke (Briefe)*, 1:90.

## Notes to Chapter Three

1. E. Egli and G. Finsler, *Huldreich Zwinglis Sämtliche Werke* (Zurich, 1905–), 2:149. Hereafter cited as *Zwinglis Sämtliche Werke*.
2. *Ibid.*, 5:722.
3. H. Bullinger, *Reformationsgeschichte*, ed. J. J. Hottinger (Frauenfeld, 1838), 1:29.
4. E. Egli, ed., *Actensammlung zur Geschichte der Zürcher Reformation in den Jahren 1519–1533* (Zurich, 1879), p. 234.
5. Egli and Finsler, *Zwinglis Sämtliche Werke*, 1:88–136.
6. *Ibid.*, 1:458–465.
7. *Ibid.*, 1:470–471.
8. T. van Braght, *The Bloody Theater or The Martyrs' Mirror* (Scottdale, 1951), pp. 984–987.
9. A. J. F. Zieglschmid, ed., *Die älteste Chronik der Hutterischen Brüder* (Ithaca, 1943), p. 43. Hereafter cited as *Hutterischen Brüder*.
10. Thomas Müntzer, *Schriften und Briefe*, ed. G. Franz (Gütersloh, 1968), pp. 491–513.
11. *Bibliotheca reformatoria Neerlandica*, S. Cramer and F. Pijper, eds., 10 vols. ('S-Gravenhage, 1903–1914), 7:124.
12. Menno Simons, *Complete Writings*, ed. J. C. Wenger (Scottdale, Pa., 1956), p. 437.
13. *Ibid.*, p. 774.
14. Zieglschmid, *Hutterischen Brüder*, p. 87.
15. H. Fischer, *Jacob Hutter: Leben, Frömmigkeit, Briefe* (Newton, 1956), p. 28f.
16. Zeiglschmid, *Hutterischen Brüder*, p. 435.
17. 'Address to the Schoolmasters,' *Mennonite Quarterly Review* 5 (1931): 241–244.
18. P. Wackernagel, *Das deutsche Kirchenlied* (Leipzig, 1870), 3:817.
19. H. J. Hillerbrand, *A Fellowship of Discontent* (New York, 1967), p. 57.
20. S. Castellio, *De haereticis an sint persequendi*, ed. S. v. d. Woude (Geneva, 1954), p. 19.
21. G. Schramm, 'Neue Ergebnisse der Antitrinitarierforschung,' *Jahrbücher für Geschichte Osteuropas* NF 8 (1960): 428ff.
22. S. Dunin-Borkowski, 'Quellenstudien zur Vorgeschichte der Unitarier des 16. Jahrhunderts,' *75 Jahre Stella Matutina* (Feldkirch, 1931), 1:91–138.
23. A. von Harnack, *History of Dogma* (New York, 1958), 7:23, 118ff.
24. J. Gauss, 'Der junge Michael Servet,' *Zwingliana* 12 (1966): 410–459.
25. *The Two Treatises of Servetus on the Trinity*, ed. E. M. Wilbur (Cambridge, Mass., 1932), p. 3.

26. Quoted in E. M. Wilbur, *A History of Unitarianism* (Cambridge, Mass., 1945), p. 180.
27. D. Cantimori, *Italienische Häretiker der Spätrenaissance* (Basel, 1949), 345ff., 81ff.
28. *Corpus reformatorum* (Berlin, 1837–; Leipzig, 1906–), 45 : 169. Hereafter cited as *CorpRef*.
29. G. Schramm, 'Antitrinitarier in Polen 1556–1658, ein Literaturbericht,' *Bibliothèque d'Humanisme et Renaissance* 21 (1959) : 473–511.
30. *CorpRef*, 45 : 676.
31. M. Martini, *Fausto Socino et la penseé socienne* (Paris, 1967).
32. Cantimori, *Italienische Häretiker*, p. 336ff.
33. *Ibid.*, p. 342.
34. *Ibid.*, p. 484.
35. P. Wizecionko, 'Die Theologie des Rakower Katechismus,' *Kirche im Osten* 6 (1963) : 73–116.

## Notes to Chapter Four

1. *CorpRef* (Berlin, 1834–; Leipzig, 1906–), 49 : 167.
1a. A useful survey of various interpretations is found in A. Ganoczy, *Calvin, théologien de l'église* (Paris, 1964).
2. John Calvin, *Opera Selecta*, ed. P. Barth et al. (2d ed., Munich, 1952), 1 : 23.
3. *Institutes of the Christian Religion*, 1.18 : 4.
4. *Ibid.*, 3.21 : 5.
5. *Ibid.*, 3.23 : 5.
6. *Ibid.*, 3.3 : 9.
7. *Ibid.*, 3.14 : 18.
8. *CorpRef*, 38 : 13. The tract is analyzed by F. Wendel, *Origin and Development of Calvin's Religious Thought* (New York, 1964).
9. *Ibid.*, 59 : 21.
10. P. Sprenger, *Das Rätsel um die Bekehrung Calvins* (Neukirchen, 1960), p. 9ff.
11. *CorpRef*, 59 : 25.
12. *Ibid.*, 50 : 30.
13. *Ibid.*, 49 : 204.
14. *Ibid.*, 39a : 5ff.
15. *Ibid.*, 38.2 : 153.
16. *Ibid.*, 49 : 225.
17. *Ibid.* 33 : 356–416.
18. *Ibid.*, 33 : 377.
19. *Ibid.*, 39 : 214.
20. *Ibid.*, 38 : 5ff.
21. *Ibid.*, 49 : 168.

## Notes to Chapter Five

1. *Neue und vollständigere Sammlung der Reichsabschiede:* II. Theil ed. H. Chr. Senckenberg (Frankfurt, 1747), p. 273ff.
2. *Deutsche Reichstagsakten, Jüngere Reihe*, Vol. 7 (Munich, 1929), 7: 1262–65; 1274–88.
3. *Ibid.*, 7: 1143ff.
4. Martin Luther, *Werke: Kritische Gesamtausgabe* (Weimar, 1883–), 6: 515. Hereafter cited as *D. Martin Luthers Werke*.
5. The letter is in E. Egli and G. Finsler, *Huldreich Zwinglis Sämtliche Werke* (Zurich, 1905–), 4: 512–519; English translation H. A. Oberman, *Forerunners of the Reformation* (New York, 1966), pp. 268–278.
6. *D. Martin Luthers Werke*, 17.2: 134.
7. Egli and Finsler, *Zwinglis Sämtliche Werke*, 3: 776.
8. *Ibid.*, 3: 807.
9. *Ibid.*, 3: 476f.
10. *D. Martin Luthers Werke*, 26: 499ff.
11. *Die Bekenntnisschriften der evangelisch-Lutherischen Kirche* (3d ed.; Göttingen, 1956), p. 62.
12. *Ibid.*, p. 62.
13. W. Köhler, *Das Marburger Religionsgespräch 1529: Versuch einer Rekonstruktion* (Leipzig, 1929), p. 27. Our analysis follows W. Köhler, *Zwingli und Luther* (Gütersloh, 1953), p. 67 ff.
14. *Ibid.*, p. 13.
15. *Ibid.*, p. 15.
16. K. E. Förstemann, *Urkundenbuch zu der Geschichte des Reichstages zu Augsburg im Jahre 1530* (Osnabrück, 1966), 1: 7f.
17. *Die Bekenntnisschriften der evangelisch-Lutherischen Kirche*, pp. 31–137.
18. E. A. Koch, *Neue und vollständigere Sammlung der Reichstagsabschiede* (Frankfurt, 1797), 2: 306–332.
19. E. Fabian, *Die Entstehung des Schmalkaldischen Bundes* (2d ed.; Tübingen, 1962), pp. 349–353.
20. Quoted by P. Joachimsen, *Die Reformation als Epoche der deutschen Geschichte* (Munich, 1951), p. 212.
21. E. Bircher, 'Ulrich Zwinglis militärische Auffassungen,' *Allgemeine Schweizerische Militärzeitung* 77 (1931): 503f.
22. Egli and Finsler, *Zwinglis Sämtliche Werke*, 3: 551.
23. *Ibid.*, 10: 147.
24. J. C. Mörikofer, *Ulrich Zwingli, nach den urkundlichen Quellen* (Leipzig, 1897), 2: 142.
25. Quoted by O. Farner, *Huldrych Zwingli* (Zurich, 1960), 4: 308.
26. *Heinrich Bullingers Reformationsgeschichte*, ed. J. J. Hottinger (Frauenfeld, 1838), 2: 185–191.

27. Quoted by O. Farner, *Huldrych Zwingli*, 4:477.
28. *Ulrich Zwingli, Eine Auswahl aus seinen Schriften*, ed. G. Finsler et al. (Zurich, 1918), p. 15.
29. *D. Martin Luthers Werke*, 19:113.
30. *Ibid.*, 12:1ff.
31. *Ibid.*, 26:200.
32. *Ibid. (Briefe)*, 8:638.
33. *Ibid.*, 9:199.
34. M. Lenz, ed., *Briefwechsel Landgraf Philip's des Grossmütigen*, 3 vols. (Leipzig, 1880–1891), 1:185f.
35. *Ibid.*, 3:98.
36. *Ibid.*, 3:39–72.
37. *CorpRef*, 4:199.
38. *Ibid.*, 4:475.
39. L. Pastor, 'Die Correspondenz des Cardinals Contarini,' *Historisches Jahrbuch der Görres-Gesellschaft* (Münster, 1880–82: Munich, 1883–; 1950–), 1 (1880): 478–481.
40. *CorpRef*, 39:261.
41. Charles-Quint (Charles V), *Commentaires*, ed. K. de Lettenhove (Bruxelles, 1862), p. 100.
42. K. T. Hergang, ed., *Das Augsburger Interim* (Leipzig, 1855), pp. 20–155.
43. K. Lanz, *Correspondenz des Kaisers Karl V.* (Leipzig, 1846), 3:483.
44. *Ibid.*, 3:624.
45. E. Walder, *Religionsvergleiche des 16. Jahrhunderts* (2d ed.; Bern, 1960), pp. 68–71.

## Notes to Chapter Six

1. N. Harpsfield, *The Life and Death of Sir Thomas More*, ed. E. V. Hitchcock and R. W. Chambers (London, 1932), p. 147.
2. 'Bishop Hooper's Visitation of Gloucester,' *English Historical Review* 19 (1904): 102.
3. S. R. Cattley and G. Townsend, eds., *The Acts and Monuments of John Foxe*, 8 vols. (London, 1843–49), 4:218. Hereafter cited as Foxe, *Acts and Monuments*.
4. *Ibid.*, 5:414–415.
5. R. Holinshed, *The Chronicles of England, Scotlande, and Irelande* (London, 1587), p. 908.
6. Quoted by F. Bridgett, *Life of St. John Fisher* (4th ed.; London, 1922), p. 148.
7. J. S. Brewer, ed., *Letters and Papers, Foreign and Domestic*, 21 vols. (London, 1862–1910), 4:4167.
8. D. Wilkins. *Concilia Magnae Britanniae et Hiberniae*, 4 vols. (London, 1737), 3:742.

9. Public Record Office, *State Papers*, 6.1 : 22.
10. *Ibid.*, 1.70 : 35.
11. Brewer, *Letters and Papers*, 5 : 1013.
12. *Statutes of the Realm*, 3 : 427.
13. W. Tyndale, *Doctrinal Treatises, Obedience of a Christian Man* (Cambridge, 1848), p. 191.
14. *Ibid.*, p. 48.
15. M. Goldast, *Monarchia S. Romani Imperii* (Frankfurt, 1613), 3 : 22–45.
16. S. Gardiner, *De vera obedientia oratio*, ed. B. A. Heywood (London, 1870), p. 50.
17. J. Foxe, *Acts and Monuments*, 8 : 110.
18. D. Erasmus. *Opus Epistolarum Des. Erasmi*, 3049.
19. N. Harpsfield, *The Life and Death of Sir Thomas More*, p. 204.
20. *Statutes of the Realm*, 3 : 469.
21. H. Latimer, *Works*, G. E. Corrie, ed., 2 vols. (Cambridge, 1844–1845), 1 : 123.
22. *Statutes of the Realm*, 3 : 576.
23. As quoted in M. H. Dodds and R. Dodds, *The Pilgrimage of Grace, 1536–1537* (Cambridge, Eng., 1915), 1 : 347.
24. *State Papers*, 1 : 463.
25. C. Hardwick, *A History of the Articles of Religion* (London, 1890), pp. 237–258.
26. H. Gee and W. J. Hardy, *Documents Illustrative of English Church History* (London, 1896), p. 269ff.
27. C. Lloyd, *Formularies of Faith put forth by Authority during the Reign of Henry VIII* (Oxford, 1856), pp. 21–213.
28. *Miscellaneous Writings and Letters of Thomas Cranmer*, ed. J. E. Cox (Cambridge, Eng., 1846), p. 95.
29. Gee and Hardy, *Documents*, pp. 275–281.
30. *Ibid.*, pp. 303–319.
31. Brewer, *Letters and Papers*, 15 : 824.
32. Foxe, *Acts and Monuments*, 5 : 402.
33. *Ibid.*, 5 : 438.
34. C. Lloyd, *Formularies of Faith Put forth by Authority During the Reign of Henry VIII* (Oxford, 1856), pp. 213–377.
35. E. Hall, *Chronicle of the Reign of Henry VIII* (London, 1806), pp. 864f.
36. Foxe, *Acts and Monuments*, 5 : 16.
37. *Ibid.*, 5 : 689.
38. Brewer, *Letters and Papers*, 15.1 : 56.
39. Foxe, *Acts and Monuments*, 6 : 106.
40. Gee and Hardy, *Documents*, p. 417f.
41. J. Strype, *Ecclesiastical Memorials Relating Chiefly to Religion*, 3 vols. (Oxford, 1822), 2 : 65.
42. Gee and Hardy, *Documents*, p. 369f.

43. *Calendar of State Papers, Venetian,* ed. R. Brown et al. 9 vols. (London, 1894–1898), 2:1287.
44. Gee and Hardy, *Documents,* p. 386.
45. Thomas Cranmer, *Miscellaneous Writings and Letters* (Cambridge, Eng., 1846), pp. 564–565.
46. *Ibid.,* p. 566.
47. *Journals of the House of Commons* (London, 1803), p. 52.
48. *The Zurich Letters,* ed. H. Robinson, 2 vols. (Cambridge, Eng., 1842), 1:3.
49. Quoted in S. Clarke, *The Marrow of Ecclesiastical History* (London, 1675), 2:94.
50. *The Public Speaking of Queen Elizabeth,* ed. G. P. Rice (New York, 1954), p. 94.
51. C. Hardwick, *History of the Articles of Religion* (Cambridge, 1851), pp. 325–329.
52. J. Jewel, *An Apology of the Church of England,* ed. J. E. Booty (Ithaca, 1963), p. 121.
53. *Correspondence of Matthew Parker, 1535–1575* (Cambridge, Eng., 1853), p. 291.
54. Gee and Hardy, *Documents,* pp. 477–480.
55. *The Zurich Letters,* 1:55.
56. P. Wilburn, *A checke or reproofe* (London, 1581), p. 15.
57. *The Seconde Parte of a Register* (London, 1915), 2:52.
58. W. Haller, *The Rise of Puritanism* (New York, 1938), p. 3.
59. M. M. Knappen, ed., 'The Diary of Samuel Ward,' *Two Elizabethan Puritan Diaries* (Chicago, 1933), p. 110.
60. Gee and Hardy, *Documents,* pp. 417–422.
61. *The Zurich Letters,* 1:67.
62. J. Strype, *The Life and Acts of Matthew Parker* (Oxford, 1821), 3:67.
63. Gee and Hardy, *Documents,* p. 467ff.
64. J. H. Primus, *The Vestments Controversy* (Kampen, 1960), p. 108.
65. *Correspondence of Matthew Parker, 1535–1575,* p. 279.
66. W. H. Frere and C. E. Douglas, eds., *Puritan Manifestoes* (London, 1954), pp. 8–19.
67. J. Ayre, ed., *John Whitgift Works* (Cambridge, 1851), 1:184.
68. *The Remains of Edmund Grindal, D.D.,* ed. W. Nicholson (Cambridge, 1843), p. 387.
69. G. Hickes, *Bibliotheca Scriptorum Ecclesiae Anglicanae* (London, 1709), pp. 247–315.
70. T. F. Knox, ed., *The First and Second Diaries of the English College, Douay* (London, 1878), p. XXXVIII.
71. W. Allen, *A True, Sincere and Modest Defence,* ed. R. M. Kingdon (Ithaca, 1965), p. 160.
72. P. Renold, ed., *Letters of William Allen and Richard Barret 1572–1598* (Oxford, 1967), p. 289.

M

## Notes to Chapter Seven

1. Quoted in R. Nürnberger, *Die Politisierung des französischen Protestantismus* (Tübingen, 1948), p. 43.
2. *Le Journal d'un Bourgeois de Paris,* ed. V. L. Vourilly (Paris, 1910), p. 101.
3. R. Hari, 'Les Placards de 1534.' *Aspects de la Propagande Religieuse* (Geneva, 1957), pp. 114–115.
4. See *Bulletin de la Societé de l'Histoire du Protestantisme français* 33 (1884): 15ff.
5. M. Weiss, *La Chambre Ardente* (Paris, 1889), p. 291.
6. A. C. Keller, 'Michel de L'Hôpital and the Edict of Toleration of 1562,' *Bibliotheque d'Humanisme et Renaissance* 14 (1952): 301–310.
7. Nürnberger, *Die Politisierung des französischen Protestantismus,* p. 91.
8. *Bekenntnisschriften und Kirchenordnungen der nach Gottes Wort reformierten Kirche,* p. 90.
9. *Ibid.,* p. 98.
10. *CorpRef* (Berlin, 1834–; Leipzig, 1906–), 42: 544f.
11. Quoted in H. J. Hillerbrand, *The Protestant Reformation* (New York, 1968), p. 232.
12. E. Walder, *Religionsvergleiche des 16. Jahrhunderts* (Bern, 1961), 2: 13–71.
13. *Konung Gustaf den förstes Registratur,* ed. J. A. Nordström (Stockholm, 1861), 1: 139.
14. *Ibid.,* 1: 147f.
15. *Handlingar rörande Skandinaviens historia* (Stockholm, 1816–65), 17: 205.
16. Olavus Petri, *Samlade skifter,* ed. B. Hesselmann, 4 vols. (Stockholm, 1914–1917).
17. S. Ingebrand, *Olavus Petris reformatoriska åskådning* (Uppsala, 1964).
18. *Svenska Riksdagsakter,* eds. E. Hilderbrand and O. Alin, 4 vols. (Stockholm, 1887). 1: 82–87.
19. *Ibid.,* 1: 86.
20. S. Tunberg, *Västeraas Riksdag 1527* (Uppsala, 1915).
21. T. v. Haag, 'Die apostolische Sukzession in Schweden,' *Kyrkohistorik Arsskrift* 44 (1945): 1–168.
22. S. Kjöllerström, 'Gustav Vasa und die Bischofs Weihe (1523–31),' *Festschrift für Joh. Heckel,* ed. S. Grundmann (Köln–Graz, 1959), p. 180.
23. H. Elmquist, *Örebro möte aar 1529,* ed. H. Holmberg (Örebro, 1929), pp. 69–73.
24. *Svenska Rigsdagsakter,* 1: 390–392.

25. S. Kjöllerström, 'Kirche und Staat in Schweden nach der Reformation,' *Zeitschrift der Savigny-Stiftung für Rechtsgeschichte, Kanonistische Abteilung* 41 (1955); 271–289.
26. O. Garstein, *Rome and the Counter-Reformation in Scandinavia Until the Establishment of the S. Congregatio de Propaganda Fide in 1622* (Copenhagen, 1963), 125ff.
27. M. Scaduto, 'Le missioni di A. Possevino in Piemonte,' *Archivum historicum Societatis Jesu* 28 (1959): 51–191.
28. John Knox, *History of the Reformation in Scotland*, ed. W. Croft-Dickenson (London, 1950), 1:2. Hereafter cited as Knox, *History*.
29. *Ibid.*, 2:224.
30. *Ibid.*, 1:13–15, 18.
31. G. McGregor, *The Thundering Scot: A Portrait of John Knox* (Philadelphia, 1957).
32. D. Kalderwood, *The History of the Kirk of Scotland*, ed. T. Thomson and D. Laing (Edinburgh, 1848), 3:242.
33. Knox, *History*, 1:109.
34. D. Laing, ed., *The Work of John Knox* (Edinburgh, 1846–), 3:101.
35. Knox, *History*, 2:15.
36. *The Works of John Knox*, 4:240.
37. Knox, *History*, 1:137.
38. *The Works of John Knox*, 4:371ff.
39. *Ibid.*, 4:416.
40. Knox, *History*, 1:162.
41. *Ibid.*, 1:335.
42. *Ibid.*, 2:81.
43. *Correspondence of Matthew Parker 1535–75* (Cambridge, Eng., 1853), p. 105.
44. Knox, *History*, 2:284ff.
45. *Ibid.*, 2:306.
46. J. Pelikan, *Obedient Rebels* (New York, 1964), pp. 147–158.
47. D. Bartel, 'Martin Luther und Polen,' *Vierhundertfünfzig Jahre Lutherische Reformation 1517–1967. Festschrift für Franz Lau* (Göttingen, 1967), pp. 27–42.
48. E. W. Zeeden, 'Calvins Einwirken auf die Reformation in Polen-Litauen,' *Syntagma Friburgense* (Lindau, 1956), p. 323f.
49. G. Schramm, *Der Polnische Adel und die Reformation, 1548–1607* (Wiesbaden, 1965), p. 318ff.

## Notes to Chapter Eight

1. L. v. Pastor, *History of the Popes* (St. Louis, 1915–), 9:217.
2. *Concilium Tridentinum. Diariorum, actorum, epistularum, tractatum nova collectio*, ed. Görres–Gesellschaft (Freiburg, 1901–), 12:131–145.

3. *Bullarium romanum*, ed. F. Gaude et al. (Rome, 1845–), 6 : 344f.
4. T. Brieger, *Aleander und Luther 1521* (Gotha, 1884), p. 48.
5. *Concilium Tridentinum. Diariorum, actorum, epistularum, tracta·tum nova collectio*, 4 : 2.
6. *Ibid.*, 2 : 60; Session IV.

## Notes to Chapter Nine

1. A sophisticated statement is that of K. Holl, *The Cultural Significance of the Reformation* (New York, 1959), first published in 1921.
2. H. A. Oberman, *Forerunners of the Reformation: The Shape of Late Medieval Thought* (New York, 1966), p. 40.
3. See G. Edel, *Das gemeinkatholische Erbe beim jungen Luther* (Marburg, 1962).
4. J. T. McNeill, 'The Religious Initiative in Reformation History,' *The Impact of the Church Upon Its Culture*, ed. J. C. Brauer (Chicago, 1968), pp. 173–207.
5. L. Febvre, *Le problème de l'incroyance au XVIe siècle* (Paris, 1942).
6. Quoted in A. T. Hart, *The Man in the Pew 1558–1660* (London, 1966), p. 26.
7. E. W. Zeeden, *Die Entstehung der Konfessionen* (Munich, 1965) *passim*, offers abundant evidence.
8. E. W. Zeeden, 'Grundlagen und Wege der Konfessionsbildung in Deutschland im Zeitalter der Glaubenskämpfe,' *Historische Zeitschrift* 185 (1958): 249–299.
9. R. Mandrou, 'Capitalisme et protestantisme: la science et le mythe,' *Revue Historique* 90 (1966): 101–106.
10. W. H. Neuser, 'Kirche und Staat in der Reformationszeit,' *Kirche und Staat* (Berlin, 1967), p. 77.
11. W. Niesel, *Bekenntnisschriften und Kirchenordnungen der nach Gottes Wort reformierten Kirche* (Zurich, 1938), p. 33.
12. G. Wingren, *Luther on Vocation* (Philadelphia, 1957).
13. I. Asheim, *Glaube und Erziehung bei Luther* (Heidelberg, 1961).
14. D. Erasmus, *Opus Epistolarum*, ed. P. S. Allen, 1977.
15. L. Petry, 'Die Zwischenbilanz,' *Festgabe Joseph Lortz* (Wiesbaden, 1958), 2 : 317–353.
16. Martin Luther, *Werke: Kritische Gesamtausgabe* (Weimar, 1883–), 15 : 27–53.
17. Instrumentum pacis Osnabrugense . . ., K. Zeumer, *Quellensammlung zur Geschichte der deutschen Reichsverfassung* (Leipzig, 1904).
18. A. Dufour, 'Humanisme et Reformation. État de la question,' *XIIIe Congrès International des Sciences Historiques 1965. Rapports*, 3 : 57–74.
19. B. Gerrish, 'The Reformation and the Rise of Modern Science,' *The*

*Impact of the Church upon its Culture,* ed. J. C. Brauer (Chicago, 1968), pp. 231–266.
20.  P. Jourda, *Marot, l'homme et l'œuvre* (Paris, 1950).

## Note to Epilogue

1.  E. W. Kohls, 'Evangelische Bewegung und Kirchenordnung in den oberdeutschen Reichsstädten,' *Theologische Literaturzeitung* 92 (1967): 321–326.

# BIBLIOGRAPHY

## General Studies and Bibliographies

Bainton, R. H. *The Reformation of the 16th Century*. Boston: Beacon Press, 1953. Summarizes the theological currents.

——. 'Interpretations of the Reformation,' *American Historical Review* 66 (1960): 74–84. A basic introduction to the various strands of Reformation historiography.

Elton, G. R. *Reformation Europe, 1517–1559*. London: Collins, 1963. The best brief account.

——, ed. *The Reformation, 1520–1559*. Vol. 2 of New Cambridge Modern History. Cambridge, Eng.: At the University Press, 1958.

Hassinger E. *Das Werden des neuzeitlichen Europa, 1300–1600*. Braunschweig: G. Westermann, 1959. Especially valuable for its bibliography.

Hermelink, H., and Maurer, W. *Reformation und Gegenreformation*. Vol. 3 of Handbuch der Kirchengeschichte, edited by G. Krüger et al. 2d ed. Tübingen: J. C. B. Mohr, 1931. Though outdated, still exceedingly helpful for detail and bibliography.

Hillerbrand, H. J. *The Reformation: A Narrative History Related by Contemporary Observers and Participants*. New York: Harper & Row, 1965.

International Committee of Historical Sciences. *Bibliographie de la réforme: 1450–1648*. Leiden: Brill, 1960–. Fasc. 1, *Allemagne, Pays Bas*, 3d ed., 1964; Fasc. 2, *Belgique, Suède, Norvège, Danemark, Irlande, États-Unis d'Amérique*, 1960; Fasc. 3, *Italie, Espagne, Portugal*, 1961; Fasc. 4, *France, Angleterre, Suisse*, 1963; Fasc. 5, *Pologne, Hongrie, Tchécoslovaquie, Finlande*, 1965; Fasc. 6, *Autriche*, 1967. Difficult to use but virtually comprehensive.

Iserloh, E., Glazik, J. et al. *Reformation, Katholische Reformation und Gegenreformation*. Vol. 4 of Handbuch der Kirchengeschichte, edited by G. Krüger et al. Freiburg: Herder, 1967. For narrative and bibliography the best introduction to 16th-century ecclesiastical history.

Léonard, E. G. *A History of Protestantism.* Vol. 1 of *The Reformation.* Translated by J. M. H. Reid and edited by H. H. Rowley. London: Nelson, 1965. Volume 1 of a 3-volume history with a detailed bibliography.

Moeller, B. 'Probleme der Reformationsgeschichtsforschung,' *Zeitschrift für Kirchengeschichte* 76 (1965): 1–17. A perceptive essay that is both analytic and programmatic.

Ritter, G. *Die Neugestaltung Europas im 16. Jahrhundert.* Berlin: Verlag des Druckhauses Tempelhof, 1950. A perceptive narrative of the interaction of religion and politics in the 16th century, with special attention to Germany.

Swidler, L. 'Catholic Reformation Scholarship in Germany.' *Journal of Ecumenical Studies* 2 (1965): 189–233.

Zeeden, E. W. 'Probleme und Aufgaben der Reformationsgeschichtsschreibung,' *Geschichte in Wissenschaft und Unterricht* 6 (1955): 201–217.

————. 'Zeitalter der europäischen Glaubenskämpfe, Gegenreformation und katholische Reform,' *Saeculum* 7 (1956): 231–368. A useful bibliographical survey.

### The Reformation in Germany

#### BIBLIOGRAPHIES AND GENERAL STUDIES

*Deutsche Reichstagsakten: Jüngere Reihe.* Vols. 1–4, Munich: Königliche Akademie der Wissenschaften, 1893–1905. Vol. 7, Munich: Königliche Akademie der Wissenschaften, 1929. The monumental edition of the sources pertaining to the German diets.

Janssen, J. *Geschichte des deutschen Volkes seit dem Ausgang des Mittelalters.* 8 vols. Freiburg: Herder, 1876–94. The monumental Catholic history that stressed the religious vitality of the late Middle Ages.

Lau, F. and Bizer, E. *Reformationsgeschichte Deutschlands.* Vol. 3 of *Die Kirche in ihrer Geschichte.* Edited by K. D. Schmidt and E. Wolf. Göttingen: Vandenhoeck und Ruprecht, 1964. An uneven work but useful for its detailed treatment of the time, 1530–35.

Lortz, J. *The Reformation in Germany.* 2 vols. New York: Herder and Herder, 1968. Originally published in German in 1939, this is an outstanding and altogether sympathetic account by an eminent Catholic historian.

Ranke, L. von. *Deutsche Geschichte im Zeitalter der Reformation.* Edited by P. Joachimsen. 6 vols. Munich, 1925–26. Translated into English under the title *History of the Reformation in Germany*. 3 vols. Philadelphia: Lea and Blanshard, 1844.

Rothert, H. *Das Tausendjährige Reich der Wiedertäufer zu Münster 1534–35*. Münster: Aschendorff, 1947. The best narrative.

Schottenloher, K. *Bibliographie zur deutschen Geschichte im Zeitalter der Glaubensspaltung 1517–1585*. 6 vols. Leipzig: Hiersemann, 1933–40; Stuttgart: Hiersemann, 1962. The indispensable bibliographical tool for the German Reformation.

Wolf, G. *Quellenkunde der deutschen Reformationsgeschichte*. 3 vols. Gotha: 1915–23. Lacks recent studies but exceedingly helpful for survey of older publications.

MARTIN LUTHER

Aland, K. *Der Weg zur Reformation: Zeitpunkt und Charakter des reformatorischen Erlebnisses Martin Luthers*. Munich: C. Kaiser, 1965.

Althaus, P. *The Theology of Martin Luther*. Translated by R. C. Schultz. Philadelphia: Fortress, 1966. An able introduction.

Bainton, R. H. *Here I Stand: A Life of Martin Luther*. New York: Abingdon, 1950; paperback ed. New York: New American Library. Widely praised standard biography.

Bizer, E. *Fides Ex Auditu*. 2d ed. Neukirchen: Verlag der Buchhandlung des Erziehungsvereins, 1958. Re-opened the scholarly controversy over the date of Luther's 'evangelical discovery.'

Bornkamm, H. 'Zur Frage der Iustitia Dei beim jungen Luther.' *Archiv für Reformationsgeschichte* 52 (1961): 16–29, 53. A critical reaction to Bizer.

————. *Wandlungen des Lutherbildes*. Würzburg: Katholische Akademie in Bayern, 1966.

Dickens, A. G. *Martin Luther and the Reformation*. London: English Universities, 1967. A lively summary of the scholarly consensus.

Ebeling, G. *Luther: Einführung in sein Denken*. Tübingen: J. C. B. Mohr, 1964. Highly imaginative and open to questions.

Fife, R. H. *The Revolt of Martin Luther*. New York: Columbia University Press, 1957. Detailed biography to 1521.

Grane, L. *Contra Gabrielem*. Copenhagen: 1962. A competent examination of Luther's theological reaction against Gabriel Biel.

Grimm, H. J. 'Luther Research Since 1920.' *Journal of Modern History* 32 (1960): 105–180. Emphasizes the main lines.

Hagen, K. G., 'Changes in the Understanding of Luther: The Development of the Young Luther.' *Theological Studies* 29 (1968): 472–496. Basic but useful.

Holl, K. *Luther*. Vol. 1 of *Gesammelte Aufsätze zur Kirchengeschichte*. Tübingen: J. C. B. Mohr, 1923. Path-breaking essays on various facets of Luther's thought that precipitated the so-called 'Luther-Renaissance.'

Kantzenbach, F. W. 'Luther Research Since 1949.' *Lutheran World* 13 (1966): 257–315.

Luther, Martin. *Werke: Kritische Gesamtausgabe.* Weimar: H. Böhlau, 1883–1968. The definitive edition of Luther's works in four series: *Werke, Tischreden, Briefe, Deutsche Bibel.*

———. *Works.* Edited by Jaroslav Pelikan. St. Louis: Concordia Publishing House, 1955–. The comprehensive English translation of Luther's writings, to comprise 55 volumes.

Pelikan, J. *Luther the Expositor.* St. Louis: Concordia Publishing House, 1959.

Pesch, O. H. *Theologie der Rechtfertigung bei Martin Luther und Thomas von Aquin.* Mainz: Matthias–Grünewald Verlag, 1967. A monumental (and conciliatory) comparison of St. Thomas and Luther.

———. 'Zur Frage nach Luthers reformatorischer Wende. Ergebnisse und Probleme der Diskussion um Ernst Bizer, *Fides ex auditu.*' *Catholica* 20 (1966): 216–243; 264–280. Summarizes the extensive discussion over Bizer.

Scheel, O. *Martin Luther.* 2 vols. Tübingen: J. C. B. Mohr (P. Siebeck), 1916–21. Incomplete, but useful for its detail.

Spitz, L. W. 'Current Accents in Luther Study: 1960–1967.' *Theological Studies* 28 (1967): 549–573. A competent summary of recent research.

Todd, J. M. *Martin Luther: A Biographical Study.* Westminster, Md.: Newman, 1964. A competent and sympathetic account by a Catholic.

Watson, P. S. *Let God be God.* Philadelphia: Muhlenberg Press, 1950. Competent and imaginative.

Zeeden, E. W. 'Die Deutung Luthers und der Reformation als Aufgabe der Geschichtswissenschaft.' *Theologische Quartalschrift* 140 (1960): 129–162.

### SPECIFIC STUDIES

Bornkamm, H. *Thesen und Thesenanschlag Luthers.* Berlin: Töpelmann, 1967.

Brandi, K. *Kaiser Karl V.* Munich: F. Bruckmann, 1937. The standard biography, to be supplemented for the final years of Charles's reign by H. Lutz, *Christianitas afflicta* (see below).

Henning, G. *Cajetan und Luther. Ein historischer Beitrag zur Begegnung von Thomismus und Reformation.* Stuttgart, 1966.

Iserloh, E. *Luthers Thesenanschlag: Tatsache oder Legende?* Wiesbaden, 1962. Rejects the traditional view that Luther actually posted the 95 Theses.

Kalkoff, P. *Der Wormser Reichstag von 1521.* Munich: R. Oldenbourg, 1922.

Kessel, E. 'Luther vor dem Reichstag in Worms 1521.' In *Festgabe für*

*Paul Kirn,* ed. E. Kaufmann. Berlin: E. Schmidt, 1961, pp. 172–190. Examines Luther's appearance before the German Diet.

Lau, F. 'Die gegenwärtige Diskussion um Luthers Thesenanschlag.' *Luther–Jahrbuch* 34 (1967): 11–59. Summarizes the extensive discussion over Iserloh.

Lorts, J. *Wie kam es zur Reformation?* 3d ed. Einsiedeln: Johannes Verlag, 1955. English translation by Otto M. Knab, *How the Reformation Came.* New York: Herder and Herder, 1964. Attempts to explore the causes of the Reformation.

Ludolphy, I. *Die Voraussetzungen der Religionspolitik Karls V.* Stuttgart: Calwer Verlag, 1965.

Maurer, W. *Von der Freiheit eines Christenmenschen: Zwei Untersuchungen zu Luthers Reformationsschriften 1520–21.* Göttingen: Vandenhoeck & Ruprecht, 1949.

Müller, G. 'Die römische Kurie und die Anfänge der Reformation.' *Zeitschrift für Religions- und Geistesgeschichte* 19 (1967): 1–32.

Seitz, O. *Der authentische Text der Leipziger Disputation (1519).* Berlin: C. A. Schwetschke, 1903.

RESPONSE TO LUTHER'S PROCLAMATION

Berger, A. E., ed. *Die Schaubühne im Dienst der Reformation.* 2 vols. Leipzig: P. Reclam, 1935–36.

——, ed. *Die Sturmtruppen der Reformation: Ausgewählte Flugschriften.* Leipzig: P. Reclam, 1939.

Betten, F. 'The Cartoon in Luther's Warfare Against the Church.' *Catholic Historical Review* 5 (1925): 252–261.

Blochwitz, G. 'Die antirömischen deutschen Flugschriften der frühen Reformationszeit (bis 1522).' *Archiv für Reformationsgeschichte* 27 (1930): 145–246.

Böckmann, P. 'Der gemeine Mann in den Flugschriften der Reformation.' *Deutsche Vierteljahrschrift für Literatur- und Geistesgeschichte* 22 (1944): 186–230.

Clemen, O. C. *Die Lutherische Reformation und der Buchdruck.* Leipzig: M. Heinsius, 1939.

——, ed. *Flugschriften aus den ersten Jahren der Reformation.* 4 vols. Halle: 1906–11; reprinted Nieuwkoop: B. de Graaf, 1967.

Gravier, M. *Luther et l'opinion publique. Essai sur la littérature satirique et polémique en langue allemande pendant le années décisives de la Réforme 1520–1530.* Paris: Aubier, 1942.

Holborn, L. 'Printing and the Growth of a Protestant Movement.' *Church History* 11 (1942): 123–137.

McSorley, H. J. *Luthers Lehre von unfreien Willen nach seiner Hauptschrift De servo Arbitrio im Lichte der biblischen und kirchlichen Tradition.* Munich: Huebner, 1967. An English version has been published under the title *Martin Luther: Right or Wrong?* New York: Paulist-Newman, 1968.

Schade, O., ed. *Satiren und Pasquille aus der Reformationszeit.* 3 vols. Hanover: C. Rümpler, 1856–58.

Uhrig, K. 'Der Bauer in der Publizistik der Reformation.' *Archiv für Reformationsgeschichte* 33 (1936): 70–125; 165–225.

## THE REFORMATION IN GERMANY: 1521–1555

Althaus, P. *Luthers Haltung im Bauernkrieg.* Basel: Schwabe, 1952. The best statement of Luther's relation to the Peasants' War.

Bluhm, H. *Martin Luther—Creative Translator.* St. Louis: Concordia, 1965.

Boisset, J. *Erasme et Luther.* Paris: Presses Universitaires de France, 1962.

Born, K. E. 'Moritz v. Sachsen und die Fürstenverschwörung gegen Karl V.' *Historische Zeitung* 191 (1960): 18–67. Extensive bibliography.

Bornkamm, H. 'Faith and Reason in the Thought of Erasmus and Luther.' In *Religion and Culture. Essays in Honor of Paul Tillich.* New York: Harper, 1959.

Burger, H.-O. 'Luther als Ereignis der Literaturgeschichte.' *Luther-Jahrbuch* 24 (1957): 86–101.

Dülfer, K. *Die Packschen Händel.* 2 vols. Marburg: Veröffentlichungen der Historischen Kommission für Hessen und Waldeck, 1958.

Fabian, E. *Die Entstehung des Schmalkaldischen Bundes und seiner Verfassung 1529 bis 1531–33.* Tübingen: Osiandersche Buchhandlung, Kommissionsverlag, 1956.

——, ed. *Die Schmalkaldischen Bundesabschiede.* Vol. 1, *1530–1532.* Tübingen: E. Fabian, 1958–.

Frantz, G. *Der deutsche Bauernkrieg.* 4th ed. Darmstadt, 1957. The standard history.

Greschat, M. 'Luthers Haltung im Bauernkrieg.' *Archiv für Reformationsgeschichte* 56 (1965): 31–47.

Hillerbrand, H. J. *Landgrave Philipp of Hesse, 1504–1567; Religion and Politics in the Reformation.* St. Louis: Foundation for Reformation Research, 1967.

Honeé, E. 'Die Vergleichsverhandlungen zwischen Katholiken und Protestanten im August 1530.' *Quellen und Forschungen aus Italienischen Archiven und Bibliotheken* 42–43 (1963): 412–434.

Hortleder, F. *Der Römischen Keyser- und Königlichen Majesteten, auch des Heiligen Reichs geistlicher und welticher Stände Handlungen und Ausschreiben von den Ursachen des Teutschen Kriegs.* 2 vols. in 1. Frankfurt, 1617. Extensive collection of sources pertaining to the events leading up to the War of Schmalkald.

Kantzenbach, F. W. *Das Ringen um die Einheit der Kirche im Jahrhundert der Reformation.* Stuttgart, 1957.

Kohls, E. W. *Die Theologie des Erasmus.* Basel: F. Reinhardt, 1966. Concentrates on the early Erasmus. See the review in *Theological Review* 64 (1968): 503–505.

Kolde, T. von. *Die älteste Redaktion der Augsburger Konfession mit Melanchthons Einleitung.* Gütersloh: 1906.

Kühn, J. *Die Geschichte des Speyrer Reichstages von 1529.* Leipzig, 1929.

Lanz, K., ed. *Correspondenz des Kaisers Karl V.* 3 vols. Leipzig: F. A. Brockhaus, 1844–46.

Lau, F. 'Der Bauernkrieg und das angebliche Ende der lutherischen Reformation als spontaner Volksbewegung.' *Luther–Jahrbuch* 26 (1959): 109–134. Seeks to show (not altogether convincingly) that the Lutheran Reformation continued to be a popular phenomenon even after the Peasants' War.

Lutz, H. *Christianitas afflicta. Europa, das Reich und die päpstliche Politik im Niedergang der Hegemonie Kaiser Karls V. 1552–1556.* Göttingen: Vandenhoeck & Ruprecht, 1964. Indispensable for the last phase of Charles's reign. Excellent bibliography.

Mehl, O. J. 'Erasmus' Streitschrift gegen Luther: Hyperaspites.' *Zeitschrift für Religions- und Geistesgeschicht* 12 (1960): 137–146.

———, 'Erasmus contra Luther.' *Luther—Jahrbuch* 29 (1962): 52–64.

Moeller, B. 'Die deutschen Humanisten und die Anfänge der Reformation.' *Zeitschrift für Kirchengeschichte* 70 (1959): 46–61.

Müller, N. K. *Luthers Äusserungen über das Recht des bewaffneten Widerstandes gegen den Kaiser.* Munich, 1914.

Nabholz, H. 'Zur Frage nach den Ursachen des Bauernkrieges (1525).' *Ausgewählte Aufsätze zur Wirtschaftsgeschichte.* Zürich: Schulthess, 1954. Examines the impact of the Reformation.

Schmidt, I. *Das göttliche Recht und seine Bedeutung im Bauernkrieg.* Jena: Frommannschen, 1939.

Simon, M. *Der Augsburger Religionsfriede.* Augsburg, 1954.

Smirin, M. *Die Volksreformation des Thomas Münzer und der grosse Bauernkrieg.* Berlin: Dietz, 1952. A Marxist study.

Spitz, L. W., 'Particularism and Peace: Augsburg 1555.' *Church History* 25 (1956): 110–126.

Stupperich, R. *Der Humanismus und die Wiedervereinigung der Konfessionen.* Leipzig: M. Heinsius, 1936.

———. 'Der Ursprung des Regensburger Buches.' *Archiv für Reformationsgeschichte* 36 (1938): 88–116. Detailed discussion of the background of the document used at the colloquy at Regensburg.

## THE EMERGENCE OF A NEW CHURCH

Burkhardt, C. A. H. *Geschichte der sächsischen Kirchen- und Schulvisitationen 1524–1545.* Leipzig: F. W. Grunoer, 1879.

Cohrs, F. *Die Evangelischen Katechismusversuche vor Luthers Enchiridion.* 5 vols. Berlin: A. Hoffmann, 1900–07.

Fendt, L. *Der lutherische Gottesdienst des 16. Jahrhunderts.* Munich: E. Reinhardt, 1923.

Mertz, G. *Das Schulwesen der deutschen Reformation im 16. Jahrhundert.* Heidelberg: C. Winter, 1902.

Meyer, H. B. *Luther und die Messe.* Paderborn: Verlag Bonifacius-Druckerei, 1965.

Vajta, V. *Die Theologie des Gottesdienstes bei Luther.* Stockholm: Svenska, 1952.

Zeeden, E. W. and Molitor, H. *Die Visitation im Dienst der kirchlichen Reform.* Münster: 1967.

### HULDRYCH ZWINGLI AND THE SWISS REFORMATION

Blanke, F., 'Zwinglis "Fidei ratio" (1530). Entstehung und Bedeutung.' *Archiv für Reformationsgeschichte* 57 (1966): 96–101.

———— et al., eds. *Zwingli Hauptschriften.* 10 vols. Zürich: Zwingli Verlag, 1940–. A useful selection of Zwingli's writings. Translates the Latin works into German.

Courvoisier, J. *Zwingli: A Reformed Theologian.* London: Epworth, 1964.

Egli, E. and Finsler, G. *Huldreich Zwinglis Sämtliche Werke.* Leipzig-Zürich: C. A. Schwetschke und Sohn, 1905–. The standard edition.

Egli, E. *Schweizerische Reformationsgeschichte.* Zürich: Zürcher & Furrer, 1910.

Farner, O. *Huldrych Zwingli.* 4 vols. Zürich: Zwingli Verlag, 1943–60. Always detailed and panegyric; often competent.

Haas, M. 'Zwingli und der erste Kappelerkrieg.' *Zwingliana* 12 (1964): 93–136.

Hausammann, S. 'Die Marburger Artikel—eine echte Kondordie?' *Zeitschrift für Kirchengeschichte* 77 (1966): 388–421.

Köhler, W. *Huldrych Zwingli.* 2d ed. Leipzig: Koehler & Amelang, 1954. The best biography; lacks detail.

————. *Zürcher Ehegericht und Genfer Konsistorium.* 2 vols. Leipzig: M. Heinsius Nachfolger, 1932–42. On the administration of ecclesiastical discipline in Zurich.

————. *Zwingli und Luther. Ihr Streit über das Abendmahl.* 2 vols. Leipzig and Gütersloh: M. Heinsius Nachfolger, 1924–53. The definitive study on Luther's controversy with Zwingli.

————. *Das Marburger Religionsgespräch 1529. Versuch einer Rekonstruktion.* Leipzig: M. Heinsius Nachfolger, 1929.

Ley, R. *Kirchenzucht bei Zwingli.* Zurich: Zwingli Verlag, 1948.

Locher, G. W. *Die Theologie Huldrych Zwinglis im Lichte seiner Christologie. Erster Teil: Die Gotteslehre.* Zurich: Zwingli Verlag, 1952. The best treatment of Zwingli's theology, which minimizes his humanist propensity.

————. 'Die Wandlung des Zwingli-Bildes in der neueren Forschung.' *Vox Theologica* 32 (1962): 169–182. Creative and competent. Translated into English in *Church History* 34 (1965): 3–24.

————. 'Grundzüge der Theologie Huldrych Zwinglis im Vergleich mit derjenigen Martin Luthers und Johannes Calvins,' *Zwingliana* 12 (1967): 545–595.

Muralt, L. 'Probleme der Zwingliforschung.' *Schweizer Beiträge zur allgemeinen Geschichte* 4 (1946): 247–267.

Pfister, R. *Die Seligkeit erwählter Heiden bei Zwingli*. Zurich: Evangelischer Verlag, 1952.

———. *Kirchengeschichte der Schweiz*. Vol. 1. Zurich: Zwingli Verlag, 1964.

Pollet, J.-V. *Huldrych Zwingli et la réforme en Suisse*. Paris: Presses Universitaires de France, 1963. Excellent bibliography.

Rich, A. *Die Anfänge der Theologie Huldrych Zwinglis*. Zurich: Zwingli Verlag, 1949.

Vasella, O. 'Die Ursachen der Reformation in der deutschen Schweiz.' *Zeitschrift für schweizerische Kirchengeschichte* 41 (1947): 401–424.

———. *der Glaubenskrise*. 2d ed. Münster, 1965.

Walton, R. *Zwingli's Theocracy*. Toronto: University of Toronto, 1968. Excellent for the relationship of Church and state.

## The Reformation in England

Baumer, F. L. *Early Tudor Theory of Kingship*. New York: Russell & Russell, 1940.

Brooks, P. *Thomas Cranmer's Doctrine of the Eucharist*. London: Macmillan, 1965. Examines ably a complicated problem.

Clebsch, W. A. *England's Earliest Protestants 1520–35*. New Haven: Yale University Press, 1964. A survey of the earliest English Protestant theologians, with suggestion of the uniqueness of the writers before 1535.

Collinson, P. *The Elizabethan Puritan Movement*. Berkeley: University of California Press, 1967. The most recent and (together with Knappen) the best study of Elizabethan Puritanism.

Dickens, A. G. *The English Reformation*. New York: Schocken Books, 1964. The best monograph on the subject.

———. *Thomas Cromwell and the English Reformation*. London: English Universities Press, 1959.

Frere, W. and Douglas, C. E., eds. *Puritan Manifestoes*. London: SPCK, 1954.

Garrett, C. H. *The Marian Exiles. A Study in the Origins of Elizabethan Puritanism*. Cambridge: At the University Press, 1938.

Haller, W. *The Rise of Puritanism*. New York: Columbia University Press, 1938. New York: Harper Torchbook Edition, 1957.

Harpsfield, N. *The Life and Death of Sir Thomas More*. London: Early English Text Society, 1963. A re-issue of the most famous of the contemporary 'lives.'

Hughes, P. *The Reformation in England*. 3 vols. New York: Macmillan, 1950–54. Detailed narrative from a sympathetic Catholic author. Bibliography is helpful but difficult to use.

Hughes, P. *Theology of the English Reformers*. London: Hodder and Stoughton, 1965.

Jordan, W. K. *Edward VI, the Young King. The Protectorship of the Duke of Somerset.* Cambridge, Mass.: Harvard University Press, 1968. The first volume of what will probably become the definitive biography.

Knappen, M. M. *Tudor Puritanism.* Chicago: University of Chicago Press, 1949.

Knowles, D. *The Religious Orders in England.* 3 vols. Cambridge, Eng.: At the University Press, 1948. III, 194–420. Valuable on the dissolution of the monasteries.

Knox, D. B. *The Doctrine of Faith in the Reign of Henry VIII.* London: J. Clarke, 1961.

Levine, M., ed. *Tudor England, 1485–1603.* Cambridge, Eng.: At the University Press, 1968. Excellent bibliographical survey with helpful annotations.

McConica, J. K. *English Humanists and Reformation Politics under Henry VIII and Edward VI.* Oxford: Clarendon, 1965. Explores the influence of Erasmian thought on the English Reformation.

Marshall, J. S. *Hooker and the Anglican Tradition.* Sewanee, Tenn.: Sewanee University Press, 1963.

Meyer, C. S. *Elizabeth I and the Religious Settlement of 1559.* St. Louis: Concordia, 1960.

Neale, J. E. 'The Elizabethan Acts of Supremacy and Uniformity.' *English Historical Review* 65 (1950): 304–332. The basic examination of the parliamentary history of the two Elizabethan statutes.

The Parker Society. *The Works of the Fathers and Early Writers of the Reformed English Church.* 55 vols. Cambridge; At the University Press, 1841–55. The comprehensive source edition of the writings of the Anglican theologians of the 16th century.

Parmiter, G. *The King's Great Matter. A Study of Anglo-papal Relations 1527–1534.* London: Longmans, 1967. New York: Barnes & Noble, 1967.

Read, C., ed. *Bibliography of British History: Tudor Period.* 2d ed. Oxford: Clarendon Press, 1959. The basic bibliographical tool for Tudor history.

Ridley, J. *Thomas Cranmer.* Oxford: Clarendon Press, 1962.

Scarisbrick, J. J. *Henry VIII.* London: Eyre & Spottiswoode, 1968. Detailed and competent, especially valuable on the Canon Law of Henry's 'divorce'.

Tyndale, William. *The Work of William Tyndale,* ed. G. E. Duffield. Philadelphia: Fortress, 1965.

Williams, G. H., ed. *English Historical Documents 1485–1558.* Oxford: At the University Press, 1967. Contains basic documents with excellent bibliography.

### John Calvin and the Reformation in France

Bailly, A. *La réforme en France jusqu'à l'Édit de Nantes.* Paris: A. Fayard, 1960.

Buisson, A. *Michel de l'Hôpital,* Paris: Albert–Buisson, 1950.

Chenevière, M.-E. *La Pensée politique de Calvin.* Paris: Editions 'Jesers,' 1937.

Dankbaar, W. F. *De sacramentsleer van Calvijn.* Amsterdam: H. J. Paris, 1941.

Doumergue, E. *Jean Calvin: Les hommes et les choses de son temps.* 7 vols. Lausanne: G. Bridel & Cie., 1899–1927. Panegyric but basic.

Dowey, E. A. *The Knowledge of God in Calvin's Theology.* New York: Columbia University Press, 1952. Explores the place of natural theology in Calvin's system.

Erlanger, P. *Le massacre de la Saint-Barthélemy.* Paris: Gallimard, 1960.

Ganoczy, A. *Calvin, théologien de l'église et du ministère.* Paris: Editions du Cerf, 1964.

———. *Le jeune Calvin.* Wiesbaden: F. Steiner, 1966.

Héritier, J. *Catherine de Medicis.* Paris: A. Fayard, 1941.

Herminjard, A. L. *Correspondance des Réformateurs dans les pays de langue française.* 9 vols. Geneva: H. Georg, 1866–97. Important source collection for the French Reformation.

Kingdon, R. M. *Geneva and the Coming of the Wars of Religion in France.* Geneva: Droz, 1956.

———. *Geneva and the Consolidation of the French Protestant Movement, 1564–1572.* Geneva: Droz, 1967. The influence of Geneva on the development of French Protestantism.

Lévis-Mirepoix, A. de. *Les guerres de Religion 1559–1610.* Paris: Fayard, 1950.

Lovy, R. J. *Les origines de la Réforme française. Meaux 1518–1546.* Paris: Diffuseur: Librairie protestante, 1959.

McDonnell, K. *John Calvin, the Church, and the Eucharist.* Princeton: Princeton University Press, 1967.

McNeill, J. T. *The History and Character of Calvinism.* New York: Oxford University Press, 1954.

———. 'Thirty Years of Calvin Study.' *Church History* 17 (1948): 207–240.

Mayer, C. A. 'Les Oeuvres de Clément Marot: L'économie de l'édition critique.' *Bibliothèque d'Humanisme et Renaissance* 29 (1967): 357–372.

Mours, S. *Le Protestantisme en France.* Vol. 1, *Au XVIᵉ siècle.* Paris: Librairie protestante, 1959. Vol. 2, *Au XVIIᵉ siècle.* Paris: Librairie protestante, 1959.

Naef, H. ' "Huguenot." Le procès d'un mot.' *Bibliothèque d'Humanisme et Renaissance* 12 (1950).

Niesel, W. *Calvins Lehre vom Abendmahl.* Munich: C. Kaiser, 1935.
———. *Calvin-Bibliographie, 1901–1959.* Munich: C. Kaiser, 1961. Covers Calvin scholarship between 1900 and 1960.
———. *The Theology of Calvin.* Translated by Harold Knight. Philadelphia: Westminster, 1956. A basic survey of Calvin's theology.
Nürnberger, R. *Die Politisierung des französischen Protestantismus.* Tübingen: J. C. B. Mohr, 1948. Examines the change in the political reflections of the French Calvinists.
Romier, L. *Les Origines politiques des guerres de religion.* Paris: Perrin, 1913–14.
Sprenger, P. *Das Rätsel um die Bekehrung Calvins.* Moers: Neukirchener Verlag, 1960. Examines the problem of the date of Calvin's conversion.
Thompson, J. W. *The Wars of Religion in France. 1559–1576.* New York: Ungar, 1957. Reprint of the 1909 edition.
Wallace, R. S. *Calvin's Doctrine of Word and Sacrament.* Edinburgh: Oliver & Boyd, 1953.
Wendel, F. *Origin and Development of Calvin's Religious Thought.* Translated by Philip Mairet. New York: Harper & Row, 1964. The most useful introduction to Calvin's thought.

*The Radical Reformation*

Armour, R. S. *Anabaptist Baptism.* Scottdale, Pa.: Herald Press, 1966.
Bender, H. S. *Conrad Grebel.* Goshen, Ind.: Mennonite Historical Society, Goshen College, 1950.
———, et al., eds. *The Mennonite Encyclopedia.* 4 vols. Scottdale, Pa.: Herald Press, 1955–59. The basic reference work for Anabaptist history.
Bergsten, T. *Balthasar Hubmaier: seine Stellung zu Reformation und Täufertum 1521–28.* Kassel: Oncken, 1961.
Blanke, F. *Brothers in Christ.* Scottdale, Pa.: Herald Press, 1961.
Bossert, G., et al., eds. *Quellen zur Geschichte der Wiedertäufer.* 12 vols. Leipzig: M. Heinsius Nachfolger, 1930–. Excellent edition of Anabaptist sources, with heavy emphasis on interrogation records.
Cantimori, D. *Italienische Haeretiker der Spätrenaissance.* Basel, 1949.
Friedmann, R. *Hutterite Studies.* Goshen, Ind.: Mennonite Historical Society, 1961. A collection of essays on various aspects of Hutterite Anabaptism.
———, ed. *Die Schriften der Huterischen Täufergemeinschaften.* Vienna: Österreichische Akademie der Wissenschaften, 1965.
Friesen, A. 'Thomas Müntzer in Marxist Thought.' *Church History* 34 (1965): 306–327.
Gauss, J. 'Der junge Michael Servet.' *Zwingliana* 12 (1966): 410–459.
Gritsch, E. W. *Reformer without a Church: The Life and Thought of*

*Thomas Muentzer*. Philadelphia: Fortress, 1967. The only English biography.

Hillerbrand, H. J. *Bibliographie des Täufertums 1520–1630*. Vol. 10 of *Quellen zur Geschichte der Täufer*. Gütersloh: Verlagshaus G. Mohn, 1962.

———. *Die politische Ethik des oberdeutschen Täufertums*. Vol. 7 of Beihefte zur Zeitschrift für Religions- und Geistesgeschichte. Leiden: Brill, 1962.

Iserloh, E. 'Zur Gestalt und Biographie Thomas Müntzers.' *Trierer Theologische Zeitschrift* 71 (1962): 248–253.

Klassen, W. *Covenant and Community. The Life, Writings, and Hermeneutics of Pilgram Marpeck*. Grand Rapids: Eerdmans, 1968.

Kühler, W., ed. *Geschiedenis van de doopsgezinden in Nederland. 1600–1735*. 3 vols. 2d ed. Haarlem, 1940–. The standard history.

Lindeboom, J. *Eeen Franc-tireur der Reformatie, Sebastian Franck*. Arnheim, 1952.

Maier, P L. *Caspar Schwenckfeld on the Person and Work of Christ*. Assen: Van Gorcum, 1959.

Mellink, A. F. *De Wederdopers in de Noordelijke Neerlanden 1531–1544*. Gronigen-Djakarta: Wolters, 1953. Examines the social background of the Dutch Anabaptists at the time of the Münster crisis.

Müntzer, Thomas. *Schriften und Briefe*. Edited by G. Franz. Gütersloh, 1968.

Oyer, J. S. *Lutheran Reformers Against Anabaptists*. The Hague: Nijhoff, 1964.

Peuckert, W. E. *Sebastian Franck*. Munich: Piper, 1943. Verbose but competent; extensive citations from primary sources.

Pippert-Bernhofer, E. *Täuferische Denkweisen und Lebensformen im Spiegel oberdeutscher Täuferverhöre*. Münster: Aschendorff, 1967. Explores the thought of South German Anabaptists.

Rupp, E. G. 'Andrew Karlstadt and Reformation Puritanism.' *Journal of Theological Studies* N.S. 10 (1959): 308–326.

———. *Patterns of Reformation*, Philadelphia: Fortress, 1970.

Schramm, G. 'Antitrinitarier in Polen 1556–1658, ein Literaturbericht,' *Bibliothèque d'Humanisme et Renaissance* 21 (1959): 473–511.

Wilbur, E. M. *Bibliography of the Pioneers of the Socinian-Unitarian Movement*. Rome: Edizione di storia e litteratura, 1950.

Williams, G. H. *The Radical Reformation*. Philadelphia: Westminster, 1962. Competent and encyclopedic.

Wrzecionko, P. 'Die Theologie des Rakower Katechismus.' *Kirche im Osten* 6 (1963): 73–116.

Yoder, J. *Täufertum und Reformation: I Die Gespräche zwischen Täufern und Reformierten in der Schweiz 1523–1548*. Karlsruhe: Schneider, 1962. An examination of the conversations, formal and informal, between Anabaptists and Reformers in Switzerland.

*The European Compass: Scotland, Sweden, Poland*

Bergendoff, C. *Olavus Petri and the Ecclesiastical Transformation in Sweden.* Philadelphia: Fortress, 1965, reprint.

Donaldson, G. *The Scottish Reformation.* New York: Cambridge University Press, 1960.

Fox, P. *The Reformation in Poland.* Baltimore: John Hopkins, 1924.

Garstein, O. *Rome and the Counter-Reformation in Scandinavia.* Vol. 1, *1539–1583.* Oslo: Universitetsforlaget, 1946–.

Hein, L. 'Das Ringen um die rechte Gestalt der Kirche in Polen im Zeitalter der Reformation.' *Kyrios* N.F. 7 (1967): 65–81.

Johannesson, G. 'Die Kirchenreformation in den nordischen Ländern,' Rapport IV of the XI$^e$ Congrès International des Sciences Historiques. Stockholm: Almquist et Wiksell, 1960. A brief introduction to various historiographical problems.

Hoffman, J. G. H. *La Réforme en Suede 1523–1572.* Paris and Neuchâtel: Niestlé & Delachaux, 1945.

Ingebrand, S. *Olavus Petris reformatoriska Åskådning.* No. 1 in Studia doctrinae christianae upsaliensia. Lund, 1964.

Innes Review, *Essays on the Scottish Reformation. 1513–1625.* Edited by D. McRoberts. Chester Springs, Pa.: Dufour Editions, 1962. A collection of excellent essays.

Kjöllerstrom, S. G. 'Gustav Vasa und die Bischofsweihe (1523–1531).' In *Für Kirche und Recht: Festschrift für Joh. Heckel,* edited by Siegfried Grundmann, pp. 164–183. Cologne–Graz: Bohlau Verlag, 1959.

———. 'Kirche und Staat in Schweden nach der Reformation.' *Zeitschrift der Savigny–Stiftung für Rechtsgeschichte, Kanonistische Abteilung* 41 (1955): 271–289.

Knox, J. *History of the Reformation in Scotland.* Edited by W. Croft-Dickinson. 2 vols. London–New York: Nelson, 1950. The classic history of the Scottish Reformation written by its chief figure.

———. *The Works of John Knox.* Edited by D. Laing. 6 vols. Edinburgh: Bannatyne Club, 1846–64. Best edition of his writings.

Lee, M. *James Stewart, Earl of Moray: A Political Study of the Reformation in Scotland.* New York: Columbia University Press, 1953.

Matl, J. 'Reformation und Gegenreformation als Kulturfaktoren bei den Slawen.' In *Festschrift Karl Eder.* Innsbruck: Universitätsverlag Wagner, 1959.

Murray, R. *Olavus Petri.* Stockholm: Svenska kyrkans diakonistyrelses, 1952.

Renwick, A. M. *The Story of the Scottish Reformation.* London: Intervarsity Fellowship, 1960.

Rhode, G. 'Die Reformation in Osteuropa.' *Zeitschrift für Ostforschung* 7 (1958): 481–500.

Ridley, J. *John Knox*. Oxford: Clarendon Press, 1968. Detailed biography with excellent bibliography.

Schramm, G. *Der polnische Adel und die Reformation*. Wiesbaden: Steiner, 1965. A creative study.

Schwaiger, G. *Die Reformation in den nordischen Ländern*. Munich: Kösel, 1962. With an extensive bibliography.

Staniewski, B. *Reformation und Gegenreformation in Polen*. Münster, 1960. Primarily an extensive bibliographical survey.

Yrwing, H. *Gustav Vasa, kröningsfrågan och Vasterås riksdag 1527*. Lund: Gleerup, 1956.

## The Catholic Response

Burns, E. M. *The Counter-Reformation*. New York: Van Nostrand, 1964.

Cristiani, L. *L'Église à l'époque du concile de Trente*. Paris: Bloud et Gay, 1948.

Elkan, A. 'Entstehung und Entwicklung des Begriffs Gegenreformation.' *Historische Zeitschrift* 112 (1914); 473–493.

Evennett, H. O. *The Spirit of the Counter-Reformation*. Cambridge, Eng.: At the University Press, 1968. Basic.

Greving, J., ed. *Corpus Catholicorum. Werke katholischer Schriftsteller im Zeitalter der Glaubensspaltung*. 29 vols. Münster. 1917–67. The writings of anti-Protestants.

Janelle, P. *The Catholic Reformation*. Milwaukee: Bruce, 1949.

Jedin, H. *Katholische Reformation oder Gegenreformation? Ein Versuch zur Klärung der Begriffe nebst einer Jubiläumsbetrachtung über das Trienter Konzil*. Luzern, 1946. The best discussion of the complicated problem of nomenclature.

———. 'Die geschichtliche Bedeutung der katholischen Kontroversliteratur im Zeitalter der Glaubensspaltung.' *Historisches Jahrbuch* 53 (1933): 304–319.

Molitor, H. 'Studien zur katholischen Reform in Deutschland.' *Römische Quartalschrift* 60 (1965).

Tavard, G. H. 'The Catholic Reform in the Sixteenth Century.' *Church History* 26 (1957): 275–288. A bibliographical survey of select literature.

## Monographs on Various Topics

Breen, Q. 'Humanism and the Reformation.' In *The Impact of the Church Upon Its Culture*, edited by J. C. Brauer. Chicago: University of Chicago Press, 1968.

Campenhausen, H. 'Reformatorisches Selbstbewusstsein und reformatorisches Geschichtsbewusstsein, bei Luther, 1517–1522.' *Archiv für*

*Reformationsgeschichte* 37 (1940): 128–150. Important for the self-understanding of Luther in the early phase of the Reformation.

Dickmann, F. 'Das Problem der Gleichberechtigung der Konfessionen im Reich im 16. und 17. Jahrhundert.' *Historische Zeitschrift* 201 (1965): 265–305.

Hassinger, E. 'Wirtschaftliche Motive und Argumente für religiöse Duldsamkeit im 16. und 18. Jahrhundert.' *Archiv für Reformationsgeschichte* 56 (1965): 218–227.

Holl, K. *The Cultural Significance of the Reformation.* New York: Meridian, 1959.

Kitch, M. J. *Capitalism and the Reformation.* London: Longmans, 1967.

Lecler, J. *Toleration and the Reformation.* 2 vols. New York: Association, 1960.

Stickler, A. M. 'Die Reformationsbewegungen des 16. Jahrhunderts als verfassungsrechtliche Revolutionen.' *Österreichisches Archiv für Kirchenrecht* 8 (1957): 38–48.

# Name Index

Adrian VI, pope, 47, 272, 274, 275
Albert of Hohenzollern, Archbishop of Mainz, 5
Aleander, papal nuncio, 22, 147, 279
Allen, William: cardinal, 221; *An Admonition to the Nobility*, 222; *A True, Sincere and Modest Defense*, 222
Andreae, Laurentius, 247, 249
Aske, Robert, 185
Augustine, St., 13

Bancroft, Richard, 218
Barnes, Robert, 170, 179, 190
Batenburg, Jan van, 82
Beaton, Thomas, cardinal, 255
Beza, Theodore, 114, 115, 243
Biandrata, Giorgio, 93, 95, 97
Biel, Gabriel, 4
Blaurer, Ambrosius, 160
Boleyn, Anne, 172
Briçonnet, Guillaume, bishop, 225
Browne, Robert: 217; *A Treatise of Reformation*, 217
Bucer, Martin: reformer, 28, 77, 112, 146, 150, 153, 198, 216; and colloquies with Catholics, 148; and Interim, 160
Bünderlin, Hans, 77

Cajetan, Thomas, cardinal, 11, 279
Calvin, John, 99–115
 life: 105 ff; first stay in Geneva,
106; expulsion, 109; return, 111; *Ordonnances écclésiastiques*, 112
thought: 101; ecumenical orientation, 111; economic views, 298
writings: commentary on Seneca's *De Clementia*, 105; *Commentary on the Psalms*, 106; *Institutes of the Christian Religion*, 99, 103, 231; *Reply to Sadoleto*, 110
Campeggio, Lorenzo, cardinal, 47, 173
Campion, Edmund, 221
Canisius, Peter, 273
Carlstadt, Andreas Bodenstein: 5, 33; life, 70; views of Communion, 122
Cartwright, Thomas, 216
Castellio, Sebastian, 89, 93
Catherine of Aragon, 171, 181
Charles V, German Emperor: 16; his election, 17; initial encounter with Luther, 23; attitude toward Luther, 24; at Augsburg (1530), 128 ff, 146; at Regensburg (1541), 149 ff; war against France, 151, 232; against Cleves, 151; against League of Schmalkald, 154 ff; and Council of Trent, 156, 279; and Henry VIII, 173; at Augsburg (1547), 158; at Augsburg (1550), 161; abdication, 166; also, 235, 274
Chieregati, Francesco, 46, 275

337

# Subject Index